Turning P[...]
Qualitative Research

Crossroads in Qualitative Inquiry

Series Editors
Norman K. Denzin, University of Illinois, Urbana-Champaign
Yvonna S. Lincoln, Texas A&M University

ABOUT THE SERIES: Qualitative methods are material and interpretive practices. They do not stand outside politics and cultural criticism. This spirit of critically imagining and pursuing a more democratic society has been a guiding feature of qualitative inquiry from the very beginning. The Crossroads in Qualitative Inquiry series will take up such methodological and moral issues as the local and the global, text and context, voice, writing for the other, and the presence of the author in the text. The Crossroads series understands that the discourses of a critical, moral methodology are basic to any effort to re-engage the promise of the social sciences for democracy in the twenty-first century. This international series creates a space for the exploration of new representational forms and new critical, cultural studies.

SUBMITTING MANUSCRIPTS: Book proposals should be sent to Crossroads in Qualitative Inquiry Series, c/o Norman K. Denzin, Institute for Communication Studies, 810 S. Wright Street, University of Illinois, Champaign, Illinois 61820, or emailed to n-denzin@uiuc.edu.

BOOKS IN THIS SERIES:

Volume 1: *Incarceration Nation: Investigative Prison Poems of Hope and Terror*, Stephen John Hartnett (2003)

Volume 2: *9/11 in American Culture*, edited by Norman K. Denzin and Yvonna S. Lincoln (2003)

Volume 3: *Turning Points in Qualitative Research: Tying Knots in the Handkerchief*, edited by Yvonna S. Lincoln and Norman K. Denzin (2003)

Turning Points in Qualitative Research

Tying Knots in a Handkerchief

EDITED BY
YVONNA S. LINCOLN
NORMAN K. DENZIN

ALTAMIRA
PRESS

A Division of
ROWMAN & LITTLEFIELD PUBLISHERS, INC.
Walnut Creek • *Lanham* • *New York* • *Oxford*

ALTAMIRA PRESS
A Division of Rowman & Littlefield Publishers, Inc.
1630 North Main Street, #367
Walnut Creek, CA 94596
www.altamirapress.com

Rowman & Littlefield Publishers, Inc.
A Member of the Rowman & Littlefield Publishing Group
4501 Forbes Boulevard, Suite 200
Lanham, MD 20706

PO Box 317
Oxford
OX2 9RU, UK

British Library Cataloguing in Publication Information Available

Library of Congress Cataloging-in-Publication Data

Turning points in qualitative research : tying knots in a handkerchief / edited by Yvonna
S. Lincoln and Norman K. Denzin.
    p. cm — (Crossroads in qualitative inquiry)
    Includes bibliographical references.
    ISBN 0-7591-0347-X (alk. paper)—ISBN 0-7591-0348-8 (pbk. : alk. paper)
    1. Sociology—Research—Methodology. 2. Ethnology—Research—Methodology. 3.
Qualitative research. I. Lincoln, Yvonna S. II. Denzin, Norman K. III. Series
    HM571 .T87 2003
                                                                2002153405

Printed in the United States of America

Contents

The "Voice from Nowhere" Gets to Speak:
Autoethnography and Personal Narratives

Introduction: Revolutions, Ruptures, and Rifts in Interpretive Inquiry

Our intentions in this reader are threefold. The first is to introduce scholars and students to the major paradigm-shaping works in the field of qualitative inquiry. In this volume, we present what we regard as the most important works in qualitative inquiry from the last half of the twentieth century to the present. Second, we offer a critical framework for interpreting these classic works, showing, third, how they can contribute to critical qualitative discourse in this new century.

This reader is predicated on the assumption that qualitative research, as practiced by sociologists, anthropologists, and educationists, experienced a series of crises, ruptures, rifts, and even revolutions beginning in the early 1980s. These crises had the effect of creating a series of what Gregory Bateson called "knots tied in a handkerchief." They benchmarked interrogations, rifts, ruptures, moral and practical dilemmas, and revolutions that changed ethnographic practices forever. These ideas and concerns circulated among old practices, as the "vehicles" of old science met fast-moving ideas of the "new ethnography." In some way, we tried to mark these dangerous intersections of ethnography in the first and second editions of the *Handbook of Qualitative Research*. Even in the relatively short time frame between the first and second editions, we found a radically altered landscape, forever transformed by a series of issues and usages that would have been unthinkable in the early 1970s.

1

It is our belief that the classics of this new qualitative inquiry and new ethnography are not those that formed the classical era but, rather, are those that comprise the articles, papers, and exemplars that signify the ruptures in thinking, road signs that mark the point of no return. Some of those signal pieces are reproduced here. These are the works we think the field needs to build on, even as it returns to them and rethinks the issues they take up. Our use of the metaphor "tying knots in a handkerchief" announces this reflexive turn.

Some readers may think the metaphor somewhat odd. We have borrowed the metaphor from Gregory Bateson's influential *Steps to an Ecology of Mind* (1972), in which Bateson himself attempts both to puzzle out and to help the reader to understand how "thinking scientifically" occurs. Bateson recounts trying to cope with fuzzy terminology, vague concepts, and abstract and unshared meanings. He reports,

> When I am faced with a vague concept and feel that the time is not yet ripe to bring that concept into strict expression, I coin some loose expression for referring to this concept and do not want to prejudge the issue by giving the concept too meaningful a term. . . . These brief Anglo-Saxon terms have for me a definite feeling-tone which reminds me all the time that the concepts behind them are vague and await analysis. It is a trick like *tying a knot in a handkerchief*. . . . I can go on using the vague concept in the valuable process of loose thinking— still continually reminded that my thoughts are loose. (1972, 83–84, emphasis added)

We are using the metaphor in precisely the same reflexive, and perhaps paradoxical, way: as a way of signifying that even as classic works are selected, issues are not closed, options are still open, and the field of qualitative research remains very much in flux. Indeed, the transformations in qualitative inquiry that gained momentum in the 1990s continue into the new century. The appeal of a critical qualitative research project across the social sciences and the humanities increases.

Some term this the "seventh moment of inquiry" (Denzin and Lincoln 2000, 2, 12).[1] This is a period of ferment and explosion, a time when classics are reexamined and new issues come to the fore. This is a historical moment defined by breaks from the past, a focus on previously silenced voices, a turn to performance texts, and a concern with moral discourse, with critical conversations about how qualitative inquiry can contribute to contemporary discourses concerning democracy, race, gender, class, nation, freedom, and community (Lincoln and Denzin 2000, 1048).

In the seventh moment, at the beginning of the twenty-first century, there is a pressing need to look back and see what issues we need to bring forward into the new century, what knots can we firmly secure, which knots should be undone, and where new knots might need to be tied.

WHICH CRISES? WHICH TURNING POINTS? WHICH KNOTS?

The decade of the 1980s was defined by the triple crises of authority, representation, and praxis. The traditional criteria for evaluating qualitative work were challenged, as it was understood that researchers created reality through their representational, textual, and interpretive practices. The two crises of authority and representation shaped the third, asking how praxis or action was to be defined under a new interpretive regime.

The crises of authority, representation, and praxis found comfort and solace in a reconfigured ethical system (Christians 2000; Keller 1985; Lincoln 1995, 1998; Lincoln and Guba 1989), in the inclusion of respondents in the shaping and framing of their own stories, in a moral mandate for social research that actually addressed problems (Schratz and Walker 1995), and in experimental, literary (Clifford and Marcus 1986), poetic (Brady 1991; Prattis 1985), and "messy" representations of lived experience (Marcus and Fischer 1986).

The peculiarly Western and masculine bent of the social sciences was effectively challenged by multiple discourses, including subaltern, indigenous, feminist, and border voices. Further challenges emerged from discourses surrounding the self-as-researcher and the researcher-as-self. The idea of the "voice from nowhere/voice from everywhere" was also criticized, as was the "god's-eye view" of inquiry. In the process, autoethnography took its place among new genres for representing lived experience (Ellis and Bochner 1996).

Enter Critical Qualitative Research

Qualitative research—interpretivist forms, phenomenology, case study research, constructivist models of inquiry, narrative inquiry, and other perspectives on such research—played pivotal roles in the ruptures, rifts, and revolutions we take up in this volume. The first knot, or turning point, in the

revolution involved qualitative research's reintroduction into the fields of sociology and education as well as its introduction into nursing and clinical research and its adoption in other fields. These events opened up a space in
which the conventional model of experimental, statistical, and quantitative research could be challenged. The rationale for and philosophy behind qualitative research (a paradigm, or model, borrowed from phenomenology) laid
bare the basic assumptions of experimental models of research and made
those assumptions the basis of an ongoing criticism of the failure of conventional science to deliver as promised on the narrative of social progress.

In the second pivotal knot, qualitative research provided an opportunity
for social scientists to explore questions that were ill explored (Guba and Lincoln 1981; Lincoln and Guba 1985), neglected (Bakan 1967), or simply not
amenable to being answered with experimental and other quantitative methods. Qualitative research also provided a vehicle for incorporating theoretical
and conceptual concerns stemming from postmodernist formulations (Best
and Kellner 1997), poststructural critiques (Cherryholmes 1988), cultural
studies (Grossberg, Nelson, and Treichler 1992), and challenges to realist conceptions of anthropology and the social sciences more broadly.

In the third knotting of the metaphorical handkerchief, qualitative research, with its emphasis on nontechnical, ordinary-language rhetorical and
narrative forms and on respondents' voices, aided and abetted the growing
movement to reconnect art and science, literary forms with scientific information, and social life with its storied (Cruikshank 1990), performative (Conquergood 1985), and narrated existence.

By the same token, qualitative research traditions, especially those explored
as formal methods by early anthropologists and sociologists, have not been
immune to influences from questions and issues arising from within the disciplines. In reciprocating fashion, while the academic disciplines have been re-
considering the contributions of qualitative and phenomenological research
to an expanded and deepened understanding of social life, qualitative research
theorists have paid increasing attention to issues begging for resolution in the
disciplines and within the practices and politics of qualitative research itself.

Normal science does not seem so "normal" anymore—nor is it likely to
seem so ever again.

Four other knots will also likely shape the future of qualitative research in
the disciplines: (1) a revolution in the way ethics and science are seen to be re-

lated; (2) a methodological revolution; (3) a crisis surrounding the purposes of ethnography—and social science more broadly; and (4) a revolution in presentation—how ethnography's results are crafted and presented.

In conventional social science, ethics as a research concern exists outside the processes of inquiry and presentation. Issues of how respondents are treated, how information about them is to be preserved as confidential, what the nature of the researcher-respondent relationship should be, and the role of deception in research were traditionally treated as a separate class of concerns, external rather than internal to the routines of methodology itself. Standards for treatment of research subjects devolved on the federal government to codify and legislate and were relegated for oversight purposes to Institutional Reviews Boards to regulate and police.

Ethics

In interpretivist social science, however, ethics has been reembedded in the practices, politics, and presentation of research results. The relationships between researchers and respondents have come under new—and entirely voluntary—scrutiny by the community of social science researchers themselves. As researchers look to their representational practices, to questions of authority and legitimacy, and to questions of agency, locus of control, and human justice, ethical considerations have come to the forefront as inquirers see these relationships as either empowering or disempowering respondents, as fostering participation and human dignity, or as having the power to negate control and agency. Reconfigured relationships and self-conscious examinations of the potential for abuses in a more intimate social science have mandated rethinking the nature of ethics in the enterprises of the human sciences.

Methodology

The methodological revolution, a knot of some complexity, was perhaps beyond comprehension a quarter century ago. At the time of the influential and now-classic McCall and Simmons *Issues in Participant Observation: A Text and Reader* (1969), the two fundamental "methods" of anthropology and sociology were interviewing and participant observation, which together were considered the backbone of ethnographic fieldwork. Margaret Mead's constant companion, a camera-cum-tripod taken with her on all her last fieldwork expeditions, served to introduce visual methods as a data collection technique (as opposed to a recording of the exotic "Other" and as added proof that the field researcher had "been there" and "done that"). The creation, amplification, and refinement of new methods followed rapidly in the last decades of the twentieth century, when researchers began to look at the adaptation of content analyses, conversation analysis, and discourse analysis (for the analysis of textual materials and conversation); extended visual analysis; adapted historical methods for documentary and records analysis (see, for instance, Gordon Allport's seminal work, funded by the Russell Sage Foundation); the extension of focus group methodologies (borrowed from marketing research); the increasing use of the Internet for textual analysis as well as data collection; and narrative analyses in a variety of forms. The invention and extension of methods for both data collection and data analysis would have been beyond belief in 1980.

Purpose

The social sciences has also undergone a kind of crisis of purpose, with its more thoughtful practitioners daring to question what ethnography's purpose might be and whom it does or should, serve. Knorr-Cetina's (1981; see also Knorr-Cetina and Mulkay 1983) incisive criticism of the academy as a preserve for an "intellectual priesthood" whose "sacerdotal" status permitted researchers a privileged place as "knowledge elites" trading knowledge as a commodity, principally among themselves, prompted a long and divisive debate about the roles and functions of academic social science. Less abstractly oriented social scientists pointed to the diminishing fund of resources for social inquiries and asked, given limited resources, What kind of research should we be doing? And those even more closely tied to their own fieldwork asked whom social science should serve—those who collect data, or those from whom it is collected?

This series of questions cut to the heart of the enterprise of social science, for they force researchers to confront the question of whether social science, as conventionally configured, serves the purpose of improving the human lot. For many humans, it has not. The "new" qualitative researcher has been drawn to more radical forms of ethnographic and interpretive work, derived from the theoretical and praxis-oriented philosophies of critical theory, action research, and participatory action research. Each of the latter forms (and their various theoretical streams) seeks to place the issues of respondents at the forefront of inquirer concerns.

There is no single answer to the question of what ethnography is for and whom it serves or should serve. Such answers are rooted in a critical cultural politics (such as that proposed by Conquergood in this volume), a communitarian ethic for field research, a feminist principle of caring (derived from the work of Nel Noddings), a feminist moral stance rooted in relatedness (grounded in the work of Carol Gilligan), a postcolonial critique (based on the work of Mohanty, Spivak, Nandy, and others), or the work of race and ethnic epistemologies (e.g., the work of Patricia Hill Collins, Gloria Anzaldùa, Emma Perez, bell hooks, Cornel West, Stanfield and Dennis, and others). There have been few places where the plurality of voices and proposals has been heard so much as in the questioning of purposes for social science and the question of whom it will ultimately serve. Whatever the proposal or the theoretical stream, purposes have been linked almost invariably with local and indigenous concerns and with the community as the relevant site.

Presentation

A final knot, perhaps the knottiest, is the revolution in presentation. Presentation, of course, is tied intimately to representation. Even as the crisis of representation grows, the proposals for presentation expand accordingly. In part, the presentational revolution has emerged from critiques that bedevil the old dissociation of science from literature, of inquiry from spirituality, and of body from mind and many of the other bicameral dualisms that have plagued the Western mind, from St. Augustine to the present. The reemphasis on the human experience as an oral experience has led to experimentation in textual representation forms borrowed straight from literature and storied forms and from performance.

We have tried, in a somewhat limited space, to bookmark some of the major streams of thought and to extend those into what we have called the future of ethnography and qualitative research more broadly. We could not have done justice to this issue even with several volumes. The veritable explosion of "messy" forms—plays, poems, performance pieces and ethnodramas; fictional representations; "skirted," "pleated," and "layered" texts; and autoethnographies—all meant to be read out loud, performed, or savored as literature and community stories, has reshaped entirely the debates around "appropriate" scientific discourse, the technical and rhetorical conventions of scientific writing, and the meaning of research itself. In the best sense of good literature, these new works are meant to provoke an ongoing conversation about life, about human purpose, about the meaning of community, about how positive social change is prompted and takes place, about cultural life and its forms, and about social justice.

We have tried, insofar as possible in a messy, intellectually jagged, multivocal, and uneven discourse, to create a sense of classics in qualitative inquiry and ethnography via the use of the knots in the handkerchief. The turning points, revolutions, rifts, ruptures, and crises that form the major sections of this book are those that have seemed to us to be the most influential in shaping qualitative research as it exists today throughout the disciplines where its influence has been felt most strongly. Each of the crises or revolutions represents a punctuation point, beyond which the golden, or classical, era of ethnography had ended and a new era begun. Even though we have argued earlier (Denzin and Lincoln 1994, 2000) that each of the historical moments circulates freely in the present, the chapters in this volume, meant to represent classical works, reference changes in thinking so profound as to merit reconsideration of entire theoretical positions or to bring about the rethinking of older—and possibly unconsidered—positions on method, ethics, representation, and other ethnographic practices.

It is our belief that the classics of this new ethnography are not those that formed the classical era. Rather, they are the articles, papers, and exemplars that signify the ruptures in thinking, road signs that mark the point of no return. It is some of those signal pieces that we reproduce here.

Revolutions, Rifts and Ruptures

Our book unfolds in the following sections:

- The Revolution of Representation
- The Revolution in Authority
- The Revolution of Legitimation
- The Ethical Revolution
- The Methodological Revolution
- The Crisis in Purpose
- The Revolution in Presentation
- The Future of Ethnography and Qualitative Research

Each of these sections is presented with a brief introduction that conveys some of the context as well as the rationales developed by ethnographers, anthropologists, performance theorists, and other qualitative researchers. While many books could be written about each of the topics—indeed, they have been written—we have tried either to choose for readers theoretical pieces that show the evolution of thinking in the various crises (knots) or to provide exemplars, as in the poetry in the "Revolution in Presentation" section. The pieces we have chosen that are theoretical represent tectonic shifts in thinking among theoreticians and practitioners; the exemplars that we have chosen are ways of carrying out the tying and untying of the knots.

Clearly these sections work not only with but also alongside, through, in resistance to, and in tandem with each other and as counteroppositional forces. Thus, even while some voices issue calls for more rigor and more attention to how we interpolate interpretation, still other voices abandon the theoretical fray altogether and simply state, "There are elements of fieldwork that transcend questions of rigor and go directly to the heart of lived experience. The only mode of presentation for the emotional, connected, embodied *living* of experience is poetic. Here are my poems."

When we speak of tying and untying knots, we are abandoning altogether the classical Greek conundrum of the Gordian knot. There will be no sword to cut through these knots. Nor do we believe that there should be, for there will be no single moment of swift clarity that creates a clean cleavage in qualitative inquiry. Rather, we understand this field as a set of discourses, a field where dialogues are created, entered, left, and revisited on many occasions and in many different forms. This ongoing hermeneusis of propositions, proposals, counters, assays, elaborations, conversations, elisions, divagations, and reconnaissances serve to enrich, extend, and embellish the sense of complexity always surrounding the deeply human and its multiple sciences.

Knots Tied and Untied

In this era, it is impossible to say with any certainty "where" we are in this field, which is in flux. Both qualitative methods and qualitative researchers are in the process of interactive, synergistic, and symbiotic change. Several knots have been untied. We no longer need to tie a knot and hope that qualitative inquiry will achieve recognition as a legitimate form of science. Indeed, now researchers frequently see position postings specifically requiring candidates to have experience and expertise in qualitative research and to be able to teach such methods to graduate students. We no longer need to tie a knot and hope that experimental texts will get a hearing. There is nearly always an audience for such texts, and audiences come not only for the ethnographic insights they are likely to find but also frequently as much for the power, the sense of deep community connection, with which they leave.

Other knots will remain tied for some time to come because they represent arenas of inquiry, exploration, and deconstruction still in ferment (e.g., the appearance of new voices onstage and arguments surrounding representational forms). Knots will also remain tied because relatively old issues of authority and legitimation in ethnography and interpretive research have not been resolved, and they likely will not be in the near future. There will be no period of what Kuhn referred to as "normal science" for some time to come. The rules surrounding authority and legitimation have been seriously eroded, and new rules are only now being proposed.

Ethics

We are, in the same manner, a long way from settling questions of ethics. We know for a certainty that federal regulations concerning, in particular, human subjects and human subjects' protection are lamentably inadequate. While they provide a sort of "quality floor," in fact they appear to be applied differentially in different settings and simply do not serve the interests of "new" social scientists or the work in which such qualitative researchers want to engage. The new interpretivist inquirer is writing her or his own rules for relationships with respondents and is also revising his or her ideas regarding what the human sciences should be about. This same interpretivist inquirer believes that the purposes of research deeply interact with our sense of whom we are with and to those whom we engage as research participants. Thus, conversations—and classroom teaching—question the possibility of objectivity, explore the meaning of community, and probe the potential of research to support and enhance social justice.

Dozens of proposals for new ethical criteria have emerged in the past decade. While the standard criteria promulgated by the federal government appear to stand aside and apart from concerns over the rigor of scientific inquiry, the new criteria are quite simply deeply embedded inside the entire inquiry process: rigor considerations, validity issues, methodological choices, stances toward research participants, and representational forms. This ethical knot will remain tied for some time to come for no other reason than that we remain conflicted rather than consensual about the roles of social research, about our identities within the research activity, and about our responsibilities to the several communities with and for whom we speak.

Methods

The methodological knot remains tied simply because the ferment in methods is not likely to come to an end soon. New methods, as well as new uses for older methods, are being invented almost daily. New venues for the application of old and revised methods—for example, the Internet (text and narrative analysis), photography, filmmaking, media representations (visual analyses), or community-centered cultures (focus groups)—arose with technological revolutions and increasing sophistication within the social science community. This is an incredibly fertile era for the revisiting of old methods and methodological strategies and the invention of new methods. The methodological knot can and should remain profitably tied for a long time to come if for no other reason than to keep interpretivists open to possibilities for new sources of data and new ways of analyzing, interpreting, and representing.

Purpose

The purpose knot will also probably remain tied. The social sciences have engaged two arguments at once around purpose, namely, whether social science should serve larger social ends such as social justice and egalitarianism and how and under what circumstances social science can feed into policy arenas more directly to achieve these ends. One thing is clear: Among a large segment of the interpretivist and qualitative community, social science research can and should serve far broader interests and stakeholders than the disciplinary communities alone. How that is done remains less clear, so we must leave this knot tied as well.

Representation

A final knot that we believe will remain tied for this historical moment is the knot of representation. The representation revolution has only recently gotten well under way, and its potential has been scarcely explored. As inquirers explore narrative, rhetorical, literary, and performance forms for ethnographic writing, this revolution can only expand. The rupture between realist and interpretivist forms of representation cannot be healed. At the same time, the remarriage of science and art and the dissolution of what are now seen as unserviceable binaries virtually ensure that the other revolutions will be joined by an increasing number of willing volunteers.

It is both useful and right that some knots remain tied, that we are reminded that there are unsolved problems, and that there is, as yet (and, it is to be hoped, not for a long time) no "normal science" agreed on by all members of every disciplinary community. It is said that the Chinese have a blessing that is also a curse: "May you live in interesting times!" We live in interesting times as qualitative inquirers and do not consider it a curse; it is a time of yeasty experimentation and, as Evelyn Waugh remarked, a season of "mellow fruitfulness." We will continue to loosen, tighten, and loosen again the knots that mark our conceptual problems. But we will always know that interesting problems—the hallmarks, the knots, of a rich intellectual life—await our energies.

NOTES

1. Denzin and Lincoln (2000, 2) define the seven moments of inquiry, all of which operate in the present, as the traditional (1900–1950); the modernist (1950–1970); blurred genres (1970–1986); the crisis of representation (1986–1990); postmodern, or experimental (1990–1995); postexperimental (1995–2000); and the future (2000–). For criticisms of this framework, see Delamont, Coffey, and Atkinson (2000).

REFERENCES

Appadurai, Arjun. 1993. "Patriotism and Its Future." *Public Culture* 5: 411–29.

Bakan, David. 1967. *On Method: Toward a Reconstruction of Psychological Investigation.* San Francisco: Jossey-Bass.

Bateson, Gregory. 1972. *Steps to an Ecology of Mind.* New York: Ballantine.

Best, Steven, and Douglas Kellner. 1997. *The Postmodern Turn.* New York: Guilford Press.

Beverley, John. 2000. "Testimonio, Subalternity, and Narrative Authority." In Norman K. Denzin and Yvonna S. Lincoln, eds., *Handbook of Qualitative Research* (2nd ed., pp. 555–65). Thousand Oaks, Calif.: Sage Publications.

Brady, Ivan A., ed. 1991. *Anthropological Poetics.* Savage, Md.: Rowman & Littlefield.

Cherryholmes, Cleo H. 1988. *Power and Criticism: Poststructural Investigations in Education.* New York: Teachers College Press.

Christians, Clifford. 2000. "Ethics and Politics in Qualitative Research." In Norman K. Denzin and Yvonna S. Lincoln, eds., *Handbook of Qualitative Research* (2nd ed., pp. 133–55). Thousand Oaks, Calif.: Sage.

Clifford, James, and George E. Marcus, eds. 1986. *Writing Culture: The Poetics and Politics of Ethnography.* Berkeley: University of California Press.

Clough, Patricia Ticineto. 1998. *The End(s) of Ethnography.* New York: Peter Lang.

Conquergood, Dwight. 1985. "Performing as a Moral Act: Ethical Dimensions of the Ethnography of Performance" *Literature in Performance* 5: 1–13.

———. 1998. "Beyond the Text: Toward a Performative Cultural Politics." In Sheron J. Dailey, ed., *The Future of Performance Studies: Visions and Revisions* (pp. 25–36). Annandale, Va.: National Communication Association.

Cruikshank, Julie, in collaboration with Angela Sidney, Kitty Smith, and Annie Ned. 1990. *Life Lived Like a Story: Life Stories of Three Yukon Elders.* Lincoln: University of Nebraska Press.

Delamont, Sara, Amanda Coffey, and Paul Atkinson. 2002. "The Twilight Years? Educational Ethnography and the Five Moments Model." *International Journal of Qualitative Studies in Education* 13: 223–38.

Denzin, Norman K., and Yvonna S. Lincoln, eds. 2000. *Handbook of Qualitative Research* (2nd ed). Thousand Oaks, Calif.: Sage.

Ellis, Carolyn, and Arthur P. Bochner, eds. 1996. *Composing Ethnography: Alternative Forms of Qualitative Writing.* Walnut Creek, Calif.: AltaMira Press.

Geertz, Clifford. 1973. *The Interpretation of Cultures.* New York: Basic Books.

Grossberg, Lawrence, Cary Nelson, and Paula Treichler, eds. 1992. *Cultural Studies.* New York: Routledge.

Guba, Egon G., and Yvonna S. Lincoln. 1981. *Effective Evaluation.* San Francisco: Jossey-Bass.

Keller, Evelyn Fox. 1985. *Reflections on Gender and Science.* New Haven, Conn.: Yale University Press.

Knorr-Cetina, Karin. 1981. *The Manufacture of Knowledge: An Essay on the Constructivist and Contextual Nature of Science.* Oxford, U.K.: Pergamon.

Knorr-Cetina, Karin, and Michael Mulkay, eds. 1983. *Science Observed: Perspectives on the Social Study of Science.* London: Sage.

Lincoln, Yvonna. 1995. "Emerging Criteria for Quality in Qualitative and Interpretive Inquiry." *Qualitative Inquiry* 1: 275–89.

———. 1998. "The Ethics of Teaching Qualitative Research." *Qualitative Inquiry* 4(3): 315–27.

Lincoln, Yvonna S., and Egon G. Guba. 1985. *Naturalistic Inquiry.* Thousand Oaks, Calif.: Sage.

———. 1989. "Ethics: The Failure of Positivist Science." *Review of Higher Education* 10(2): 135–42.

Lincoln, Yvonna S., and Norman K. Denzin. 2000. "The Seventh Moment: Out of the Past." In Norman K. Denzin and Yvonna S. Lincoln, eds. *Handbook of Qualitative Research* (pp. 1047–65). Thousand Oaks, Calif.: Sage.

Madison, D. Soyini. 1998. "Performances, Personal Narratives, and the Politics of Possibility." In Sheron J. Dailey, ed., *The Future of Performance Studies: Visions and Revisions* (pp. 276–86). Annandale, Va.: National Communication Association.

Marcus, George E., and Michael M. J. Fischer. 1986. *Anthropology as Cultural Critique: An Experimental Moment in the Human Sciences.* Chicago: University of Chicago Press.

Menchú, Rigoberta. 1984. *I, Rigoberta Menchu: An Indian Woman in Guatemala.* Edited by E. Burgos-Debray and translated by A. Wright. London: Verso.

Mienczakowski, Jim. 1992. *Synching Out Loud: A Journey into Illness.* Brisbane: Griffith University, Reprographics.

———. 1995. "The Theatre of Ethnography: The Reconstruction of Ethnography into Theatre with Emancipatory Potential." *Qualitative Inquiry* 1: 360–75.

———. 2000. "Ethnodrama: Performed Research—Limitations and Potential." In Paul Atkinson, Sara Delamont, and Amanda Coffey, eds., *Handbook of Ethnography* (pp. 468–76). London: Sage.

Mienczakowski, Jim, and Stephen Morgan. 1993. *Busting: The Challenge of the Drought Spirit.* Brisbane: Griffith University, Reprographics.

———. 2001. "Ethnodrama: Constructing Participatory, Experiential and Compelling Action Research through Performance." In Peter Reason and Hilary Bradbury, eds., *Handbook of Action Research: Participative Inquiry and Practice.* (pp. 219–27). Thousand Oaks, Calif.: Sage.

Prattis, J. Iain, ed. 1985. *Reflections: The Anthropological Muse.* Washington, D.C.: American Anthropological Association.

Rosaldo, Renato. 1989. *Culture and the Truth.* Boston: Beacon Press.

Schratz, Michael, and Rob Walker. 1995. *Research as Social Change: New Opportunities for Qualitative Research.* London: Routledge.

Smith, John K., and Deborah K. Deemer. 2000. "The Problem of Criteria in the Age of Relativism." In Norman K. Denzin and Yvonna S. Lincoln, eds., *Handbook of Qualitative Research* (2nd ed., pp. 877–96). Thousand Oaks, Calif.: Sage.

The Revolution
of Representation

The revolution in representation moves in three directions at the same time. On the one hand, this crisis signaled an understanding that qualitative researchers can no longer directly capture and hence represent lived experience. Rather, such experience is created in the social text written by the researcher. We know the other only through our practices of representation. Second, historically the ethnographer's text was written as if an objective accounting of the world could be produced. Third, ethnographies were constructed in the absence of any thought given to praxis, or the action that might be engendered by a given text. In fact, the connection of a text to a particular set of actions left the text in danger of being considered biased on account of its advocacy.

DISCOURSES OF GENDER, RACE, AND ETHNICITY

We now know that understanding is always partial, incomplete, and situated. Haraway's now-classic 1988 article "Situated Knowledges," which we reproduce here, shapes and clarifies this argument. Thus, if the written text is always incomplete, partial, and situated, then there can be, as we said previously, no god's-eye view. All writing reflects a particular standpoint: that of the inquirer/author. All texts arrive shaped implicitly or explicitly by the social, cultural, class, and gendered location of the author.

Collins and Visweswaran explore the implications of this last point. Collins writes from the standpoint of a black feminist epistemology, one that emphasizes the importance of concrete experience, dialogue, and an ethic of caring and personal accountability. Visweswaran discusses the possibilities of a feminist ethnography. She outlines competing approaches to feminist ethnography (woman centered, decentered, experimental, Third World, confessional) and compares feminist ethnography with traditional masculine views of fieldwork and writing. She valorizes first-person confessional fieldwork texts, giving special attention to Zora Neale Hurston and more recent first-person, second-wave feminist writing. Visweswaran's chapter anticipates more recent calls for dialogical, autoethnographic texts grounded in the concrete sites of everyday life.

Thus, the revolution of representation opens spaces for voices previously silenced. Challenges from feminists and scholars of color have moved ethnographic writing closer and closer to the first-person, autoethnographic text.

THE SUBALTERN SPEAKS

John Beverley enlarges this revolution, by taking up the topic of the *testimonio* and the issue of how the subaltern speaks. Gayatri Spivak's famous and difficult article "Can the Subaltern Speak?" rightly observes that if the subaltern spoke in a way that we would listen to, then s/he would not be a subaltern (Beverley 2000, 559). For Beverley, *testimonio* overcomes this objection. A *testimonio* is a first-person political text told by a narrator who is the protagonist or witness to the events that are reported on. These tellings report on torture, imprisonment, social upheaval, colonization processes, and struggles for survival. These works are intended to record and produce social change. Their truth is contained in the telling of the events that are recorded by the narrator. The author is not a researcher but rather a person who testifies on behalf of history and personal experience. In a *testimonio*, the author/narrator gives "his or her personal testimony directly, addressing a specific interlocutor." Often this is a personal story that is shared with a community.

Rigoberta Menchú's *I, Rigoberta Menchú: An Indian Woman in Guatemala* (1984) is one of the most important testimonios in recent times. In this work, Menchú tells of the torture and death of her little brother. Menchú's testimonio was used by Beverley and other academics as well as solidarity and human rights activists to mobilize international support for the Guatemalan guerrilla movement in the 1980s. Understood this way, testimonios as life-history documents connect memory and history to reflexive political action. They create spaces for the voices of previously silenced persons to be heard. In this way, the globalized postmodern subaltern has taken control of the production of her/his own history, helping to create the liberating texts for which liberal Western social scientists and critical theorists have been calling for decades.

AUTOETHNOGRAPHY

Finding a space for the subaltern voice suggests a new location for voice, that is, in personal narratives, autobiographies, and autoethnographic texts. In autoethnography, researchers conduct and write ethnographies of their own experience. If we study our own experiences, then the researcher becomes both the research subject and its object, the natural topic of autoethnography. A variety of terms and methodological strategies are associated with the meanings and uses of autoethnographies, including personal narratives, narratives of the self, writing stories, self stories, auto-observation, personal ethnography, literary tales, critical autobiography, radical empiricism, evocative narratives, reflexive ethnography, biographical method, co-constructed narrative, indigenous anthropology, anthropological poetics, and performance ethnography. The autoethnography can be read as a variation on the testimonio, or the first-person life history.

REFERENCES

Beverley, John. 2000. "Testimonio, Subalternity, and Narrative Authority." In Norman K. Denzin and Yvonna S. Lincoln, eds., *Handbook of Qualitative Research* (2nd ed., pp. 555–65). Thousand Oaks, Calif.: Sage Publications.

Menchú, Rigoberta. 1984. *I, Rigoberta Menchú: An Indian Woman in Guatemala.* Edited by E. Burgos-Debray and translated by A. Wright. London: Verso.

Spivak, Gayatri. 1988. "Can the Subaltern Speak?" In C. Nelson, L. Gossberg, and P. Treichler, eds., *Marxism and the Interpretation of Culture* (pp. 280–316). Urbana: University of Illinois Press.

1

Situated Knowledges: The Science Question in Feminism and the Privilege of Partial Perspective

Donna Haraway

Academic and activist feminist inquiry has repeatedly tried to come to terms with the question of what we might mean by the curious and inescapable term "objectivity." We have used a lot of toxic ink and trees processed into paper decrying what *they* have meant and how it hurts *us*. The imagined "they" constitute a kind of invisible conspiracy of masculinist scientists and philosophers replete with grants and laboratories. The imagined "we" are the embodied others, who are not allowed not to have a body, a finite point of view, and so an inevitably disqualifying and polluting bias in any discussion of consequence outside our own little circles, where a "mass"-subscription journal might reach a few thousand readers composed mostly of science haters. At least, I confess to these paranoid fantasies and academic resentments lurking underneath some convoluted reflections in print under my name in the feminist literature in the history and philosophy of science. We, the feminists in the debates about science and technology, are the Reagan era's "special-interest groups" in the rarified realm of epistemology, where traditionally what can count as knowledge is policed by philosophers codifying cognitive canon law. Of course, a special-interest group is, by Reaganoid definition, any collective historical subject that dares to resist the stripped-down atomism of Star

Reprinted from *Feminist Studies* 14, no. 3 (fall 1998): 575–99, by permission of the publisher, Feminist Studies Inc.

Wars, hypermarket, postmodern, media-simulated citizenship. Max Headroom doesn't have a body; therefore, he alone *sees* everything in the great communicator's empire of the Global Network. No wonder Max gets to have a naïve sense of humor and a kind of happily regressive, preoedipal sexuality, a sexuality that we ambivalently—with dangerous incorrectness—had imagined to be reserved for lifelong inmates of female and colonized bodies and maybe also white male computer hackers in solitary electronic confinement.

It has seemed to me that feminists have both selectively and flexibly used and been trapped by two poles of a tempting dichotomy on the question of objectivity. Certainly I speak for myself here, and I offer the speculation that there is a collective discourse on these matters. Recent social studies of science and technology, for example, have made available a very strong social constructionist argument for all forms of knowledge claims, most certainly and especially scientific ones.[1] According to these tempting views, no insider's perspective is privileged, because all drawings of inside-outside boundaries in knowledge are theorized as power moves, not moves toward truth. So, from the strong social constructionist perspective, why should we be cowed by scientists' descriptions of their activity and accomplishments; they and their patrons have stakes in throwing sand in our eyes. They tell parables about objectivity and scientific method to students in the first years of their initiation, but no practitioner of the high scientific arts would be caught dead *acting on* the textbook versions. Social constructionists make clear that official ideologies about objectivity and scientific method are particularly bad guides to how scientific knowledge is actually *made.* Just as for the rest of us, what scientists believe or say they do and what they really do have a very loose fit.

The only people who end up actually *believing* and, goddess forbid, acting on the ideological doctrines of disembodied scientific objectivity—enshrined in elementary textbooks and technoscience booster literature—are nonscientists, including a few very trusting philosophers. Of course, my designation of this last group is probably just a reflection of a residual disciplinary chauvinism acquired from identifying with historians of science and from spending too much time with a microscope in early adulthood in a kind of disciplinary preoedipal and modernist poetic moment when cells seemed to be cells and organisms, organisms. *Pace,* Gertrude Stein. But then came the law of the father and its resolution of the problem of objectivity, a problem solved by always already absent referents, deferred signifieds, split subjects, and the endless play of signifiers. Who wouldn't grow up warped? Gender, race, and the world itself—all seem the effects of warp speeds in the play of signifiers in a cosmic force field.

In any case, social constructionists might maintain that the ideological doctrine of scientific method and all the philosophical verbiage about epistemology were cooked up to distract our attention from getting to know the world *effectively* by practicing the sciences. From this point of view, science—the real game in town—is rhetoric, a series of efforts to persuade relevant social actors that one's manufactured knowledge is a route to a desired form of very objective power. Such persuasions must take account of the structure of facts and artifacts, as well as of language-mediated actors in the knowledge game. Here, artifacts and facts are parts of the powerful art of rhetoric. Practice is persuasion, and the focus is very much on practice. All knowledge is a condensed node in an agnostic power field. The strong program in the sociology of knowledge joins with the lovely and nasty tools of semiology and deconstruction to insist on the rhetorical nature of truth, including scientific truth. History is a story Western culture buffs tell each other; science is a contestable text and a power field; the content is the form.[2] Period.

So much for those of us who would still like to talk about *reality* with more confidence than we allow to the Christian Right when they discuss the Second Coming and their being raptured out of the final destruction of the world. We would like to think our appeals to real worlds are more than a desperate lurch away from cynicism and an act of faith like any other cult's, no matter how much space we generously give to all the rich and always historically specific mediations through which we and everybody else must know the world. But the further I get in describing the radical social constructionist program and a particular version of postmodernism, coupled with the acid tools of critical discourse in the human sciences, the more nervous I get. The imagery of force fields, of moves in a fully textualized and coded world, which is the working metaphor in many arguments about socially negotiated reality for the postmodern subject, is, just for starters, an imagery of high-tech military fields, of automated academic battlefields, where blips of light called players disintegrate (what a metaphor!) each other in order to stay in the knowledge and power game. Technoscience and science fiction collapse into the sun of their radiant (ir)reality—war.[3] It shouldn't take decades of feminist theory to sense the enemy here. Nancy Hartsock got all this crystal clear in her concept of abstract masculinity.[4]

I, and others, started out wanting a strong tool for deconstructing the truth claims of hostile science by showing the radical historical specificity, and so contestability, of every layer of the onion of scientific and technological constructions, and we end up with a kind of epistemological electroshock therapy, which far from ushering us into the high stakes tables of the game of contesting public truths, lays us out on the table with self-induced multiple personality disorder. We wanted a way to go beyond showing bias in science (that proved too easy anyhow) and beyond separating the good scientific sheep from the bad goats of bias and misuse. It seemed promising to do this by the strongest possible constructionist argument that left no cracks for reducing the issues to bias versus objectivity, use versus misuse, science versus pseudo-science. We unmasked the doctrines of objectivity because they threatened our budding sense of collective historical subjectivity and agency and our "embodied" accounts of the truth, and we ended up with one more excuse for not learning any post-Newtonian physics and one more reason to drop the old feminist self-help practices of repairing our own cars. They're just texts anyway, so let the boys have them back.

Some of us tried to stay sane in these disassembled and disassembling times by holding out for a feminist version of objectivity. Here, motivated by many of the same political desires, is the other seductive end of the objectivity problem. Humanistic Marxism was polluted at the source by its structuring theory about the domination of nature in the self-construction of man and by its closely related impotence in relation to historicizing anything women did that didn't qualify for a wage. But Marxism was still a promising resource as a kind of epistemological feminist mental hygiene that sought out own doctrines of objective vision. Marxist starting points offered a way to get to our own versions of standpoint theories, insistent embodiment, a rich tradition of critiquing hegemony without disempowering positivisms and relativisms and a way to get a nuanced theories of mediation. Some versions of psychoanalysis were of aid in this approach, especially anglophone object relations theory, which maybe did more for U.S. socialist feminism for a time than anything from the pen of Marx or Engels, much less Althusser or any of the late pretenders to sonship treating the subject of ideology and science.[5]

Another approach, "feminist empiricism," also converges with feminist uses of Marxian resources to get a theory of science which continues to insist on legitimate meanings of objectivity and which remains leery of a radical constructivism conjugated with semiology and narratology.[6] Feminists have to insist on a better account of the world; it is not enough to show radical historical contingency and modes of construction for everything. Here, we, as feminists, find ourselves perversely conjoined with the discourse of many practicing scientists, who, when all is said and done, mostly believe they are describing and discovering things *by means of* all their constructing and arguing. Evelyn Fox Keller has been particularly insistent on this fundamental matter, and Sandra Harding calls the goal of these approaches a "successor science." Feminists have stakes in a successor science project that offers a more adequate, richer, better account of a world, in order to live in it well and in critical, reflexive relation to our own as well as others' practices of domination and the unequal parts of privilege and oppression that make up all positions. In traditional philosophical categories, the issue is ethics and politics perhaps more than epistemology.

So, I think my problem, and "our" problem, is how to have *simultaneously* an account of radical historical contingency for all knowledge claims and knowing subjects, a critical practice for recognizing our own "semiotic technologies" for making meanings, *and* a no-nonsense commitment to faithful accounts of a "real" world, one that can be partially shared and that is friendly to earthwide projects of finite freedom, adequate material abundance, modest meaning in suffering, and limited happiness. Harding calls this necessary multiple desire a need for a successor science project and a postmodern insistence on irreducible difference and radical multiplicity of local knowledges. *All* components of the desire are paradoxical and dangerous, and their combination is both contradictory and necessary. Feminists don't need a doctrine of objectivity that promises transcendence, a story that loses track of its mediations just where someone might be held responsible for something, and unlimited instrumental power. We don't want a theory of innocent powers to represent the world, where language and bodies both fall into the bliss of organic symbiosis. We also don't want to theorize the world, much less act within it, in terms of Global Systems, but we do need an earthwide network of connections, including the ability partially to translate knowledges among very different—and power-differentiated—communities. We need the power of modern critical theories of how meanings and bodies get made, not in order to deny meanings and bodies, but in order to build meanings and bodies that have a chance for life.

Natural, social, and human sciences have always been implicated in hopes like these. Science has been about a search for translation, convertibility, mobility of meanings, and universality—which I call reductionism only when one language (guess whose?) must be enforced as the standard for all the translations and conversions. What money does in the exchange orders of capitalism, reductionism does in the powerful mental orders of global sciences. There is, finally, only one equation. That is the deadly fantasy that feminists and others have identified in some versions of objectivity, those in the service of hierarchical and positivist orderings of what can count as knowledge. That is one of the reasons the debates about objectivity matter, metaphorically and otherwise. Immortality and omnipotence are not our goals. But we could use some enforceable, reliable accounts of things not reducible to power moves and agonistic, high-status games of rhetoric or to scientistic, positivist arrogance. This point applies whether we are talking about genes, social classes, elementary particles, genders, races, or texts; the point applies to the exact, natural, social, and human sciences, despite the slippery ambiguities of the words "objectivity" and "science" as we slide around the discursive terrain. In our efforts to climb the greased pole leading to a usable doctrine of objectivity, I and most other feminists in the objectivity debates have alternatively, or even simultaneously, held on to both ends of the dichotomy, a dichotomy which Harding describes in terms of successor science projects versus postmodernist accounts of difference and which I have sketched in this essay as radical constructivism versus feminist critical empiricism. It is, of course, hard to climb when you are holding on to both ends of a pole, simultaneously or alternatively. It is, therefore, time to switch metaphors.

THE PERSISTENCE OF VISION

I would like to proceed by placing metaphorical reliance on a much maligned sensory system in feminist discourse: vision.[7] Vision can be good for avoiding binary oppositions. I would like to insist on the embodied nature of all vision and so reclaim the sensory system that has been used to signify a leap out of the marked body and into a conquering gaze from nowhere. This is the gaze that mythically inscribes all the marked bodies, that makes the unmarked category claim the power to see and not to be seen, to represent while escaping representation. This gaze signifies the unmarked positions of Man and White, one of the many nasty tones of the word "objectivity" to feminist ears in scientific and technological, late-industrial, militarized, racist, and male-dominant societies, that is, here, in the belly of the monster, in the United States in the late 1980s. I would like a doctrine of embodied objectivity that accommodates paradoxical and critical feminist science projects: Feminist objectivity means quite simply *situated knowledges.*

The eyes have been used to signify a perverse capacity—honed to perfection in the history of science tied to militarism, capitalism, colonialism, and male supremacy—to distance the knowing subject from everybody and everything in the interests of unfettered power. The instruments of visualization in multinationalist, postmodernist culture have compounded these meanings of disembodiment. The visualizing technologies are without apparent limit. The eye of any ordinary primate like us can be endlessly enhanced by sonography systems, magnetic resonance imaging, artificial intelligence-linked graphic manipulation systems, scanning electron microscopes, computed tomography scanners, color-enhancement techniques, satellite surveillance systems, home and office video display terminals, cameras for every purpose from filming the mucous membrane lining the gut cavity of a marine worm living in the vent gases on a fault between continental plates to mapping a planetary hemisphere elsewhere in the solar system. Vision in this technological feast becomes unregulated gluttony; all seems not just mythically about the god trick of seeing everything from nowhere, but to have put the myth into ordinary practice. And like the god trick, this eye fucks the world to make techno-monsters. Zoe Sofoulis calls this the cannibaleye of masculinist extra-terrestrial projects for excremental second birthing.

A tribute to this ideology of direct, devouring, generative, and unrestricted vision, whose technological mediations are simultaneously celebrated and presented as utterly transparent, can be found in the volume celebrating the 100th anniversary of the National Geographic Society. The volume closes its survey of the magazine's quest literature, effected through its amazing photography, with two juxtaposed chapters. The first is on "Space," introduced by the epigraph, "The choice is the universe—or nothing."[8] This chapter recounts the exploits of the space race and displays the color-enhanced "snapshots" of the outer planets reassembled from digitalized signals transmitted across vast space to let the viewer "experience" the moment of discovery in immediate vision of the "object."[9] These fabulous objects come to us simultaneously as indubitable

recordings of what is simply there and as heroic feats of technoscientific production. The next chapter, is the twin of outer space: "Inner Space," introduced
by the epigraph, "The stuff of stars has come alive."[10] Here, the reader is
brought into the realm of the infinitesimal, objectified by means of radiation
outside the wave lengths that are "normally" perceived by hominid primates,
that is, the beams of lasers and scanning electron microscopes, whose signals
are processed into the wonderful full-color snapshots of defending T cells and
invading viruses.

But, of course, that view of infinite vision is an illusion, a god trick. I would
like to suggest how our insisting metaphorically on the particularity and embodiment of all vision (although not necessarily organic embodiment and including technological mediation), and not giving in to the tempting myths of
vision as a route to disembodiment and second-birthing allows us to construct a usable, but not an innocent, doctrine of objectivity. I want a feminist
writing of the body that metaphorically emphasizes vision again, because we
need to reclaim that sense to find our way through all the visualizing tricks
and powers of modern sciences and technologies that have transformed the
objectivity debates. We need to learn in our bodies, endowed with primate
color and stereoscopic vision, how to attach the objective to our theoretical
and political scanners in order to name where we are and are not, in dimensions of mental and physical space we hardly know how to name. So, not so
perversely, objectivity turns out to be about particular and specific embodiment and definitely not about the false vision promising transcendence of all
limits and responsibility. The moral is simple: only partial perspective promises objective vision. All Western cultural narratives about objectivity are allegories of the ideologies governing the relations of what we call mind and
body, distance and responsibility. Feminist objectivity is about limited location and situated knowledge, not about transcendence and splitting of subject
and object. It allows us to become answerable for what we learn how to see.

These are lessons that I learned in part walking with my dogs and wondering how the world looks without a fovea and very few retinal cells for color vision but with a huge neural processing and sensory area for smells. It is a
lesson available from photographs of how the world looks to the compound
eyes of an insect or even from the camera eye of a spy satellite or the digitally
transmitted signals of space probe-perceived differences "near" Jupiter that
have been transformed into coffee table color photographs. The "eyes" made

available in modern technological sciences shatter any idea of passive vision; these prosthetic devices show us that all eyes, including your own organic ones, are active perceptual systems, building on translations and specific *ways of seeing*, that is, ways of life. There is no unmediated photograph or passive camera obscura in scientific accounts of bodies and machines; there are only highly specific visual possibilities, each with a wonderfully detailed, active, partial way of organizing worlds. All these pictures of the world should not be allegories of infinite mobility and interchangeability but of elaborate specificity and difference and the loving care people might take to learn how to see faithfully from another's point of view, even when the other is our own machine. That's not alienating distance; that's a *possible* allegory for feminist versions of objectivity. Understanding how these visual systems work, technically, socially, and psychically, ought to be a way of embodying feminist objectivity.

Many currents in feminism attempt to theorize grounds for trusting especially the vantage points of the subjugated; there is good reason to believe vision is better from below the brilliant space platforms of the powerful.[11] Building on that suspicion, this essay is an argument for situated and embodied knowledge and an argument against various forms of unlocatable, and so irresponsible, knowledge claims. Irresponsible means unable to be called into account. There is a premium on establishing the capacity to see from the peripheries and the depths. But here there also lies a serious danger of romanticizing and/or appropriating the vision of the less powerful while claiming to see from their positions. To see from below is neither easily learned nor unproblematic, even if "we" "naturally" inhabit the great underground terrain of the subjugated knowledges. The positionings of the subjugated are not exempt from critical reexamination, decoding, deconstruction, and interpretation; that is, from both semiological and hermeneutic modes of critical inquiry. The standpoints of the subjugated are not "innocent" positions. On the contrary, they are preferred because in principle they are least likely to allow denial of the critical and interpretive core of all knowledge. They are knowledgeable of modes of denial through repression, forgetting, and disappearing acts—ways of being nowhere while claiming to see comprehensively. The subjugated have a decent chance to be on to the god trick and all its dazzling—and, therefore, blinding—illuminations. "Subjugated" standpoints are preferred because they seem to promise more adequate, sustained, objective, transforming accounts of the world. But how to see from below is a problem requiring at least as much skill with bodies and language, with the mediations of vision, as the "highest" technoscientific visualizations.

Such preferred positioning is as hostile to various forms of relativism as to the most explicitly totalizing versions of claims to scientific authority. But the alternative to relativism is not totalization and single vision, which is always finally the unmarked category whose power depends on systematic narrowing and obscuring. The alternative to relativism is partial, locatable, critical knowledges sustaining the possibility of webs of connections called solidarity in politics and shared conversations in epistemology. Relativism is a way of being nowhere while claiming to be everywhere equally. The "equality" of positioning is a denial of responsibility and critical inquiry. Relativism is the perfect mirror twin of totalization in the ideologies of objectivity; both deny the stakes in location, embodiment, and partial perspective; both make it impossible to see well. Relativism and totalization are both "god tricks" promising vision from everywhere and nowhere equally and fully, common myths in rhetorics surrounding Science. But it is precisely in the politics and epistemology of partial perspectives that the possibility of sustained, rational, objective inquiry rests.

So, with many other feminists, I want to argue for a doctrine and practice of objectivity that privileges contestation, deconstruction, passionate construction, webbed connections, and hope for transformation of systems of knowledge and ways of seeing. But not just any partial perspective will do; we must be hostile to easy relativisms and holisms built out of summing and subsuming parts. "Passionate detachment"[12] requires more than acknowledged and self-critical partiality. We are also bound to seek perspective from those points of view, which can never be known in advance, that promise something quite extraordinary, that is, knowledge potent for constructing worlds less organized by axes of domination. From such a viewpoint, the unmarked category would *really* disappear—quite a difference from simply repeating a disappearing act. The imaginary and the rational—the visionary and objective vision—hover close together. I think Harding's plea for a successor science and for postmodern sensibilities must be read as an argument for the idea that the fantastic element of hope for transformative knowledge and the severe check and stimulus of sustained critical inquiry are jointly the ground of any believable claim to objectivity or rationality not riddled with breathtaking denials and repressions. It is even possible to read the record of scientific revolutions in terms of this feminist doctrine of rationality and objectivity. Science has been utopian and visionary from the start; that is one reason "we" need it.

A commitment to mobile positioning and to passionate detachment is dependent on the impossibility of entertaining innocent "identity" politics and epistemologies as strategies for seeing from the standpoints of the subjugated in order to see well. One cannot "be" either a cell or molecule—or a woman, colonized person, laborer, and so on—if one intends to see and see from these positions critically. "Being" is much more problematic and contingent. Also, one cannot relocate in any possible vantage point without being accountable for that movement. Vision is *always* a question of the power to see—and perhaps of the violence implicit in our visualizing practices. With whose blood were my eyes crafted? These points also apply to testimony from the position of "oneself." We are not immediately present to ourselves. Self-knowledge requires a semiotic-material technology to link meanings and bodies. Self-identity is a bad visual system. Fusion is a bad strategy of positioning. The boys in the human sciences have called this doubt about self-presence the "death of the subject" defined as a single ordering point of will and consciousness. That judgment seems bizarre to me. I prefer to call this doubt the opening of nonisomorphic subjects, agents, and territories of stories unimaginable from the vantage point of the cyclopean, self-satiated eye of the master subject. The Western eye has fundamentally been a wandering eye, a traveling lens. These peregrinations have often been violent and insistent on having mirrors for a conquering self—but not always. Western feminists also *inherit* some skill in learning to participate in revisualizing worlds turned upside down in earth-transforming challenges to the views of the masters. All is not to be done from scratch.

The split and contradictory self is the one who can interrogate positionings and be accountable, the one who can construct and join rational conversations and fantastic imaginings that change history.[13] Splitting, not being, is the privileged image for feminist epistemologies of scientific knowledge. "Splitting" in this context should be about heterogeneous multiplicities that are simultaneously salient and incapable of being squashed into isomorphic slots or cumulative lists. This geometry pertains within and among subjects. Subjectivity is multidimensional; so, therefore, is vision. The knowing self is partial in all its guises, never finished, whole, simply there and original; it is always constructed and stitched together imperfectly, and *therefore* able to join with another, to see together without claiming to be another. Here is the promise of objectivity: a scientific knower seeks the subject position, not of identity, but of objectivity, that is, partial connection. There is no way to "be" simultaneously in all, or wholly in any, of the privileged (i.e., subjugated) positions structured by gender, race, nation, and class. And that is a short list of critical positions. The search for such a "full" and total position is the search for the fetishized perfect subject of oppositional history, sometimes appearing in feminist theory as the essentialized Third World Woman.[14] Subjugation is not grounds for an ontology; it might be a visual clue. Vision requires instruments of vision; an optics is a politics of positioning. Instruments of vision mediate standpoints; there is no immediate vision from the standpoints of the subjugated. Identity, including self-identity, does not produce science; critical positioning does, that is, objectivity. Only those occupying the positions of the dominators are self-identical, unmarked, disembodied, unmediated, transcendent, born again. It is unfortunately possible for the subjugated to lust for and even scramble into that subject position—and then disappear from view. Knowledge from the point of view of the unmarked is truly fantastic, distorted, and irrational. The only position from which objectivity could not possibly be practiced and honored is the standpoint of the master, the Man, the One God, whose Eye produces, appropriates, and orders all difference. No one ever accused the God of monotheism of objectivity, only of indifference. The god trick is self-identical, and we have mistaken that for creativity and knowledge, omniscience even.

Positioning is, therefore, the key practice in grounding knowledge organized around the imagery of vision, and much Western scientific and philosophic discourse is organized in this way. Positioning implies responsibility for our enabling practices. It follows that politics and ethics ground struggles for and contests over what may count as rational knowledge. That is, admitted or not, politics and ethics ground struggles over knowledge projects in the exact, natural, social, and human sciences. Otherwise, rationality is simply impossible, an optical illusion projected from nowhere comprehensively. Histories of science may be powerfully told as histories of the technologies. These technologies are ways of life, social orders, practices of visualization. Technologies are skilled practices. How to see? Where to see from? What limits to vision? What to see for? Whom to see with Who gets to have more than one point of view? Who gets blinded? Who wears blinders? Who interprets the visual field?

What other sensory powers do we wish to cultivate besides vision? Moral and political discourse should be the paradigm for rational discourse about the imagery and technologies of vision. Sandra Harding's claim, or observation, that movements of social revolution have most contributed to improvements in science might be read as a claim about the knowledge consequences of new technologies of positioning. But I wish Harding had spent more time remembering that social and scientific revolutions have not always been liberatory, even if they have always been visionary. Perhaps this point could be captured in another phrase: the science question in the military. Struggles over what will count as rational accounts of the world are struggles over *how* to see. The terms of vision: the science question in colonialism, the science question in exterminism,[15] the science question in feminism.

The issue in politically engaged attacks on various empiricisms, reductionisms, or other versions of scientific authority should not be relativism—but location. A dichotomous chart expressing this point might look like this:

universal rationality	ethnophilosophies
common language	heteroglossia
new organon	deconstruction
unified field theory	oppositional positioning
world system	local knowledges
master theory	webbed accounts

But a dichotomous chart misrepresents in a critical way the positions of embodied objectivity that I am trying to sketch. The primary distortion is the illusion of symmetry in the chart's dichotomy, making any position appear, first, simply alternative and, second, mutually exclusive. A map of tensions and resonances between the fixed ends of a charged dichotomy better represents the potent politics and epistemologies of embodied, therefore accountable, objectivity. For example, local knowledges have also to be in tension with the productive structurings that force unequal translations and exchanges—material and semiotic—within the webs of knowledge and power. Webs can have the property of being systematic, even if being centrally structured global

systems with deep filaments and tenacious tendrils into time, space, and consciousness, which are the dimensions of world history. Feminist accountability requires a knowledge tuned to resonance, not to dichotomy. Gender is a
field of structured and structuring difference, in which the tones of extreme
localization, of the intimately personal and individualized body, vibrate in the
same field with global high-tension emissions. Feminist embodiment, then, is
not about fixed location in a reified body, female or otherwise, but about
nodes in fields, inflections in orientations, and responsibility for difference in
material-semiotic fields of meaning. Embodiment is significant prosthesis;
objectivity cannot be about fixed vision when what counts as an object is precisely what world history turns out to be about.

How should one be positioned in order to see, in this situation of tensions,
resonances, transformations, resistances, and complicities? Here, primate vision is not immediately a very powerful metaphor or technology for feminist
political-epistemological clarification, because it seems to present to consciousness already processed and objectified fields; things seem already fixed
and distanced. But the visual metaphor allow some to go beyond fixed ap-
pearances, which are only the end products. The metaphor invites us to investigate the varied apparatuses of visual production, including the prosthetic
technologies interfaced with our biological eyes and brains. And here we find
highly particular machineries for processing regions of the electromagnetic
spectrum into our pictures of the world. It is in the intricacies of these visualization technologies in which we are embedded that we will find metaphors
and means for understanding and intervening in the patterns of objectification in the world—that is, the patterns of reality for which we must be accountable. In these metaphors, we find means for appreciating simultaneously
both the concrete, "real" aspect and the aspect of semiosis and production in
what we call scientific knowledge.

I am arguing for politics and epistemologies of location, positioning, and
situating, where partiality and not universality is the condition of being heard
to make rational knowledge claims. These are claims on people's lives. I am arguing for the view from a body, always a complex, contradictory, structuring,
and structured body, versus the view from above, from nowhere, from sim-
plicity. Only the god trick is forbidden. Here is a criterion for deciding the science question in militarism, that dream science/technology of perfect
language, perfect communication, final order.

Feminism loves another science: the sciences and politics of interpretation, translation, stuttering, and the partly understood. Feminism is about the sciences of the multiple subject with (at least) double vision. Feminism is about a critical vision consequent upon a critical positioning in unhomogeneous gendered social space.[16] Translation is always interpretive, critical, and partial. Here is a ground for conversation, rationality, and objectivity—which is power-sensitive, not pluralist, "conversation." It is not even the mythic cartoons of physics and mathematics—incorrectly caricatured in antiscience ideology as exact, hypersimple knowledges—that have come to represent the hostile other to feminist paradigmatic models of scientific knowledge, but the dreams of the perfectly known in high-technology, permanently militarized scientific productions and positionings, the god trick of a Star Wars paradigm of rational knowledge. So location is about vulnerability; location resists the politics of closure, finality, or to borrow from Althusser, feminist objectivity resists "simplification in the last instance." That is because feminist embodiment resists fixation and is insatiably curious about the webs of differential positioning. There is no single feminist standpoint because our maps require too many dimensions for that metaphor to ground our visions. But the feminist standpoint theorists' goals of an epistemology and politics of engaged, accountable positioning remains eminently potent. The goal is better accounts of the world, that is, "science."

Above all, rational knowledge does not pretend to disengagement: to be from everywhere and so nowhere, to be free from interpretation, from being represented, to be fully self-contained or fully formalizable. Rational knowledge is a process of ongoing critical interpretation among "fields" of interpreters and decoders. Rational knowledge is power-sensitive conversation.[17] Decoding and transcoding plus translation and criticism; all are necessary. So science becomes the paradigmatic model, not of closure, but of that which is contestable and contested. Science becomes the myth, not of what escapes human agency and responsibility in a realm above the fray, but, rather, of accountability and responsibility for translations and solidarities linking the cacophonous visions and visionary voices that characterize the knowledges of the subjugated. A splitting of senses, a confusion of voice and sight, rather than clear and distinct ideas, becomes the metaphor for the ground of the rational. We seek not the knowledges ruled by phallogocentrism (nostalgia for the presence of the one true Word) and disembodied vision. We seek those rules by partial sight and limited voice—not partiality for its own sake but, rather, for the sake of the connections and unexpected openings situated knowledges make possible. Situated knowledges are about communities, not about isolated individuals. The only way to find a larger vision is to be somewhere in particular. The science question in feminism is about objectivity as positioned rationality. Its images are not the products of escape and transcendence of limits (the view from above) but the joining of partial views and halting voices into a collective subject position that promises a vision of the means of ongoing finite embodiment, of living within limits and contradictions—of views from somewhere.

OBJECTS AS ACTORS: THE APPARATUS OF BODILY PRODUCTION

Throughout this reflection on "objectivity," I have refused to resolve the ambiguities built into referring to science without differentiating its extraordinary range of contexts. Through the insistent ambiguity, I have foregrounded a field of commonalities binding exact, physical, natural, social, political, biological, and human sciences; and I have tied this whole heterogeneous field of academically (and industrially, e.g., in publishing, the weapons trade, and pharmaceuticals) institutionalized knowledge production to a meaning of science that insists on its potency in ideological struggles. But, partly in order to give play to both the specificities and the highly permeable boundaries of meanings in discourse on science, I would like to suggest a resolution to one ambiguity. Throughout the field of meanings constituting science, one of the commonalities concerns the status of any object of knowledge and of related claims about the faithfulness of our accounts to a "real world," no matter how mediated for us and no matter how complex and contradictory these worlds may be. Feminists, and others who have been most active as critics of the sciences and their claims or associated ideologies, have shied away from doctrines of scientific objectivity in part because of the suspicion that an "object" of knowledge is a passive and inert thing. Accounts of such objects can seem to be either appropriations of a fixed and determined world reduced to resource for instrumentalist projects of destructive Western societies, or they can be seen as masks for interests, usually dominating interests.

For example, "sex" as an object of biological knowledge appears regularly in the guise of biological determinism, threatening the fragile space for social constructionism and critical theory, with their attendant possibilities for active and transformative intervention, which were called into being by feminist concepts of gender as socially, historically, and semiotically positioned difference. And yet, to lose authoritative biological accounts of sex, which set up productive tensions with gender, seems to be to lose too much; it seems to be to lose not just analytic power within a particular Western tradition but also the body itself as anything but a blank page for social inscriptions, including those of biological discourse. The same problem of loss attends the radical "reduction" of the objects of physics or of any other science to the ephemera of discursive production and social construction.[18]

But the difficulty and loss are not necessary. They derive partly from the analytic tradition, deeply indebted to Aristotle and to the transformative history of "White Capitalist Patriarchy" (how may we name this scandalous Thing?) that turns everything into a resource for appropriation, in which an object of knowledge is finally itself only matter for the seminal power, the act, of the knower. Here, the object both guarantees and refreshes the power of the knower, but any status as *agent* in the productions of knowledge must be denied the object. It—the world—must, in sort, be objectified as a thing, not as an agent; it must be matter for the self-formation of the only social being in the productions of knowledge, the human knower. Zoe Sofoulis[19] identified the structure of this mode of knowing in technoscience as "resourcing"—as the second birthing of Man through the homogenizing of all the world's body into resource for his perverse projects. Nature is only the raw material of culture, appropriated, preserved, enslaved, exalted, or otherwise made flexible for disposal by culture in the logic of capitalist colonialism. Similarly, sex is only matter to the act of gender; the productionist logic seems inescapable in traditions of Western binary oppositions. This analytical and historical narrative logic accounts for my nervousness about the sex/gender distinction in the recent history of feminist theory. Sex is "resourced" for its representations as gender, which "we" can control. It has seemed all but impossible to avoid the trap of an appropriationist logic of domination built into the nature/culture opposition and its generative lineage, including the sex/gender distinction.

It seems clear that feminist accounts of objectivity and embodiment—that is, of a world—of the kind sketched in this essay require a deceptively simple maneuver within inherited Western analytical traditions, a maneuver begun in dialectics but stopping short of the needed revisions. Situated knowledges require that the object of knowledge be pictured as an actor and agent, not as a screen or a ground or a resource, never finally as slave to the master that closes off the dialectic in his unique agency and his authorship of "objective" knowledge. The point is paradigmatically clear in critical approaches to the social and human sciences, where the agency of people studied itself transforms the entire project of producing social theory. Indeed, coming to terms with the agency of the "objects" studied is the only way to avoid gross error and false knowledge of many kinds in these sciences. But the same point must apply to the other knowledge projects called sciences. A corollary of the insistence that ethics and politics covertly or overtly provide the bases for objectivity in the sciences as a heterogeneous whole, and not just in the social sciences, is granting the status of agent/actor to the "objects" of the world. Actors come in many and wonderful forms. Accounts of a "real" world do not, then, depend on a logic of "discovery" but on a power-charged social relation of "conversation." The world neither speaks itself nor disappears in favor of a master decoder. The codes of the world are not still, waiting only to be read. The world is not raw material for humanization; the thorough attacks on humanism, another branch of "death of the subject" discourse, have made this point quite clear. In some critical sense that is crudely hinted at by the clumsy category of the social or of agency, the world encountered in knowledge projects is an active entity. Insofar as a scientific account has been able to engage this dimension of the world as object of knowledge, faithful knowledge can be imagined and can make claims on us. But no particular doctrine of representation or decoding or discovery guarantees anything. The approach I am recommending is not a version of "realism," which has proved a rather poor way of engaging with the world's active agency.

My simple, perhaps simple-minded, maneuver is obviously not new in Western philosophy, but it has a special feminist edge to it in relation to the science question in feminism and to the linked question of gender as situated difference and the question of female embodiment. Ecofeminists have perhaps been most insistent on some version of the world as active subject, not as resource to be mapped and appropriated in bourgeois, Marxist, or masculinist projects. Acknowledging the agency of the world in knowledge makes room for some unsettling possibilities, including a sense of the world's independent sense of humor. Such a sense of humor is not comfortable for humanists and others committed to the world as resource. There are, however, richly evocative figures to promote feminist visualizations of the world as witty agent. We need not lapse into appeals to a primal mother resisting her translation into resource. The Coyote or Trickster, as embodied in Southwest native American accounts, suggests the situation we are in when we give up mastery but keep searching for fidelity, knowing all the while that we will be hoodwinked. I think these are useful myths for scientists who might be our allies. Feminist objectivity makes room for surprises and ironies at the heart of all knowledge production; we are not in charge of the world. We just live here and try to strike up noninnocent conversations by means of our prosthetic devices, including our visualization technologies. No wonder science fiction has been such a rich writing practice in recent feminist theory. I like to see feminist theory as a reinvented coyote discourse obligated to its sources in many heterogeneous accounts of the world.

Another rich feminist practice in science in the last couple of decades illustrates particularly well the "activation" of the previously passive categories of objects of knowledge. This activation permanently problematizes binary distinctions like sex and gender, without eliminating their strategic utility. I refer to the reconstructions in primatology (especially, but not only, in women's practice as primatologists, evolutionary biologists, and behavioral ecologists) of what may count as sex, especially as female sex, in scientific accounts.[20] The *body*, the object of biological discourse, becomes a most engaging being. Claims of biological determinism can never be the same again. When female "sex" has been so thoroughly retheorized and revisualized that it emerges as practically indistinguishable from "mind," something basic has happened to the categories of biology. The biological female peopling current biological behavioral accounts has almost no passive properties left. She is structuring and active in every respect; the "body" is an agent, not a resource. Difference is theorized biologically as situational, not intrinsic, at every level from gene to foraging pattern, thereby fundamentally changing the biological politics of the body. The relations between sex and gender need to be categorically reworked within these frames of knowledge. I would like to suggest that this trend in explanatory strategies in biology is an allegory for interventions faithful to projects of feminist objectivity. The point is not that these new pictures of the biological female are simply true or not open to contestation and conversation—quite the opposite. But these pictures foreground knowledge as situated conversation at every level of its articulation. The boundary between animal and human is one of the stakes in this allegory, as is the boundary between machine and organism.

So I will close with a final category useful to a feminist theory of situated knowledges: the apparatus of bodily production. In her analysis of the production of the poem as an object of literary value, Katie King offers tools that clarify matters in the objectivity debates among feminists. King suggests the term "apparatus of literary production" to refer to the emergence of literature at the intersection of art, business, and technology. The apparatus of literary production is a matrix from which "literature" is born. Focusing on the potent object of value called the "poem," King applies her analytic framework to the relation of women and writing technologies.[21] I would like to adapt her work to understanding the generation—the actual production and reproduction— of bodies and other objects of value in scientific knowledge projects. At first glance, there is a limitation to using King's scheme inherent in the "facticity" of biological discourse that is absent from literary discourse and its knowledge claims. Are biological bodies "produced" or "generated" in the same strong sense as poems? From the early stirrings of Romanticism in the late eighteenth century, many poets and biologists have believed that poetry and organisms are siblings. *Frankenstein* may be read as a mediation on this proposition. I continue to believe in this potent proposition but in a postmodern and not a Romantic manner. I wish to translate the ideological dimensions of "facticity" and "the organic" into a cumbersome entity called a "material-semiotic actor." This unwieldy term is intended to portray the object of knowledge as an active, meaning-generating part of apparatus of bodily production, without ever implying the immediate presence of such objects or, what is the same thing, their final or unique determination of what can count as objective knowledge at a particular historical juncture. Like "poems," which are sites of literary production where language too is an actor independent of intentions and authors, bodies as objects of knowledge are material-semiotic generative nodes. Their *boundaries* materialize in social interaction. Boundaries are drawn by mapping practices; "objects" do not preexist as such. Objects are boundary projects. But boundaries shift from within; boundaries are very tricky. What boundaries provisionally contain remains generative, productive of meanings and bodies. Siting (sighting) boundaries is a risky practice.

Objectivity is not about disengagement but about mutual *and* usually unequal structuring, about taking risks in a world where "we" are permanently mortal, that is, not in "final" control. We have, finally, no clear and distinct ideas. The various contending biological bodies emerge at the intersection of biological research and writing, medical and other business practices, and technology, such as the visualization technologies enlisted as metaphors in this essay. But also invited into that node of intersection is the analogue to the lively languages that actively intertwine in the production of literary value: the coyote and the protean embodiments of the world as witty agent and actor. Perhaps the world resists being reduced to mere resource because it is—not mother/matter/mutter—but coyote, a figure of the always problematic, always potent tie between meaning and bodies. Feminist embodiment, feminist hopes for partiality, objectivity, and situated knowledges, turn on conversations and codes at this potent node in fields of possible bodies and meanings. Here is where science, science fantasy and science fiction converge in the objectivity question in feminism. Perhaps our hopes for accountability, for politics, for ecofeminism, turn on revisioning the world as coding trickster with whom we must learn to converse.

NOTES

This essay originated as commentary on Sandra Harding's "The Science Question in Feminism," at the Western Division meetings of the American Philosophical Association, San Francisco, March 1987. Support during the writing of this paper was generously provided by the Alpha Fund of the Institute for Advanced Study, Princeton, New Jersey. Thanks especially to Joan Scott, Judy Butler, Lila Abu-Lughod, and Dorinne Kondo.

1. For example, see Karin Knorr-Cetina and Michael Mulkay, eds., *Science Observed: Perspectives on the Social Study of Science* (London: Sage 1983); Wiebe E. Bijker, Thomas P. Hughes, and Trevor Pinch, eds., *The Social Construction of Technological System* (Cambridge: MIT Press, 1987); and esp. Bruno Latour's *Les microbes, guerre et pais, suivi de irréductions* (Paris: Métailié, 1984) and *The Pasteurization of France, Followed by Irreductions: A Politico-Scientific Essay* (Cambridge: Harvard University Press, 1988). Borrowing from Michel Tournier's *Vendredi* (Paris: Gallimard, 1967), *Les microbes* (p. 171), Latour's brilliant and maddening aphoristic polemic against all forms of reductionism, makes the essential point for feminists: "Méfiez-vous de la pureté; c'est le vitriol de l'ame" (Beware of purity; it is the vitriol of the soul). Latour is not otherwise a notable feminist theorist, but he might be made into one by readings as perverse as those he makes of the laboratory, that great machine for making significant mistakes faster than anyone else can, and so gaining world-changing power. The laboratory for Latour is the railroad industry of epistemology,

where facts can only be made to run on the tracks laid down from the laboratory out. Those who control the railroads control the surround territory. How could we have forgotten? But now it's not so much the bankrupt railroads we need as the satellite network. Facts run on light beams these days.

2. For an elegant and very helpful elucidation of a noncartoon version of this argument, see Hayden White, *The Content of the Form: Narrative Discourse and Historical Representation* (Baltimore: Johns Hopkins University Press, 1987). I still want more: and unfulfilled desire can be a powerful seed for changing the stories.

3. In "Through the Lumen: Frankenstein and the Optics of Re-Origination" (Ph.D. diss. University of California at Santa Cruz, 1988), Zoe Sofoulis has produced a dazzling (she will forgive me the metaphor) theoretical treatment of technoscience, the psychoanalysis of science fiction culture, and the metaphorics of extraterrestrialism, including a wonderful focus on the ideologies and philosophies of light, illumination, and discovery in Western mythics of science and technology. My essay was revised in dialogue with Sofoulis's arguments and metaphors in her dissertation.

4. Nancy Hartsock, *Money, Sex, and Power: An Essay on Domination and Community* (Boston: Northeastern University Press, 1984).

5. Crucial to this discussion are Sandra Harding, *The Science Quesiton in Feminism* (Ithaca, N.Y.: Cornell University Press, 1987); Evelyn Fox Keller, *Reflections on Gender and Science* (New Haven, Conn.: Yale University Press, 1984); Nancy Hartsock, "The Feminist Standpoint: Developing the Ground for a Specifically Feminist Historical Materialism," in *Discovering Reality: Feminist Perspectives on Epistemology, Metaphysics, and Philosophy of Science*, eds. Sandra Harding and Merrill B. Hintikka (Dordrecht, The Netherlands: Reidel, 1983): 283–310; Jane Flax's "Political Philosophy and the Patriarchal Unconscious," in *Discovering Reality* 245–891; and "Postmodernism and Gender Relations in Feminist Theory," *Signs* 12 (summer 1983): 621–43; Evelyn Fox Keller and Christine Grontkowski, "The Mind's Eye," in *Discovering Reality* 207–24; Hilary Rose, "Women's Work, Women's Knowledge," in *What Is Feminism? A Re-Examination*, eds. Juliet Mitchell and Ann Oakley (New York: Pantheon, 1986), 161–83; Donna Haraway, "A Manifesto for Cyborgs: Science, Technology, and Socialist Feminism in the 1980s," *Socialist Review*, no. 80 (March–April 1985): 65–107; and Rosalind Pollack Petchesky, "Fetal Images: The Power of Visual Culture in the Politics of Reproduction," *Feminist Studies* 13 (summer 1987): 263–92.

Aspects of the debates about modernism and postmodernism affect feminist analyses of the problem of "objectivity." Mapping the fault line between modernism and postmodernism in ethnography and anthropology—in which the high stakes are

the authorization or prohibition to craft *comparative* knowledge across "cultures"—
Marilyn Strathern made the crucial observation that it is not the written ethnography
that is parallel to the work of art as object-of-knowledge, but the culture. The Romantic
and modernist natural-technical objects of knowledge, in science and in other cultural
practice, stand on one side of this divide. The postmodernist formation stands on the
other side, with its "anti-aesthetic" of permanently split, problematized, always receding
and deferred "objects" of knowledge and practice, including signs, organisms, systems,
selves, and cultures. "Objectivity" in a postmodern framework cannot be about
unproblematic objects; it must be about specific prosthesis and always partial
translations. At root, objectivity is about crafting comparative knowledge: How may a
community name things to be stable and to be like each other? In postmodernism, this
query translates into a question of the politics of redrawing of boundaries in order to
have noninnocent conversations and connections. What is at stake in the debates about
modernism and postmodernism is the pattern of relationships between and within
bodies and language. This is a crucial matter for feminists. See Marilyn Strathern, "Out
of Context: The Persuasive Fictions of Anthropology," *Current Anthropology* 28 (June
1987): 251–81, and "Partial Connections," Munro Lecture, University of Edinburgh,
November 1987, unpublished manuscript.

6. Harding, 24–26, 161–62.

7. John Varley's science fiction short story, "The Persistence of Vision," in *The
Persistence of Vision* (New York: Dell, 1978), 263–316, is part of the inspiration for
this section. In the story, Varley constructs a utopian community designed and built
by the deaf-blind. He then explores these people's technologies and other mediations
of communication and their relations to sighted children and visitors. In the story,
"Blue Champagne," in *Blue Champagne* (New York: Berkeley, 1986), 17–79, Varley
transmutes the theme to interrogate the politics of intimacy and technology for a
paraplegic young woman whose prosthetic device, the golden gypsy, allows her full
mobility. But because the infinitely costly device is owned by an intergalactic
communications and entertainment empire, for which she works as a media star
making "feelies," she may keep her technological, intimate, enabling, other self only
in exchange for her complicity in the commodification of all experience. What are
her limits to the reinvention of experience for sale? Is the personal political under
the sign of simulation? One way to read Varley's repeated investigations of finally
always limited embodiments, differently abled beings, prosthetic technologies, and
cyborgian encounters with their finitude, despite their extraordinary transcendence
of "organic" orders, is to find an allegory for the personal and political in the
historical mythic time of the late twentieth century, the era of techno-biopolitics.
Prosthesis becomes a fundamental category for understanding our most intimate

selves. Prosthesis is semiosis, the making of meanings and bodies, not for transcendence, but for power-charged communication.

8. C. D. B. Bryan, *The National Geographic Society: 100 Years of Adventure and Discovery* (New York: Harry N. Abrams, 1987), 352.

9. I owe my understanding of the experience of these photographs to Jim Clifford, University of California at Santa Cruz, who identified their "land ho!" effect on the reader.

10. Bryan, 454.

11. See Hartsock, "The Feminist Standpoint: Developing the Ground for a Specifically Feminist Historical Materialism"; and Chela Sandoval, *Yours in Struggle: Women Respond to Racism* (Oakland, Calif.: Center for Third World Organizing, n.d.); Harding; and Gloria Anzaldua, *Borderlands/La Frontera* (San Francisco: Spinsters/Aunt Lute, 1987).

12. Annette Kuhn, *Women's Pictures: Feminism and Cinema* (London: Routledge & Kegan Paul, 1982), 3–18.

13. Joan Scott reminded me that Teresa de Lauretis put it like this: Difference among women may be better understood as differences within women. . . . But once understood in their constitutive power—once it is understood, that is, that these differences not only constitute each woman's consciousness and subjective limits but all together define the female subject of feminism in its very specificity, is inherent and at least for now irreconcilable contradiction—these differences, then, cannot be again collapsed into a fixed identity, a sameness of all women as Woman, or a representation of Feminism as a coherent and available image. See Theresa de Lauretis, "Feminist Studies/Critical Studies: Issues, Terms, and Contexts," in her *Feminist Studies/Critical Studies* (Bloomington: Indiana University Press, 1986), 14–15.

14. Chandra Mohanty, "Under Western Eyes," *Boundary* 2 and 3 (1984): 333–58.

15. See Sofoulis, unpublished manuscript.

16. In *The Science Question in Feminism* (p. 18), Harding suggests that gender has three dimensions, each historically specific: gender symbolism, the social-sexual division of labor, and processes of constructing individual gendered identity. I would enlarge her point to note that there is no reason to expect the three dimensions to covary or codetermine each other, at least not directly. That is, extremely steep gradients between contrasting terms in gender symbolism may very well not correlate with sharp social-sexual divisions of labor or social power, but they may be

closely related to sharp racial stratification or something else. Similarly, the processes of gendered subject formation may not be directly illuminated by knowledge of the sexual division of labor or the gender symbolism in the particular historical situation under examination. On the other hand, we should expect mediated relations among the dimensions. The mediations might move through quite different social axes of organization of both symbols, practice, and identity, such as race—and vice versa. I would suggest also that science, as well as gender or race, might be usefully broken up into such a multipart scheme of symbolism, social practice, and subject position. More than three dimensions suggest themselves when the parallels are drawn. The different dimensions of, for example, gender, race and science might mediate relations among dimensions on a parallel chart. That is, racial divisions of labor might mediate the patterns of connection between symbolic connections and formations of gendered or racial subjectivity might mediate the relations between scientific social division of labor and scientific symbolic patterns. The chart below begins an analysis by parallel dissections. In the chart (and in reality?), both gender and science are analytically asymmetrical; that is, each term contains and obscures a structuring hierarchicalized binary opposition, sex/gender and nature/science. Each binary opposition orders the silent term by a logic of appropriation, as resource to product, nature to culture, potential to actual. Both poles of the opposition are constructed and structure each other dialectically. Within each voiced or explicit term, further asymmetrical splittings can be excavated, as from gender, masculine to feminine, and from science, hard sciences to soft sciences. This is a point about remembering how a particular analytical tool works, willy-nilly, intended or not. The chart reflects common ideological aspects of discourse on science and gender and may help as an analytical tool to crack open mystified units like Science or Woman.

GENDER

1) symbolic system
2) social division of labor (by sex, by race, etc.)
3) individual identity/subject position (desiring/desired; autonomous relations)
4) material culture (e.g., gender paraphernalia and daily gender technologies, the narrow tracks on which sexual difference runs)
5) dialectic of construction and discovery

SCIENCE

symbolic system
social division of labor (e.g., by craft or industrial logics)
individual identity/subject position (knower/known; scientist/other)

material culture (e.g., laboratories, the narrow tracks on which facts run)

dialectic of construction and discovery

17. Katie King, "Canons without Innocence" (Ph.D. diss., University of California at Santa Cruz, 1987).

18. Evelyn Fox Keller, in "The Gender/Science System: Or, Is Sex to Gender As Nature Is to Science?" (*Hypatia* 2 [fall 1987]: 37–49), has insisted on the important possibilities opened up by the construction of the intersection of the distinction between sex and gender, on the one hand, and nature and science, on the other. She also insists on the need to hold to some nondiscursive grounding in "sex" and "nature," perhaps what I am calling the "body" and "world."

19. See Sofoulis, chap. 3.

20. Donna Haraway, *Primate Visions: Gender, Race, and Nature in the World of Modern Science* (New York: Routledge & Kegan Paul), spring 1989.

21. Katie King, prospectus for "The Passing Dreams of Choice . . . Once Before and After: Audre Lorde and the Apparatus of Literary Production" (*MS*, University of Maryland, College Park, 1987).

2

Toward an Afrocentric Feminist Epistemology

Patricia Hill Collins

A small girl and her mother passed a statue depicting a European man who had barehandedly subdued a ferocious lion. The little girl stopped, looked puzzled and asked, "Mama, something's wrong with that statute. Everybody knows that a man can't whip a lion." "But darling," her mother replied, "you must remember that the man made the statue."

—As told by Katie G. Cannon

Black feminist thought, like all specialized thought, reflects the interests and standpoint of its creators. Tracing the origin and diffusion of any body of specialized thought reveals its affinity to the power of the group that created it (Mannheim 1936). Because elite white men and their representatives control structures of knowledge validation, white male interests pervade the thematic content of traditional scholarship. As a result, Black women's experiences with work, family, motherhood, political activism, and sexual politics have been routinely distorted in, or excluded from, traditional academic discourse.

Black feminist thought as specialized thought reflects the thematic content of African-American women's experiences. But because Black women have had to struggle against white male interpretations of the world in order to express a self-defined standpoint, Black feminist thought can best be viewed as subjugated knowledge. The suppression of Black women's efforts for self-definition in traditional sites of knowledge production has led African-American women to use alternative sites such as music, literature, daily conversations, and everyday behavior as important locations for articulating the core themes of a Black feminist consciousness.

Investigating the subjugated knowledge of subordinate groups—in this case a Black women's standpoint and Black feminist thought—requires more ingenuity than that needed to examine the standpoints and thought of dominant groups. I found my training as a social scientist inadequate to the task of studying the subjugated knowledge of a Black women's standpoint. This is because subordinate groups have long had to use alternative ways to create independent self-definitions and self-valuations and to rearticulate them through our own specialists. Like other subordinate groups, African-American women have not only developed a distinctive Black women's standpoint, but have done so by using alternative ways of producing and validating knowledge.

Epistemology is the study of the philosophical problems in concepts of knowledge and truth. The techniques I use in this volume to rearticulate a Black women's standpoint and to further Black feminist thought may appear to violate some of the basic epistemological assumptions of my training as a social scientist. In choosing the core themes in Black feminist thought that merited investigation, I consulted established bodies of academic research. But I also searched my own experiences and those of African-American women I know for themes we thought were important. My use of language signals a different relationship to my material than that which currently prevails in social science literature. For example, I often use the pronoun "our" instead of "their" when referring to African-American women, a choice that embeds me in the group I am studying instead of distancing me from it. In addition, I occasionally place my own concrete experiences in the text. To support my analysis, I cite few statistics and instead rely on the voices of Black women from all walks of life. These conscious epistemological choices signal my attempts not only to explore the thematic content of Black feminist thought but to do so in a way that does not violate its basic epistemological framework.

One key epistemological concern facing Black women intellectuals is the question of what constitutes adequate justifications that a given knowledge claim, such as a fact or theory, is true. In producing the specialized knowledge of Black feminist thought, Black women intellectuals often encounter two distinct epistemologies: one representing elite white male interests and the other expressing Afrocentric feminist concerns. Epistemological choices about who to trust, what to believe, and why something is true are not benign academic issues. Instead, these concerns tap the fundamental question of which versions of truth will prevail and shape thought and action.

THE EUROCENTRIC, MASCULINIST KNOWLEDGE VALIDATION PROCESS

Institutions, paradigms and other elements of the knowledge validation procedure controlled by elite white men constitute the Eurocentric masculinist knowledge validation process. The purpose of this process is to represent a white male standpoint. Although it reflects powerful white males interest, various dimensions of the process are not necessarily managed by white men themselves. Scholars, publishers, and other experts represent specific interests and credentialing processes, and their knowledge claims must satisfy the political and epistemological criteria of the contexts in which they reside (Kuhn 1962; Mulkay 1979).

Two political criteria influence the knowledge validation process. First, knowledge claims are evaluated by a community of experts whose members represent the standpoints of the groups from which they originate. Within the Eurocentric masculinist process this means that a scholar making a knowledge claim must convince a scholarly community controlled by white men that a given claim is justified. Second, each community of experts must maintain its credibility as defined by the larger group in which it is situated and from which it draws its basic, taken-for-granted knowledge. This means that scholarly communities that challenge basic beliefs held in the culture at large will be deemed less credible than those which support popular perspectives.

When white men control the knowledge validation process, both political criteria can work to suppress Black feminist thought. Given that the general culture shaping the taken-for-granted knowledge of the community of experts is permeated by widespread notions of Black and female inferiority, new knowledge claims that seem to violate these fundamental assumptions are likely to be viewed as anomalies (Kuhn 1962). Moreover, specialized thought challenging notions of Black and female inferiority is unlikely to be generated from within a white-male-controlled academic community because both the kinds of questions that could be asked and the explanations that would be found satisfying would necessarily reflect a basic lack of familiarity with Black women's reality.

The experiences of African-American women scholars illustrate how individuals who wish to rearticulate a Black women's standpoint through Black feminist thought can be suppressed by a white-male-controlled knowledge validation process. Exclusion from basic literacy, quality educational experiences, and faculty and administrative positions has limited Black women's access to influential academic positions (Zinn et al. 1986). While Black women can produce knowledge claims that contest those advanced by the white male community, this community does not grant that Black women scholars have competing knowledge claims based in another knowledge validation process. As a consequence, any credentials controlled by white male academicians can be denied to Black women producing Black feminist thought on the grounds that it is not credible research.

Black women with academic credentials who seek to exert the authority that our status grants us to propose new knowledge claims about African-American women face pressures to use our authority to help legitimate a system that devalues and excludes the majority of Black women. When an outsider group—in this case, African-American women—recognizes that the insider group—namely, white men—requires special privileges from the larger society, a special problem arises of keeping the outsiders out and at the same time having them acknowledge the legitimacy of this procedure. Accepting a few "safe" outsiders addresses this legitimation problem (Berger and Luckmann 1966). One way of excluding the majority of Black women from the knowledge validation process is to permit a few Black women to acquire positions of authority in institutions that legitimate knowledge, and to encourage us to work within the taken-for-granted assumptions of Black female inferiority shared by the scholarly community and by the culture at large. Those Black women who accept these assumptions are likely to be rewarded by their institutions, often at significant personal cost. Those challenging the assumptions run the risk of being ostracized.

African-American women academicians who persist in trying to rearticulate a Black women's standpoint also face potential rejection of our knowledge claims on epistemological grounds. Just as the material realities of the powerful and the dominated produce separate standpoints, each group may also have distinctive epistemologies or theories of knowledge. Black women scholars may know that something is true but be unwilling or unable to legitimate our claims using Eurocentric, masculinist criteria for consistency with substantiated knowledge and criteria for methodological adequacy. For any body of knowledge, new knowledge claims must be consistent with an existing body of knowledge that the group controlling the interpretive context accepts as true. The methods used to validate knowledge claims must also be acceptable to the group controlling the knowledge validation process.

The criteria for the methodological adequacy of positivism illustrate the epistemological standards that Black women scholars would have to satisfy in legitimating Black feminist thought using a Eurocentric masculinist epistemology. While I describe Eurocentric masculinist approaches as a single process, many schools of thought or paradigms are subsumed under this one process. Moreover, my focus on positivism should be interpreted neither to mean that all dimensions of positivism are inherently problematic for Black women nor that nonpositivist frameworks are better. For example, most traditional frameworks that women of color internationally regard as oppressive to women are not positivist, and Eurocentric feminist critiques of positivism may have less political importance for women of color (Narayan 1989).

Positivist approaches aim to create scientific descriptions of reality by producing objective generalizations. Because researchers have widely differing values, experiences, and emotions, genuine science is thought to be unattainable unless all human characteristics except rationality are eliminated from the research process. By following strict methodological rules, scientists aim to distance themselves from the values, vested interests, and emotions generated by their class, race, sex, or unique situation. By decontextualizing themselves, they allegedly become detached observers and manipulators of nature (Jaggar 1983; Harding 1986). Moreover, this researcher decontextualization is paralleled by comparable efforts to remove the objects of study from their contexts. The result of this entire process is often the separation of information from meaning (Fausto-Sterling 1989).

Several requirements typify positivist methodological approaches. First, research methods generally require a distancing of the researcher from her or his "object" of study by defining the researcher as a "subject" with full human subjectivity and by objectifying the "object" of study (Keller 1985; Asante 1987; hooks 1989). A second requirement is the absence of emotions from the research process (Hochschild 1975; Jaggar 1983). Third, ethics and values are deemed inappropriate in the research process, either as the reason for scientific inquiry or as part of the research process itself (Richards 1980; Haan et al. 1983). Finally, adversarial debates, whether written or oral, become the preferred method of ascertaining truth: the arguments that can withstand the greatest assault and survive intact become the strongest truths (Moulton 1983).

Such criteria ask African-American women to objectify ourselves, devalue our emotional life, displace our motivations for furthering knowledge about Black women, and confront in an adversarial relationship those with more social, economic and professional power. It therefore seems unlikely that Black women would use a positivist epistemological stance in rearticulating a Black women's standpoint. Black women are more likely to choose an alternative epistemology for assessing knowledge claims, one using different standards that are consistent with Black women's criteria for substantiated knowledge and with our criteria for methodological adequacy. If such an epistemology exists, what are its contours? Moreover, what is its role in the production of Black feminist thought?

THE CONTOURS OF AN AFROCENTRIC FEMINIST EPISTEMOLOGY

Africanist analyses of the Black experience generally agree on the fundamental elements of an Afrocentric standpoint (Okanlawon 1972). Despite varying histories, Black societies reflect elements of a core African value system that existed prior to and independently of racial oppression (Jahn 1961; Mbiti 1969; Diop 1974; Zahan 1979; Sobel 1979; Richards 1980, 1990; Asante 1987; Myers 1988). Moreover, as a result of colonialism, imperialism, slavery, apartheid, and other systems of racial domination, Black people share a common experience of oppression. These two factors foster shared Afrocentric values that permeate the family structure, religious institutions, culture, and community life of Blacks in varying parts of Africa, the Caribbean, South America, and North America (Walton 1971; Gayle 1971; Smitherman 1977; Shimkin et al. 1978; Walker 1980; Sudarkasa 1981; Thompson 1983; Mitchell and Lewter 1986; Asante 1987; Brown 1989). This Afrocentric consciousness permeates the shared history of people of African descent through the framework of a distinctive Afrocentric epistemology (Turner 1984).

Feminist scholars advance a similar argument by asserting that women share a history of gender oppression, primarily through sex/gender hierarchies (Eisenstein 1983; Hartsock 1983b; Andersen 1988). These experiences transcend divisions among women created by race, social class, religion, sexual orientation, and ethnicity and form the basis of a women's standpoint with a corresponding feminist consciousness and epistemology (Rosaldo 1974; D. Smith 1987; Hartsock 1983a; Jaggar 1983).

Because Black women have access to both the Afrocentric and the feminist standpoints, an alternative epistemology used to rearticulate a Black women's standpoint should reflect elements of both traditions. The search for the distinguishing features of an alternative epistemology used by African-American women reveals that values and ideas Africanist scholars identify as characteristically "Black" often bear remarkable resemblance to similar ideas claimed by feminist scholars as characteristically "female."[1] This similarity suggests that the material conditions of race, class, and gender oppression can vary dramatically and yet generate some uniformity in the epistemologies of subordinate groups. Thus the significance of an Afrocentric feminist epistemology may lie in how such an epistemology enriches our understanding of how subordinate groups create knowledge that fosters resistance.

The parallels between the two conceptual schemes raise a question: Is the worldview of women of African descent more intensely infused with the overlapping feminine/Afrocentric standpoints than is the case for either African-American men or white women? While an Afrocentric feminist epistemology reflects elements of epistemologies used by African-Americans and women as groups, it also paradoxically demonstrates features that may be unique to Black women. On certain dimensions Black women may more closely resemble Black men; on others, white women; and on still others Black women may stand apart from both groups. Black women's both/and conceptual orientation, the act of being simultaneously a member of a group and yet standing apart from it, forms an integral part of Black women's consciousness. Black women negotiate these contradictions, a situation Bonnie Thornton Dill (1979) labels the "dialectics of Black womanhood," by using this both/and conceptual orientation.

Rather than emphasizing how a Black women's standpoint and its accompanying epistemology are different from those in Afrocentric and feminist analyses, I use Black women's experiences to examine points of contact between the two. Viewing an Afrocentric feminist epistemology in this way challenges additive analyses of oppression claiming that Black women have a more accurate view of oppression than do other groups. Such approaches suggest that oppression can be quantified and compared and that adding layers of oppression produces a potentially clearer standpoint (Spelman 1982). One implication of standpoint approaches is that the more subordinated the group, the purer the vision of the oppressed group. This is an outcome of the origins of standpoint approaches in Marxist social theory, itself an analysis of social structure rooted in Western either/or dichotomous thinking. Ironically, by quantifying and ranking human oppressions, standpoint theorists invoke criteria for methodological adequacy characteristic of positivism. Although it is tempting to claim that Black women are more oppressed than everyone else and therefore have the best standpoint from which to understand the mechanism, processes, and effects of oppression, this simply may not be the case.

Like a Black women's standpoint, an Afrocentric feminist epistemology is rooted in the everyday experiences of African-American women. In spite of diversity that exists among women, what are the dimensions of an Afrocentric feminist epistemology?

CONCRETE EXPERIENCE AS A CRITERION OF MEANING
"My aunt used to say, 'A heap see, but a few know,'" remembers Carolyn Chase, a 31-year-old inner-city Black woman (Gwaltney 1980, 83). This saying depicts two types of knowing—knowledge and wisdom—and taps the first dimension of an Afrocentric feminist epistemology. Living life as Black women requires wisdom because knowledge about the dynamics of race, gender, and class oppression has been essential to Black women's survival. African-American women give such wisdom high credence in assessing knowledge.

Allusions to these two types of knowing pervade the words of a range of African-American women. Zilpha Elaw, a preacher of the mid-1800s, explains the tenacity of racism: "The pride of a white skin is a bauble of great value with many in some parts of the United States, who readily sacrifice their intelligence to their prejudices, and possess more knowledge than wisdom" (Andrews 1986, 85). In describing differences separating African-American and white women, Nancy White invokes a similar rule: "When you come right down to it, white women just *think* they are free. Black women know they ain't free" (Gwaltney 1980, 147). Geneva Smitherman, a college professor specializing in African-American linguistics, suggests that "from a black perspective, written documents are limited in what they can teach about life and survival in the world. Blacks are quick to ridicule 'educated fools,' . . . they have 'book learning' but no 'mother wit,' knowledge, but not wisdom" (Smitherman 1977, 76). Mabel Lincoln eloquently summarizes the distinction between knowledge and wisdom: "To black people like me, a fool is funny—you know, people who love to break bad, people you can't tell anything to, folks that would take a shotgun to a roach" (Gwaltney 1980, 68).

African-American women need wisdom to know how to deal with the "educated fools" who would "take a shotgun to a roach." As members of a subordinate group, Black women cannot afford to be fools of any type, for our objectification as the Other denies us the protections that white skin, maleness, and wealth confer. This distinction between knowledge and wisdom, and the use of experience as the cutting edge dividing them, has been key to Black women's survival. In the context of race, gender, and class oppression, the distinction is essential. Knowledge without wisdom is adequate for the powerful, but wisdom is essential to the survival of the subordinate.

For most African-American women those individuals who have lived through the experiences about which they claim to be experts are more believable and credible than those who have merely read or thought about such experiences. Thus concrete experience as a criterion for credibility frequently is invoked by Black women when making knowledge claims. For instance, Hannah Nelson describes the importance personal experience has for her: "Our speech is most directly personal, and every black person assumes that every other black person has a right to a personal opinion. In speaking of grave matters, your personal experience is considered very good evidence. With us, distant statistics are certainly not as important as the actual experience of a sober person" (Gwaltney 1980, 7). Similarly, Ruth Shays uses her concrete experiences to challenge the idea that formal education is the only route to knowledge: "I am the kind of person who doesn't have a lot of education, but both my mother and my father had good common sense. Now, I think that's all you need. I might not know how to use thirty-four words where three would do, but that does not mean that I don't know what I'm talking about. . . . I know what I'm talking about because I'm talking about myself. I'm talking about what I have lived" (Gwaltney 1980, 27, 33). Implicit in Ms. Shays's self-assessment is a critique of the type of knowledge that obscures the truth, the "thirty-four words" that cover up a truth that can be expressed in three.

Even after substantial mastery of white masculinist epistemologies, many Black women scholars invoke our own concrete experiences and those of other African-American women in selecting topics for investigation and methodologies used. For example, Elsa Barkley Brown (1986) subtitles her essay on Black women's history, "how my mother taught me to be an historian in spite of my academic training." Similarly, Joyce Ladner (1972) maintains that growing up as a Black woman in the South gave her special insights in conducting her study of Black adolescent women. Lorraine Hansberry alludes to the potential epistemological significance of valuing the concrete: "In certain peculiar ways, we have been conditioned to think not small—but tiny. And the thing, I think, which has strangled us most is the tendency to turn away from the world in search of the universe. That is chaos in science—can it be anything else in art?" (1969, 134).

Experience as a criterion of meaning with practical images as its symbolic vehicles is a fundamental epistemological tenet in African-American thought systems (Mitchell and Lewter 1986). "Look at my arm!" Sojourner Truth proclaimed: "I have ploughed, and planted, and gathered into barns, and no man could head me! And ain't I a woman?" (Loewenberg and Bogin 1976, 235). By invoking concrete practical images from her own life to symbolize new meanings, Truth deconstructed the prevailing notions of woman. Stories, narratives, and Bible principles are selected for their applicability to the lived experiences of African-Americans and become symbolic representations of a whole wealth of experience. Bible tales are often told for the wisdom they express about everyday life, so their interpretation involves no need for scientific historical verification. The narrative method requires that the story be told, not torn apart in analysis, and trusted as core belief, not "admired as science" (Mitchell and Lewter 1986, 8).

June Jordan's essay about her mother's suicide illustrates the multiple levels of meaning that can occur when concrete experiences are used as a criterion of meaning. Jordan describes her mother, a woman who literally died trying to stand up, and the effect her mother's death had on her own work:

I think all of this is really about women and work. Certainly this is all about me as a woman and my life work. I mean I am not sure my mother's suicide was something extraordinary. Perhaps most women must deal with a similar inheritance, the legacy of a woman whose death you cannot possibly pinpoint because she died so many, many times and because, even before she became your mother, the life of that woman was taken.... I came too late to help my mother to her feet. By way of everlasting thanks to all of the women who have helped me to stay alive I am working never to be late again. (Jordan 1985, 26)

While Jordan has knowledge about the concrete act of her mother's death, she also strives for wisdom concerning the meaning of that death.

Some feminist scholars offer a similar claim that women as a group are more likely than men to use concrete knowledge in assessing knowledge claims. For example, a substantial number of the 135 women in a study of women's cognitive development were "connected knowers" and were drawn to the sort of knowledge that emerges from first-hand observation (Belenky et al. 1986). Such women felt that because knowledge comes from experience, the best way of understanding another person's ideas was to develop empathy and share the experiences that led the person to form those ideas.

In valuing the concrete, African-American women invoke not only an Afrocentric tradition but a women's tradition as well. Some feminist theorists suggest that women are socialized in complex relational nexuses where contextual rules versus abstract principles govern behavior (Chodorow 1978; Gilligan 1982). This socialization process is thought to stimulate characteristic ways of knowing (Hartsock 1983a; Belenky et al. 1986). These theorists suggest that women are more likely to experience two modes of knowing: one located in the body and the space it occupies and the other passing beyond it. Through their child-rearing and nurturing activities, women mediate these two modes and use the concrete experiences of their daily lives to assess more abstract knowledge claims (D. Smith 1987).

Although valuing the concrete may be more representative of women than men, social class differences among women may generate differential expression of this women's value. One study of working-class women's ways of knowing found that both white and African-American women rely on common sense and intuition (Luttrell 1989). These forms of knowledge allow for subjectivity between the knower and the known, rest in the women themselves (not in higher authorities), and are experienced directly in the world (not through abstractions).

Amanda King, a young African-American mother, describes how she used the concrete to assess the abstract and points out how difficult mediating these two modes of knowing can be:

> The leaders of the ROC [a labor union] lost their jobs too, but it just seemed like they were used to losing their jobs. . . . This was like a lifelong thing for them, to get out there and protest. They were like, what do you call them—intellectuals. . . . You got the ones that go to the university that are supposed to make all the speeches, they're the ones that are supposed to lead, you know, put this little revolution together, and then you got the little ones . . . that go to the factory everyday, they be the ones that have to fight. I had a child and I thought I don't have the time to be running around with these people. . . . I mean I understand some of that stuff they were talking about, like the bourgeoisie, the rich and the poor and all that, but I had surviving on my mind for me and my kid. (Byerly 1986, 198)

For Ms. King abstract ideals of class solidarity were mediated by the concrete experience of motherhood and the connectedness it involved.

In traditional African-American communities Black women find considerable institutional support for valuing concrete experience. Black women's centrality in families, churches, and other community organizations allows us to share our concrete knowledge of what it takes to be self-defined Black women with younger, less experienced sisters. "Sisterhood is not new to Black women," asserts Bonnie Thornton Dill, but "while Black women have fostered and encouraged sisterhood, we have not used it as the anvil to forge our political identities" (1983, 134). Though not expressed in explicitly political terms, this relationship of sisterhood among Black women can be seen as a model for a whole series of relationships African-American women have with one another (Gilkes 1985; Giddings 1988).

Given that Black churches and families are both woman-centered, Afrocentric institutions, African-American women traditionally have found considerable institutional support for this dimension of an Afrocentric feminist epistemology. While white women may value the concrete, it is questionable whether white families—particularly middle-class nuclear ones—and white community institutions provide comparable types of support. Similarly, while

Black men are supported by Afrocentric institutions, they cannot participate in Black women's sisterhood. In terms of Black women's relationships with one another, African-American women may find it easier than others to recognize connectedness as a primary way of knowing, simply because we are encouraged to do so by a Black women's tradition of sisterhood.

THE USE OF DIALOGUE IN ASSESSING KNOWLEDGE CLAIMS

"Dialogue implies talk between two subjects, not the speech of subject and object. It is a humanizing speech, one that challenges and resists domination," asserts bell hooks (1989, 131). For Black women new knowledge claims are rarely worked out in isolation from other individuals and are usually developed through dialogues with other members of a community. A primary epistemological assumption underlying the use of dialogue in assessing knowledge claims is that connectedness rather than separation is an essential component of the knowledge validation process (Belenky et al. 1986, 18).

This belief in connectedness and the use of dialogue as one of its criteria for methodological adequacy has Afrocentric roots. In contrast to Western, either/or dichotomous thought, the traditional African worldview if holistic and seeks harmony. "One must understand that to become human, to realize the promise of becoming human, is the only important task of the person," posits Molefi Asante (1987, 1985). People become more human and empowered only in the context of a community, and only when they "become seekers of the type of connections, interactions, and meetings that lead to harmony" (p. 185). The power of the word generally (Jahn 1961), and dialogues specifically, allows this to happen.

Not to be confused with adversarial debate, the use of dialogue has deep roots in an African-based oral tradition and in African-American culture (Sidran 1971; Smitherman 1977; Kochman 1981; Stanback 1985). Ruth Shays describes the importance of dialogue in the knowledge validation process of enslaved African-Americans:

> They would find a lie if it took them a year. . . . The foreparents found the truth because they listened and they made people tell their part many times. Most often you can hear a lie. . . . Those old people was everywhere and knew the truth of many disputes. They believed that a liar should suffer the pain of his lies, and they had all kinds of ways of bringing liars to judgment. (Gwaltney 1980, 32)

The widespread use of the call-and-response discourse mode among African-Americans illustrates the importance placed on dialogue. Composed of spontaneous verbal and nonverbal interaction between speaker and listener in which all of the speaker's statements, or "calls," are punctuated by expressions, or "responses," from the listener, this Black discourse mode pervades African-American culture. The fundamental requirement of this interactive network is active participation of all individuals (Smitherman 1977, 108). For ideas to be tested and validated, everyone in the group must participate. To refuse to join in, especially if one really disagrees with what has been said, is seen as "cheating" (Kochman 1981, 28).

June Jordan's analysis of Black English points to the significance of this dimension of an alternative epistemology:

> Our language is a system constructed by people constantly needing to insist that we exist. . . . Our language devolves from a culture that abhors all abstraction, or anything tending to obscure or delete the fact of the human being who is here and now/the truth of the person who is speaking or listening. Consequently, *there is no passive voice construction possible in Black English.* For example, you cannot say, "Black English is being eliminated." You must say, instead, "White people eliminating Black English." The assumption of the presence of life governs all of Black English . . . every sentence assumes the living and active participation of at least two human beings, the speaker and the listener. (Jordan 1985, 129)

Many Black women intellectuals invoke the relationships and connectedness provided by use of dialogue. When asked why she chose the themes she did, novelist Gayl Jones replied: "I was . . . interested . . . in oral traditions of storytelling—Afro-American and others, in which there is always the consciousness and importance of the hearer" (Tate 1983, 91). In describing the difference in the way male and female writers select significant events and relationships, Jones points out that "with many women writers, relationships within family, community, between men and women, and among women— from slave narratives by black women writers on—are treated as complex and significant relationships, whereas with many men the significant relationships are those that involve confrontations—relationships outside the family and community" (in Tate 1983, 92). Alice Walker's reaction to Zora Neale Hurston's book, *Mules and Men,* is another example of the use of dialogue in assessing knowledge claims. In *Mules and Men* Hurston chose not to become a detached observer of the stories and folktales she collected but instead, through extensive dialogues with the people in the communities she studies, placed herself in the center of her analysis. Using a similar process, Walker tests the truth of Hurston's knowledge claims:

> When I read *Mules and Men* I was delighted. Here was this perfect book! The "perfection" of which I immediately tested on my relatives, who are such typical Black Americans they are useful for every sort of political, cultural, or economic survey. Very regular people from the South, rapidly forgetting their Southern cultural inheritance in the suburbs and ghettos of Boston and New York, they sat around reading the book themselves, listing to me read the book, listening to each other read the book, and a kind of paradise was regained. (Walker 1977, xii)

Black women's centrality in families and community organizations provides African-American women with a high degree of support for invoking dialogue as a dimension of an Afrocentric feminist epistemology. However, when African-American women use dialogues in assessing knowledge claims, we might be invoking a particularly female way of knowing as well. Feminist scholars contend that men and women are socialized to seek different types of autonomy—the former based on separation, the latter seeking connectedness—and that this variation in types of autonomy parallels the characteristic differences between male and female ways of knowing (Chodorow 1978; Keller 1983; Belenky et al. 1986). For instance, in contrast to the visual metaphors (such as equating knowledge with illumination, knowing with seeing, and truth with light) that scientists and philosophers typically use, women tend to ground their epistemological premises in metaphors suggesting finding a voice, speaking, and listening (Belenky et al. 1986). The words of the Black woman who struggled for her education at Medgar Evers College resonate with the importance placed on voice: "I was basically a shy and reserved person prior to the struggle at Medgar, but I found my voice—and I used it! Now, I will never lose my voice again!" (Nicola-McLaughlin and Chandler 1988, 195).

While significant differences exist between Black women's family experiences and those of middle-class white women, African-American women clearly are affected by general cultural norms prescribing certain familial roles for women. Thus in terms of the role of dialogue in an Afrocentric feminist epistemology, Black women may again experience a convergence of the values of the African-American community and women's experiences.

THE ETHIC OF CARING

"Ole white preachers used to talk wid dey tongues widdout sayin' nothin'. But Jesus told us slaves to talk wid our hearts" (Webber 1978, 127). These words of an ex-slave suggest that ideas cannot be divorced from the individuals who create and share them. This theme of talking with the heart taps the ethic of caring, another dimension of an alternative epistemology used by African-American women. Just as the ex-slave used the wisdom in his heart to reject the ideas of the preachers who talked "wid dey tongues widdout sayin' nothin'," the ethic of caring suggests that personal expressiveness, emotions, and empathy are central to the knowledge validation process.

One of three interrelated components comprising the ethic of caring is the emphasis placed on individual uniqueness. Rooted in a tradition of African humanism, each individual is thought to be a unique expression of a common spirit, power, or energy inherent in all life.[2] When Alice Walker "never doubted her powers of judgment because her mother assumed they were sound," she invokes the sense of individual uniqueness taught to her by her mother (Washington 1984, 145). The polyrhythms in African-American music, in which no one main beat subordinates the others, is paralleled by the theme of individual expression in Black women's quilting. Black women quilters place strong color and patterns next to one another and see the individual differences not as detracting from each piece but as enriching the whole quilt (Brown 1989). This belief in individual uniqueness is illustrated by the value placed on personal expressiveness in African-American communities (Smitherman 1977; Kochman 1981; Mitchell and Lewter 1986). Johnetta Ray, an inner-city resident, describes this Afrocentric emphasis on individual uniqueness: "No matter how hard we try, I don't think black people will ever develop much of a herd instinct. We are profound individualists with a passion for self-expression" (Gwaltney 1980, 228).

A second component of the ethic of caring concerns the appropriateness of emotions in dialogues. Emotion indicates that a speaker believes in the validity of an argument. Consider Ntozake Shange's description of one of the goals of her work: "Our [Western] society allows people to be absolutely neurotic and totally out of touch with their feelings and everyone else's feelings, and yet be very respectable. This, to me, is a travesty. . . . I'm trying to change the idea of seeing emotions and intellect as distinct faculties" (Tate 1983, 156). The Black women's blues tradition's history of personal expressiveness heals this either/or dichotomous rift separating emotion and intellect. For example, in her rendition of "Strange Fruit," Billie Holiday's lyrics blend seamlessly with the emotion of her delivery to render a trenchant social commentary on southern lynching. Without emotion, Aretha Franklin's (1967) cry for "respect" would be virtually meaningless.

A third component of the ethic of caring involves developing the capacity for empathy. Harriet Jones, a 16-year-old Black woman, explains to her interviewer why she chose to open up to him: "Some things in my life are so hard for me to bear, and it makes me feel better to know that you feel sorry about those things and would change them if you could" (Gwaltney 1980, 11). Without her belief in his empathy, she found it difficult to talk. Black women writers often explore the growth of empathy as part of an ethic of caring. For example, the growing respect that the Black slave woman Dessa and the white woman Rufel gain for one another in Sherley Anne Williams's *Dessa Rose* stems from their increased understanding of each other's positions. After watching Rufel fight off the advances of a white man, Dessa lay awake thinking: "The white woman was subject to the same ravishment as me; this the thought that kept me awake. I hadn't knowed white mens could use a white woman like that, just take her by force same as they could with us" (1986, 220). As a result of her new-found empathy, Dessa observed, "it was like we had a secret between us" (p. 220).

These components of the ethic of caring—the value placed on individual expressiveness, the appropriateness of emotions, and the capacity for empathy—pervade African-American culture. One of the best examples of the interactive nature of the importance of dialogue and the ethic of caring in assessing knowledge claims occurs in the use of the call-and-response discourse mode in traditional Black church services. In such services both the minister and the congregation routinely use voice rhythm and vocal inflection to convey meaning. The sound of what is being said is just as important as the words themselves in what is, in a sense, a dialogue of reason and emotion. As a result it is nearly impossible to filter out psychomotive meaning (Smitherman 1977, 135, 137). While the ideas presented by a speaker must have validity (i.e., agree with the general body of knowledge shared by the Black congregation), the group also appraises the way knowledge claims are presented.

There is growing evidence that the ethic of caring may be part of women's experience as well (Noddings 1984). Certain dimensions of women's ways of knowing bear striking resemblance to Afrocentric expressions of the ethic of caring. Belenky et al. (1986) point out that two contrasting epistemological orientations characterize knowing; one an epistemology of separation based on impersonal procedures for establishing truth and the other, an epistemology of connection in which truth emerges through care. While these ways of knowing are not gender specific, disproportionate numbers of women rely on connected knowing.

The emphasis placed on expressiveness and emotion in African-American communities bears marked resemblance to feminist perspectives on the importance of personality in connected knowing. Separate knowers try to subtract the personality of an individual from his or her ideas because they see personality as biasing those ideas. In contrast, connected knowers see personality as adding to an individual's ideas and feel that the personality of each group member enriches a group's understanding. The significance of individual uniqueness, personal expressiveness, and empathy in African-American communities thus resembles the importance that some feminist analyses place on women's "inner voice" (Belenky et al. 1986).

The convergence of Afrocentric and feminist values in the ethic of caring seems particularly acute. White women may have access to a women's tradition valuing emotion and expressiveness, but few Eurocentric institutions except the family validate this way of knowing. In contrast, Black women have long had the support of the Black church, an institution with deep roots in the African past and a philosophy that accepts and encourages expressiveness and an ethic of caring. Black men share in this Afrocentric tradition. But they must resolve the contradictions that confront them in searching for Afrocentric models of masculinity in the face of abstract, unemotional notions of masculinity imposed on them (Hoch 1979). The differences among race/gender groups thus hinge on differences in their access to institutional supports valuing one type of knowing over another. Although Black women may be denigrated within white-male-controlled academic institutions, other institutions, such as Black families and churches, which encourage the expression of Black female power seem to do so, in part, by way of their support for an Afrocentric feminist epistemology.

THE ETHIC OF PERSONAL ACCOUNTABILITY

An ethic of personal accountability is the final dimension of an alternative epistemology. Not only must individuals develop their knowledge claims through dialogue and present them in a style proving their concern for their ideas, but people are expected to be accountable for their knowledge claims. Zilpha Elaw's description of slavery reflects this notion that every idea has an owner and that the owner's identity matters: "Oh, the abominaionts of slavery! ... Every case of slavery, however lenient its inflictions and mitigated its atrocities, indicates an oppressor, the oppressed, and oppression" (Andrews 1986, 98). For Elaw abstract definitions of slavery mesh with the concrete identities of its perpetrators and its victims. African-Americans consider it essential for individuals to have personal positions on issues and assume full responsibility for arguing their validity (Kochman 1981).

Assessments of an individual's knowledge claims simultaneously evaluate an individual's character, values, and ethics. African-Americans reject the Eurocentric, masculinist belief that probing into an individual's personal viewpoint is outside the boundaries of discussion. Rather, all views expressed and actions taken are thought to derive from a central set of core beliefs that cannot be other than personal (Kochman 1981, 23). "Does Aretha really *believe* that Black women should get 'respect,' or is she just mouthing the words?" is a valid question in an Afrocentric feminist epistemology. Knowledge claims made by individuals respected for their moral and ethical connections to their ideas will carry more weight than those offered by less respected figures.

An example drawn from an undergraduate course composed entirely of Black women which I taught might help to clarify the uniqueness of this portion of the knowledge validation process. During one class discussion I asked the students to evaluate a prominent Black male scholar's analysis of Black feminism. Instead of severing the scholar from his context in order to dissect the rationality of this thesis, my students demanded facts about the author's personal biography. They were especially interested in concrete details of his life, such as his relationships with Black women, his marital status, and his social class background. By requesting data on dimensions of his personal life routinely excluded in positivist approaches to knowledge validation, they invoked concrete experience as a criterion of meaning. They used this information to assess whether he really cared about his topic and drew on this ethic of caring in advancing their knowledge claims about his work. Furthermore,

they refused to evaluate the rationality of his written ideas without some indication of his personal credibility as an ethical human being. The entire exchange could only have occurred as a dialogue among members of a class that
had established a solid enough community to employ an alternative epistemology in assessing knowledge claims.

The ethic of personal accountability is clearly an Afrocentric value, but is it
feminist as well? While limited by its attention to middle-class, white women,
Carol Gilligan's (1982) work suggests that there is a female model for moral
development whereby women are more inclined to link morality to responsibility, relationships, and the ability to maintain social ties. If this is the case,
then African-American women again experience a convergence of values from
Afrocentric and female institutions.

The use of an Afrocentric feminist epistemology in traditional Black church
services illustrates the interactive nature of all four dimensions and also serves
as a metaphor for the distinguishing features of an Afrocentric feminist way of
knowing. The services represent more than dialogues between the rationality
used in examining biblical texts and stories and the emotion inherent in the use
of reason for this purpose. The rationale for such dialogues involves the task of
examining concrete experiences for the presence of an ethic of caring. Neither
emotion nor ethics is subordinated to reason. Instead, emotion, ethics, and reason are used as interconnected, essential components in assessing knowledge
claims. In an Afrocentric feminist epistemology, values lie at the heart of the
knowledge validation process such that inquiry always has an ethical aim.

Alternative knowledge claims in and of themselves are rarely threatening to
conventional knowledge. Such claims are routinely ignored, discredited, or
simply absorbed and marginalized in existing paradigms. Much more threatening is the challenge that alternative epistemologies offer to the basic process
used by the powerful to legitimate their knowledge claims. If the epistemology
used to validate knowledge comes into question, then all prior knowledge
claims validated under the dominant model become suspect. An alternative
epistemology challenges all certified knowledge and opens up the question of
whether what has been taken to be true can stand the test of alternative ways
of validating truth. The existence of a self-defined Black women's standpoint
using an Afrocentric feminist epistemology calls into question the content of
what currently passes as truth and simultaneously challenges the process of
arriving at that truth.

NOTES

1. In critiques of the Eurocentric, masculinist knowledge validation process, what Africanist scholars label "white" and "Eurocentric" feminist scholars describe as "male-dominated" and "masculinst." Although he does not emphasize its patriarchal and racist features, Morris Berman's *The Reenchantment of the World* (1981) provides an important discussion of Western thought. Afrocentric analyses of this same process can be found in Asante (1987) and Richards (1980, 1990). For feminist analyses see Hartsock (1983a, 1983b) and Harding (1986), especially chapter seven, "Other 'Others' and Fractured Identities: Issues for Epistemologists," pp. 163–96.

2. In discussing the West African Sacred Cosmos, Mechal Sobel notes that *Nyam*, a root word in many West African languages, connotes an enduring spirit, power, or energy possessed by all life. Despite the persuasiveness of this important concept in African humanism (see Jahn 1961, for example), its definition remains elusive. Sobel observes, "every individual analyzing the various Sacred Cosmos of West Africans has recognized the reality of this force, but no one has yet adequately translated this concept into Western terms" (1979, 13). For a comprehensive discussion of African spirituality, see Richards (1990).

BIBLIOGRAPHY

Andersen, Margaret L. 1988. *Thinking about Women: Sociological Perspectives on Sex and Gender.* 2d ed. New York: Macmillan.

Andrews, William L. 1986. *Sisters of the Spirit: Three Black Women's Autobiographies of the Nineteenth Century.* Bloomington: Indiana University Press.

Asante, Molefi Kete. 1987. *The Afrocentric Idea.* Philadelphia: Temple University Press.

Belenky, Mary Field, Blythe McVicker Clinchy, Nancy Rule Goldberger, and Jill Mattuck Tarule. 1986. *Women's Ways of Knowing.* New York: Basic Books.

Berger, Peter L., and Thomas Luckmann. 1966. *The Social Construction of Reality.* New York: Doubleday.

Berman, Morris. 1981. *The Reenchantment of the World.* New York: Bantam Books.

Brown, Elsa Barkley. 1986. *Hearing Our Mothers' Lives.* Atlanta: Fifteenth Anniversary of African-American and African Studies, Emory University (unpublished).

————. 1989. "African-American Women's Quilting: A Framework for Conceptualizing and Teaching African-American Women's History." *Signs* 14(4): 921–29.

Byerly, Victoria. 1986. *Hard Times Cotton Mills Girls.* Ithaca, NY: Cornell University Press.

Chodorow, Nancy. 1978. *The Reproduction of Mothering.* Berkeley: University of California Press.

Dill, Bonnie Thornton. 1979. "The Dialectics of Black Womanhood." *Signs* 4(3): 543–55.

————. 1983. "Race, Class, and Gender: Prospects for an All-Inclusive Sisterhood." *Feminist Studies* 9(1): 131–50.

Diop, Cheikh. 1974. *The African Origin of Civilization: Myth or Reality.* New York: L. Hill.

Eisenstein, Hester. 1983. *Contemporary Feminist Thought.* Boston: G. K. Hall.

Fausto-Sterling, Anne. 1989. "Life in the XY Corral." *Women's International Forum* 12(3): 319–31.

Franklin, Aretha. 1967. *I Never Loved A Man the Way I Love You.* Atlantic Recording Corp.

Gayle, Addison, ed. 1971. *The Black Aesthetic.* Garden City, NY: Doubleday.

Giddings, Paula. 1988. *In Search of Sisterhood: Delta Sigma Theta and the Challenge of the Black Sorority Movement.* New York: William Morrow.

Gilkes, Cheryl Townsend. 1980. "' Holding Back the Ocean with a Broom: Black Women and Community Work." In *The Black Woman,* ed. La Frances Rodgers-Rose, 217–32: Beverly Hills, Calif.: Sage.

————. 1985. "'Together and in Harness': Women's Traditions in the Sanctified Church." *Signs* 10(4): 678–99.

Gilligan, Carol. 1982. *In a Different Voice.* Cambridge, MA: Harvard University Press.

Gwaltney, John Langston. 1980. *Drylongso, A Self-Portrait of Black America.* New York: Vintage.

Haan, Norma, Robert Bellah, Paul Rabinow, and William Sullivan, eds. 1983. *Social Science as Moral Inquiry.* New York: Columbia University Press.

Hansberry, Lorraine. 1969. *To Be Young, Gifted and Black.* New York: Signet.

Harding, Sandra. 1986. *The Science Question in Feminism.* Ithaca, NY: Cornell University Press.

———. 1987. "Introduction: Is There a Feminist Method?" In *Feminism and Methodology,* ed. Sandra Harding, 1–14. Bloomington: Indiana University Press.

Hartsock, Nancy M. 1983a. "The Feminist Standpoint: Developing the Ground for a Specifically Feminist Historical Materialism." In *Discovering Reality,* ed. Sandra Harding and Merrill B. Hintikka, 283–310. Boston: D. Reidel.

———. 1983b. *Money, Sex, and Power.* Boston: Northeastern University Press.

Hoch, Paul. 1979. *White Hero Black Beast: Racism, Sexism and the Mask of Masculinity.* London: Pluto Press.

Hochschild, Arlie Russell. 1975. "The Sociology of Feeling and Emotion: Selected Possibilities." In *Another Voice: Feminist Perspectives on Social Life and Social Science,* ed. Marcia Millman and Rosabeth Kanter, 280–307. Garden City, NY: Anchor.

hooks, bell. 1989. *Talking Back: Thinking Feminist, Thinking Black.* Boston: South End Press.

Jaggar, Alison M. 1983. *Feminist Politics and Human Nature.* Totawa, NJ: Rosman and Allanheld.

Jahn, Janheinz. 1961. *Muntu: An Outline of Neo-African Culture.* London: Faber and Faber.

Jordan, June. 1985. *On Call.* Boston: South End Press.

Keller, Evelyn Fox. 1983. "Gender and Science." In *Discovering Reality,* ed. Sandra Harding and Merrill B. Hintikka, 187–206. Boston: D. Reidel.

———. 1985. *Reflections on Gender and Science.* New Haven, CT: Yale University Press.

Kochman, Thomas. 1981. *Black and White Styles in Conflict.* Chicago: University of Chicago Press.

Kuhn, Thomas. 1962. *The Structure of Scientific Revolutions.* 2d ed. Chicago: University of Chicago Press.

Ladner, Joyce. 1972. *Tomorrow's Tomorrow.* Garden City, NY: Doubleday.

———. 1986. "Black Women Face the 21st Century: Major Issues and Problems." *Black Scholar* 17(5): 12–19.

Loewenberg, Bert J., and Ruth Bogin, eds. 1976. *Black Women in Nineteenth-Century American Life.* University Park: Pennsylvania State University Press.

Luttrell, Wendy. 1989. "Working-Class Women's Ways of Knowing: Effects of Gender, Race, and Class." *Sociology of Education* 62(1): 33–46.

Mannheim, Karl. 1936. *Ideology and Utopia.* New York: Harcourt, Brace & World.

Mbiti, John S. 1969. *African Religions and Philosophy.* London: Heinemann.

Mitchell, Henry H., and Nicholas Cooper Lewter. 1986. *Soul Theology: The Heart of American Black Culture.* San Francisco: Harper and Row.

Moulton, Janice. 1983. "A Paradigm of Philosophy: The Adversary Method." In *Discovering Reality,* ed. Sandra Harding and Merrill B. Hintikka, 149–64. Boston: D. Reidel.

Mulkay, Michael. 1979. *Science and the Sociology of Knowledge.* Boston: Unwin Hyman.

Myers, Linda James. 1988. *Understanding an Afrocentric World View: Introduction to an Optimal Psychology.* Dubuque, IA: Kendall/Hunt.

Narayan, Uma. 1989. "The Project of Feminist Epistemology: Perspectives from a Nonwestern Feminist." In *Gender/Body/Knowledge: Feminist Reconstructions of Being and Knowing,* ed. Alison M. Jaggar and Susan R. Bordo, 256–69. New Brunswick, NJ: Rutgers University Press.

Nicola-McLaughlin, Andree, and Zula Chandler. 1988. "Urban Politics in the Higher Education of Black Women: A Case Study." In *Women and the Politics of Empowerment,* ed. Ann Bookman and Sandra Morgen, 180–201. Philadelphia: Temple University Press.

Noddings, Nel. 1984. *Caring: A Feminine Approach to Ethics and Moral Education.* Berkeley: University of California Press.

Okanlawon, Alexander. 1972. "Africanism—A Synthesis of the African World-View." *Black World* 21(9): 40–44, 92–97.

Richards, Dona. 1980. "European Mythology: The Ideology of 'Progress.'" In *Contemporary Black Thought,* ed. Molefi Kete Asante and Abdulai S. Vandi, 59–79. Beverly Hills, Calif.: Sage.

———. 1990. "The Implications of African-American Spirituality." In *African Culture: The Rhythms of Unity*, ed. Molefi Kete Asante and Kariamu Welch Asante, 207–31. Trenton, NJ: Africa World Press.

Rosaldo, Michelle Z. 1974. "Women, Culture, and Society: A Theoretical Overview." In *Women, Culture and Society*, ed. Michelle Rosaldo and Louise Lamphere, 17–42. Stanford: Stanford University Press.

Shimkin, Demitri B., Edith M. Shimkin, and Dennis A. Frate, eds. 1978. *The Extended Family in Black Societies*. Chicago: Aldine.

Sidran, Ben. 1971. *Black Talk*. New York: Da Capo Press.

Smith, Dorothy. 1987. *The Everyday World as Problematic*. Boston: Northeastern University Press.

Smitherman, Geneva. 1977. *Talkin and Testifyin: The Language of Black America*. Boston: Houghton Mifflin.

Sobel, Mechal. 1979. *Trabelin' On: The Slave Journey to an Afro-Baptist Faith*. Princeton, NJ: Princeton University Press.

Spelman, Elizabeth V. 1982. "Theories of Race and Gender: The Erasure of Black Women." *Quest* 5(4): 36–62.

Stanback, Marsha Houston. 1985. "Language and Black Women's Place: Evidence from Black Middle Class." In *For Alma Mater: Theory and Practice of Feminist Scholarship*, ed. P. A. Trechler, Cheris Kramarae, and R. Shafford, 177–93. Urbana: University of Illinois Press.

Sudarkasa, Niara. 1981. "Interpreting the African Heritage in Afro-American Family Organization." In *Black Families*, ed. Harriette Pipes McAdoo, 37–53. Beverly Hills, Calif.: Sage.

Tate, Claudia, ed. 1983. *Black Women Writers at Work*. New York: Continuum Press.

Thompson, Robert Farris. 1983. *Flash of the Spirit: African and Afro-American Art and Philosophy*. New York: Vintage.

Turner, James E. 1984. "Foreword: Africana Studies and Epistemology: A Discourse in the Sociology of Knowledge." In *The Next Decade: Theoretical and Research*

Issues in Africana Studies, ed. James E. Turner, v–xxv. Ithaca, NY: Cornell University African Studies and Research Center.

Walker, Alice. 1977. "Zora Neale Hurston: A Cautionary Tale and a Partisan View." Foreword to *Zora Neale Hurston: A Literary Biography*, by Robert Hemenway, xi–xvii. Urbana: University of Illinois Press.

Walker, Sheila S. 1980. "African Gods in the Americas: The Black Religious Continuum." *Black Scholar* 11(8): 25–36.

Walton, Ortiz M. 1971. "Comparative Analysis of the African and Western Aesthetics." In *The Black Aesthetic*, ed. Addison Gayle, 154–64. Garden City, NY: Doubleday.

Washington, Mary Helen. 1984. "I Sign My Mother's Name: Alice Walker, Dorothy West and Paule Marshall." In *Mothering the Mind: Twelve Studies of Writers and Their Silent Partners*, ed. Ruth Perry and Martine Watson Broronley, 143–63. New York: Holmes and Meier.

Webber, Thomas L. 1978. *Deep Like the Rivers*. New York: W. W. Norton.

Williams, Sherley A. 1986. *Dessa Rose*. New York: William Morrow.

Zinn, Maxine Baca, Lynn Weber Cannon, Elizabeth Higginbotham, and Bonnie Thornton Dill. 1986. "The Costs of Exclusionary Practices in Women's Studies." *Signs* 11 (2): 290–303.

Zahan, Dominique. 1979. *The Religion, Spirituality, and Thought of Traditional Africa*. Chicago: University of Chicago Press.

3

Defining Feminist Ethnography

Kamala Visweswaran

In a recent essay, Renato Rosaldo describes driving through the Santa Cruz mountains, and the following interchange with a physicist who has asked him to define what anthropologists have discovered. As Rosaldo replies in dismay, "You mean something like $E = mc^2$?" it suddenly occurs to him: "There's one thing that we know for sure. We all know a good description when we see one. We haven't discovered any laws of culture, but we do think there are really classic ethographies, really telling descriptions of other cultures, like the Trobriand islanders, the Tikopika, and the Nuer."[1]

Malinowski, Firth, Evans-Pritchard. This essay is in part a questioning of the discipline's canonization of "classic ethnographies." To ask why it is that the classics most often cited are those written by men, and why it is that what women anthropologists write is so easily dismissed as "subjective," is to invite a mumbled answer of "sexism." Yet, within the latest "experimental" moment of ethnography, ethnographies written by women are again consigned to the margins of what is valorized.[2]

My aim in writing this essay is to describe and suggest possibilities for a "feminist ethnography." Part of this exercise is restitutive, which involves

Reprinted from Kamala Visweswaran, *Fictions of Feminist Thought* (Minneapolis: University of Minnesota Press, 1994), 17–39.

rereading and assigning new value to texts ignored or discarded. In other disciplinary terms—those of literary criticism—this exercise would be called
"questioning the canon." Some of the things I will look at are the ways in
which female ethnographers confront their biases as Western women, and the
processes of identification (or lack thereof) that inform description.

The other part of this exercise is exploratory. So along with the older texts
I will reevaluate, I suggest more recent autobiographical and novelistic attempts for consideration. Most of this essay focuses on locating feminist
ethnography in the recent challenge mounted by experimental ethnography
to ethnographic authority. Anthropology in general can learn from the challenge to ethnographic authority, but this challenge needs to be pushed to its
limits. I argue that feminist ethnography can benefit from experimental
ethnography's concern for the constitution of subjectivities, but perhaps more
important, that experimental ethnography can benefit from a feminist evaluation of some of its assumptions. I will begin by briefly describing competing
mode of analysis within feminist anthropology, then consider women's accounts that can be read as feminist or experimental ethnography. In so doing,
I level critiques at both the assumptions of feminist anthropology and experimental ethnography.

COMPETING APPROACHES IN FEMINIST ANTHROPOLOGY

It is not inaccurate to say that the women's movement in the United States inspired feminist scholarship. But it might be more accurate to say that the
women's movement provoked key lines of questioning and demanded answers from academic feminists. The disciplines of anthropology and history
were perhaps hardest hit with questions like these: Were women oppressed
everywhere, at all historical times, or only in modern capitalist society? Were
there female models of power and resistance to "male domination" outside of
Western or modern cultures? Infused by feminism's "second wave" and its
analysis of patriarchy, this generation of feminist anthropologists tended to
cast their arguments against a backdrop of "universal womanhood." For this
reason, feminists in the 1970s were sometimes placed in contradictory positions: arguing against essentialism or biological universals on the one hand,
but deploying cultural relativism to assert universal sisterhood on the other.

It was in Michelle Rosaldo's work that the tension between relativism and
universals was most strikingly evident. In a 1981 article, "The Use and Abuse

of Anthropology," she argued for the universal sexual asymmetry of women in relation to men, while taking issue with those feminists who portrayed women of other cultures as "ourselves undressed"—heroines with less sophisticated tools than we, but fighting the same battle against male oppression. In this formula, the oppression of women was the universal product; it was the multiplicands in each society that were relatively different.

It is odd that the study of culture, radical because it emphasizes the nonnatural bases of difference, sparked the opposite effect in feminist anthropology and much feminist theorizing. While women's oppression had different names, it was all part of the same transhistoric phenomenon. For Rosaldo, Mary Daly (the author of *Gyn-Ecology*) probably came to mind as a feminist theorist, who in seeking to prove the commonality of women's oppression wound up with a cross-cultural catalog of women as victims. Audre Lorde's criticism of Daly is by now well known.[3]

Rosaldo opened her essay by arguing that what we now need it not more data (read: fieldwork), but more questions (read: theory). As I see it, this separation of theory from experience loses sight of the fundamentally restitutive value of feminism, and the potential of a feminist ethnography that has yet to be expressed: locating the self in the experience of oppression in order to liberate it. As Susan Griffin says,

A theory of liberation must be created to articulate the feeling of oppression, to describe this oppression as real, as unjust, and to point to a cause. In this way the idea is liberating. It restores to the oppressed a belief in the self and in the *authority* of the self to determine what is real [emphasis mine].[4]

Rosaldo's separation of experience and theory corresponds to the development of what might be termed "woman-centered" and "decentered" approaches in feminist anthropology. Just as James Clifford noted a late-nineteenth-century division of labor between ethnographers and theorists in anthropology, a similar division exists among feminist anthropologists.[5] The "ethnographers," drawing on the "compensatory scholarship" phase in anthropology ("bringing women back in"), have matured into the chronicles of women's life history Jane Atkinson and Susan Geiger have so thoroughly documented.[6] The theorists, on the other hand, continue to take a more comparative tack, using field data explicitly to deconstruct

Western categories of analysis,[7] or reanalyzing data about women pulled from traditional ethnographies.[8] In contrast to the ethnographer's centering of women in the text, theoretical approaches are becoming increasingly more decentered. That is, if one wants to understand anything about women, don't start with women, but with their relations to men; or analyze relationships among men. This approach is illustrated by Sherry Ortner's analysis of a Sherpa nunnery where women recede from the analysis as the primary analytic category.[9]

It is my contention that a very obvious element has been left out of the above equations for research on women. A woman-centered ethnographic approach need not sacrifice relationality, the virtue of a decentered approach. But rather than foreground men's relationships to one another (which classical ethnography does quite well), or women's relationships to men, perhaps a feminist ethnography could focus on women's relationships to other women, and the power differentials between them. Research on communities of women is a step in this direction,[10] yet relationships between women of the colonizer and women of the colonized also demand systematic attention in the present "postcolonial" world.

There are, however, barriers to this kind of study within the discipline. At birth, feminist anthropology, like her sister subdisciplines, needed to imagine a universal self or "we." The other established was that of "man." Unfortunately, feminist anthropologists have uncritically continued to promulgate this assumption.

Marilyn Strathern's (1987) essay that evaluates feminist anthropology in light of experimental ethnography is a telling example of this assumption.[11] She proposes that feminism and anthropology, instead of being mutually reconcilable, actually work at cross-purposes. She compares the feminist emphasis on experience "as knowledge which cannot be appropriated by others" with experimental ethnography's emphasis on experience, and concludes that while the goal of experimental ethnography is to create a (positive) relation with the other, the goal of feminist anthropology is to attack it. Thus,

> Feminist theory suggests that one can acknowledge the self by becoming conscious of oppression from the other. This creates a natural kinship between those who are similarly oppressed. Thus one may seek to regain a common past which is also one's own.[12]

While Third World women broached the problems of racism, classism, and homophobia that prohibited a universalizing "we" within the American women's movement, it is not a little ironic that feminists in anthropology, versed as they are in the tenets of cultural relativism, maintain an us/them split that does not call into question their own positions as members of dominant Western societies. Insisting on the opposition between a unified female self and male other removes the power categories that exist between all anthropologists and their subjects; the ways in which female anthropologists may pass as honorary males in some societies, or as persons of higher status by virtue of their membership in Western culture.

In experimental ethnography, "pursuit of the other" becomes problematic, not taken for granted. The text is marked by disaffections, ruptures, and incomprehensions. Skepticism, and perhaps a respect for the integrity of difference, replaces the ethnographic goal of total understanding and representation. Feminist anthropology, I would argue, stands to benefit from reevaluating its assumptions about "the other" in terms of experimental ethnography. In the next section, however, I would like to demonstrate how experimental ethnography stands to benefit from a feminist questioning of its assumptions.

"CONFESSIONAL FIELD LITERATURE" AND EXPERIMENTAL ETHNOGRAPHY

A number of pioneer women anthropologists (continuing through the mid-seventies) portrayed women's lives through the use of third-person objective accounts.[13] Many of the writings I will consider, however, have been dismissed as "popularized accounts," or as "confessional field literature." Often judged as "inadequate science," these first-person narratives have been consigned to the margins of anthropological discourse. In traditional ethnographic practice, if the first-person narrative is allowed to creep into the ethnographic text, it is confined to the introduction or postscript;[14] if a book is devoted to the first-hand experiences of the novice ethnographer, it is after a monograph written in the proper objective manner has been produced.[15]

Proponents of a more experimental mode of writing ethnography[16] have also dismissed such accounts, calling them "fables of rapport," in the end shoring up traditional boundaries of ethnographic authority by showing the process of the ethnographer's "mastery" of culture. George Marcus and Dick

Cushman distinguish confessional field literature from experimental ethnography by telling us that

> what is at issue in the self-reflectiveness of recent ethnographies is not merely
> a methodologically oriented re-telling of field conditions and experiences,
> such as is to be found in the confessional fieldwork literature which has ap-
> peared over the last fifteen years. While such works have certainly helped to
> stimulate the kind of questioning of the tacit assumptions of research prac-
> tice that now has led to a more trenchant critical perspective on ethno-
> graphic writing itself, their main aim has been to demystify the process of
> anthropological fieldwork whose veil of public secrecy has been increasingly
> embarrassing to a "scientific discipline." Such accounts, because they are typ-
> ically conceived and published as ends in themselves—as separate books or
> articles—are at best seldom more than tenuously related to their author's
> ethnographic enterprises. The writers of experimental ethnographies, in
> contrast, often represent fieldwork experiences as a vital technique for struc-
> turing their narratives of description and analysis.[17]

Thus texts by Paul Rabinow, Jean-Paul Dumont, and Vincent Crapanzano are heralded as exemplars of this new genre,[18] while earlier efforts are treated as so many more throwaway paperback novels. What Clifford and others have missed is that for women writers of this genre, subjective accounts are often first accounts. Moreover, they are as likely to generate tales of distance or alienation as empathic fables of rapport.

The writers I will discuss see the fieldwork experience not only as central to their analyses, but also as definitive of its shaping into first-person narratives. While due respects are paid them for "paving the way" for experimental ethnography, there has been little acknowledgment that these books, radical before their time, had to carve out a space for themselves within a dominant positivist paradigm. Often lumped together with "fieldwork anthologies."[19] I would argue that anthologies like Saberwal and Henry's (1969) *Stress and Response in Fieldwork* are geared more toward shoring up anthropology as a positive science than are the first-person narratives I review.

These accounts comprise a tradition of women ethnographers, not always professionally trained, often writing in a novelistic or fictive voice about culture. Some of these women were the wives of male anthropologists, men who, upon completion of their fieldwork, continued publishing for a professional audience. Kevin Dwyer[20] has noted that in such cases the male seems to adopt the "objective" explanatory mode, and the female a "subjective, anecdotal" mode.[21] Dwyer suggests comparing the books of Laura Bohannon, Elizabeth Fernea, Margery Wolf (and I would add Marion Benedict) with those of their anthropologist husbands to get some idea of this contrast. This division of labor, for example, is marked in Marion and Burton Benedict's book *Men, Women, and Money in the Seychelles*. The book opens with Marion Benedict's novelized account of her experiences with a Seychelloise fortune-teller, followed by Burton Benedict's account of the Seychelles economy. The preface to the book reads: "Each of us appears to have had a perception of the field which could not include material gathered by the other, yet each of us recognizes the validity of what the other has written."[22]

Other writers, regardless of their marital status, have also been consigned to the genre of confessional or popular literature: Jean Briggs, Hortense Powdermaker, and Elizabeth Marshall Thomas. We might ask why it is that this genre consists largely of women, and why it is that women more frequently adopt first-person narrative as a means to convey their ethnographic experiences.

One cannot convincingly argue that this was a choice circumscribed by lack of training, since Bohannon, Briggs, and Powdermaker were professional anthropologists. What is it, then, about the power of the fieldwork experience that cannot be contained in the traditional introductory and concluding margins of anthropological discourse? I shall argue that first-person narratives are being selected by women as part of an implicit critique of positivist assumptions and as a strategy of communication and self-discovery. This strategy is evinced in texts that predate second-wave feminism, for example, Zora Neale Hurston's (1938) *Tell My Horse* or Ella Deloria's (1944) *Speaking of Indians* (discussed in the concluding section), and in a host of texts produced at the onset of second-wave American feminism: Jean Briggs's (1970) *Never in Anger*, Elizabeth Fernea's (1969) *Guests of the Sheikh*, Hortense Powdermaker's (1966) *Stranger and Friend*, and Laura Bohannon's (1964) *Return to Laughter*. Finally, first-person narratives of communication and self-discovery are present in texts such as Marjorie Shostak's (1981) *Nisa* and Manda Cesara's (1982) *Reflections of a Woman Anthropologist*, produced at the ebb tide of second-wave feminism.[23]

READING CONFESSIONAL FIELD LITERATURE
AS EXPERIMENTS IN FEMINIST ETHNOGRAPHY

During her fieldwork among the Inuit, Briggs finds herself adopted by an Eskimo family as a "Kapluna" (white) daughter, but constantly bridling under
male authority. Issues of autonomy are important to her and influence her relationship with Eskimo women. She tells us,

> On one occasion I nonplussed Allaq by asking why it was that men "bossed"
> women and made all the daily decisions. Allaq, very resourceful when con-
> fronted with idiotic Kapluna questions was silent for only a minute, then said:
> "Because the Bible says that's the way it should be." Wanting to know whether
> the situation was rationalized in terms of women's inferiority, I prodded her,
> telling her that some Kapluna men also boss their women because they believe
> that women have less *ihuna* (judgment or mind) than men. She assured me this
> was not the case among Eskimos.[24]

Briggs continues to question Inuit sex roles and rebels against what she
comes to see as repressive igloo life, affirming her need for self-expression.
The Eskimo with whom she lives see her as angry and irritable. Finally, one
day she loses her temper and is ostracized by the community. Briggs is never
able to fully comprehend her ostracism, and the dispute evolves into a permanent misunderstanding that she can never repair. The last pages of her
book call into question the very nature of ethnographic understanding.

Brigg's difficulties sprang in part from her positionality in Eskimo Culture. Questions of positionality more often confront female than male
fieldworkers, and the female ethnographer is more likely to be faced with a
decision over which world she enters.[25] I will discuss three examples among
many.

Elizabeth Fernea's book, *Guests of the Sheikh*, like Briggs's account, marks
points of rupture and acts of transgression, underscoring the problems of
identification. Living in what is typically described as a "sex-segregated society," Fernea is consigned to the women's world with sometimes disastrous
consequences. Although Fernea's identification with Iraqi women is such that
she grows used to wearing a veil, and worries about being caught without it,
she is unable to entirely accept the restrictions placed on her freedom of
movement. When other women of the village ask her out, they insist she first
get permission from her husband, "Mr. Bob." No amount of explaining will

convince the women that she does not need to get permission from her husband to move freely.

One day Fernea accepts an invitation to go driving in the country with the (female) schoolteacher, and her somewhat disreputable (male) cousin. Fernea's best friend, Laila, wants to accompany them, so Fernea asks Laila if she should first get permission from her father. Laila says no, and Fernea does not pursue the matter.

Upon return to the village, however, Laila's friends are furious with Fernea for having placed their reputations in jeopardy. For an unmarried woman to be seen with an unmarried man, especially one as unsavory as the schoolteacher's cousin, was to risk extreme censure and possibly death, as a father would be forced to act to protect the reputations of other women in the family. Soon the issue is a village matter. If the schoolteacher's cousin were to gossip about the two women in the coffee shops, then the good names of the women and the honor of the entire tribe would be at stake.

Although she and Laila were close in age, Laila's family held Fernea, married and therefore more mature, responsible for Laila's conduct. Fernea's husband is also lectured for "letting his wife go out alone." The incident eventually blows over, but Fernea is either unwilling or unable to describe fully what happens to Laila, alluding only to the likelihood that she was beaten for her disobedience.

I pull my second example from Hortense Powdermaker's book *Stranger and Friend*, the title of which astutely suggests the intrinsic duality of the anthropologist. Observing Lesu women practicing ritual dances. Powdermaker sought a way to stay awake during the long evening sessions. She soon began to practice with the women as a means of relieving the tedium of observation. When she is asked to participate in the upcoming festivities, however, Powdermaker is taken by surprise. Fearing a refusal would be seen by the women as a rejection, she self-consciously agrees, and recounts:

There I was on my proper place in the circle; the drums began; I danced. Something happened. I forgot myself and was one with the dancers. Under the full moon and for the brief time of the dance, I ceased to be an anthropologist from a modern society. I danced. When it was over I realized that for this short period, I had been emotionally a part of the rite. Then out came my notebook.[26]

Later, being invited to watch ceremonial circumcision of the village boys, Powdermaker decides,

> since I had been identified with the women, even to the extent of dancing with them, it seemed unwise in the hostile atmosphere between the sexes to swerve suddenly from the women's group to the men's. Or perhaps I was unable to switch my identifications so quickly.
> From then on the quality of my relationships with the women as different. I had their confidence as I had not had it before. They came of their own accord to visit me and talked intimately about their lives.[27]

It is with the illness of Powdermaker's friend and "best informant" that she feels her uselessness and the tribe's withdrawing into itself. Then she realizes that "no matter how intimate and friendly I was with the natives, I was never truly a part of their lives."[28]

My third example is drawn from Laura Bohannon's "anthropological novel," *Return to Laughter*. Bohannon was perhaps even more acutely aware than were her contemporaries of the disciplinary boundaries surrounding truth and fiction, hence the nom de plume Elenore Smith Bowen. Profound crises of identity mark Bohannon's account, initiated by a confusion over which role, as a woman, she should assume:

> We reached Udama's hut. There the bride was handed to her mother-in-law. The women scrambled in the hut after them. I tried to follow. Udama herself stopped me. "You must make up your mind," she announced loudly so all could hear, "whether you wish to be an important guest or one of the senior women of the homestead. If you are an important guest we will again lead out the bride so you may see her. If you are one of us, you may come inside, but you must dance with us."[29]

Bohannon says that without stopping to consider the ramifications, she went inside. But it is her refusal to remain in the women's world, and her determination to enter the men's world, that eventually earns her the title "witch." Caught in a battle between two powerful village elders. Bohannon, almost against her will, is forced to play out her role as witch.

Bohannon is confronted throughout her fieldwork experience with a number of moral dilemmas, some of which involve decisions to dispense medication or aid those afflicted with smallpox banished from the Tiv homestead. But perhaps the moral problem that upsets Bohannon the most involves what she regards as callous jokes villagers lay on the helpless. One in particular haunts Bohannon and recurs as a motif signifying the limitations of cultural understanding: the villagers tell an old blind man a snake is in front of him on the path, then laugh watching him try to run. In the end, Bohannon feels she can come to terms with the villagers' sense of humor because she comprehends the tragedies of Tiv everyday life, in particular the effects of a devastating smallpox epidemic on the village. Finally, there is a "return to laughter."

> Many of my moral dilemmas had sprung from the very nature of my work, which had made me a trickster: one who seems to be what he is not and who professes faith in what he does not believe. But this realization is of little help. It is not enough to be true to one's self. The self may be bad and need to be changed, or it may change unawares into something strange and new. I had changed. . . .
>
> I had held that knowledge is worth the acquisition. I had willingly accepted the supposition that one cannot learn save by suppressing one's prejudices, or, at the very least, holding them morally in abeyance. The trouble lay in my careless assumption that it would be only my "prejudices" that were to be involved, and never my "principles"—it had not occurred to me that the distinction between "prejudice" and "principle" is itself a matter of prejudice.
>
> It is an error to assume that to know is to understand and that to understand is to like. The greater the extent to which one has lived and participated in a genuinely foreign culture and understood it, the greater the extent to which one realizes that one could not, without violence to one's personal integrity, be of it.[30]

Bohannon's closing words are marked by an awareness of the integrity and ineffability of difference. Recognizing that her "principles" (her use of quotation marks around the word is quite deliberate)—those of positivist science—are a matter of prejudice, Bohannon is a long way from shoring up the boundaries of positivist science. Her questioning does not stop with the distinction between prejudice and principle but extends to the very nature of self.

More recent works by women anthropologists have also been excluded from consideration as experimental ethnography. Marjorie Shostak's book *Nisa*, for example, reveals a complex negotiation of positionality within a single gender domain. Shostak is puzzled by !Kung women's insistence on talking to her about sex. Thinking that the fault must lie with her questions (their misunderstanding what she wanted to talk about), she says,

> All Kung women it seemed, loved to talk and joke about sex. I was still willing to talk about it, but I was not quite as interested as I had been four years earlier. I now wanted to focus on less romantic matters: on friendship, on women as providers, on childcare, and on avenues for self expression and creativity— issues that had also become more relevant to my own life.
>
> Although I made it quite explicit that *my* work involved a broader scope than it had years before, I found conversations drifting, if not being totally diverted, toward sexual topics. Also, the women usually reported on their daily activities in a dutiful manner, but when they discussed their relationships with men— either fanciful or factual—they often expressed delight in *our* work.[31]

Shostak finally decides that talking about sex "may have been easier than talking about more troublesome matters," and concludes that while her "prior reputation may have magnified their tendency to make sex a prime topic of conversation . . . certainly it did not create that tendency."[32] Shostak's attempt to balance the !Kungs' agenda with her own is expressed in her equivocation between "my work" and "our work" in the passage cited above.

Such speculation, however, shows the extent to which full comprehension of a cultural other may be blocked by the ethnographer's own conceptual categories. !Kung women may in fact be talking about what is most important to them. Shostak's insistence that sex talk is the fluff before getting down to the brass tacks of emotional relationships is, I think, belied by her own narrative. !Kung women may not articulate "emotional relationships," or, more important, sex is perhaps the idiom through which they describe emotional relationships between men and women. The fact that Nisa alone is able to describe emotional relationships in ways that approximate Western terms is accounted for by her continual contact with anthropologists. Still, Shostak recounts Nisa's own resistance to speak of emotional affairs:

> During our first interview, I asked about the years I had been away. She asked, "You mean about men?" I explained that I hoped we would review everything that had happened to her, men included, but that I now wanted to hear about

the truly important things. For the next hour, she talked about lovers, mostly those of the past. No matter how I tried to lead the discussion elsewhere, I met with little success. It was only during later interviews that she seemed to feel comfortable enough with me to discuss some of the more "personal" issues in her life.[33]

The conclusion to this compelling book indicates another ruptured understanding. Nisa has adopted Shostak as a niece, relationships between aunts and uncles with their nieces and nephews being emotionally charged among the !Kung, and particularly significant in Nisa's own life as well.[34] When a girl did not get along with her parents, she simply went off to live with grandparents or aunts and uncles who succored and cared for the wayward child. On the last page of the book, Nisa's words to Shostak are, "My niece, my niece . . . you are someone who truly thinks of me." Shostak's reply represents her failure to either accept or understand Nisa's meaning: "Almost every experience I have in life is colored and enriched by the !Kung world and the way Nisa looked at it. I will always think of her and hope she will think of me, as a distant sister."[35] Is Shostak's denial of the kinship Nisa constructs for them due to her feminist bias toward the category "sister" and its positive emotional connotations, or is it perhaps a more subtle repudiation of their unequal child-teacher relationship, with an assertion of one in which they are "equal"?

Unlike Shostak, Manda Cesara, an economic anthropologist, did not set out to study women. During the course of her fieldwork, however, her perspective shifts. She tells us,

> My outburst of anger against the condition of Western women or that of oppressed women generally surprised even me. I was not the least bit interested in the study of women as a graduate student. I came to Lenda to study the broad problem of the interaction between religion, kinship, and economic activities.[36]

Cesara's identity as a Western woman is confronted in the field by her failing marriage. Changing notions of her own sexuality are shaped by how she comes to understand "Lenda" sexuality and marriage. She recounts a discussion with a Lenda man on the nature of Western marriage:

> "Would you like to take your wife to friends, beer drinks, dances and hold her hand and show the world you love her?"

"That's what you do really?" he asked, I nodded affirmatively. "No," he said. "If I took my wife, I could not talk to other women. I could not explore what others are like."

I looked at him with as much gravity as I could muster.

"Would you like to be ostracized from couples when you are single? Would you accept, upon meeting a nice married woman, that you should not be attracted to her and could not marry? Would you like to feel alone? Would you like to feel there are few women, or that you may never find one because most are married?" He looked at me with great fright. "No," he said. I took a deep long, satisfying breath. "Then don't complain about your women," I said.[37]

Despite Cesara's feeling of affinity for Lenda women, she is unable to establish relationships with them. She reports:

I seem to be misreading women somehow. Anyway it is a darned lot easier and more pleasant to work with Lenda men than with Lenda women. It's the men who are the talkers here. Women are taciturn, proud, and I would say managerial. Sometimes I have the impression that women see me as foolish for talking to men.[38]

Cesara's book is decidedly experimental. She pastes together, montagelike, field notes, diary pages, letters, and analytic streams of consciousness. Like Elenore Smith Bowen, Manda Cesara is a pen name. And like many a male experimental ethnographer, *Reflections of a Woman Anthropologist* follows the author's first published traditional ethnography.

It is not difficult to read the works discussed above as "accounts which deal with fieldwork as an intellectual odyssey," qualifying them as a kind of experimental ethnography.[39] It is more difficult to read them as "fables of rapport." More precisely, they can be read as the fables of "imperfect rapport" Rabinow's and Dumont's books exhibit. The women ethnographers I have discussed glossed the fieldwork experience in terms of its disjunctions and gendered misunderstandings long before "experimental ethnography" appeared as a historical moment in anthropological practice. Briggs and Bohannon, in particular, question anthropology as a positivist endeavor. Giving these women the credit they deserve is one way experimental ethnography can incorporate a feminist critique of its assumptions. A second criticism of experimental ethnography's assumptions follows.

WOMEN AND NATIVES: RECALCITRANT SUBJECTS?

Focus on women's lives has been made an epistemological problem by male ethnographers such as Edwin Ardener and, more recently, Roger Keesing.[40] Ardener attempted to explain men's willingness to provide cultural models for the anthropologist and women's reluctance to do so with the idea of "muted discourse." While Ardener was criticized for biologism and essentialism,[41] the boldest argument of his paper—that men and women in different cultures might have separate realities—has been ignored.

In Keesing's reassessment of Ardener's theory, he attempts to analyze historic and structural reasons for his previous failures to elicit detailed information about women from women. While Keesing's sex was a large barrier, so was the fact that he was commissioned by Kwaio men to record the *kastom* of their society. Women, not initially seeing their activities as a part of this endeavor, saw no point in talking to Keesing. Keesing concludes that "what women can and will say about themselves and their society can never . . . be taken as direct evidence of what they know and don't know, or of women's status."[42] Of course, we might consider whether "what men can and will say about themselves and their society is direct evidence of what they know"; however, I choose to see Keesing's report as a welcome rejoinder to feminist anthropologists who returned from fieldwork claiming they could not study gender because it was not "at issue" in that society. Indeed, the fact that it was not at issue may have been the issue. Perhaps women chose not to discuss gender issues with an outsider. I would argue that a feminist anthropology cannot assume the willingness of women to talk, and that one avenue open to it is an investigation of when and why women do talk—assessing what strictures are placed on their speech, what avenues of creativity they have appropriated, what degrees of freedom they possess. Thus far epistemological problems about women as subjects have been framed in terms of anthropological models (like Ardener's), when much feminist theory outside the discipline takes the problematic of voicing as its starting point. Yet feminist theories of language have not informed ethnography. In fact, I would argue that feminist anthropologists stand to learn not only from women's speech, but women's silences as well. Like Adrienne Rich, we might learn how to plot those silences, very possibly strategies of resistance, in the text.

Silence can be a plan
rigorously executed

the blueprint to a life

It is a presence
it has a history a form

Do not confuse it
with any kind of absence.[43]

According to James Clifford, it is the intercultural dialogic production of texts that constitutes one of the key moments in experimental ethnography: "With expanded communication and intercultural influence, people interpret others, and themselves, in a bewildering diversity of idioms—a global condition of what Bakhtin called 'heteroglossia.'"[44] Yet heteroglossia is not a ready-made solution. It assumes voices, most likely male ones, and does not confront problems of coming to voice. Experimental ethnography's critique of anthropology's scientific ethos should also explicitly name patriarchy, and examine the way in which the scientific voice is at once patriarchal. This voice, Griffin says,

> rarely uses a personal pronoun, never speaks as "I" or "we," and almost always implies that it has found absolute truth, or at least has the authority to do so. In writing . . . this paternal voice became quite real to me, and I was afraid of it. . . . You will recognize this voice from its use of such phrases as "it is decided" or "the discovery was made."[45]

This is my second feminist critique of experimental ethnography's assumptions.

Clifford's analysis of the prospects for experimental ethnography envisions coauthored, joint texts. As Rabinow points out, proponents of experimental ethnography go only so far in their critique of anthropological representations; they stop just short of calling themselves into question.[46] Marcus and Cushman note that experiments with dispersed authority risk "giving up the game."[47] On the contrary, I argue that dispersed authority represents anthropology's last grasp of the "other." I am not surprised that no inclusion of work done in ethnic studies or so-called indigenous anthropology is made in experimental ethnography, but I am dismayed. This, despite the fact these writings explicitly challenge the authority of representations . . . of themselves. Self writing about like selves has thus far not been on the agenda of experimental ethnography. To accept "native" authority is to give up the game.

If we have learned anything about anthropology's encounter with colonialism, the question is not really whether anthropologists can represent people better, but whether we can be accountable to people's own struggles for self-representation and self-determination. Paula Gunn Allen, a teacher and critic of native American literature, argues that

> when a people has no control over public perceptions of it, when its sense of self is denied at every turn in the books, films, television, and radio shows it is forced to imbibe, it cannot help but falter. But when its image is shaped by its own people, the hope for survival can be turned into a much greater hope: it can become a hope for life, for vitality, for affirmation.[48]

Thus when the "other" drops out of anthropology, becomes subject, participant, and *sole* author, not "object" then, in Kevin Dwyer's words, we will have established a "hermeneutics of vulnerability" and an "anthropology which calls itself into question."[49] Another way in which feminist theory can make a contribution to the study of colonialism is through a critique of the politics of representation itself.

This is my point, alluded to at the outset of this essay, about experimental ethnography not pushing the challenge to traditional anthropology far enough. What would your alternate ethnographic canon look like if it included books like John Langston Gwaltney's *Drylongso*, Maxine Hong Kingston's *Woman Warrior* or essays like Renato Rosaldo's "When Natives Talk Back"?[50] This is not a uniquely feminist criticism, but it can be expressed in feminist ways.

What would experimental ethnography's concern with the constitution of subjectivities, the politics of *identity*, look like if it addressed a politics of *identification*? If it addressed the dynamics of autobiography and community, rather than authority and disaffection? For a movement that claims interest in experimenting with how selves are constituted or represented, experimental ethnography has been strangely reluctant to embrace other forms of writing, such as the novel, short story, diary, or autobiography.[51] At a time when literary critics read such texts as expressive of culture, why can't anthropologists? Novels, much less

novels by Zora Neale Hurston or Ella Deloria, would never be considered anthropology in the old canon, but perhaps they can be in the new one.

[. . .]

Barbara Hernstein Smith, in her seminal essay "Contingencies of Value," reminds us that "the entry of marginal texts into the modern curriculum not only
'opens up' the canon but opens to question the idea of a canon."[52] For what is at
stake, as Cornel West reminds us, is not simply the canon, but a cultural and historical crisis, namely, "the decolonization of the Third World associated with the
historical agency of those . . . exploited, devalued and degraded by European civilization" that renders a radical reordering of the canon necessary.[53] If this essay
has questioned the place of confessional ethnography, "anthropological novels,"
and writings by people of color in the alternative canon of experimental ethnography, perhaps we too can consider the project of feminist ethnography as one
that continually challenges the very notion of a canon.

NOTES

I wish here to acknowledge some of the influences that have shaped this essay, but
were not mentioned in the version that appeared in *Inscriptions*. Before *Writing
Culture* appeared, I was fortunate to have attended one (very crowded) session of a
seminar on experimental ethnography given by Paul Rabinow and James Clifford in
the fall of 1984. Certainly some of my thinking here, in ways that I cannot fully detail,
stems from that event and Deborah Gordon's very insightful presentation there.

1. Renato Rosaldo, "Where Objectivity Lies: The Rhetoric of Anthropology," in *The
Rhetoric of Human Sciences*, ed. John Nelson and Donald McCloskey (Madison:
University of Wisconsin Press, 1987).

2. In Marcus and Cushman's (1982) reviews of "experimental ethnography," for
example, texts authored by women ethnographers account for only 9 of 117 references.
Of those 9 texts, only Jean Briggs's *Never in Anger* is considered in this essay.

3. Audre Lorde, *Sister/Outsider* (Trumansburg, N.Y.: Crossing, 1984)

4. Susan Griffin, "The Way of All Ideology," in *Feminist Theory*, ed. N. Keohane et al.
(Chicago: University of Chicago Press, 1982).

5. James Clifford, "On Ethnographic Authority," *Representations* 2 (spring 1983):
121. See also Marilyn Strathern, "Out of Context: The Persuasive Fictions of
Anthropology," *Current Anthropology* 28, no. 3 (June 1987).

6. Jane Atkinson, "Review Essay: Anthropology," *Signs* 8, no. 2 (1982): 236–58; Susan Geiger, "Women's Life History: Method and Content," *Signs* 11, no. 2 (1986): 334–51.

7. For example, Carol MacCormack and Marilyn Strathern, *Nature, Culture and Gender* (Cambridge: Cambridge University Press, 1980).

8. See Jane Collier and Michelle Rosaldo, "Politics and Gender in Simple Societies," and Sherry Ortner, "Gender and Sexuality in Hierarchical Societies," in *Sexual Meanings*, ed. Sherry Ortner and Harriet Whitehead (Cambridge: Cambridge University Press, 1981).

9. See, for example, Sherry Ortner's 1983 paper "The Founding of a Sherpa Nunnery and the Problem of Women as an Analytic Category," in which women recede from the analysis as the primary analytic category. In *Feminist Revisions*, ed. Louise Tilly and Vivien Pataraka (Ann Arbor: University of Michigan Press, 1983).

10. See Susan Kreiger's ethnography of a midwestern lesbian community, *The Mirror Dance: Identity in a Women's Community* (Philadelphia: Temple University Press, 1983), and more recently, Lila Abu-Lughod's *Writing Women's Worlds: Bedouin Stories* (Berkeley: University of California Press, 1993).

11. Marilyn Strathern, "An Awkward Relationship: The Case of Feminism and Anthropology," *Signs* 12 (winter 1987): 276–92.

12. Marilyn Strathern, "An Awkward Relationship."

13. See, for example, Margaret Mead, *Coming of Age in Samoa* (New York: Morrow, 1928); Ruth Landes, *The Ojibwa Woman* (1937; reprint, New York: Norton, 1969); Phyllis Kaberry, *Aboriginal Woman* (New York: Humanities, 1939); Audrey Richards, *Chisungu* (London: Tavistock, 1956); and Marilyn Strathern, *Women in Between* (London: Seminar Press, 1972).

14. See, for example, Renato Rosaldo's analysis of Evans-Pritchard's *Nuer*, in "From the Door of His Tent," in *Writing Culture*, ed. James Clifford and George Marcus (Berkeley: University of California Press, 1986), and Barbara Tedlock, "From Participant Observation to the Observation of Participation: The Emergence of Narrative Ethnography," *Journal of Anthropological Research* 47 (spring 1991).

15. See George E. Marcus and Dick Cushman, "Ethnographies as Texts," *Annual Review of Anthropology* 11 (1982): 25–69.

16. See Clifford, "On Ethnographic Authority."

17. Marcus and Cushman, "Ethnographies as Texts," 26.

18. Paul Rabinow, *Reflections of Fieldwork in Morocco* (Berkeley: University of California Press, 1977); Jean-Paul Dumont, *The Headman and I* (Austin: University of Texas Press, 1978); and Vincent Crapanzano, *Tuhami* (Chicago: University of Chicago Press, 1980).

19. Other examples are Morris Freilick, ed., *Marginal Natives: Anthropologists at Work* (New York: Harper & Row, 1970); George Spindler, ed. *Being an Anthropologist: Fieldwork in Eleven Cultures* (New York: Holt, Rinehart and Winston, 1970); Solon T. Kimball, ed., *Crossing Cultural Boundaries: The Anthropological Experience* (San Francisco: Chandler, 1972); T. N. Madan, ed., *Encounter and Experience* (1975); and M. N. Srinivas et al., eds., *The Fieldworker and the Field* (Delhi: Oxford University Press, 1979). However, not all the papers in Peggy Golde's edited collection, *Women in the Field* (Berkeley: University of California Press, 1970), represent the notion of anthropology as positivist science, especially those by Lederman and Briggs.

20. Kevin Dwyer, "On the Dialogic of Fieldwork," *Dialectical Anthropology* 2, no. 2 (1979): 121.

21. Clearly there are several exceptions, one of which is Robert and Yolanda Murphy's collaboration on *Women of the Forest* (New York: Columbia University Press, 1974).

22. Marion and Burton Benedict, *Men, Women, and Money in the Seychelles* (Berkeley: Univeristy of California Press, 1982), vii.

23. Zora Neale Hurston, *Tell My Horse* (1938; reprint, New York: Harper & Row, 1978); Ella Deloria, *Speaking of Indians* (New York: Friendship, 1944); Jean Briggs, *Never in Anger* (Cambridge, Mass.: Harvard University Press, 1970); Elizabeth Fernea, *Guests of the Sheik* (New York: Doubleday, 1969); Elenore Smith Bowen (a.k.a. Laura Bohannon), *Return to Laughter* (New York: Doubleday, 1964); Manda Cesara, *Reflections of a Woman Anthropologist: No Hiding Place* (New York: Academic, 1982); and Marjorie Shostak, *Nisa: The Life and Words of a !Kung Woman* (Cambridge, Mass.: Harvard University Press, 1981).

24. Briggs, *Never in Anger*, 107.

25. Suzanne Kirschner's analysis of Briggs and Powdermaker emphasizes the place of women's empathy in cross-cultural understanding, derived from being placed more frequently in vulnerable roles (such as daughter), and suggests a different understanding of positionality than the one I employ. See her "Then What Have I to Do with Thee? On Identity, Fieldwork, and Ethnographic Knowledge," *Cultural Anthropology* 2, no. 2 (1987).

26. Powdermaker, *Stranger and Friend*, 112.

27. Powdermaker, *Stranger and Friend*, 113.

28. Powdermaker, *Stranger and Friend*, 116.

29. Bohannon (a.k.a. Elenore Smith Bowen), *Return to Laughter*, 123.

30. Bohannon (a.k.a. Elenore Smith Bowen), *Return to Laughter*, 291–92.

31. Shostak, *Nisa*, 354. Emphasis mine.

32. Shostak, *Nisa*, 356.

33. Shostak, *Nisa*, 356.

34. Shostak, *Nisa*, 50, 52, 62.

35. Shostak, *Nisa*, 371; see also Mary Pratt, "Fieldwork in Common Places," in *Writing Culture*, ed. James Clifford and George Marcus (Berkeley: University of California Press, 1986).

36. Cesara, *Reflections of a Woman Anthropologist*, 112.

37. Cesara, *Reflections of a Woman Anthropologist*, 73.

38. Cesara, *Reflections of a Woman Anthropologist*, 86.

39. See G. Marcus and D. Cushman, "Ethnographies as Texts."

40. Edwin Ardener, "Belief and the Problem of Women," reprinted in *Perceiving Women*, ed. Shirley Ardener (New York: Wiley, 1972); Roger Keesing, "Kwaio Women Speak: The Micropolitics of Autobiography in a Solomon Island Society," *American Anthropologist* 87, no. 1 (1984): 27–39.

41. See Nicole-Claude Mathieu, "Man-Culture and Woman-Nature," *Feminist Studies International Quarterly* 1 (1978): 55–56.

42. Keesing, "Kwaio Women Speak," 27.

43. Adrienne Rich, cited in Joanne Feit Dehil, "Cartographies of Silence: Rich's Common Language and the Woman Poet," *Feminist Studies* 1 6, no. 3 (1980): 539.

44. Clifford, "On Ethnographic Authority," 119.

45. Susan Griffin, *Women and Nature* (New York: Harper & Row, 1978), xv.

46. See Paul Rabinow, "Discourse and Power: On the Limits of Ethnographic Texts," *Dialectical Anthropology* 110 (1985): 1–22.

47. Marcus and Cushman, "Ethnographies as Texts," 44.

48. Paula Gunn Allen, introduction to *Spider Woman's Granddaughters: traditional Tales and Contemporary Writing by Native American Women* (New York: Fawcett Columbine, 1989), 17.

49. Kevin Dwyer, "On the Dialogic of Fieldwork," *Dialectical Anthopology* 2 (1977): 143–51.

50. See John Gwaltney, *Dylongso* (New York: Vintage, 1982); Renato Rosaldo, "When Natives Talk Back: Chicano Anthropology since the Late 60s," Renato Rosaldo Lecture Series Monograph, vol. 2, series 1984–85 (Mexican American Studies and Research Center, University of Arizona, Tucson, spring 1986); and Maxine Hong Kingston, *The Woman Warrior: Memoirs of a Girlhood among Ghosts* (New York: Knopf, 1976) and *Chinamen* (New York: Knopf, 1980).

In the 1988 version of this essay, I advocated reading the novels of women of color, including those of Paula Gunn Allen and Cherrie Moraga, as ethnography. While I feel this proposal has productive consequences for anthropology, I do recognize that for many such writers, the struggle is to have their novels read as "literature," and not automatically as sociology and anthropology. For example, Maxine Hong Kingston's novels *The Woman Warrior* and *Chinamen* were marketed as nonfiction when they first appeared. Zora Neale Hurston, responding to the criticisms of Richard Wright and others who accused her of ignoring the problems of racial oppression in her work, said "she had wanted at long last to write a black novel, not a treatise on Sociology" (see Henry Louis Gates, "Zora Neale Hurston: A Negro Way of Saying," afterword to *Tell My Horse* [New York: Harper & Row, 1990], 294). Therefore, in this version of the essay, I have decided to restrict my claim that the novel may be considered as ethnography to a review of the writings of women like Ella Deloria and Zora Neale Hurston, who also worked as anthropologists.

51. However, see Michael Fischer, "Ethnicity and the Postmodern Arts of Memory," in *Writing Culture*, ed. James Clifford and George Marcus.

52. Barbara Hernstein Smith, "Contingencies of Value," *Critical Inquiry* (September, 1983): 326.

53. Cornel West, "Minority Discourse and the Pitfalls of Canon Formation," *Yale Journal of Criticism* 1, no. 1 (1987): 194.

4

The Torture and Death of Her Little Brother, Burnt Alive in Front of Members of Their Families and the Community

Rigoberta Menchú, translated by Ann Wright

My mother said that when a woman sees her son tortured, burnt alive, she is incapable of forgiving, incapable of getting rid of her hate.

—*Rigoberta Menchú*

. . . but next winter the requital will come [they thought], and they fed the blaze with branches of the great thorn trees, because in the fire of warriors, which is the fire of war, even the thorns weep.

—*Miguel Angel Asturias, Men of Maize*

It was in 1979, I remember, that my younger brother died, the first person in my family to be tortured. He was sixteen years old. After the family's farewell, each of us went their own way: he stayed in the community since, as I said, he was secretary of the community. He was the youngest of my brothers, though I have two little sisters who are younger. One of them went with my mother and the other stayed in the community, learning and training in self-defence.

Reprinted from Rigoberta Menchú, *I, Rigoberta Menchú: An Indian Woman in Guatemala*, trans. Ann Wright, ed. Elisabeth Burgos-Debray (London: Verson, 1984), 172–82.

My mother, unable to find any other solution had gone off somewhere else. My brothers too, because they were being hunted, and so as not to expose the community to danger. . . . The thing is that the government put about this image of us, of our family, as if we were monsters, as if we were some kind of foreigners, aliens. But my father was Quiche, he was no Cuban. The government called us communists and accused us of being a bad influence. So, in order not to expose the community to danger and to weed out this "bad influence," we had to go away to different places. But my young brother had stayed there in the community.

On 9 September 1979 my brother was kidnapped. It was a Sunday, and he'd gone down to another village—he worked in other villages as well as his own. His name was Petrocinio Menchú Tum—Tum is my mother's name. Well, my brother had a job to do. He was very fond of organising work. So he went round organising in various places, and the army discovered him and kidnapped him. After 9 September my mother and the rest of us began to worry. At that time—and I still thank God they didn't kill all of us—my mother nonetheless went to the authorities to enquire after him. If they kill me because of my son, she said, let them kill me. I wasn't there at the time; I was in Huehuetenango when my brother was captured. They say that the day he fell, my mother was at home and my other brothers were not far away. Mother went into the village to find out where her son was, but nobody could give her any news of his whereabouts. However, he had been betrayed by someone in the community. As I said before, there are people who'll turn their hand to anything when you least expect it. Out of pure necessity, often they'll sell their own brothers. This man from the community had been a *compañero*, a person who'd always collaborated and who had been in agreement with us. But, they offered him fifteen *quetzals*—that's to say fifteen dollars—to turn my brother in, and so he did. The army didn't know who he was. That day my brother was going to another village with a girl when they caught him. The girl and her mother followed along after him. From the first moment they tied his hands behind his back, they started to drive him along with kicks. My brother fell, he couldn't protect his face. The first part of him to begin to bleed was his face. They took him over rough ground where there were stones, fallen tree trunks. He walked about two kilometers being kicked and hit all the time. Then they started to threaten the girl and her mother. They were risking their lives by following my brother and finding out where he was being taken. Apparently they said to them: "Do you want us to do the same to you, do you want us to rape you right here?" That's what this thug of a soldier said. And he told the *señora* that if they didn't go away they'd be tortured just like he was going to be because he was a communist and a subversive, and subversives deserved to be punished and to die.

It's an unbelievable story. We managed to find out how he died, what tortures they inflicted on him from start to finish. They took my brother away, bleeding from different places. When they'd done with him, he didn't look like a person any more. His whole face was disfigured with beating, from striking against the stones, the tree trunks; my brother was completely destroyed. His clothes were torn from his falling down. After that they let the women go. When he got to the camp, he was scarcely on his feet, he couldn't walk any more. And his face, he couldn't see any more, they'd even forced stones into his eyes, my brother's eyes. Once he arrived in the camp they inflicted terrible tortures on him to make him tell where the guerrilla fighters were and where his family was. What was he doing with the Bible, they wanted to know, why were the priests guerrillas? Straight away they talked of the Bible as if it were a subversive tract, they accused priests and nuns of being guerrillas. They asked him what relationship the priests had with the guerrillas, what relationship the whole community had with the guerrillas. So they inflicted those dreadful tortures on him. Day and night they subjected him to terrible, terrible pain. They tied him up, they tied his testicles, my brother's sexual organs, they tied them behind with string and forced him to run. Well, he couldn't stand that, my little brother, he couldn't bear that awful pain and he cried out, he asked for mercy. And they left him in a well, I don't know what it's called, a hole with water and a bit of mud in it, they left him naked there all night. There were a lot of corpses there in the hole with him and he couldn't stand the smell of all those corpses. There were other people there who'd been tortured. He recognized several catechists there who'd been kidnapped from other villages and were suffering as badly as he was. My brother was tortured for more than sixteen days. They cut off his fingernails, they cut off his fingers, they cut off his skin, they burned parts of his skin. Many of the wounds, the first ones, swelled and were infected. He stayed alive. They shaved his head, left just the skin, and also they cut the skin off his head and pulled it down on either side and cut off the fleshy part of his face. My brother suffered tortures on every part of his body, but they took care not to damage the arteries or veins so that he would survive the tortures and not die. They gave him food so that he'd hold out and not die from his wounds. There were twenty men with him who had been tortured or were still undergoing torture. There was also a woman. They had raped her and then tortured her.

As soon as she heard, my mother got in touch with me and I came home. My brother had been missing for three days when I got home. Most of all it was a matter of comforting my mother, because we knew that our enemies were criminals and, well, we wouldn't be able to do anything. If we went to claim him, they'd kidnap us at once. Mother did go, the first days, but they threatened her and said that if she came again she'd get the same treatment as her son was getting. And they told her straight out that her son was being tortured, so not to worry.

Then, on 23 September, we heard that the military were putting out bulletins around the villages. They didn't come to my village because they knew the people were prepared, ready for them at the moment's notice. In other villages, where we also had *compañeros*, they handed out bulletins and propaganda announcing punishment for the guerrillas. Saying they had such and such a number of guerrillas in their power and that they were going to carry out punishment in such and such a place. Well, when we got this news, it must have been about 11 in the morning, I remember, on the 23rd, my mother said: "My son will be among those who are punished." It was going to be done in public, that is, they were calling the people out to witness the punishment. Not only that, a bulletin said (we'd managed to get hold of a copy) that any who didn't go to witness the punishment were themselves accomplices of the guerrillas. That was how they threatened the people. So my mother said: "Come along then, if they're calling out everyone, we'll have to go." My father also came home at once, saying it was an opportunity we couldn't miss, we must go and see. We were in a frenzy. My brothers arrived. We were all together at home, my brothers, my little sisters, Mother, Father and me. We were preparing the midday meal when we heard the news and we didn't even finish preparing it or remember to take a bit of food to eat on the way. We just went.

We had to cross a long mountain ridge to get to another village—Chajul, where the punishment took place. Mother said: "We've got to be there tomorrow!" We knew it was a long way off. Se we set out at 11 in the morning on the 23rd for Chajul. We crossed long stretches of mountain country on foot. We walked through some of the night, with pine torches, in the mountains. About

8 o'clock the next morning we were entering the village of Chajul. The soldiers had the little village surrounded. There were about five hundred of them. They'd made all the people come out of their houses, with threats that if they didn't go to watch the punishments they'd suffer the same punishment, the same tortures. They stopped us on the road, but they didn't know we were relatives of one of the tortured. They asked us where we were going. My father said: "To visit the saint at Chajul." There's a saint there that many people visit. The soldier said: "No chance of that, get going, go over there. And if you get there, you'll see that no-one leaves this village." We said, "All right." About twenty soldiers, it must have been, stopped us at different points before we reached the village. They all threatened us the same way. They were waiting for the men whom they hadn't found when they emptied the houses, in case they'd gone to work, to make them come back to the village to see the punishments.

When we reached the village there were many people who'd been there since early morning: children, women, men. Minutes later, the army was surrounding the people who were there to watch. There were machines, armored cars, jeeps, all kinds of weapons. Helicopters started to fly over the village so that guerrilla fighters wouldn't come. That's what they were afraid of. The officer opened the meeting. I remember he started by saying that a group of guerrillas they'd caught were about to arrive and that they were going to suffer a little punishment. A little punishment, because there were greater punishments, he said, but you'll see the punishment they get. And that's for being communists! For being Cubans, for being subversives! And if you get mixed up with communists and subversives, you'll get the same treatment as these subversives you'll be seeing in a little while. My mother was just about 100 per cent certain her son would be amongst those being brought in. I was still not sure, though, because I knew my brother wasn't a criminal and didn't deserve such punishments.

Well, a few minutes later three army lorries came into the village. One went a little ahead, the middle one carried the tortured people and the third one brought up the rear. They guarded them very closely, even with armoured cars. The lorry with the tortured came in. They started to take them out one by one. They were all wearing army uniforms. But their faces were monstrously disfigured, unrecognisable. My mother went closer to the lorry to see if she could recognise her son. Each of the tortured had different wounds on the face. I mean, their faces all looked different. But my mother recognized her son, my little brother, among them. They put them in a line. Some of them were very nearly half dead, or they were nearly in their last agony, and others, you could see that they were; you could see that very well indeed. My brother was very badly tortured, he could hardly stand up. All the tortured had no nails and they had cut off part of the soles of their feet. They were barefoot. They forced them to walk and put them in a line. They fell down at once. They picked them up again. There was a squadron of soldiers there ready to do exactly what the officer ordered. And the officer carried on with his rigmarole, saying that we had to be satisfied with our lands, we had to be satisfied with eating bread and chile, but we mustn't let ourselves be led astray by communist ideas. Saying that all the people had access to everything, that they were content. If I remember alright, he must have repeated the word "communist" a hundred times. He started off with the Soviet Union, Cuba, Nicaragua; he said that the same communists from the Soviet Union had moved on to Cuba and then Nicaragua and that now they were in Guatemala. And that those Cubans would die a death like that of these tortured people. Every time he paused in his speech, they forced the tortured up with kicks and blows from their weapons.

No-one could leave the meeting. Everyone was weeping. I, I don't know, every time I tell this story, I can't hold back my tears, for me it's a reality I can't forget, even though it's not easy to tell of it. My mother was weeping; she was looking at her son. My brother scarcely recognized us. Or perhaps . . . My mother said he did, that he could still smile at her, but I, well, I didn't see that. They were monstrous. They were all fat, fat, fat. They were all swollen up, all wounded. When I drew closer to them, I saw that their clothes were damp. Damp from the moisture oozing out of their bodies. Somewhere around halfway through the speech, it would be about an hour and a half, two hours on, the captain made the squad of soldiers take the clothes off the tortured people, saying that it was so that everyone could see for themselves what their punishment had been and realize that if we got mixed up in communism, in terrorism, we'd be punished the same way. Threatening the people like that, they wanted to force us to do just as they said. They couldn't simply take the clothes off the tortured men, so the soldiers brought scissors and cut the clothes apart from the feet up and took the clothes off the tortured bodies. They all had the marks of different tortures. The captain devoted himself to explaining each of the different tortures. This is perforation with needles, he's say, this is a wire burn. He went on like that explaining each torture and describing each tortured man. There were three people who looked like bladders. I mean, they were inflated, although they had no wounds on their bodies. But they were inflated, inflated. And the officer said, that's from something we put in them that hurts them. The important thing is that they should know that it hurts and that the people should know it's no easy thing to have that done to your body.

In my brother's case, he was cut in various places. His head was shaved and slashed. He had no nails. He had no soles to his feet. The earlier wounds were suppurating from infection. And the woman *compañera*, of course I recognized her; she was from a village near ours. They had shaved her private parts. The nipple of one of her breasts was missing and her other breast was cut off. She had the marks of bites on different parts of her body. She was bitten all over, that *compañera*. She had no ears. All of them were missing part of the tongue or had had their tongues split apart. I found it impossible to concentrate, seeing that this could be. You could only think that these were human beings and what pain those bodies had felt to arrive at that unrecognizable state. All the people were crying, even the children. I was watching the children. They were crying and terrified, clinging to their mothers. We didn't know what to do. During his speech, the captain kept saying his government was democratic and gave us everything. What more could we want? He said that the subversives brought foreign ideas, exotic ideas that would only lead us to torture, and he'd point to the bodies of the men. If we listened to these exotic slogans, he said, we'd die like them. He said they had all kinds of weapons that we could choose to be killed with. The captain gave a panoramic description of all the power they had, the capacity they had. We, the people, didn't have the capacity to confront them. This was really all being said to strike terror into the people and stop anyone from speaking. My mother wept. She almost risked her own life by going to embrace my brother. My other brothers and my father held her back so she wouldn't endanger herself. My father was incredible; I watched him and he didn't shed a tear, but he was full of rage. And that was a rage we all felt. But all the rest of us began to weep, like everyone else. We couldn't believe it, I couldn't believe that had happened to my little brother. What had he done to deserve that? He was just an innocent child and that had happened to him.

After he'd finished talking the officer ordered the squad to take away those who'd been "punished," naked and swollen as they were. They dragged them along, they could no longer walk. Dragged them along to this place, where they lined them up all together within sight of everyone. The officer called to the worst of his criminals—the *Kaibiles*, who wear different clothes from other soldiers. They're the ones with the most training, the most power. Well, he called the *Kaibiles* and they poured petrol over each of the tortured. The captain said, "This isn't the last of their punishments, there's another one yet. This is what we've done with all the subversives we catch, because they have to die by violence. And if this doesn't teach you a lesson, this is what'll happen to you too. The problem is that the Indians let themselves be led by the communists. Since no-one's told the Indians anything, they go along with the communists." He was trying to convince the people but at the same time he was insulting them by what he said. Anyway, the lined up the tortured and poured petrol on them; and then the soldiers set fire to each one of them. Many of them begged for mercy. They looked half dead when they were lined up there, but when the bodies began to burn they began to plead for mercy. Some of them screamed, many of them leapt but uttered no sound—of course, that was because their breathing was cut off. But—and to me this was incredible—many of the people had weapons with them, the ones who'd been on their way to work had machetes, others had nothing in their hands, but when they saw the army setting fire to the victims, everyone wanted to strike back, to risk their lives doing it, despite all the soldiers' arms. . . . Faced with its own cowardice, the army itself realized that the whole people were prepared to fight. You could see that even the children were enraged, but they didn't know how to express their rage.

Well, the officer quickly gave the order for the squad to withdraw. They all fell back holding their weapons up and shouting slogans as if it were a celebration. They were happy! They roared with laughter and cried, "Long live the Fatherland! Long live Guatemala! Long live our President! Long live the army, long live Lucas!" The people raised their weapons and rushed at the army, but they drew back at once, because there was the risk of a massacre. The army had all kinds of arms, even planes flying overhead. Anyway, if there'd been a confrontation with the army, the people would have been massacred. But nobody thought about death. I didn't think that I might die, I just wanted to do something, even kill a soldier. At that moment I wanted to show my aggression. Many people hurried off for water to put out the fires, but no-one fetched it in time. It needed lots of people to carry the water—the water supply is in one particular place and everyone goes there for it—but it was a long way off and nothing could be done. The bodies were twitching about. Although the fire had gone out, the bodies kept twitching. It was a frightful thing for me to accept that. You know, it wasn't just my brother's life. It was many lives, and you don't think that the grief is just for yourself but for all the relatives of that others: God knows if they found relatives of theirs there or not! Anyway, they were Indians, our brothers. And what you think is that Indians are already being killed off by malnutrition, and when our parents can hardly give us enough to live on, and make such sacrifices so that we can grow up, then they burn us alive like that. Savagely. I said, this is impossible, and that was precisely the moment for me, personally, when I finally felt firmly convinced that if it's a sin to kill a human being, how can what the regime does to us not be a sin?

Everyone set to work, so that in two hours there were coffins for all the bodies. Everyone busied themselves with finding a blanket to put over them. I remember they picked bunches of flowers and put them beside them. The people of Guatemala are mostly Christian. They express their faith one way or another; they went to fetch the priest (I suppose that priest's since been murdered as well) to ask him, since he was a long way from the village, to bless the blanket to put over the corpses. When the fires died out, for a while nobody knew what to do: it was both terrifying to see the burned, tortured bodies and at the same time it gave you courage, strength to keep on going. My mother was half dead with grief. She embraced her son, she spoke to him, dead and tortured as he was. She kissed him and everything, though he was burnt. I said to her: "Come, let's go home." We couldn't bear to watch, we couldn't bear to keep looking at the dead. It wasn't through cowardice, rather that it filled us with rage. It was intolerable. So, all the people promised to give all the dead and tortured a Christian burial. Then my mother said, "I can't stay here." So we had to go, to leave it all behind and leave off looking. My father and my brothers were there, grieving. We just saw that the people . . . there were flowers, there was everything. The people decided to bury them there, not to take them home. There would have been a wake in one of the houses, but the people said, they didn't die in a house, it's fitting that this place should be sacred to them. We left them there. And it started to rain; it rained heavily. There they were getting wet, the people watching over the corpses. None of them left that spot. They all stayed.

But we went home. It was as though we were drunk or struck dumb; none of us uttered a word. When we got home Father said: "I'm going back to work." Then he started to talk to us. He said, rightly, that if so many people were brave enough to give their lives, their last moments, their last drop of blood, then wouldn't we be brave enough to do the same? And my mother, too, said: "It's not possible that other mothers should suffer as I have suffered. The people cannot endure that, their children being killed. I've decided too to abandon everything I shall go away." And we all said the same: there was nothing else you could say. Though, for myself, I didn't know what would be the most effective: to take up arms, to go to fight—which was what I most wanted to do—or to go to some other village and continue consciousness-raising among the people. My father said: "I may be old, but I'm joining the guerrillas. I'll avenge my son with arms." But I also considered that the community was important, since I had experience in organising people. We concluded that the most important thing was to organise the people so that they wouldn't have to suffer the way we had, see that horror film that was my brother's death.

The next day my father sorted out his things and left the house without delay. "Whether I return or not," he said, "I know the house will remain. I'll try to attend to everything in the community; that's always been my dream. Well, I'm going now." And my father left. Mother stayed in the house, not knowing what to do. She couldn't bear it, she remembered the whole thing. She cried from moment to moment, remembering. But most of the time she didn't cry; she tried to be cheerful. She said that her son was the one who had been a lot of trouble to bring up, because he'd nearly died as a little child. She had to go into a lot of debt to cure him. And then for this to happen to him. It made her very sad. But there were times when she cheered up. I remember that during this time Mother was very close to the *compañeros* in the mountains. Since we still had my brother's clothes—his trousers and shirts—my mother gave them away to one of the *compañeros* in the mountains, saying it was only just that they should be used by the *compañeros* because they were her son's clothes and her son had always been against the whole situation we were facing. And since the *compañeros* were against it too, they should use the clothes. Sometimes my mother was mad. All the neighbours would come and look. And mother thought: "If I start crying in front of the neighbours, what sort of example will that be?" "No crying; fighting's what we want," she'd say, and she'd act tough, and in spite of the fact that she was always a little ill and felt very tired, she'd battle on.

I stayed in the house a week longer. Then I made up my mind and said: "I must go." So I left, keener than ever to work. I knew that my mother also had to leave home. There was hardly any communication between us, either about where we were going or what we were going to do. I had the chance to say goodbye to my brothers, but I didn't know what they were going to do either. Each of us took our own decision. And so I left.

5

The Way We Were, Are, and Might Be: Torch Singing as Autoethnography

Stacy Holman Jones

A BEGINNING, TENTATIVE

Two ideas:

1. Torch singing—performing songs of unrequited love—is, for audiences and singers, a type of autoethnographic performance. Torch singing is how the body *does* and *undoes* the experience of unrequited love (adapted from Jones 1996: 132).[1]

2. Torch singing is, for me, an autoethnographic performance, a doing and undoing of my own love in the act of research.

These are ideas about subjectivity, and because of this, they conjure stories of my own desires and disappointments. I'd like to tell a few of those stories. Then I'll return to the idea that torch singing is an autoethnographic performance—a performance that invites us to experience the longing and participate in the revolution of unrequited love.

AN ENDING, REPEATED

Katie rushes to cross a busy New York City street. She is late for her shift to collect signatures and distribute leaflets urging her government to "Ban the

Reprinted from *Ethnographically Speaking*, ed. Arthur P. Bochner and Carolyn Ellis (Walnut Creek, Calif.: AltaMira Press, 2002), 44–56.

Bomb." She is in charge, informed, and loud. She is Jewish, political, and proud.

Katie looks up from her work—her cause, her passion—and sees Hubbell (once her work, her cause, and her passion) emerge from a car across the street. He is beautiful, intractable, All-American.

Hubbell waves. Katie rushes to cross the busy New York City street. They kiss, then embrace. A beautiful, perhaps intractable, and certainly All-American woman moves into the scene. She is Hubbell's fiancée. Katie, Hubbell, and the fiancée make small talk and empty promises to meet for drinks, then say good-bye. Katie returns to her work to Ban the Bomb.

But this isn't the end. Now Hubbell crosses the busy New York City street. He tells Katie that she never gives up (he means her work). She says that she only gives up when she is absolutely forced to (she means her work, too, including Hubbell). They kiss, embrace, and say good-bye.

Hubbell returns to his fiancée. Katie returns, once again, to her work. Barbra sings, "Memories . . ."

A PERFORMANCE, HIDDEN

I am crying. I cry each time I see the final scene between Katie and Hubbell in *The Way We Were*. I have to see only that last scene, hear only those last sounds. "Memories . . ."

I cry for Katie and Hubbell, for the way they tried, but just couldn't make their relationship work. I cry for Katie's refusal to give up on her causes or her passions. I cry for how she feels forced to choose between her work and her love. Most of all, I cry for how much I feel like Katie during the last moments of the film, listening to that song.

Today, as I watch the final moments of *The Way We Were*, my husband comes into the room. As Katie rushes to cross the busy New York City street, I feel my husband's eyes on me. He knows I will cry at the end, and he watches me, waiting. When Hubbell returns to his fiancée and Katie to her work, I get up from the couch and rush into my office. I sit at my desk and cry, not wanting my husband to see me. I don't want him to see me weep for my own longings, refusals, and choices. I want to be alone with Katie and Hubbell and that song of unrequited love. I lay my head on the desk and sing "The Way We Were." I play the final scene over in my head, only this time I am Katie and you are Hubbell.

The scene ends the same, with you returning to your fiancée and me to my work. And I cry again, only this time I don't feel the stab of unrequited desire and the ache of lost opportunities. No, I feel strangely . . . curious. I am curious about whether this story has another sort of ending. I am curious about whether I can play Katie with all of her caring and conviction.

A READER, IMAGINED

Our meeting does not happen by chance. I don't catch a glimpse of you across some downtown street. No, when I visit my parents and our hometown, I call you. I give my name to the receptionist and wait for you to come on the line. My heart is pounding. I fight the urge to hang up. You are surprised to hear from me, and at first the conversation is awkward and hesitant. We ask each other about families and jobs, about spouses and children. After a while, we settle into a comfortable rhythm and move on to questions of happiness and ambitions. As the conversation winds down, I (trying to be casual) say we should get together for a drink the next time I'm in town. You suggest we have lunch the next day.

I don't sleep at all that night.

I wait for you in the front of a small Thai restaurant. I sit on a hard chair next to the door. Each time it swings open, I hold my breath. I try standing, but imagine I look too expectant. I sit again, then pick up a day-old newspaper and pretend to read. The door opens and you explode into the tiny space (or so it seems to me). When I stand to meet your embrace, I can't feel my legs beneath me.

We're seated at a table next to the window. I order a large glass of water, which I drink greedily when it arrives at the table. I don't remember being this nervous about speaking to anyone—ever. The first moments pass in a haze. We discuss Thai food and order something from the menu. We return to questions of families and careers. And then something odd happens.

You say you know about the book I wrote, an ethnography on women's music. I don't believe this, but I am flattered that you mention it. You say you haven't seen it, but you know it's a *feminist* book, which doesn't surprise you. You say you are proud of me, that you knew I would become an author. I think about how many times I have imagined you reading my words. I think about my story about you and me and Billie Holiday and feminism and I wonder if I was wrong.

A MEMORY, INSCRIBED

The story about you and me and Billie Holiday and feminism? Oh yes, well, you wouldn't have seen that. I wrote that story when I first began researching torch singing—songs about unrequited love typically sung by women. Mind if I indulge in a bit of background here? I'll try to keep it brief.

The torch song is quite an old form, descending from the French chanson, or song-poem, which dates to the eleventh century. Torch songs tell stories of desire, seduction, and heartbreak. They are designed to arouse "intense emotion in both singer and audience" (Clements 1998, 32). A great chanson evokes a "powerful melancholy that can make listeners experience longing and consolation, often simultaneously" (Clements 1998, 32). However, the torch singer does not leave her audiences despairing or languishing in the afterglow of catharsis. No, she uses her story to understand the past and to "nurture the future" (Moore 1989, 45, 53).

Yes, the afterglow of catharsis! Okay, well maybe I got a bit carried away there. . . . I'm getting to the story about you. . . . When I began my research on torch singing, I started with Billie Holiday, one of my favorites. I tried to remember the first time I heard Holiday's voice. I tried to remember what her words and her songs of unrequited love meant to me then. I sat down at my desk, and I wrote. . . .

Some days I wonder if, after all the hours I've spent in seminar rooms and alone in front of my computer writing, I have been reduced to making lists of words, to scripting fragments. Unable to express in finely wrought sentences the injustice of oppression or the beauty of a solution, I make lists that signify worlds, words that set off explosions of thought and feeling.

A recent list:

shared experience of oppression

the abyss of representation

demanding voice and redress

a red dress

a smoky voice

Billie Holiday

This list makes me think of you. Why you? Why now? I think of the cassette tapes you made for me—tapes that now reside, sticky with age, in a blue shoebox. A blue shoebox buried deep in an ocean of report cards, prom photos, pages filled with the rush and slope of your words. I add

homemade tapes

to the list, and then something clicks and tilts and I'm in Ames, Iowa, in our steamy, windowless downtown apartment. I see your guitar-calloused finger-tips pressing the eject button, offering me Laurie Anderson and The Specials and this or that Beatle and R.E.M. Your recorded undergraduate music education course packed in tight against my own cassette rebellion—Prince and Sting and Billie. Torchers every one.

I find Billie in the bargain bin at your favorite music store. You detest the tinny piano and her pleading voice. Your guitar-calloused fingertips press the eject button.

You use those fingertips to educate me in the finer-points of a scornful, noisy, jealous love.

I hear this music in and around your smile and biting remarks, in and around the fury of your anger. And over what? That I wanted to go to graduate school. That I wanted more for myself than you.

After it was over, you said you were sorry it happened the way it did. You said you treated me like an animal.

And I said yes, but only because you couldn't coax and tame me into your note-filled consciousness without a fight.

You said you were sorry. Don't be. I still have them. I still hear their voices. Laurie and Sting and Billie. Every one.

The cursor blinks, waiting for an explanation. I delete homemade tapes from the list. I add

feminist theory

because that is what remains. You gave me music, but I gave myself Billie Holiday.

A CURIOSITY, CONFESSED
I think about this story of you and me and Billie Holiday and feminism and know I was wrong. Looking at you now, in the Thai restaurant, I decide not to

tell you the story I've been telling myself all these years. I rewrite it then and there. Instead of pitting your wants and desires for marriage and family against my own for a career and an intellectual life, I say that you taught me to write my book.

You look confused. I say it was your curiosity—about music and about life—that inspired me to be intellectually and emotionally curious. You still look confused. I say that your desire to learn everything you could about the music you loved—songs and performers and recordings and performances and playing—inspired me to listen more closely, to really feel and think about music. But more than that—more than music—you taught me how to ask questions and piece together answers. You taught me how to be a thinker. You made me want to be a writer. It took me a long time to understand that. I say these words to you and I mean them. You don't look confused anymore. Instead, you look away.

AN AUTHOR, BLINKING

A few weeks before our lunch, I found a poem lurking in a file titled "Music and Literature." I didn't remember writing this poem or placing it among the ideas I've collected about music and literature. It begins with these words, written by Peggy Phelan (1993, 16): "All seeing is hooded with loss. . . . In looking at the other . . . the subject seeks to see" herself. Then, my words about you . . .

> I feel the slipping away, welcome it.
> Turn over the memory of a long, lost
> other. Blurring vision and breath coming fast,
> swallowing so hard the longing catches in my throat.
>
> Your eyes, green like mine, on me. Steadily
> watching myself reflected in your gaze. Look
> at you seeing me, better one, now two, three, now four,
> recognizable at last, this image in green, is mine.
>
> I blink, dismantle the sudden need. Strip motives bare.
> Symptom of too much criticism, discourse, disguise.
> Fashioning shards of regret into bone—no children, two
> mortgages, no investments, save your own mind.

I want to live the torch song I think, write, dream about.
Waking surfaces the absurdity of this dim remembrance.
I get back to work on the novel, the essay, the poem, the book.
I do.

Here, now, I watch you looking out the window of the Thai restaurant. I think of the poem filed under "Music and Literature," and wonder if I will revise it as well. Then I suddenly remember a scene in Milan Kundera's (1991) novel *Immortality*. In the scene, Paul, a character in the novel, speaks to Kundera, a character in the novel and also the author of the novel. I can hear their exchange:

> "My wife adores Mahler," [Paul] continued. "She told me that two weeks before the premiere of his Seventh Symphony he locked himself up in a noisy hotel room and spent the whole night rewriting the orchestration."
>
> "Yes," I agreed, "it was in Prague, in 1906. The name of the hotel was the Blue Star."
>
> "I visualize him sitting in the hotel room, surrounded by manuscript paper," Paul continued, refusing to let himself be interrupted. "He was convinced that his whole work would be ruined if the melody were played by a clarinet instead of an oboe during the second movement."
>
> "That is precisely so," I said, thinking of my novel. (Kundera 1991, 335)

"That is precisely so," I say, thinking of my poem and my work and my curiosity. You look at me, finally, with eyes green like mine. You say that no one knows you better than I do. That no one knows me better than you.

I blink. I am sitting here with you, thinking of a hundred things, and all I can do is blink.

A BLUE STAR, WHISPERED

You suggest that we leave the restaurant, that we get some air. We walk into a brilliant daylight and stand facing each other in the parking lot. You ask to kiss me. I hear you say that no one knows you better than I do. That no one knows me better than you. I close my eyes. I feel your lips on mine and I fall back into some other place, some other romance. Your urgent, familiar kiss returns to me. I hear you whisper something about a hotel.

I am awake now, eyes open, standing in the parking lot and looking into green eyes unfamiliar to me. I think about Mahler and music and memory. I

see Katie in an earlier scene, before she and Hubbell parted. She is crying, oh,
I want, I want . . .

Kundera (1991, 314) says, "memory does not make films, it makes photographs." Obviously he has not seen *The Way We Were* or the noon movie of
you and me in the parking lot of a Thai Restaurant, with a hotel between us,
waiting for an answer.

I ask if you mean the Blue Star. I am nervous, and I laugh. You don't blink;
you smile. I ask you how? How can we live two lives? How can we be purposefully duplicitous and ever be sure or right or true again?

You say we all live two lives. You say it's like that book, *The Unbearable
Lightness of Being.* You say our mistake would be to burden others with the du-
plicity of our true selves, the facts of our being.

Kundera interrupts. He says he was wrong about the unbearable lightness
of being. He says, "What is unbearable in life is not being but being one's self"
(1991, 258).

I hear Kundera. I look at you, smiling. I'm not sure.

A TORCH SONG

We make empty promises to phone each other. I look at you, then walk away.

I stop and turn around and ask if you were wrong. I ask if we were wrong.
I ask you and Kundera and Katie and myself.

You say that I never give up.

I say that I give up only when I am absolutely forced to, and I mean both
you and my work. Then I say that I can listen to both Billie Holiday *and* "The
Way We Were." That I can be Katie *and* myself. That I can have love *and* feminism. You look confused. I say that you taught me to write this book, and now
I'm going to write it.

I get in my car and start the engine. Barbra's voice begins low as I put the
car in gear. She sings "Memories." I cry, just hearing that song. I sing along. I
drive away from you and back to somewhere else, someone else.

TWO IDEAS, REVISITED

I began this essay by proposing two ideas. First, that torch singing is a kind of
autoethnographic performance. To borrow a phrase about ethnography from
Joni Jones, torch singing is how the body does and undoes the experience of
unrequited love (1996, 132). Second, torch singing is, for me, an autoethno-

graphic performance. A "doing" and "undoing" of my own love in the act of research. I also said that these ideas were about subjectivity. Let's return to that.

Autoethnography and torch singing are storytelling activities (Van Maanen 1995, 3; Hamm 1979, 292). Autoethnography and torch singing both enact a life story within larger cultural and social contexts and histories (Reed-Danahay 1997, 9; Moore 1989, 43). Further, these stories are often deeply nostalgic; they are often lamentations (Clements 1998, 32; Ellis and Flaherty 1992, 35). Why do we tell such tales? To inscribe our own melancholy, mourning, and release, and to evoke these same emotions in our readers and our audiences. More than this, though, we seek to create a live, charged exchange with an audience (Dolan 1993, 151).

Within this exchange, performers and audiences inhabit and move outside the "subject" of the text. As an ethnographer, I am not the people I work with and write about, even when I am writing about myself. Nor is the actor the character she performs. Nor is the torch singer the woman she sings about. And the woman (or man) in the audience? She is not the woman in the song or the character on stage or the "subject" of the ethnography. Why? Because the stories of torch and autoethnography are incomplete. They are partial, fragmented performances of subjectivity (Abu-Lughod 1993, 9). And yet because these stories move from and in and through real bodies, their performance can move us in our bodies, hearts, and minds (Pobryn 1993, 71). That is why we can feel Billie Holiday's pain and defiance when she sings "My Man": "It cost me a lot, but there's one thing that I've got, it's my man, it's my man. . . " (quoted in White 1987, 117). And that is why, when we hear Fanny Brice or Barbra Streisand sing "My Man," we feel a different sort of pain and defiance. Torch singing and autoethnography allow us to "try on" the subjectivity of another—to gauge how the "glove" fits and doesn't fit and to show the "seams" of our acts to an audience (Anna Deavere Smith, quoted in Capo and Langellier 1994, 72). In performing "others," we discover how the body, heart, and mind does and undoes unrequited love or the experience of immigration or the dilemmas of doing fieldwork and writing ethnographic accounts (see, for example, Holiday 1992; Conquergood 1985; Jones 1996; Behar 1996).

The example of torch singing points up an interesting question about the force and effect of subjectivity in performances and in texts. Does torch performance afford performers and audiences access to the longing and consolation of another and nothing more? Does the torch singer enable an audience to confirm (and perhaps become complicit with) the experience of victimization or, worse, to dismiss the performance as unproductive for women's lives? (See, for example, Moore 1989; Paglia 1996.) These are also valid questions for the autoethnographer. And if I wish to answer "no" to both sets of questions, I must examine how the performance of torch songs and autoethographic texts moves audiences both within themselves and within the world.

Here is my answer. First, the torch song and the autoethnography are both acts of love (see Tedlock 1991, 69; Anna Deavere Smith quoted in Crawford 1996, 167). Their performance (in writing or on stage) is a conscious act of being in love with another and staying true to that love in our representations. The torch singer and the autoethnographer invite audiences into this love. As performers, we ask our listeners to live in our—and their own—desire for the other, even when this desire may seem destructive and painful and politically impotent.

However, being in love is not always (or only) easy or natural or cathartic. Being in love can also be startling and alienating and instructive. For the torch singer, this means infusing the lyrics with not only the pain and longing, but also the irony and wisdom of unrequited love. How does the torch singer perform both "sides" of being in love? In "Lover, Come Back to Me," Billie Holiday sings the rote, lyrical meaning of the song (lover, come back), adding a contrapuntal discourse just beneath and behind the beat—a discourse that says, "Lover, please stay away—I am immensely enjoying this state of freedom" (Davis 1998, 175). The torch singer encourages audiences to say, in Bertolt Brecht's terms, "Yes, I have felt like that too—Just like me—It's only natural—It'll never change," as well as, "I'd never have thought it—That's not the way—That's extraordinary, hardly believable—It's got to stop" (1964, 71).

How does Holiday inspire her audiences to engage this "doubled" meaning of her lyrics? She invites us to participate in the performance, to meet her halfway in creating a heightened emotional atmosphere and embarking on the passionate journey wrought in her material (Clements 1998, 32). She works on our inner thoughts and feelings as well as our presence in the world around us. She engages us as individuals and as social beings (Moore 1989, 45). Music scholar Will Friedwald notes, "Billie Holiday's art is the kind that takes you deeper inside yourself and ultimately out again" (1990, 126). Angela Davis adds, "in her phrasing, her timing, the timbre of her voice, the social roots of pain and despair in women's emotional lives are given a lyrical legibility"

(1998, 177). It is this inward, then outward, journey that makes torch performances profoundly moving in ways that are, at times, difficult to express. Autoethnographies also move from the inside of the author to outward expression while working to take readers inside themselves and ultimately out again (Denzin 1997, 208). Readers and audiences are invited to share in the emotional experience of an author. The test of such texts and performances comes down to whether they evoke in readers a "feeling that the experience described is authentic, that it is believable and possible" (Ellis 1995, 318–19). In telling their stories, autoethnographers ask readers to embark on a collaborative journey that tacks between individual experience and social roles, relationships, and structures (Jackson 1989, 18). As Michael Jackson notes, the stories of autoethnography begin "with the experience of one person, but others make it over to themselves and give it new uses and interpretations" (1989, 18).

This is what thinking about torch singing as autoethnography (and autoethnography as torch singing) teaches me: Create a highly charged atmosphere and heightened emotional state with and for my audience. Then use this energy to understand and critique my own relationships, as well as the place of these relationships in larger social structures and histories (Moore 1989, 45). Within the intimate, sensual contact among readers and texts, torch singing and autoethnography create a space of "critical vigilance" in which "communities of resistance are forged to sustain us"; a place where we come to know that "we are not alone" (adapted from hooks 1995, 220–21).[2] In these spaces and places, torch singing and autoethnography become memory and performance, passion and cause, unbearable and light, a torch song and a political protest. They become the way we were, the way we are, and the way we might be.

I type these last words and save the file. I have been and remain done and undone by my subjectivity and the ways my subjectivity touches and blurs with and hinges on the subjectivities of others. I leave my office and return to the living room. I watch the last scene of the film again. I see Katie spy Hubbell across a busy New York street. I watch Hubbell return to his fiancée and Katie return to her work. I hear Barbra sing. I let my husband see me cry.

NOTES

1. Joni Jones writes that performance ethnography "honors the embodied acts of interaction and dialogue. Indeed, performance ethnography is how the body does culture" (1996, 132).

2. hooks writes these words about African American performance artists. She views African American performance as a place where identities, subjugated knowledges, and historical memories must be reclaimed (1995, 220). These goals can also be said to motivate and sustain feminist performance practices, including torch singing and, in many cases, autoethnography.

REFERENCES

Abu-Lughod, Lila. 1993. *Writing Women's Worlds: Bedouin Stories.* Berkeley: University of California Press.

Behar, Ruth. 1996. *The Vulnerable Observer: Anthropology That Breaks Your Heart.* Boston: Beacon Press.

Brecht, Bertolt. 1964. *Brecht on Theater: The Development of an Aesthetic*, ed. and trans. John Willet, 1957. Reprint, New York: Hill and Wang.

Capo, Kay Ellen, and Kristin M. Langellier. 1994. "Anna Deavere Smith on 'Fires in the Mirror,'" *Text and Performance Quarterly* 14(1): 62–75.

Clements, Marcelle. 1998. "Sighing, a French Sound Endures." *New York Times* (October 18), AR1, 32–35.

Conquergood, Dwight. 1985. *Between Two Worlds: The Hmong Shaman in America* (documentary film). Chicago: Siegel Productions.

Crawford, Lyall. 1996. "Personal Ethnography." *Communication Monographs* 63: 158–70.

Davis, Angela Y. 1998. *Blues Legacies and Black Feminism: Gertrude "Ma" Rainey, Bessie Smith, and Billie Holiday.* New York: Pantheon.

Denzin, Norman K. 1997. *Interpretive Ethnography: Ethnographic Practices for the 21st Century.* Thousand Oaks, Calif.: Sage.

Dolan, Jill. 1993. *Presence and Desire: Essays on Gender, Sexuality, Performance.* Ann Arbor: University of Michigan Press.

Ellis, Carolyn. 1995. *Final Negotiations: A Story of Love, Loss and Chronic Illness.* Philadelphia: Temple University Press.

Ellis, Carolyn, and Michael G. Flaherty. 1992. "An Agenda for the Interpretation of Lived Experience." In *Investigating Subjectivity: Research on Lived Experience*, ed. Carolyn Ellis and Michael G. Flaherty (pp. 1–13). Newbury Park, Calif.: Sage.

Friedwald, Will. 1990. *Jazz Singing: America's Great Voices from Bessie Smith to Bebop and Beyond.* New York: Scribner's Sons.

Hamm, Charles. 1979. *Yesterdays: Popular Song in America.* New York: W. W. Norton.

Holiday, Billie. 1992. *Lady Sings the Blues,* written with William Dufty. 1956. Reprint, New York: Penguin.

hooks, bell. 1995. "Performance Practice As a Site of Opposition." In *Let's Get It On: The Politics of Black Performance,* ed. Catherine Ugwu (pp. 210–32). Seattle, Wash.: Bay Press.

Jackson, Michael. 1989. *Paths toward a Clearing: Radical Empiricism and Ethnographic Inquiry.* Bloomington: Indiana University Press.

Jones, Joni L. 1996. "The Self As Other: Creating the Role of Joni the Ethnographer for 'Broken Circles.'" *Text and Performance Quarterly* 16(2): 131–45.

Kundera, Milan. 1991. *Immortality,* trans. Peter Kusi. New York: Perennial Classics.

———. 1985. *The Unbearable Lightness of Being,* trans. Michael Henry Heim. New York: Harper & Row.

Moore, John. 1989. "'The Hieroglyphics of Love': The Torch Singers and Interpretation." *Popular Music* 8(1): 31–58.

Paglia, Camille. 1996. "The Way She Was." In *Diva: Barbra Streisand and the Making of a Superstar,* ed. Ethlie Ann Vare (pp. 221–26). New York: Boulevard Books.

Phelan, Peggy. 1993. *Unmarked: The Politics of Performance.* New York: Routledge.

Pobryn, Elspeth. 1993. "Moving Selves and Stationary Others: Ethnography's Ontological Dilemma." In *Sexing the Self: Gendered Positions in Cultural Studies,* ed. Elspeth Pobryn (pp. 58–81). New York: Routledge.

Reed-Danahay, Deborah E. 1997. "Introduction." In *Autoethnography: Rewriting the Self and the Social,* ed. Deborah E. Reed-Danahay (pp. 1–17). Oxford, U.K.: Berg.

Sayre, Henry M. 1989. *The Object of Performance: The American Avant-Garde since 1970.* Chicago: University of Chicago Press.

Stark, Ray, producer, and Sidney Pollack, director. 1973. *The Way We Were* (film). Burbank, Calif.: Raystar Productions.

Streisand, Barbra. 1974. "The Way We Were." On *The Way We Were* (recording). Burbank, Calif.: Columbia.

Tedlock, Barbara. 1991. "From Participant Observation to the Observation of Participation: The Emergence of Narrative Ethnography." *Journal of Anthropological Research* 47: 69–94.

Van Maanen, John. 1995. "An End to Innocence: The Ethnography of Ethnography." In *Representation in Ethnography*, ed. John Van Maanen (pp. 1–35). Thousand Oaks, Calif.: Sage.

White, John. 1987. *Billie Holiday*. New York: Universe.

The Revolution in Authority

The crisis or revolution of representation opened up the text to new voices, including women, persons of color, and subalterns. This crisis created the demand for different writing forms. In its challenges to the white, male voice, the crisis in representation undermined from within the very authority of the text itself. The revolution of authority centers on this erosion. It challenges the claim that just because "the ethnographer was there, you are there, too."

Clifford's seminal essay "Ethnographic Authority" traces the formation and breakup of the predominant form of modern fieldwork authority. This breakup challenges the authority and ability of the ethnographer to claim that the written text objectively establishes the presence of the other for the reader. In tracing this collapse Clifford shows that authority can only be established textually. The older, realist ethnographic texts presumed a single vantage point: white patriarchy. Indeed, Clough (1998, 17) asserts that an oedipal logic of realist narrativity underwrites classic ethnography's claim to authority. Today, many different forms of authority are available to the writer, including the experiential, the interpretive, the dialogical, and the polyphonic. No single form of authority is authoritative, nor does any single form represent so-called scientific discourse.

REFERENCE

Clough, Patricia Ticineto. 1998. *The End(s) of Ethnography.* New York: Peter Lang.

6

On Ethnographic Authority

James Clifford

The 1724 Frontispiece of Father Lafitau's *Moeurs des sauvages ameriquains* portrays the ethnographer as a young woman sitting at a writing table amidst artifacts from the New World and from classical Greece and Egypt. The author is accompanied by two cherubs who assist in the task of comparison and by the bearded figure of Time who points toward a tableau representing the ultimate source of the truths issuing from the writer's pen. The image toward which the young woman lifts her gaze is a bank of clouds where Adam, Eve, and the serpent appear. Above them stand the redeemed man and woman of the Apocalypse on either side of a radiant triangle bearing the Hebrew script for Yahweh.

The frontispiece for Malinowski's *Argonauts of the Western Pacific* is a photograph with the caption "A Ceremonial Act of the Kula." A shell necklace is being offered to a Trobriand chief who stands at the door of his dwelling. Behind the man presenting the necklace is a row of six bowing youths, one of them sounding a conch. All the figures stand in profile, their attention apparently concentrated on the rite of exchange, a real event of Melanesian life. But on closer inspection one of the bowing Trobrianders may be seen to be looking at the camera.

Lafitau's allegory is the less familiar: his author transcribes rather than originates. Unlike Malinowski's photo, the engraving makes no reference to ethnographic experience—despite Lafitau's five years of research among the Mohawks, research that has earned him a respected place among the field-workers of any generation. His account is presented not as the product of first-hand observation but of writing, in a crowded workshop. The fron-tispiece from *Argonauts*, like all photographs, asserts presence, that of the scene before the lens. But it suggests also another presence—the ethnographer actively composing his fragment of Trobriand reality. Kula exchange, the sub-ject of Malinowski's book, has been made perfectly visible, centered in the perceptual frame. And a participant's glance redirects our attention to the ob-servational standpoint we share, as readers, with the ethnographer and his camera. The predominant mode of modern fieldwork authority is signaled; "You are there, because I was there."

The present essay traces the formation and breakup of this authority in twentieth-century social anthropology. It is not a complete account, nor is it based on a fully realized theory of ethnographic interpretation and textuality.[1] Such a theory's contours are problematic, since the activity of cross cultural representation is now more than usually in question. The present predicament is linked to the breakup and redistribution of colonial power in the decades af-ter 1950 and to the echoes of that process in the radical cultural theories of the 1960s and 1970s. After the Negritude movement's reversal of the European gaze, after anthropology's *crise de conscience* with respect to its liberal status within the imperial order, and now that the West can no longer present itself as the unique purveyor of anthropological knowledge about others, it has be-come necessary to imagine a world of generalized ethnography. With ex-panded communication and intercultural influence, people interpret others, and themselves, in a bewildering diversity of idioms—a global condition of what Bakhtin called "heteroglossia."[2] This ambiguous, multi-vocal world makes it increasingly hard to conceive of human diversity as inscribed in bounded, independent cultures. Difference is an effect of inventive syncretism. In recent years works like Edward Said's *Orientalism* and Paulin Hountondji's *Sur la "philosophie africaine"* have cast radical doubt on the procedures by which alien human groups can be represented, without proposing systematic, sharply new methods or epistemologies. These studies suggest that while ethnographic writing cannot entirely escape the reductionist use of dichotomies and essences, it can at least struggle self-consciously to avoid portraying abstract, a-historical "others."[3] It is more than ever crucial for different peoples to form complex concrete images of one another, as well as of the relationships of knowledge and power that connect them. But no sovereign scientific method or ethical stance can guarantee the truth of such images. They are constituted—the critique of colonial modes of representation has shown at least this much—in specific historical relations of dominance and dialogue.

The experiments in ethnographic writing surveyed below do not fall into a clear reformist direction or evolution. They are ad hoc inventions and cannot be seen in terms of a systematic analysis of post-colonial representation. They are perhaps best understood as components of that "toolkit" of engaged theory recently recommended by Deleuze and Foucault.

> The notion of theory as a toolkit means (i) The theory to be constructed is not a system but an instrument, a *logic* of the specificity of power relations and the struggles around them; (ii) That this investigation can only be carried out step by step on the basis of reflection (which will necessarily be historical in some of its aspects) on given situations.[4]

We may contribute to a practical reflection on cross cultural representation by undertaking an inventory of the better, though imperfect, approaches currently at hand. Of these, ethnographic fieldwork remains an unusually sensitive method. Participant observation obliges its practitioners to experience, at a bodily as well as intellectual level, the vicissitudes of translation. It requires arduous language learning, some degree of direct involvement and conversation, and often a derangement of personal and cultural expectations. There is, of course, a myth of fieldwork, and the actual experience, hedged around with contingencies, rarely lives up to the ideal. But as a means for producing knowledge from an intense, intersubjective engagement, the practice of ethnography retains a certain exemplary status. Moreover, if fieldwork has for a time been identified with a uniquely Western discipline and a totalizing science of "anthropology," these associations are not necessarily permanent. Current styles of cultural description are historically limited and undergoing important metamorphoses.

The development of ethnographic science cannot ultimately be understood in isolation from more general political-epistemological debates about writing and the representations of otherness. However, in the present discussion I have maintained a focus on professional anthropology and specifically on developments within interpretive ethnography since 1950.[5] The current crisis—or better, dispersion—of ethnographic authority makes it possible to mark off a rough period, bounded by the years 1900 and 1960, during which a new conception of field research established itself as the norm for European and American anthropology. Intensive fieldwork pursued by university trained specialists, emerged as a privileged, sanctioned source of data about exotic peoples. It is not a question, here, of the dominance of a single research method. "Intensive" ethnography was variously defined.[6] Moreover, the hegemony of fieldwork was established earlier and more thoroughly in America and England that it was in France. The early examples of Boas and the Torres Straits Expedition were matched only belatedly by the funding of the Institut d'Ethnologie in 1925 and the much-publicized Mission Dakar-Djibouti of 1932.[7] Nevertheless, by the mid-1930s one can fairly speak of a developing international consensus: valid anthropological abstractions were to be based, wherever possible, on intensive cultural descriptions by qualified scholars. By the mid-1930s the new style had been made popular, institutionalized, and embodied in specific textual practices.

It has recently become possible to identify and take a certain distance from these conventions.[8] If ethnography produces cultural interpretations through intense research experiences, how is unruly experience transformed into an authoritative written account? How, precisely, is a garrulous, overdetermined, cross cultural encounter shot through with power relations and personal cross purposes circumscribed as an adequate version of a more-or-less discrete "other world," composed by an individual author?

In analyzing this complex transformation one must bear in mind the fact that ethnography is from beginning to end enmeshed in writing. This writing includes, minimally, a translation of experience into textual form. The process is complicated by the action of multiple subjectivities and political constraints beyond the control of the writer. In response to these forces ethnographic writing enacts a specific strategy of authority. This has classically involved an unquestioned claim to appear as the purveyor of truth in the text. A complex cultural experience is enunciated by an individual: *We the Tikopia*, by Raymond Firth; *Nous avons mangé la forêt*, by Georges Condominas; *Coming of Age in Samoa*, by Margaret Mead; *The Nuer*, by Evans-Pritchard.

The discussion that follows first locates this authority historically—in the development of a twentieth-century science of participant-observation. It then proceeds to a critique of underlying assumptions and a review of emerging textual practices.

[...]

In the 1920s, the new fieldworker-theorist brought to completion a powerful new scientific and literary genre, the ethnography, a synthetic cultural description based on participant-observations.[9] The new style of representation depended on institutional and methodological innovations circumventing the obstacles to rapid knowledge of other cultures that had preoccupied the best representatives of Codrington's generation. These may be briefly summarized.

First, the persona of the fieldworker was validated, both publicly and professionally. In the popular domain, visible figures like Malinowski, Mead, and Griaule communicated a vision of ethnography as both scientifically demanding and heroic. The professional ethnographer was trained in the latest analytic techniques and modes of scientific explanation. This conferred an advantage over amateurs in the field: the professional could claim to get to the heart of a culture more quickly, grasping its essential institutions and structures. A prescribed attitude of cultural relativism distinguished the fieldworker from missionaries, administrators, and others whose view of natives was, presumably, less dispassionate, who were preoccupied with the problems of government, or conversion. In addition to scientific sophistication and relativist sympathy, a variety of normative standards for the new form of research emerged: the fieldworker was to live in the native village, use the vernacular, stay a sufficient (but seldom specified) length of time, investigate certain classic subjects, and so on.

Second, it was tacitly agreed that the new-style ethnographer, whose sojourn in the field seldom exceeded two years, and more frequently was much less, could efficiently "use" native languages without "mastering" them. In a significant article of 1939 Margaret Mead argued that the ethnographer following the Malinowskian prescription to avoid interpreters and to conduct research in the vernacular did not, in fact, need to attain "virtuosity" in native tongues, but could "use" the vernacular to ask questions, maintain rapport, and generally get along in the culture while obtaining good research results in particular areas of concentration.[10] This, in effect, justified her own practice, which featured relatively short stays and a focus on specific domains, like childhood, or "personality." These foci would function as "types" for a cultural synthesis. But her attitude toward language "use" was broadly characteristic of an ethnographic generation that could, for example, credit an authoritative study called *The Nuer*, that was based on the only eleven months of difficult research. Mead's article provoked a sharp response from Robert Lowie, writing from the older Boasian tradition, more philological in its orientation.[11] But his was a rearguard action; the point had been generally established that valid research could, in practice, be accomplished on the basis of a one or two-year familiarity with a foreign vernacular (even though, as Lowie suggested, no one would credit a translation of Proust that was based on an equivalent knowledge of French).

Third, the new ethnography was marked by an increased emphasis on the power of observation. Culture was construed as an ensemble of characteristic behaviors, ceremonies and gestures, susceptible to recording and explanation by a trained onlooker. Mead pressed this point furthest (indeed, her own powers of visual analysis were extraordinary). As a general trend the participant-*observer* emerged as a research norm. Of course, successful fieldwork mobilized the fullest possible range of interactions, but a distinct primacy was accorded to the visual: interpretation was tied to description. After Malinowski, a general suspicion of "privileged informants" reflected this systematic preference for the (methodical) observations of the ethnographer over the (interested) interpretations of indigenous authorities.

Fourth, certain powerful theoretical abstractions promised to help academic ethnographers "get to the heart" of a culture more rapidly than someone undertaking, for example, a thorough inventory of customs and beliefs. Without spending years getting to know natives, their complex languages and habits, in intimate detail, the researcher could go after selected data that would yield a central armature of structure of the cultural whole. Rivers' "genealogical method," followed by Radcliffe-Brown's model of "social structure," provided this sort of shortcut. One could, it seemed, elicit kin terms without a deep understanding of local vernacular, and the range of necessary contextual knowledge was conveniently limited.

Fifth, since culture, seen as a complex whole, was always too much to master in a short research span, the new ethnographer tended to focus thematically or particular institutions. The aim was not to contribute to a complete inventory or description of custom, but rather to get at the whole through one or more of its parts. We have noted the privilege given, for a time, to social structure. An individual life-cycle, a ritual complex like the Kula ring or the

Naven ceremony could also serve, as could categories of behavior like "economics," "politics," and the like. In the predominantly synecdochic rhetorical stance of the new ethnography, parts were assumed to be microcosms or analogies of wholes. This setting of institutional foregrounds against cultural backgrounds in the portrayal of a coherent world lent itself to realist literary conventions.

Sixth, the wholes thus represented tended to be synchronic, products of short-term research activity. The intensive fieldworker could plausibly sketch the contours of an "ethnographic present"—the cycle of a year, a ritual series, patterns of typical behavior. To introduce long-term historical inquiry would have impossibly complicated the task of the new-style fieldwork. Thus, when Malinowski and Radcliffe-Brown established their critique of the "conjectural history" of the diffusionists it was all to easy to exclude diachronic processes as objects of fieldwork, with consequences that have by now been sufficiently denounced.

These innovations served to validate an efficient ethnography based on scientific participant-observation. Their combined effect may be seen in what may well be the *tour de force* of the new ethnography, Evans-Pritchard's *The Nuer*, published in 1940. Based on eleven months of research conducted—as the book's remarkable introduction tells us—in almost impossible conditions, Evans-Pritchard nonetheless was able to compose a classic. He arrived in Nuerland on the heels of a punitive military expedition and at the urgent request of the government of the Anglo-Egyptian Sudan. He was the object of constant and intense suspicion. Only in the final few months could he converse at all effectively with informants who, he tells us, were skilled at evading his questions. In the circumstances his monograph is a kind of miracle.

While advancing limited claims and making no secret of the restraints on his research, Evans-Pritchard manages to present his study as a demonstration of the effectiveness of theory. He focuses on Nuer political and social "structure," analyzed as an abstract set of relations between territorial segments, lineages, age-sets, and other more fluid groups. This analytically derived ensemble is portrayed against an "ecological" backdrop composed of migratory patterns, relationships with cattle, notions of time and space. Evans-Pritchard sharply distinguishes his method from what he calls "haphazard" (Malinowskian) documentation. *The Nuer* is not an extensive compendium of observations and vernacular texts in the style of Malinowski's *Argonauts* and

Coral Gardens. Evans-Pritchard argues rigorously that "facts can only be selected and arranged in the light of theory." The frank abstraction of a political-
social structure offers the necessary framework. If I am accused of describing
facts as exemplifications of my theory, he then goes on to note, I have been understood.[12]

[. . .]

"Participant-observation" serves as shorthand for a continuous tacking between the "inside" and "outside" of events: on the one hand grasping the sense
of specific occurrences and gestures empathetically, on the other stepping
back to situate these meanings in wider contexts. Particular events thus acquire deeper or more general significance, structural rules, and so forth. Understood literally, participant-observation is a paradoxical, misleading
formula. But it may be taken seriously if reformulated in hermeneutic terms
as a dialectic of experience and interpretation. This is how the method's most
persuasive recent defenders have restated it, in the tradition that leads from
Dilthey, via Weber, to "symbols and meanings anthropologists" like Geertz.
Experience and interpretation have, however, been accorded different em-
phases when presented as claims to authority. In recent years, there has been
a marked shift of emphasis from the former to the latter. This section and the
one that follows will explore the rather different claims of experience and interpretation as well as their evolving interrelation.

The growing prestige of the fieldworker-theorist downplayed (without eliminating) a number of processes and mediators that had figured more promi-
nently in previous methods. We have seen how language mastery was defined as
a level of use adequate for amassing a discrete body of data in a limited period
of time. The tasks of textual transcription and translation along with the crucial
dialogical role of interpreters and "privileged informants" were relegated to a
secondary, sometimes even despised, status. Fieldwork was now centered on the
experience of the participant-observing scholar. A sharp image, or narrative,
made its appearance—that of an outsider entering a culture, undergoing a kind
of initiation leading to "rapport" (minimally, acceptance and empathy, but usually implying something akin to friendship). Out of this experience emerged, in
unspecified ways, a representational text authored by the participant-observer.
As we shall see, this version of textural production obscures as much as it reveals. But it is worth taking seriously its principal assumption, that the experience of the researcher can serve as a unifying source of authority in the field.

Experiential authority is based on a "feel" for the foreign context, a kind of accumulated savvy and sense of the style of a people or place. Such an appeal is frequently explicit in the texts of the early professional participant-observers. Margaret Mead's claim to grasp the underlying principle or ethos of a culture through a heightened sensitivity to form, tone, gesture, and behavioral styles, or Malinowski's stress on his life in the village and the comprehension derived from the "imponderable" of daily existence, are prominent cases in point. Many ethnographies, Colin Turnbull's *The Forest People* for example, are still cast in the experiential mode, asserting, prior to any specific research hypothesis or method, the "I was there" of the ethnographer as insider and participant.

Of course, it is difficult to say very much about experience. Like "intuition" one has it or not, and its invocation often smacks of mystification. Nevertheless one should resist the temptation to translate all meaningful experience into interpretation. If the two are reciprocally related, they are not identical. It makes sense here to hold them apart, if only because appeals to experience often act as validations for ethnographic authority. The most serious argument for the role of experience in the historical and cultural sciences is contained in the general notion of *Verstehen*.[13] In Dilthey's influential view, understanding others arises initially from the sheer fact of coexistence in a shared world. But this experiential world, an intersubjective ground for objective forms of knowledge, is precisely what is missing or problematic for an ethnographer entering an alien culture. Thus during the early months in the field (and indeed throughout the research) what is going on its language-learning in the broadest sense. Dilthey's "common sphere" must be established and re-established, building up a shared experiential world in relation to which all "facts," "texts," "events," and their interpretations will be constructed. This process of living one's way into an alien expressive universe is, in his scheme, always subjective in nature. But it quickly becomes dependent on what he calls "permanently fixed expressions," stable forms to which understanding can return. The exegesis of these fixed forms provides the content of all systematic historical-cultural knowledge. Thus experience, for Dilthey, is closely linked to interpretation (and he is among the first modern theorists to compare the understanding of cultural forms to the reading of "texts"). But this sort of reading or exegesis cannot occur without an intense, personal participation, an active at-homeness in a common universe.[14]

Following Dilthey, ethnographic "experience" can be seen as the building-up of a common, meaningful world, drawing on intuitive styles of feeling, perception, and a common, meaningful world, drawing on intuitive styles of feeling, perception, and guesswork. This activity makes use of clues, traces, gestures, and scraps of sense prior to the development of developed, stable interpretations. Such piecemeal forms of experience may be classified as esthetic and/or divinatory. There is space here for only a few words about such styles of comprehension as they related to ethnography. An evocation of an esthetic mode is conveniently provided by A. L. Kroeber's 1931 review of Mead's *Growing up in New Guinea.*

> First of all, it is clear that she possesses to an outstanding degree the faculties of swiftly apperceiving the principal currents of a culture as they impinge on individuals, and of delineating these with compact pen-pictures of astonishing sharpness. The result is a representation of quite extraordinary vividness and semblance to life. Obviously, a gift of intellectualized but strong sensationalism underlies this capacity; also, obviously, a high order of intuitiveness, in the sense of the ability to complete a convincing picture from clues, for clues is all that some of her data can be, with only six months to learn a language and enter the inwards of a whole culture, besides specializing on child behavior. At any rate, the picture, so far as it goes, is wholly convincing to the reviewer, who unreservedly admires the sureness of insight and efficiency of stroke of the depiction.[15]

[. . .]

Precisely because it is hard to pin down, "experience" has served as an effective guarantee of ethnographic authority. There is, of course, a telling ambiguity in the term. Experience evokes a participatory presence, a sensitive contact with the world to be understood, a rapport with its people, a concreteness of perception. And experience suggests also a cumulative, deepening knowledge ("her ten years' experience of new Guinea"). The senses work together to authorize an ethnographer's real, but ineffable, feel or flair for his or her people. But it is worth noticing that this "world," when conceived as an experiential creation, is subjective, not dialogical or intersubjective. The ethnographer *accumulates* personal knowledge of the field. (The possessive form, "my people," has until recently been familiarly used in anthropological circles; but the phrase in effect signifies "my experience.")

It is understandable, given their vagueness, that experiential criteria of authority—unexamined beliefs in the "method" of participant-observation, in the power of rapport, empathy, and so on—have come under criticism by hermeneutically sophisticated anthropologists. In recent years the second moment in the dialectic of experience and interpretation has received increasing attention and elaboration.[16] Interpretation, based on a philological model of textual "reading," has emerged as a sophisticated alternative to the now apparently naïve claims for experiential authority. Interpretive anthropology demystifies much of what had previously passed unexamined in the construction of ethnographic narratives, types, observations, and descriptions. It contributes to an increasing visibility of the creative (and in a broad sense, poetic) processes by which "cultural" objects are invented and treated as meaningful.

What is involved in looking at culture as an assemblage of texts to be interpreted? A classic account has been provided by Paul Ricoeur, notably in his 1971 essay, "The Model of the Text: Meaningful Action Considered as a Text."[17] Clifford Geertz, in a number of stimulating and subtle discussions has adapted Ricoeur's theory to anthropological fieldwork.[18] "Textualization" is understood as a prerequisite to interpretation, the constitution of Dilthey's "fixed expressions." It is the process through which unwritten behavior, speech, beliefs, oral tradition or ritual, come to be marked as a corpus, a potentially meaningful ensemble separated out from an immediate discursive or performative situation. In the moment of textualization this meaningful corpus assumes a more or less stable relation to a context, and we are familiar with the end result of this process in much of what counts as ethnographic thick description. For example, we say that a certain institution or segment of behavior is typical of, or a communicative element within, a surrounding culture. (Geertz's famous cockfight becomes an intensely significant locus of Balinese culture.) Fields of synecdoches are created in which parts are related to wholes—and by which the whole, what we often call culture, is constituted.

[. . .]

Interpretive anthropology, by viewing cultures as assemblages of texts, loosely and sometimes contradictorily united, and by highlighting the inventive poesis at work in all collective representations, has contributed significantly to the defamiliarization of ethnographic authority. But in its mainstream realist strands it does not escape the general strictures of those critics of "colonial" representation who, since 1950, have rejected discourses that portray the cultural realities of other peoples without placing their own reality in jeopardy. In Leiris's early critiques, by way of Maquet, Asad and many others, the unreciprocal quality of ethnographic interpretation has been called to account.[19] Henceforth, neither the experience nor the interpretive activity of the scientific researcher can be considered innocent. It becomes necessary to conceive ethnography, not as the experience and interpretation of a circumscribed "other" reality, but rather as a constructive negotiation involving at least two, and usually more, conscious, politically significant subjects. Paradigms of experience and interpretation are yielding to paradigms of discourse, of dialogue and polyphony. The remaining sections of my essay will survey these emergent modes of authority.

[. . .]

To say that an ethnography is composed of discourses and that its different components are dialogically related, is not to say that its textual form should be that of a literal dialogue. Indeed, as Crapanzano recognizes in *Tuhami*, a third participant, real or imagined, must function as mediator in any encounter between two individuals.[20] The fictional dialogue is, in fact, a condensation, a simplified representation of complex, multi-vocal processes. An alternative way of representing this discursive complexity is to understand the overall course of the research as an ongoing negotiation. The case of Marcel Griaule and the Dogon is well known and particularly clear-cut. Griaule's account of his instruction in Dogon cosmological wisdom, *Dieu d'Eau* (*Conversations with Ogotemmêli*), was an early exercise in dialogical ethnographic narration. But beyond this specific interlocutory occasion, a more complex process was at work. For it is apparent that the content and timing of the Griaule team's long-term research, spanning decades, was closely monitored and significantly shaped by Dogon tribal authorities.[21] This is no longer news. Many ethnographers have commented on the ways, both subtle and blatant, in which their research was directed or circumscribed by their informants. In his provocative discussion of this issue, Ioan Lewis even calls anthropology a form of "plagiarism."[22]

[. . .]

It is intrinsic to the breakup of monological authority that ethnographies no longer address a single general type of reader. The multiplication of possible readings reflects the fact that self-conscious "ethnographic" consciousness can no longer be seen as the monopoly of certain Western cultures and social classes. Even in ethnographies lacking vernacular texts, indigenous readers will decode differently the textualized interpretations and lore. Polyphonic works are particularly open to readings not specifically intended. Trobriand readers may find Malinowski's interpretations tiresome but his examples and extensive transcriptions still evocative. And Ndembu will not gloss as quickly as European readers over the different voices embedded in Turner's works.

Recent literary theory suggests that the ability of a text to make sense in a coherent way depends less on the willed intentions of an originating author than on the creative activity of a reader. In Barthes' words, if a text is "a tissue of quotations drawn from innumerable centers of culture," then "a text's unity lies not in its origin but in its destination."[23] The writing of ethnography, an unruly, multisubjective activity, is given coherence in particular acts of reading. But there is always a variety of possible readings (beyond merely individual appropriations), readings beyond the control of any single authority. One may approach a classic ethnography seeking simply to grasp the meanings that the researcher derives from represented cultural facts. But, as we have suggested, one may also read against the grain of the text's dominant voice, seeking out other, half-hidden authorities, reinterpreting the descriptions, texts and quotations gathered together by the writer. With the recent questioning of colonial styles of representation, with the expansion of literacy and ethnographic consciousness, new possibilities for reading (and thus for writing) cultural descriptions are emerging.[24]

The textual embodiment of authority is a recurring problem for recent experiments in ethnography.[25] An older, realist mode—figured in the frontispiece to *Argonauts of the Western Pacific* and based on the construction of a cultural *tableau vivant* designed to be seen from a single vantage point, that of the writer and reader—can now be identified as only one possible paradigm for authority. Political and epistemological assumptions are built into this and other styles, assumptions the ethnographic writer can no longer afford to ignore. The modes of authority reviewed in this essay—experiential, interpretive, dialogical, polyphonic—are available to all writers of ethnographic texts, Western and non-Western. None is obsolete, none pure: there is room for invention within each paradigm. For example, interpretation—as conceived by Gadamer—can aspire to a radical dialogism. We have seen, too, how new approaches tend to rediscover discarded practices. Polyphonic authority looks with renewed sympathy to compendia of vernacular texts—expository forms distinct from the focused monograph tied to participant-observation. And now that naïve claims to the authority of experience have been subjected to hermeneutic suspicion, we may anticipate a renewed attention to the subtle interplay of personal and disciplinary components in ethnographic research.

Experiential, interpretive, dialogical, and polyphonic processes are at work, discordantly, in any ethnography. But coherent presentation presupposes a controlling mode of authority. I have argued that this imposition of coherence on an unruly textual process is now, inescapably, a matter of strategic choice. I have tried to distinguish important styles of authority as they have become visible in recent decades. If ethnographic writing is alive, as I believe it is, it is struggling within and against these possibilities.

NOTES

An early version of this essay was presented at the American Anthropological Association in December of 1980. For helpful criticisms I would like to thank Talal Asad, Vincent Crapanzano, Joel Fineman, Thomas Laquer, Joan Larcom, George Marcus, T. N. Pandey, Mary Pratt, Richard Randolph, Renato Rosaldo, George Stocking, Sharon Traweek, Steven Webster.

1. Only English, American, and French examples are discussed. If it is likely that the modes of authority analyzed here are able widely to be generalized, no attempt has been made to extend them to other national traditions. It is assumed, also, in the antipositivist tradition of Dilthey, that ethnography is a process of interpretation, not of explanation. Modes of authority based on natural-scientific epistemologies are not discussed. In its focus on participant-observation as an intersubjective process at the heart of twentieth-century ethnography, the essay scants a number of contributing sources of authority: for example, the weight of accumulated "archival" knowledge about particular groups, of a cross cultural comparative perspective, and of statistical survey work.

2. See M. Bakhtin, "Discourse in the Novel" (1935), in Michael Holquist, ed., *The Dialogic Imagination: Four Essays by M. M. Bakhtin* (Austin: University of Texas Press, 1981), pp. 259–442. "Heteroglossia" assumes that "languages do not *exclude* each other, but rather intersect with each other in many different ways (the Ukranian language, the language of the epic poem, of early Symbolism, of the student, of a particular generation of children, of the run-of-the-mill intellectual, of the Nietzschean and so on). It might even seem that the very word "language" loses

all meaning in this process-for apparently there is no single plane on which all these 'languages' might be juxtaposed to one another." What is said of languages applies equally to "cultures" and "subcultures." See also V. N. Vološinov (Bakhtin?), *Marxism and the Philosophy of Language* (New York: Seminar Press, 1973), esp. Chaps. 1–3; and Tzvetan Todorov, *Mikhail Bakhtine: le principe dialogique* (Paris: Seuil, 1981), pp. 88–93.

3. Edward Said, *Orientalism* (New York: Pantheon, 1978); Paulin Hountondji, *Sur la "philosophie africaine"* (Yaounde, Cameroon: 1980); for more on this ambiguous predicament, J. Clifford, review of Said, *History and Theory*, 19:2 (1980), 204–23.

4. Michel Foucault, *Power/Knowledge* (New York: Pantheon, 1980), p. 145; see also "Intellectuals and Power: A Conversation between Michel Foucault and Gilles Deleuze," in Foucault, *Language, Counter-Memory, Practice* (Ithaca, N.Y.: Cornell University Press, 1977), pp. 208–209. A recent unpublished essay by Edward Said, "The Text's Slow Politics and the Prompt Language of Criticism," has sharpened my conception of a historically contingent, engaged theory.

5. I have not attempted to survey new styles of ethnographic writing that may be originating from outside the West. As Said, Hountondji, and others have shown, a considerable work of ideological "clearing," an oppositional, critical work remains, and it is to this that non-Western intellectuals have been devoting a great part of their energies. My essay remains inside, but at the experimental boundaries of, a realist cultural science elaborated in the Occident. It does not consider, as areas of innovation, the "para-ethnographic" genres of oral history, the non-fiction novel, the "new journalism," travel literature, and the documentary film.

6. Compare, for example, Marcel Griaule's idea of team research (with repeated visits to the field) and Malinowski's extended solo sojourn: Griaule, *Méthode de l'ethnographie* (Paris: Presses Universitaires de France, 1957); Malinowski, *Argonauts of the Western Pacific* (London: 1922), chapter 1.

7. Victor Karady, "Le problème de la légitimité dans l'organisation historique de l'ethnologie française." *Review française de sociologie* 23:1 (1982), 17–36; George Stocking, "The Ethnographer's Magic: the Development of Fieldwork in British Anthropology from Tylor to Malinowski." *History of Anthroplogy* 1 (1983), forthcoming.

8. In the present crisis of authority, ethnography has emerged as a subject of historical scrutiny. For new critical approaches see: François Hartog, *Le miroir d'Hérodote: essai sur la représentation de l'autre* (Paris: 1980); K. O. L. Burridge, *Encountering Aborigines* (New York: Pergamon Press, 1973), chapter 1; Michéle

Duchet, *Anthropologie et Histoire au siècle des lumières* (Paris: Flammarion, 1971); James Boon, "Comparative De-enlightenment: Paradox and Limits in the History of Ethnology," *Daedalus*, spring 1980, 73–90; Michel de Certeau, "Writing vs. Time: History and Anthropology in the Works of Lafitau," *Yale French Studies*, 59 (1980), 37–64; Edward Said, *Orientalism*; George Stocking, ed., "Observers Observed: Essays on Ethnographic Fieldwork." *History of Anthropology* 1 (1983), Madison, Wis.: forthcoming.

9. I am indebted to two important unpublished papers by Robert Thornton of the University of Capetown: "The Rise of Ethnography in South Africa: 1860–1920."and "The Rise of the Ethnographic Monograph in Eastern and Southern Africa."

10. Margaret Mead, "Native Languages as Field-Work Tools," *American Anthropologist*, 41:2 (1939), 189–205.

11. Robert Lowie, "Native Languages as Ethnographic Tools," *American Anthropologist*, 421: 1 (1940), 81–89.

12. E. Evans-Pritchard, *The Nuer* (New York, Oxford: 1969), p. 261.

13. The concept is sometimes too readily associated with intuition or empathy, but as a description of ethnographic knowledge, *Verstehen* properly involves a critique of empathetic experience. The exact meaning of the term is a matter of debate among Dilthey scholars. See Rudolf Makkreel, *Dilthey: Philosopher of the Human Sciences* (Princeton, N.J.: Princeton University Press, 1975), pp. 6–7, and *passim*.

14. This bare summary is drawn from H. P. Rickman, ed., *W. Dilthey: Selected Writings* (Cambridge, U.K.: Cambridge University Press, 1976), pp. 168–245. "The Construction of the Historical World in the Human Studies," Vol. VII of the *Gesammelte Schriften* (Leipzig: 1914).

15. *American Anthropologist*, 33 (1931), p. 248.

16. For example: Clifford Geertz, *The Interpretation of Cultures* (New York: Basic Books, 1973): "From the Native's Point of View: on the Nature of Anthropological Understanding," in K. Basso and H. Selby, eds., *Meaning in Anthropology* (Albuquerque: University of New Mexico Press, 1976), pp. 221–38; Paul Rabinow and William Sullivan, eds., *Interpretive Social Science* (Berkeley: University of California Press, 1979); Irene and Thomas Winner, "The Semiotics of Cultural Texts," *Semiotica*, 18:2 (1976), 101–56; Dan Sperber, "L'Interprétation en Anthropologie," *L'Homme*, XXI:I (1981), 69–92.

17. *Social Research*, 38 (1971), 529–562.

18. See especially, "Thick Description: Toward an Interpretive Theory of Culture," chapter 1 of *The Interpretation of Cultures.*

19. Michel Leiris, "L'ethnographe devant le colonialisme," *Les Temps Modernes,* 58 (1950); reprinted in Leiris, *Brisées* (Paris: Mercure de France, 1966), pp. 125–45; Jacques Maquet, "Objectivity in Anthropology," *Current Anthropology* 5 (1964), 47–55; Talal Asad, ed., *Anthropology and the Colonial Encounter* (London: Ithaca Press, 1973).

20. Crapanzano, *Tuhami,* pp. 147–51.

21. James Clifford, "Power and Dialogue in Ethnography: Marcel Griaule's Initiation," *History of Anthropology* 1, forthcoming.

22. I. Lewis, *The Anthropologist's Muse* (London: London School of Economics, 1973).

23. R. Barthes, *Image, Music, Text* (New York: Hill and Wang, 1977), pp. 145, 148.

24. An extremely suggestive model of polyphonic exposition is offered by the projected four-volume edition of the ethnographic texts written, provoked, and transcribed between 1896 and 1914 by James Walker, on the Pine Ridge Sioux Reservation. Two titles have appeared so far: James Walker, *Lakota Belief and Ritual,* Raymond DeMallie and Elaine Jahner, eds., and *Lakota Society,* Raymond DeMallie, ed. (Lincoln: University of Nebraska Press, 1980). These engrossing volumes in effect re-open the textual homogeneity of Walker's classic monograph of 1917, *The Sun Dance,* a summary of the individual statements here published in translation. These statements, by more than thirty named "authorities," complement and transcend Walker's synthesis. A long section of *Lakota Belief and Ritual* was written by Thomas Tyon, Walker's interpreter. And the collection's fourth volume will be a translation of the writings of George Sword, an Oglala warrior and judge encouraged by Walker to record and interpret the traditional way of life. The first two volumes present the unpublished texts of knowledgeable Lakota and Walker's own descriptions in identical formats. Ethnography appears as a process of collective production. It is essential to note that the Colorado Historical Society's decision to publish these texts was provoked by increasing requests from the Oglala Community at Pine Ridge for copies of Walker's materials to use in Oglala history classes.

25. For a very useful and complete survey of recent experimental ethnographies see George Marcus and Dick Cushman, "Ethnographies as Texts," *Annual Review of Anthropology,* 11 (1982), pp. 25–69; Steven Webster, "Dialogue and Fiction in Ethnography," *Dialectical Anthropology* 7:2 (1982); and Hussein Fahim, ed., *Indigenous Anthropology in Non-Western Countries* (Durham, N.C.: Carolina Academic Press, 1982).

III

The Revolution
of Legitimation

The crisis and revolution in legitimation challenges traditional, postpositivist arguments concerning the text, its validity, and its claims to scientific authority. The legitimation crisis reevaluates the qualitative research process and the criteria used to evaluate a text. A call for validity represents a text's call to power and persuasion. This plea refers to a set of rules that reference a reality outside the text, rules concerning knowledge, its production, and representation. Without validity, is it argued, there is no truth; without truth, there can be no trust in a text's claims to legitimacy (or authority).

There are three basic positions on the issues of validity and the other criteria that are used to evaluate a text: foundational, quasi-foundational, and nonfoundational. Foundationalists apply the same positivistic criteria to qualitative research as are employed in quantitative inquiry, contending that is there is nothing special about qualitative research that demands a special set of evaluative criteria. Quasi-foundationalists contend that a set of criteria unique to qualitative research must be developed (see Smith and Deemer 2000). Nonfoundationalists reject in advance all epistemological criteria. (Nonfoundationalists are sometimes called antifoundationalists.) Nonfoundationalists argue that evaluative criteria are moral and political and reflect the standpoint of the theorist and some interpretive community.

Three positions on the legitimacy of the interpretive text are staked out in this part. Geertz, in an essay that achieved near canonical status in the 1980s, argued that the social sciences need thick descriptions of human interaction. Geertz's ethnographer inscribes social discourse, writing it down, turning it from a passing event into an account that exists in its inscriptions (Geertz 1973, 19). Geertz's thick description has five characteristics. It is interpretive of the flow of social discourse. This interpreting consists of trying to rescue the "said" of such discourse from the "saying." Such description is close-up, microscopic. As an interpretive practice, thick description creates the world it describes. These descriptions make culture public and readable, turning it into a text.

Cultural interpretation, based on thick description, stays close to the ground, close to experience. The task of theory, for Geertz, is not to codify either abstractions or generalizations. Rather, the task is to generalize within cases, within the particular. Cultural theory is not predictive. Theory directs us to recover the "said" while helping us construct an interpretation that makes these "saids" meaningful (Geertz 1973, 27).

Conquergood (1998) contests the textual turn in Geertz, the move that turns culture into a text. This move, he argues, makes it difficult to rethink or recapture culture as a performance, as a set of performance practices. He asserts that the culture-as-text model displays a Eurocentric, print-based bias that potentially silences the subaltern (30). Conquergood is clear on the thrust of the performance paradigm: "Instead of endeavoring to rescue the *said* from the *saying*, a performance paradigm struggles to recuperate the *saying* from the *said*, to put mobility, action, and agency back into play" (31).

This rift, or rupture, between the textual and performance paradigms is still unresolved.

Avoiding the textual-performance dispute, Seale returns the conversation to the foundational and quasi-foundational framework discussed previously. He reviews a variety of postpositivist, constructivist, and relativist criteria, finding fault in each. Seale endorses a version of "subtle realism"; that is, there is a world out there that is constructed. Seale suggests that we view research as a craft skill. He then offers a constructionist version of triangulation as a way of deepening understanding from within a fallibilistic epistemology. He suggests that this view of triangulation can be useful for poststructuralists and postmodernists by enhancing the quality of politically driven research projects.

In this move, Seale divorces craft skills from philosophical, or paradigm, positions. In this framework, triangulation, member checking, analytic induction, and grounded theory simply become craft skills. This position allows Seale to be on both sides of the fence at the same time. While we are not in agreement with his position, largely because of the equivocation within it, his work represents the position of many of those practicing qualitative work today, especially those engaged in discourse and conversational analyses.

Lather thickens the argument and ties another knot. She offers a playful reversal on the notion of rock and soft place: "To recast a familiar metaphor, the 'rock' is the unquestionable need for trustworthiness in data generated by alternative paradigms . . . and the 'soft place' is the positivist claim to neutrality" (65). She reconceptualizes validity within the contexts of openly ideological research. She reviews three openly value-based research programs: feminist research, neo-Marxist critical ethnography, and Freirian "empowering" research. She assesses recent work within each paradigm in terms of four guidelines: triangulation (multiple data sources, methods, theoretical schemes), construct validity (theoretical reflexivity), face validity (member checks), and catalytic validity (praxis).

Returning at the end of her piece to her title, Lather observes that "what is at first impression the 'hard place' of validity coefficients . . . is, in fact, a soft spot" (78). The "rock" is not positivism's validity, but rather the need to establish the trustworthiness of qualitative data, a "new rigor of softness." (78). Such inquiry will critically use triangulation, reflexivity, member checks, and praxis and increasingly our ability to have faith in the findings of a given piece of research while maintaining its more open-ended qualities.

Thus, Lather is aligned with Seale. Another knot remains untied, and the need for other more openly ideological, interpretive, nonfoundational models of legitimation remains.

REFERENCES

Conquergood, Dwight. 1998. "Beyond the Text: Toward a Performative Cultural Politics." In Sheron J. Dailey, ed., *The Future of Performance Studies: Visions and Revisions* (pp. 25–36). Annandale, Va.: National Communication Association.

Geertz, Clifford. 1973. *The Interpretation of Cultures.* New York: Basic Books.

Smith, John K., and Deborah K. Deemer. 2000. "The Problem of Criteria in the Age of Relativism." In Norman K. Denzin and Yvonna S. Lincoln, eds., *Handbook of Qualitative Research* (2nd ed., pp. 877–96). Thousand Oaks, Calif.: Sage.

7

Thick Description: Toward an Interpretive Theory of Culture

Clifford Geertz

I

In her book, *Philosophy in a New Key*, Susanne Langer remarks that certain ideas burst upon the intellectual landscape with a tremendous force. They resolve so many fundamental problems at once that they seem also to promise that they will resolve all fundamental problems, clarify all obscure issues. Everyone snaps them up as the open sesame of some new positive science, the conceptual center-point around which a comprehensive system of analysis can be built. The sudden vogue of such a *grande idée*, crowding out almost everything else for a while, is due, she says, "to the fact that all sensitive and active minds turn at once to exploiting it. We try it in every connection, for every purpose, experiment with possible stretches of its strict meaning, with generalizations and derivatives."

After we have become familiar with the new idea, however, after it has become part of our general stock of theoretical concepts, our expectations are brought more into balance with its actual uses, and its excessive popularity is ended. A few zealots persist in the old key-to-the-universe view of it; but less driven thinkers settle down after a while to the problems the idea has really

Reprinted from Clifford Geertz, *The Interpretation of Cultures: Selected Essays* (New York: Basic, 1973), 3–30.

generated. They try to apply it and extend it where it applies and where it is capable of extension; and they desist truth, a seminal idea in the first place, a permanent and enduring part of our intellectual armory. But it no longer has the grandiose, all-promising scope, the infinite versatility of apparent application, it once had. The second law of thermodynamics, or the principle of natural selection, or the notion of unconscious motivation, or the organization of the means of production does not explain everything, not even everything human, but it still explains something; and our attention shifts to isolating just what that something is, to disentangling ourselves from a lot of pseudoscience to which, in the first flush of its celebrity, it has also given rise.

Whether or not this is, in fact, the way all centrally important scientific concepts develop, I don't know. But certainly this pattern fits the concept of culture, around which the whole discipline of anthropology arose, and whose domination that discipline has been increasingly concerned to limit, specify, focus, and contain. It is to this cutting of the culture concept down to size, therefore actually insuring its continued importance rather than undermining it, that the essays below are all, in their several ways and from their several directions, dedicated. They all argue, sometimes explicitly, more often merely through the particular analysis they develop, for a narrowed, specialized, and so I imagine, theoretically more powerful concept of culture to replace E. B. Tylor's famous "most complex whole," which, its originative power not denied, seems to me to have reached the point where it obscures a good deal more than it reveals.

The conceptual morass into which the Tylorean kind of *pot-au-feu* theorizing about culture can lead, is evident in what is still one of the better general introductions to anthropology, Clyde Kluckhohn's *Mirror for Man*. In some twenty-seven pages of his chapter on the concept, Kluckhohn managed to define culture in turn as: (1) "the total way of life of a people"; (2) "the social legacy the individual acquires from his group"; (3) "a way of thinking, feeling, and believing"; (4) "an abstraction from behavior"; (5) a theory on the part of the anthropologist about the way in which a group of people in fact behave; (6) a "store-house of pooled learning"; (7) "a set of standardized orientations to recurrent problems"; (8) "learned behavior"; (9) a mechanism for the normative regulation of behavior; (10) "a set of techniques for adjusting both to the external environment and to other men"; (11) "a precipitate of history"; and turning, perhaps in desperation, to similes, as a map, as a sieve, and as a matrix. In the face of this sort of theoretical diffusion, even a somewhat constricted and not entirely standard concept of culture, which is at least internally coherent and, more important, which has a definable argument to make is (as, to be fair, Kluckhohn himself keenly realized) an improvement. Eclecticism is self-defeating not because there is only one direction in which it is useful to move, but because there are so many: it is necessary to choose.

The concept of culture I espouse, and whose utility the essays below attempt to demonstrate, is essentially a semiotic one. Believing, with Max Weber, that man is an animal suspended in webs of significance he himself has spun, I take culture to be those webs, and the analysis of it to be therefore not an experimental science in search of law but an interpretive one in search of meaning. It is explication I am after, construing social expressions on their surface enigmatical. But this pronouncement, a doctrine in a clause, demands itself some explication.

II

Operationalism as a methodological dogma never made much sense so far as the social sciences are concerned, and except for a few rather too well-swept corners—Skinnerian behaviorism, intelligence testing, and so on—it is largely dead now. But it had, for all that, an important point to make, which, however we may feel about trying to define charisma or alienation in terms of operations, retains a certain force: if you want to understand what a science is, you should look in the first instance not at its theories or its findings, and certainly not at what its apologists say about it; you should look at what the practitioners of it do.

In anthropology, or anyway social anthropology, what the practitioners do is ethnography. And it is in understanding what ethnography is, or more exactly *what doing ethnography is*, that a start can be made toward grasping what anthropological analysis amounts to as a form of knowledge. This, it must immediately be said, is not a matter of methods. From one point of view, that of the textbook, doing ethnography is establishing rapport, selecting informants, transcribing texts, taking genealogies, mapping fields, keeping a diary, and so on. But it is not these things, techniques and received procedures, that define the enterprise. What defines it is the kind of intellectual effort it is: an elaborate venture in, to borrow a notion from Gilbert Ryle, "thick description."

Ryle's discussion of "thick description" appears in two recent essays of his (now reprinted in the second volume of his *Collected Papers*) addressed to the general question of what, as he puts it, "*Le Penseur*" is doing: "Thinking and Reflecting" and "The Thinking of Thoughts." Consider, he says, two boys rapidly contracting the eyelids of their right eyes. In one, this is an involuntary twitch; in the other, a conspiratorial signal to a friend. The two movements are, as movements, identical; from an I-am-a-camera, "phenomenalistic" observation of them alone, one could not tell which was twitch and which was wink, or indeed whether both or either was twitch or wink. Yet the difference, however unphotographable, between a twitch and a wink is vast; as anyone unfortunate enough to have had the first taken for the second knows. The winker is communicating, and indeed communicating in a quite precise and special way: (1) deliberately, (2) to someone in particular, (3) to impart a particular message, (4) according to a socially established code, and (5) without cognizance of the rest of the company. As Ryle points out, the winker has done two things, contracted his eyelids and winked, while the twitcher has done only one, contracted his eyelids. Contracting your eyelids on purpose when there exists a public code in which so doing counts as a conspiratorial signal is winking. That's all there is to it: a speck of behavior, a fleck of culture, and— *violà!*—a gesture.

That, however, is just the beginning. Suppose, he continues, there is a third boy, who, "to give malicious amusement to his cronies," parodies the first boy's wink, as amateurish, clumsy, obvious, and so on. He, of course, does this in the same way the second boy winked and the first twitched: by contracting his right eyelids. Only this boy is neither winking nor twitching, his is parodying someone else's, as he takes it, laughable, attempt at winking. Here, too, a socially established code exists (he will "wink" laboriously, over obviously, perhaps adding a grimace—the usual artifices of the clown); and so also does a message. Only now it is not conspiracy but ridicule that is in the air. If the others think he is actually winking, his whole project misfires as completely, though with somewhat different results, as if they think he is twitching. One can go further: uncertain of his mimicking abilities, the would-be satirist may practice at home before the mirror, in which case he is not twitching, winking, or parodying, but rehearsing; though so far as what a camera, a radical behaviorist, or a believer in protocol sentences would record he is just rapidly contracting his right eyelids like all the others. Complexities are possible, if not practically without end, at least logically so. The original winker might, for example, actually have been fake-winking, say, to mislead outsiders into imag-

ining there was a conspiracy afoot when there in fact was not, in which case
our descriptions of what the parodist is parodying and the rehearser rehearsing of course shift accordingly. But the point is that between what Ryle calls
the "thin description" of what the rehearser (parodist, winker, twitcher . . .) is
doing ("rapidly contracting his right eyelids") and the "thick description" of
what he is doing ("practicing a burlesque of a friend taking a wink to deceive
an innocent into thinking a conspiracy is in motion") lies the object of
ethnography: a stratified hierarchy of meaningful structures in terms of which
twitches, winks, fake-winks, parodies, rehearsals of parodies are produced,
perceived, and interpreted, and without which they would not (not even the
zero-form twitches, which, *as a cultural category*, are as much nonwinks as
winks are nontwitches) in fact exist, no matter what anyone did or didn't do
with his eyelids.

Like so many of the little stories Oxford philosophers like to make up for
themselves, all this winking, fake-winking, burlesque-fake-winking, rehearsed-
burlesque-fake-winking, may seem a bit artificial. In way of adding a more empirical note, let me give, deliberately unpreceded by any prior explanatory
comment at all, a not untypical excerpt from my own field journal to demonstrate that, however evened off for didactic purposes, Ryle's example presents
an image only to exact of the sort of piled-up structures of inference and implication through which an ethnographer is continually trying to pick his way:

> The French [the informant said] had only just arrived. They set up twenty or so
> small forts between here, the town, and the Marmusha area up in the middle of
> the mountains, placing them on promontories so they could survey the coun-
> tryside. But for all this they couldn't guarantee safety, especially at night, so al-
> though the *mezrag*, trade-pact, system was supposed to be legally abolished it in
> fact continued as before.
>
> One night, when Cohen (who speaks fluent Berber), was up there, at Mar-
> musha, two other Jews who were traders to a neighboring tribe came by to pur-
> chase some goods from him. Some Berbers, from yet another neighboring tribe,
> tried to break into Cohen's place, but he fired his rifle in the air. (Traditionally,
> Jews were not allowed to carry weapons; but at this period things were so un-
> settled many did so anyway.) This attracted the attention of the French and the
> marauders fled.
>
> The next night, however, they came back, one of them disguised as a woman
> who knocked on the door with some sort of a story. Cohen was suspicious and

didn't want to let "her" in, but the other Jews said, "oh, it's all right, it's only a woman." So they opened the door and the whole lot came pouring in. They killed the two visiting Jews, but Cohen managed to barricade himself in an adjoining room. He heard the robbers planning to burn him alive in the shop after they removed his goods, and so he opened the door and, laying about him wildly with a club, managed to escape through a window.

He went up to the fort, then, to have his wounds dressed, and complained to the local commandant, one Captain Dumari, saying he wanted his *'ar* —i.e., four or five times the value of the merchandise stolen from him. The robbers were from a tribe which had not yet submitted to French authority and were in open rebellion against it, and he wanted authorization to go with his *mezrag*-holder, the Marmusha tribal *sheikh*, to collect the indemnity that, under traditional rules, he had coming to him. Captain Dumari couldn't officially give him permission to do this, because of the French prohibition of the *mezrag* relationship, but he gave him verbal authorization, saying, "If you get killed, it's your problem."

So the *sheikh*, the Jew, and a small company of armed Marmushans went off ten or fifteen kilometers up into the rebellious area, where there were of course no French, and, sneaking up, captured the thief-tribe's shepherd and stole its herds. The other tribe soon came riding out on horses after them, armed with rifles and ready to attack. But when they saw who the "sheep thieves" were, they thought better of it and said, "all right, we'll talk." They couldn't really deny what had happened—that some of their men had robbed Cohen and killed the two visitors—and they weren't prepared to start the serious feud with the Marmusha a scuffle with the invading party would bring on. So the two groups talked, and talked, and talked, there on the plain amid the thousands of sheep, and decided finally on five-hundred-sheep damages. The two armed Berber groups then lined up on their horses at opposite ends of the plain, with the sheep herded between them, and Cohen, in his black gown, pillbox hat, and flapping slippers, went out alone among the sheep, picking out, one by one and at his own good speed, the best ones for his payment.

So Cohen got his sheep and drove them back to Marmusha. The French, up in their fort, heard them coming from some distance ("Ba, ba, ba" said Cohen, happily, recalling the image) and said, "What the hell is that?" And Cohen said, "That is my *'ar*." The French couldn't believe he had actually done what he said he had done, and accused him of being a spy for the rebellious Berbers, put him in prison, and took his sheep. In the town, his family, not having heard from him in so long a time, thought he was dead. But after a while the French released him and he came back home, but without his sheep. He then went to the Colonel in the town, the Frenchman in charge of the whole region, to complain. But the Colonel said, "I can't do anything about the matter. It's not my problem."

Quoted raw, a note in a bottle, this passage conveys, as any similar one similarly presented would do, a fair sense of how much goes into ethnographic description of even the most elemental sort—how extraordinarily "thick" it is. In finished anthropological writings, including those collected here, this fact—that what we call our data are really our own constructions of other people's constructions of what they and their compatriots are up to—is obscured because most of what we need to comprehend a particular event, ritual, custom, idea, or whatever is insinuated as background information before the thing itself is directly examined. (Even to reveal that this little drama took place in the highlands of central Morocco in 1912—and was recounted therein 1968—is to determine much of our understanding of it.) There is nothing particularly wrong with this, and it is in any case inevitable. But it does lead to a view of anthropological research as rather more of an observational and rather less of an interpretive activity than it really is. Right down at the factual base, the hard rock, insofar as there is any, of the whole enterprise, we are already explicating: and worse, explicating explications. Winks upon winks upon winks.

Analysis, then, is sorting out the structures of signification—what Ryle called established codes, a somewhat misleading expression, for it makes the enterprise sound too much like that of the cipher clerk when it is much more like that of the literary critic—and determining their social ground and import. Here, in our text, such sorting would begin with distinguishing the three unlike frames of interpretation ingredient in the situation, Jewish, Berber, and French, and would then move on to show how (and why) at that time, in that place, their copresence produced a situation in which systematic misunderstanding reduced traditional form to social farce. What tripped Cohen up, and with him the whole, ancient pattern of social and economic relationships within which he functioned, was a confusion of tongues.

I shall come back to this too-compacted aphorism later, as well as to the details of the text itself. The point for now is only that ethnography is thick description. What the ethnographer is in fact faced with—except when (as, of course, he must do) he is pursuing the more automatized routines of data collection—is a multiplicity of complex conceptual structures, many of them superimposed upon or knotted into one another, which are at once strange, irregular, and inexplicit, and which he must contrive somehow first to grasp and then to render. And this is true at the most down-to-earth, jungle field work levels of this activity: interviewing informants, observing rituals, eliciting kin terms, tracing property lines, censusing households ... writing his journal. Doing ethnography is like trying to read (in the sense of "construct a reading of") a manuscript—foreign, faded, full of ellipses, incoherencies, suspicious emendations, and tendentious commentaries, but written not in conventionalized graphs of sound but in transient examples of shaped behavior.

III

Culture, this acted document, thus is public, like a burlesqued wink or a mock sheep raid. Though ideational, it does not exist in someone's head; though unphysical, it is not an occult entity. The interminable, because unterminable, debate within anthropology as to whether culture is "subjective" or "objective," together with the mutual exchange of intellectual insults ("idealist!"—"materialist!"; "mentalist!"—"behaviorist!"; "impressionist!"—"positivist!") which accompanies it, is wholly misconceived. Once human behavior is seen as (most of the time; there are true twitches) symbolic action—action which, like phonation in speech, pigment in painting, line in writing, or sonance in music, signifies—the question as to whether culture is patterned conduct or a frame of mind, or even the two somehow mixed together, loses sense. The thing to ask about a burlesqued wink or a mock sheep raid is not what their ontological status is. It is the same as that of rocks on the one hand and dreams on the other—they are things of this world. The thing to ask is what their import is: what it is, ridicule or challenge, irony or anger, snobbery or pride, that, in their occurrence and through their agency, is getting said.

This may seem like an obvious truth, but there are a number of ways to obscure it. One is to imagine that culture is a self-contained "super-organic" reality with forces and purposes of its own; that is, to reify it. Another is to claim that it consists in the brute pattern of behavioral events we observe in fact to occur in some identifiable community or other; that is, to reduce it. But though both these confusions still exist, and doubtless will be always with us, the main source of theoretical muddlement in contemporary anthropology is a view which developed in reaction to them and is right now very widely

held—namely, that, to quote Ward Goodenough, perhaps its leading proponent, "culture [is located] in the minds and hearts of men."

Variously called ethnoscience, componential analysis, or cognitive anthropology (a terminological wavering which reflects a deeper uncertainty), this
school of thought holds that culture is composed of psychological structures
by means of which individuals or groups of individuals guide their behavior.
"A society's culture," to quote Goodenough again, this time in a passage which
has become the *locus classicus* of the whole movement, "consists of whatever it
is one has to know or believe in order to operate in a manner acceptable to its
members." And from this view of what culture is follows a view, equally assured, of what describing it is—the writing out of systematic rules, an ethnographic algorithm, which, if followed, would make it possible so to operate, to
pass (physical appearance aside) for a native. In such a way, extreme subjec-
tivism is married to extreme formalism, with the expected result: an explosion
of debate as to whether particular analyses (which come in the form of tax-
onomies, paradigms, tables, trees, and other ingenuities) reflect what the natives "really" think or are merely clever simulations, logically equivalent but
substantively different, of what they think.

As, on first glance, this approach may look close enough to the one being
developed here to be mistaken for it, it is useful to be explicit as to what di-
vides them. If, leaving our winks and sheep behind for the moment, we take,
say, a Beethoven quartet as an admittedly rather special but, for these purposes, nicely illustrative, sample of culture, no one would, I think, identify it
with its score, with the skills and knowledge need to play it, with the understanding of it possessed by its performers or auditors, nor, to take care, en pas-
sant, of the reductionists and reifiers, with a particular performance of it or
with some mysterious entity transcending material existence. The "no one" is
perhaps too strong here, for there are always incorrigibles. But that a
Beethoven quartet is a temporally developed tonal structure, a coherent sequence of modeled sound—in a word, music—and not anybody's knowledge
of or belief about anything, including how to play it, is a proposition to which
most people are, upon reflection, likely to assent.

To play the violin it is necessary to possess certain habits, skills, knowledge,
and talents, to be in the mood to play, and (as the old joke goes) to have a violin. But violin playing is neither the habits, skills, knowledge, and so on, nor
the mood, nor (the notion believers in "material culture" apparently embrace)

the violin. To make a trade pact in Morocco, you have to do certain things in certain ways (among others, cut, while chanting Quranic Arabic, the throat of a lamb before the assembled, undeformed, adult male members of your tribe) and to be possessed of certain psychological characteristics (among others, a desire for distant things). But a trade pact is neither the throat cutting nor the desire, though it is real enough, as seven kinsmen of our Marmusha sheikh discovered when, on an earlier occasion, they were executed by him following the theft of one mangy, essentially valueless sheepskin from Cohen.

Culture is public because meaning is. You can't wink (or burlesque one) without knowing what counts as winking or how, physically, to contract your eyelids, and you can't conduct a sheep raid (or mimic one) without knowing what it is to steal a sheep and how practically to go about it. But to draw from such truths the conclusion that knowing how to wink is winking and know-ing how to steal a sheep is sheep raiding is to betray as deep a confusion as, taking thin descriptions for thick, to identify winking with eyelid contractions or sheep raiding with chasing woolly animals out of pastures. The cognitivist fallacy—that culture consists (to quote another spokesman for the movement, Stephen Tyler) of "mental phenomena which can [he means "should"] be an-alyzed by formal methods similar to those of mathematics and logic"—is as destructive of an effective use of the concept as are the behaviorist and ideal-ist fallacies to which it is a misdrawn correction. Perhaps, as its errors are more sophisticated and its distortions subtler, it is even more so.

The generalized attack on privacy theories of meaning is, since early Husserl and late Wittgenstein, so much a part of modern thought that it need not be developed once more here. What is necessary is to see to it that the news of it reaches anthropology; and in particular that it is made clear that to say that culture consists of socially established structures of meaning in terms of which people do such things as signal conspiracies and join them or per-ceive insults and answer them, is no more to say that it is a psychological phe-nomenon, a characteristic of someone's mind, personality, cognitive structure, or whatever, than to say one's mind, personality, cognitive structure, or whatever, than to say that Tantrism, genetics, the progressive form of the verb, the classification of wines, the Common law, or the notion of "a condi-tional curse" (as Westermarck defined the concept of 'ar in terms of which Co-hen pressed his claim to damages) is. What, in a place like Morocco, most prevents those of us who grew up winking other winks or attending other sheep from grasping what people are up to is not ignorance as to how cognition works (though, especially as, one assumes, it works the same among them as it does among us, it would greatly help to have less of that too) as a lack of familiarity with the imaginative universe within which their acts are signs. As Wittgenstein has been invoked, he may as well be quoted:

> We . . . say of some people that they are transparent to us. It is, however, important as regards this observation that one human being can be a complete enigma to another. We learn this when we come into a strange country with entirely strange traditions; and, what is more, even given a mastery of the country's language, we do not *understand* the people. (And not because of not knowing what they are saying to themselves.) We cannot find our feet with them.

IV

Finding our feet, an unnerving business which never more than distantly succeeds, is what ethnographic research consists of as a personal experience; trying to formulate the basis on which one imagines, always excessively, one has found them is what anthropological writing consists of as a scientific endeavor. We are not, or at least I am not, seeking either to become natives (a compromised word in any case) or to mimic them. Only romantics or spies would seem to find point in that. We are seeking, in the widened sense of the term in which it encompasses very much more than talk, to converse with them, a matter a great deal more difficult, and not only with strangers, than is commonly recognized. "If speaking for someone else seems to be a mysterious process," Stanley Cavell has remarked, "that may be because speaking to someone does not seem mysterious enough."

Looked at in this way, the aim of anthropology is the enlargement of the universe of human discourse. That is not, of course, its only aim—instruction, amusement, practical counsel, moral advance, and the discovery of natural order in human behavior are others; nor is anthropology the only discipline which pursues it. But it is an aim to which a semiotic concept of culture is peculiarly well adapted. As interworked systems of construable signs (what, ignoring provincial usages, I would call symbols), culture is not a power, something to which social events, behaviors, institutions, or processes can be causally attributed; it is a context, something within which they can be intelligibly—that is, thickly—described.

The famous anthropological absorption with the (to us) exotic—Berber horsemen, Jewish peddlers, French Legionnaires—is, thus, essentially a device for displacing the dulling sense of familiarity with which the mysteriousness of our own ability to relate perceptively to one another is concealed from us. Looking at the ordinary in places where it takes unaccustomed forms brings out not, as has so often been claimed, the arbitrariness of human behavior (there is nothing especially arbitrary about taking sheep theft for insolence in Morocco), but the degree to which its meaning varies according to the pattern of life by which it is informed. Understanding a people's cultures exposes their normalness without reducing their particularity. (The more I manage to follow what the Moroccans are up to, the more logical, and the more singular, they seem.) It renders them accessible: setting them in the frame of their own banalities, it dissolves their opacity.

It is this maneuver, usually too casually referred to as "seeing things from the actor's point of view," too bookishly as "the *verstehen* approach," or too technically as "emic analysis," that so often leads to the notion that anthropology is a variety of either long-distance mind reading or cannibal-isle fantasizing, and which, for someone anxious to navigate past the wrecks of a dozen sunken philosophies, must therefore be executed with a great deal of care. Nothing is more necessary to comprehending what anthropological interpretation is, and the degree to which it is interpretation, than an exact understanding of what it means—and what it does not mean—to say that our formulations of other peoples' symbol systems must be actor-oriented.[1]

What it means is that descriptions of Berber, Jewish, or French culture must be cast in terms of the constructions we imagine Berbers, Jews, or Frenchmen to place upon what they live through, the formulae they use to define what happens to them. What it does not mean is that such descriptions are themselves Berber, Jewish, or French—that is, part of the reality they are ostensibly describing; they are anthropological—that is, part of a developing system of scientific analysis. They must be cast in terms of the interpretations to which persons of a particular denomination subject their experience, because that is what they profess to be descriptions of; they are anthropological because it is, in fact, anthropologists who profess them. Normally, it is not necessary to point out quite so laboriously that the object of study is one thing and the study of it another. It is clear enough that the physical world is not physics and *A Skeleton Key to Finnegan's Wake* not *Finnegan's Wake*. But, as in the study of culture, analysis penetrates into the very body of the object—that is, *we begin with our own interpretations of what our informants are up to, or think they are up to, and then systematize those*—the line between (Moroccan) culture as a natural fact and (Moroccan) culture as a theoretical entity tends to get blurred. All the more so, as the latter is presented in the form of an actor's-eye description of (Moroccan) conceptions of everything from violence, honor, divinity, and justice, to tribe, property, patronage, and chiefship.

In short, anthropological writings are themselves interpretations, and second and third order ones to boot. (By definition, only a "native" makes first order ones: it's *his* culture.)[2] They are, thus, fictions: fictions, in the sense that they are "something made," "something fashioned"—the original meaning of *fictio*—not that they are false, unfactual, or merely "as if" thought experiments. To construct actor-oriented descriptions of the involvements of a Berber chieftain, a Jewish merchant, and a French soldier with one another in 1912 Morocco is clearly an imaginative act, not all that different from constructing similar descriptions of, say, the involvements with one another of a provincial French doctor, his silly, adulterous wife, and her feckless lover in nineteenth-century France. In the latter case, the actors are represented as not having existed and the events was not having happened, while in the former they are represented as actual, or as having been so. This is a difference of no mean importance; indeed, precisely the one Madame Bovary had difficulty grasping. But the importance does not lie in the fact that their story was created while Cohen's was only noted. The conditions of their creation, and the point of it (to say nothing of the manner and the quality) differ. But the one is as much a *fictio*—"a making"—as the other.

Anthropologists have not always been as aware as they might be of this fact: that although culture exists in the trading post, the hill fort, or the sheep run, anthropology exists in the book, the article, the lecture, the museum display, or, sometimes nowadays, the film. To become aware of it is to realize that the line between mode of representation and substantive content is as undrawable in cultural analysis as it is in painting; and that fact in turn seems to threaten the objective status of anthropological knowledge by suggesting that its source is not social reality but scholarly artifice.

It does threaten it, but the threat is hollow. The claim to attention of an ethnographic account does not rest on its author's ability to capture primitive facts in faraway places and carry them home like a mask or a carving, but on

the degree to which he is able to clarify what goes on in such places, to reduce
the puzzlement—what manner of men are these?—to which unfamiliar acts
emerging out of unknown backgrounds naturally give rise. This raises some
serious problems of verification, all right—or, if "verification" is too strong a
word for so soft a science (I, myself, would prefer "appraisal"), of how you can
tell a better account from a worse one. But that is precisely the virtue of it. If
ethnography is thick description and ethnographers those who are doing the
describing, then the determining question for any given example of it, whether
a field journal squib or a Malinowski-sized monograph, is whether it sorts
winks from twitches and real winks from mimicked ones. It is not against a
body of uninterpreted data, radically thinned descriptions, that we must measure the cogency of our explications, but against the power of the scientific
imagination to bring us into touch with the lives of strangers. It is not worth it,
as Thoreau said, to go round the world to count the cats in Zanzibar.

V

Now, this proposition, that it is not in our interest to bleach behavior of the
very properties that interest us before we being to examine it, has sometimes
been escalated into a larger claim: namely, that as it is only those properties
that interest us, we need not attend, save cursorily, to behavior at all. Culture
is most effectively treated, the argument goes, purely as a symbolic system (the
catch phrase is, "in its own terms"), by isolating its elements, specifying the internal relationships among those elements, and then characterizing the whole
system in among those elements, and then characterizing the whole system in
some general way—according to the core symbols around which it is organized, the underlying structures of which it is a surface expression, or the ideological principles upon which it is based. Though a distinct improvement
over "learned behavior" and "mental phenomena" notions of what culture is,
and the source of some of the most powerful theoretical ideas in contemporary anthropology, this hermetical approach to things seems to me to run the
danger (and increasingly to have been overtaken by it) of locking cultural
analysis away from its proper object, the informal logic of actual life. There is
little profit in extricating a concept from the defects of psychologism only to
plunge it immediately into those of schematicism.

Behavior must be attended to, and with some exactness, because it is
through the flow of behavior—or, more precisely, social action—that cultural

forms find articulation. They find it as well, of course, in various sorts of artifacts, and various states of consciousness; but these draw their meaning from the role they play (Wittgenstein would say their "use") in an ongoing pattern of life, not from any intrinsic relationships they bear to one another. It is what Cohen, the sheikh, and "Captain Dumari" were doing when they tripped over one another's purposes—pursuing trade, defending honor, establishing dominance—that created our pastoral drama, and that is what the drama is, therefore, "about." Whatever, or wherever, symbol systems "in their own terms" may be, we gain empirical access to them by inspecting events, not by arranging abstracted entities into unified patterns.

A further implication of this is that coherence cannot be the major test of validity for a cultural description. Cultural systems must have a minimal degree of coherence, else we would not call them systems; and, by observation, they normally have a great deal more. But there is nothing so coherent as a paranoid's delusion or a swindler's story. The force of our interpretations cannot rest, as they are now so often made to do, on the tightness with which they hold together, or the assurance with which they are argued. Nothing has done more, I think, to discredit cultural analysis than the construction of impeccable depictions of formal order in whose actual existence nobody can quite believe.

If anthropological interpretation is constructing a reading of what happens, then to divorce it from what happens—from what, in this time or that place, specific people say, what they do, what is done to them, from the whole vast business of the world—is to divorce it from its applications and render it vacant. A good interpretation of anything—a poem, a person, a history, a ritual, an institution, a society—takes us into the heart of that of which it is the interpretation. When it does not do that, but leads us instead somewhere else—into an admiration of its own elegance, of its author's cleverness, or of the beauties of Euclidean order—it may have its intrinsic charms; but it is something else than what the task at hand—figuring out what all that rigamarole with the sheep is about—calls for.

The rigamarole with the sheep—the sham theft of them, the reparative transfer of them, the political confiscation of them—is (or was) essentially a social discourse, even if, as I suggested earlier, one conducted in multiple tongues and as much in action as in words.

Claiming his 'ar, Cohen invoked the trade pact; recognizing the claim, the sheikh challenged the offenders' tribe; accepting responsibility, the offenders' tribe paid the indemnity; anxious to make clear to sheikhs and peddlers alike who was now in charge here, the French showed the imperial hand. As in any discourse, code does not determine conduct, and what was actually said need not have been. Cohen might not have, given its illegitimacy in Protectorate eyes, chosen to press his claim. The sheikh might, for similar reasons, have rejected it. The offenders' tribe, still resisting French authority, might have decided to regard the raid as "real" and fight rather than negotiate. The French, were they more *habile* and less *dur* (as, under Mareschal Lyautey's seigniorial tutelage, they later in fact became) might have permitted Cohen to keep his sheep, winking—as we say—at the continuance of the trade pattern and its limitation to their authority. And there are other possibilities: the Marmushans might have regarded the French action as too great an insult to bear and gone into dissidence themselves; the French might have attempted not just to clamp down on Cohen but to bring the sheikh himself more closely to heel; and Cohen might have concluded that between renegade Berbers and Beau Geste soldiers, driving trade in the Atlas highlands was no longer worth the candle and retired to the better-governed confines of the town. This, indeed, is more or less what happened, somewhat further along, as the Protectorate moved toward genuine sovereignty. But the point here is not to describe what did or did not take place in Morocco. (From this simple incident one can widen out into enormous complexities of social experience.) It is to demonstrate what a piece of anthropological interpretation consists in: tracing the curve of a social discourse; fixing it into an inspectable form.

The ethnographer "inscribes" social discourse; *he writes it down*. In so doing, he turns it from a passing event, which exists only in its own moment of occurrence, into an account, which exists in its inscriptions and can be reconsulted. The sheikh is long dead, killed in the process of being, as the French called it, "pacified"; "Captain Dumari," his pacifier, lives, retired to his souvenirs, in the south of France; and Cohen went last year, part refugee, part pilgrim, part dying patriarch, "home" to Israel. But what they, in my extended sense, "said" to one another on an Atlas plateau sixty years ago is—very far from perfectly—preserved for study. "What," Paul Ricoeur, from whom this whole idea of the inscription of action is borrowed and somewhat twisted, asks, "what does writing fix?"

Not the event of speaking, but the "said" of speaking, where we understand by the "said" of speaking that intentional exteriorization constitutive of the aim of

discourse thanks to which the *sagen*—the saying—wants to become *Aus-sage*—
the enunciation, the enunciated. In short, what we write is the *noema*
["thought," "content," "gist"] of the speaking. It is the meaning of the speech
event, not the event as event.

This is not itself so very "said"—if Oxford philosophers run to little stories,
phenomenological ones run to large sentences; but it brings us anyway to a
more precise answer to our generative question, "What does the ethnographer
do?"—he writes.[3] This, too, may seem a less than startling discovery, and to
someone familiar with the current "literature," an implausible one. But as
the standard answer to our question has been, "He observes, he records, he
analyzes"—a kind of *veni, vidi, vici* conception of the matter—it may have
more deep-going consequences than are at first apparent, not the least of
which is that distinguishing these three phases of knowledge-seeking may not,
as a matter of fact, normally be possible; and, indeed, as autonomous "operations" they may not in fact exist.

The situation is even more delicate, because, as already noted, what we inscribe (or try to) is not raw social discourse, to which, because, save very mar-
ginally or very specially, we are not actors, we do not have direct access, but
only that small part of it which our informants can lead us into understanding.[4] This is not as fatal as it sounds, for, in fact, not all Cretans are liars, and
it is not necessary to know everything in order to understand something. But
it does make the view of anthropological analysis as the conceptual manipulation of discovered facts, a logical reconstruction of a mere reality, seem
rather lame. To set forth symmetrical crystals of significance, purified of the
material complexity in which they were located, and then attribute their existence to autogenous principles of order, universal properties of the human
mind, or vast, a priori *weltanschauungen*, is to pretend a science that does not
exist and imagine a reality that cannot be found. Cultural analysis is (or
should be) guessing at meanings, assessing the guesses, and drawing explanatory conclusions from the better guesses, not discovering the Continent of
Meaning and mapping out its bodiless landscape.

VI

So, there are three characteristics of ethnographic description: it is interpretive;
what it is interpretive of is the flow of social discourse; and the interpreting

involved consists in trying to rescue the "said" of such discourse from its per-
ishing occasions and fix it in perusable terms. The *kula* is gone or altered; but,
for better or worse, *The Argonauts of the Western Pacific* remains. But there is,
in addition, a fourth characteristic of such description, at least as I practice it:
it is microscopic.

This is not to say that there are no large-scale anthropological interpretations of whole societies, civilizations, world events, and so on. Indeed, it is
such extension of our analyses to wider contexts that, along with their theoretical implications, recommends them to general attention and justifies our
constructing them. No one really cares anymore, not even Cohen (well . . .
maybe, Cohen), about those sheep as such. History may have its unobtrusive
turning points, "great noises in a little room"; but his little go-round was
surely not one of them.

It is merely to say that the anthropologist characteristically approaches
such broader interpretations and more abstract analyses from the direction of
exceedingly extended acquaintances with extremely small matters. He confronts the same grand realities that others—historians, economists, political
scientists, sociologists—confront in more fateful settings: Power, Change,
Faith, Oppression, Work, Passion, Authority, Beauty, Violence, Love, Prestige;
but he confronts them in contexts obscure enough—places like Marmusha
and lives like Cohen's—to take the capital letters off them. These all-too-human
constancies, "those big words that make us all afraid," take a homely form in
such homely contexts. But that is exactly the advantage. There are enough
profundities in the world already.

Yet, the problem of how to get from a collection of ethnographic miniatures
on the order of our sheep story—an assortment of remarks and anecdotes—to
wall-sized culturescapes of the nation, the epoch, the continent, or the civilization is not so easily passed over with vague allusions to the virtues of concreteness and the down-to-earth mind. For a science born in Indian tribes,
Pacific islands, and African lineages and subsequently seized with grander ambitions, this has come to be a major methodological problem, and for the
most part a badly handled one. The models that anthropologists have themselves worked out to justify their moving from local truths to general visions
have been, in fact, as responsible for undermining the effort as anything their
critics—sociologists obsessed with sample sizes, psychologists with measures,
or economists with aggregates—have been able to devise against them.

Of these, the two main ones have been: the Jonesville-is-the-USA "microcosmic" model; and the Easter-Island-is-a-testing-case "natural experiment" model. Either heaven in a grain of sand, or the farther shores of possibility.

The Jonesville-is-America writ small (or America-is-Jonesville writ large) fallacy is so obviously one that the only thing that needs explanation is how people have managed to believe it and expected others to believe it. The notion that one can find the essence of national societies, civilizations, great religions, or whatever summed up and simplified in so-called "typical" small towns and villages is palpable nonsense. What one finds in small towns and villages is (alas) small-town or village life. If localized, microscopic studies were really dependent for their greater relevance upon such a premise—that they captured the great world in the little—they wouldn't have any relevance.

But, of course, they are not. The locus of study is not the object of study. Anthropologists don't study villages (tribes, towns, neighborhoods . . .); they study in villages. You can study different things in different places, and some things—for example, what colonial domination does to established frames of moral expectation—you can best study in confined localities. But that doesn't make the place what it is you are studying. In the remoter provinces of Morocco and Indonesia I have wrestled with the same questions other social scientists have wrestled with in more central locations—for example, how comes it that men's most importunate claims to humanity are cast in the accents of group pride?—and with about the same conclusiveness. One can add a dimension—one much needed in the present climate of size-up-and-solve social science; but that is all. There is a certain value, if you are going to run on about the exploitation of the masses in having seen a Javanese sharecropper turning earth in a tropical downpour or a Moroccan tailor embroidering kaftans by the light of a twenty-watt bulb. But the notion that this gives you the thing entire (and elevates you to some moral vantage ground from which you can look down upon the ethically less privileged) is an idea which only someone too long in the bush could possibly entertain.

The "natural laboratory" notion has been equally pernicious, not only because the analogy is false—what kind of a laboratory is it where *none* of the parameters are manipulable?—but because it leads to a notion that the data derived from ethnographic studies are purer, or more fundamental, or more solid, or less conditioned (the most favored word is "elementary") than those derived from other sorts of social inquiry. The great natural variation of cultural forms is, of course, not only anthropology's great (and wasting) resource, but the ground of its deepest theoretical dilemma: how is such variation to be squared with the biological unity of the human species? But it is not, even metaphorically, experimental variation, because the context in which it occurs varies along with it, and it is not possible (though there are those who try) to isolate the y's from x's to write a proper function.

The famous studies purporting to show that the Oedipus complex was backwards in the Trobriands, sex roles were upside down in Tchambuli, and the Pueblo Indians lacked aggression (it is characteristic that they were all negative—"but not in the South"), are, whatever their empirical validity may or may not be, not "scientifically tested and approved" hypotheses. They are interpretations, or misinterpretations, like any others, arrived at in the same way as any others, and as inherently inconclusive as any others, and the attempt to invest them with the authority of physical experimentation is but methodological sleight of hand. Ethnographic findings are not privileged, just particular: another country heard from. To regard them as anything more (or *anything less*) than that distorts both them and their implications, which are far profounder than mere primitivity, for social theory.

Another country head from: the reason that protracted descriptions of distant sheep raids (and a really good ethnographer would have gone into what kind of sheep they were) have general relevance is that they present the sociological mind with bodied stuff on which to feed. The important thing about the anthropologist's findings is their complex specificness, their circumstantiality. It is with the kind of material produced by long-term, mainly (though not exclusively) qualitative, highly participative, and almost obsessively finecomb field study in confined contexts that the mega-concepts with which contemporary social science is afflicted—legitimacy, modernization, integration, conflict, charisma, structure . . . meaning—can be given the sort of sensible actuality that makes it possible to think not only realistically and concretely *about* them, but, what is more important, creatively and imaginatively *with* them.

The methodological problem which the microscopic nature of ethnography presents is both real and critical. But it is not to be resolved by regarding a remote locality as the world in a teacup or as the sociological equivalent of a cloud chamber. It is to be resolved—or, anyway, decently kept at bay—by realizing that social actions are comments on more than themselves; that where an interpretation comes from does not determine where it can be impelled to go. Small facts speak to large issues, winks to epistemology, or sheep raids to revolution, because they are made to.

VII

Which brings us, finally, to theory. The besetting sin of interpretive approaches to anything—literature, dreams, symptoms, culture—is that they tend to resist, or to be permitted to resist, conceptual articulation and thus to escape systematic modes of assessment. You either grasp an interpretation or you do not, see the point of it or you do not, accept it or you do not. Imprisoned in the immediacy of its own detail, it is presented as self-validating, or, worse, as validated by the supposedly developed sensitivities of the person who presents it; any attempt to cast what it says in terms other than its own is regarded as a travesty—as, the anthropologist's severest term of moral abuse, ethnocentric.

For a field of study which, however, timidly (though I, myself, am not timid about the matter at all), asserts itself to be a science, this just will not do. There is no reason why the conceptual structure of a cultural interpretation should be any less formulable, and thus less susceptible to explicit canons of appraisal, than that of, say, a biological observation or a physical experiment— no reason except that the terms in which such formulations can be cast are, if not wholly nonexistent, very nearly so. We are reduced to insinuating theories because we lack the power to state them.

At the same time, it must be admitted that there are a number of characteristics of cultural interpretation which make the theoretical development of it more than usually difficult. The first is the need for theory to stay rather closer to the ground than tends to be the case in sciences more able to give themselves over to imaginative abstraction. Only short flights of ratiocination tend to be effective in anthropology; longer ones tend to drift off into logical dreams, academic bemusements with formal symmetry. The whole point of a semiotic approach to culture is, as I have said, to aid us in gaining access to the conceptual world in which our subjects lives so that we can, in some extended sense of the term, converse with them. The tension between the pull of this need to penetrate an unfamiliar universe of symbolic action and the requirements of technical advance in the theory of culture between the need to grasp and the need to analyze, is, as a result, both necessarily great and essentially irremovable. Indeed, the further theoretical development goes, the deeper the tension gets. This is the first condition for cultural theory: it is not its own master. As it is unseverable from the immediacies thick description presents, its freedom to shape itself in terms of its internal logic is rather limited. What generality it contrives to achieve grows out of the delicacy of its distinctions, not the sweep of its abstractions.

And from this follows a peculiarity in the way, as a simple matter of empirical fact, our knowledge of culture . . . cultures . . . a culture . . . grows: in spurts. Rather than following a rising curve of cumulative findings, cultural analysis breaks up into a disconnected yet coherent sequence of bolder and bolder sorties. Studies do build on other studies, not in the sense that they take up where the others leave off, but in the sense that, better informed and better conceptualized, they plunge more deeply into the same things. Every serious cultural analysis starts from a sheer beginning and ends where it manages to get before exhausting its intellectual impulse. Previously discovered facts are mobilized, previously developed concepts used, previously formulated hypotheses tried out; but the movement is not from already proven theorems to newly proven ones, it is from an awkward fumbling for the most elementary understanding to a supported claim that one has achieved that and surpassed it. A study is an advance if it is more incisive—whatever that may mean—than those that preceded it; but it less stands on their shoulders than, challenged and challenging, runs by their side.

It is for this reason, among others, that the essay, whether of thirty pages or three hundred, has seemed the natural genre in which to present cultural interpretations and the theories sustaining them, and why, if one looks for systematic treatises in the field, one is so soon disappointed, the more so if one finds any. Even inventory articles are rare here, and anyway of hardly more than bibliographical interest. The major theoretical contributions not only lie in specific studies—that is true in almost any field—but they are very difficult to abstract from such studies and integrate into anything one might call "culture theory" as such. Theoretical formulations hover so low over the interpretations they govern that they don't make much sense or hold much interest apart from them. This is so, not because they are not general (if they are not general, they are not theoretical), but because, stated independently of their applications, they seem either commonplace or vacant. One can, and this in fact is how the field progresses conceptually, take a line of theoretical attack developed in connection with one exercise in ethnographic interpretation and employ it in another, pushing it forward to greater precision and broader relevance; but one cannot write a "general Theory of Cultural Interpretation." Or, rather, one can, but there appears to be little profit in it, because the essential task of theory building here is not to codify abstract regularities but to make thick description possible, not to generalize across cases but to generalize within them.

To generalize within cases is usually called, at least in medicine and depth psychology, clinical inference. Rather than beginning with a set of observations and attempting to subsume them under a governing law, such inference begins with a set of (presumptive) signifiers and attempts to lace them within an intelligible frame. Measures are matched to the theoretical predictions, but symptoms (even when they are measured) are scanned for theoretical peculiarities—that is, they are diagnosed. In the study of culture the signifiers are not symptoms or clusters of symptoms, but symbolic acts of clusters of symbolic acts, and the aim is not therapy but the analysis of social discourse. But the way in which theory is used—to ferret out the unapparent import of things—is the same.

Thus we are lead to the second condition of cultural theory: it is not, at least in the strict meaning of the term, predictive. The diagnostician doesn't predict measles; he decides that someone has them, or at the very most *anticipates* that someone is rather likely shortly to get them. But this limitation, which is real enough, has commonly been both misunderstood and exaggerated, because it has been taken to mean that cultural interpretation is merely post facto: that, like the peasant in the old story, we first shoot the holes in the fence and then paint the bull's-eyes around them. It is hardly to be denied that there is a good deal of that sort of thing around, some of it in prominent places. It is to be denied, however, that it is the inevitable outcome of a clinical approach to the use of theory.

It is true that in the clinical style of theoretical formulation, conceptualization is directed toward the task of generating interpretations of matters already in hand, not toward projecting outcomes of experimental manipulations or deducing future states of a determined system. But that does not mean that theory has only to fit (or, more carefully, to generate cogent interpretations of) realities past; it has also to survive—intellectually survive—realities to come. Although we formulate our interpretations of an outburst of winking or an instance of sheep-raiding after its occurrence, sometimes long after, the theoretical framework in terms of which such an interpretation is made must be capable of continuing to yield defensible interpretations as new social phenomena swim into view. Although one starts any effort at thick description, beyond the obvious and superficial, from a state of general bewilderment as to what the devil is going on—trying to find one's feet—one does not start (or ought not) intellectually empty-handed. Theoretical ideas are not created wholly anew in each study; as I have said, they are adopted from other, related studies, and, refined in the process, applied to new interpretive problems. If they cease being useful with respect to such problems, they tend to stop being used and are more or less abandoned. If they continue being useful, throwing up new understandings, they are further elaborated and go on being used.[5]

Such a view of how theory functions in an interpretive science suggests that the distinction, relative in any case, that appears in the experimental or observational sciences between "description" and "explanation" appears here as one, even more relative, between "inscription" ("thick description") and "specification" ("diagnosis")—between setting down the meaning particular social actions have for the actors whose actions they are, and stating, as explicitly as we can manage, what the knowledge thus attained demonstrates about the society in which it is found and, beyond that, about social life as such. Our double task is to uncover the conceptual structures that inform our subjects' acts, the "said" of social discourse, and to construct a system of analysis in whose terms what is generic to those structures, what belongs to them because they are what they are, will stand out against the other determinants of human behavior. In ethnography, the office of theory is to provide a vocabulary in which what symbolic action has to say about itself—that is, about the role of culture in human life—can be expressed.

Aside from a couple of orienting pieces concerned with more foundational matters, it is in such a manner that theory operates in the essays collected here. A repertoire of very general, made-in-the-academy concepts and systems of concepts—"integration," "rationalization," "symbol," "ideology," "ethos," "revolution," "identity," "metaphor," "structure," "ritual," "world view," "actor," "function," "sacred," and, of course, "culture" itself—is woven into the body of thick-description ethnography in the hope of rendering mere occurrences scientifically eloquent.[6] The aim is to draw large conclusions from small, but very densely textured facts; to support broad assertions about the role of culture in the construction of collective life by engaging them exactly with complex specifics.

Thus it is not only interpretation that goes all the way down to the most immediate observational level: the theory upon which such interpretation conceptually depends does so also. My interest in Cohen' story, like Ryle's in winks, grew out of some very general notions indeed. The "confusion of tongues" model—the view that social conflict is not something that happens when, out of weakness, indefiniteness, obsolescence, or neglect, cultural forms cease to operate, but rather something which happens when, like burlesqued winks, such forms are pressed by unusual situations or unusual intentions to operate in unusual ways—is not an idea I got from Cohen's story. It is one, instructed by colleagues, students, and predecessors, I brought to it.

Our innocent-looking "note in a bottle" is more than a portrayal of the frames of meaning of Jewish peddlers, Berber warriors, and French proconsuls, or even of their mutual interference. It is an argument that to rework the pattern of social relationships is to rearrange the coordinates of the experienced world. Society's forms are culture's substance.

[. . .]

NOTES

1. Not only other peoples': anthropology *can* be trained on the culture of which it is itself a part, and it increasingly is; a fact of profound importance, but which, as it raises a few tricky and rather special second order problems, I shall put to the side for the moment.

2. The order problem is, again, complex. Anthropological works based on other anthropological works (Lévi-Strauss', for example) may, of course, be fourth order or higher, and informants frequently, even habitually, make second order interpretations—what have come to be known as "native models." In literate cultures, where "native" interpretation can proceed to higher levels—in connection with the Maghreb, one has only to think of Ibn Khaldun; with the United States, Margaret Mead—these matters become intricate indeed.

3. Or, again, more exactly, "inscribes." Most ethnography is in fact to be found in books and articles, rather than in films, records, museum displays, or whatever; but even in them there are, of course, photographs, drawings, diagrams, tables, and so on. Self-consciousness about modes of representation (not to speak of experiments with them) has been very lacking in anthropology.

4. So far as it has reinforced the anthropologist's impulse to engage himself with his informants as persons rather than as objects, the notion of "participant observation" has been a valuable one. But, to the degree it has lead the anthropologist to block from his view the very special, culturally bracketed nature of his own role and to imagine himself something more than an interested (in both senses of that word) sojourner, it has been our most powerful source of bad faith.

5. Admittedly, this is something of an idealization. Because theories are seldom if ever decisively disproved in clinical use but merely grow increasingly awkward, unproductive, strained, or vacuous, they often persist long after all but a handful of people (though they are often most passionate) have lost much interest in them. Indeed, so far as anthropology is concerned, it is almost more of a problem to get exhausted ideas out of the literature than it is to get productive ones in, and so a great deal more of theoretical discussion than one would prefer is critical rather than constructive, and whole careers have been devoted to hastening the demise of moribund notions. As the field advances one would hope that this sort of intellectual weed control would become a less prominent part of our activities. But, for the moment, it remains true that old theories tend less to die than to go into second editions.

6. The overwhelming bulk of the following chapters concern Indonesia rather than Morocco, for I have just begun to face up to the demands of my North African material, which, for the most part, was gathered more recently. Field work in Indonesia was carried out in 1952–1954, 1957–1958, and 1971; in Morocco in 1964, 1965–1966, 1968–1969, and 1972.

8

Quality in Qualitative Research

Clive Seale

A lot of effort has been expended by methodologists over the years, trying to give some guidance to qualitative researchers in improving or judging the quality of qualitative research. You could say that all methodological writing is ultimately directed at such a goal, because the idea of writing about how one can do research is presumably aimed at giving other people some good ideas on how they might proceed with their own studies. Explicit discussions of quality in social research, though, began from concerns designated with words such as *validity* and *reliability*, developed within the quantitative or scientific tradition, and then moved on under the pressure of critique from the qualitative research community. At first, this led qualitative methodologists to spawn new terms that either substituted for the scientific language of earlier periods or added new ideas to them. More recently, with postmodernist perspectives in fashion, the whole issue of whether we ought to be trying to generate criteria for judging the quality of research has become controversial. Maybe we should be letting a thousand flowers bloom, people say. The result is that practicing researchers now have to find their way through a mass of conflicting positions, and methodology is in danger of getting a bad name. I want to suggest

Reprinted from *Qualitative Inquiry* 5, no. 4 (1999): 465–78. Copyright 1999 by Sage Publications Inc.

a way through, following in the spirit of an earlier era, when the call to produce grounded theory empowered researchers concerned to reclaim their craft from the "theoretical capitalist(s)" of the day (Glaser & Strauss, 1967, p. 10). The appeal to scientific foundations made by Glaser and Strauss may no longer be as easily sustainable, but the need for a new conceptualization of the relationship between qualitative social research, theory, and indeed philosophy is as pressing now as it was in the 1960s.

Philosophy is often presented as underpinning the craft of social research, being an arena where various attempts at providing foundations for judging truth claims have come and gone, yet present day opinion seems nowadays, paradoxically, to conclude on antifoundationalism as itself being a philosophical foundation for social research. I think it is time for social researchers to exploit this paradox, by breaking free from the obligation to fulfill philosophical schemes through research practice, while remaining aware of the value of philosophical and political reflexivity for their craft. A confident view of social research as a craft skill could then emerge, relatively autonomous from social theory or philosophy, yet drawing on these arenas of discourse as a resource. The search for overarching criteria for judging quality under this vision is thereby held at a distance, and the elusive nature of quality (we somehow recognize it when we see it, but we cannot prespecify it with methodological rules) is preserved. This also means that we do not have to abandon skills developed under one paradigm because another paradigm has come along.

It is worth summarizing some key shifts in criteriology, which is a kind of offshoot of broader debates in the philosophy of science, to show how I have reached this conclusion. Then I shall make some statements about philosophical positions and foundationalism, after which I shall use the example of triangulation to demonstrate how social researchers might operate within a conception of research as a craft skill in a way that preserves a commitment to producing good quality research.

CRITERIOLOGY

Qualitative creation mythology, in the modernist phase of qualitative inquiry, emphasized difference by making overdrawn contrasts with the supposed "positivism" of quantitative work. In the methodological debate about quality criteria, this, initially, involved substituting new terms for words such as *va-*

lidity and *reliability* to reflect interpretivist conceptions while retaining a sense that social researchers in both traditions shared similar scientific orientations. A typical example here is LeCompte and Goetz (1982) who argued that techniques for establishing validity and reliability should be somewhat different in, say, an ethnography compared with an experiment. They drew up a scheme intended as a qualitative parallel to Campbell and Stanley's (1966) influential account of validity and reliability in quasi-experimental designs, inventing new concepts such as *internal* and *external reliability* to legitimate a degree of difference that nevertheless allowed them to advocate pragmatic combinations of quantitative and qualitative work.

Qualitative criteriologists since LeCompte and Goetz progressively moved away from modernist commitments, leading to conceptions of validity and reliability very far removed from positivist or realist perspectives, and constructivism shifted into postmodernism. The urge to generate criteria for judging good quality studies seems irrepressible in these methodological writings, perhaps in part due to the requirement that social researchers impress the worth of their efforts on skeptical audiences, such as research-funding bodies.

A sometimes bewildering variety of new concepts arose. For example, Altheide and Johnson's (1994) review of interpretivist positions on validity identifies "successor validity, catalytic validity, interrogated validity, transgressive validity, imperial validity, simulacra/ironic validity, situated validity, and voluptuous validity" (p. 488). A glance at Kirk and Miller (1986), though, shows Altheide and Johnson to have omitted from this list "apparent," "instrumental," and "theoretical" validity. Additionally, Kirk and Miller (1986) demonstrate the ease with which new forms of reliability can be conceptualized, dividing this into the "quixotic," the "diachronic," and the "synchronic." This proliferation of concepts reflects the difficulties that qualitative methodologists, committed to creating some overarching system for specifying quality, have had in making their ideas stick. This is in marked contrast to parallel authors in the quantitative tradition where a consensus around certain ideas (for example, the distinction between validity and reliability, or between internal and external validity) has been more easy to sustain. In qualitative research, the project of criteriology experiences particular contradictions because of the difficulty in regulating and constraining an endeavor whose guiding philosophy often stresses creativity, exploration, conceptual flexibility, and a freedom of spirit. Additionally, though, conceptual proliferation is a marker of the paradigm shifts and crises of legitimation and representations, which have characterize "moments" in the recent history of qualitative methods (Denzin & Lincoln, 1994).

The work of Lincoln and Guba reflects these more recent shifts. Lincoln and Guba (1985) argue that establishing the trustworthiness of a research report lies at the heart of issues conventionally discussed as validity and reliability so that four questions have, from within the modernist paradigm, been asked of research reports, namely their truth value, applicability, consistency, and neutrality. Truth value, though, assumes a "single tangible reality that an investigation is intended to unearth and display" (Lincoln & Guba, 1985, p. 294), whereas the naturalistic researcher makes "the assumption of multiple constructed realities" (p. 295). Applicability depends on generalizing from a sample to a population, on the untested assumption that the "receiving" population is similar to that of the "sending" sample; the naturalistic inquirer, on the other hand, would claim the potential uniqueness of every local context, requiring empirical study of both sending and receiving contexts for applicability to be established. They are similarly critical of the other two conventional criteria. Consistency, they say, depends on naïve realism assumptions; neutrality depends on an artificial separation of values from inquiry. They criticize LeCompte and Goetz, whom they identify with such questions, for their dependence on axioms such as "naïve realism and linear causality" (Lincoln & Guba, 1985, p. 293).

Instead, Lincoln and Guba (1985) propose their own four-point criterion list for naturalistic inquirers. A concern with credibility should replace truth value and "the most crucial technique for establishing credibility" is through "member checks" (Lincoln & Guba, 1985, p. 314). Transferability should replace applicability, or external validity as conventionally conceived. Dependability is proposed as a replacement for consistency, or reliability as conventionally conceived, to be fulfilled by peer auditing procedures. Auditing is also useful in establishing confirmability, a criterion designed to replace the conventional criterion of neutrality or objectivity. Auditing is an exercise in reflexivity, which involves the provision of a methodologically self-critical account of how the research was done. Trustworthiness is always negotiable and open-ended, not being a matter of final proof whereby readers are compelled to accept an account. This, Lincoln and Guba (1985) claim, "stands in marked contrast to that of conventional inquiry" (p. 329), which claims to be "utterly unassailable" once relevant procedures have been carried out. This is, in fact, a rather overdrawn contrast if we consider the fallibilistic spirit of Campbell and Stanley's (1966) account of threats to validity and reliability. The criteria offered by Lincoln and Guba in 1985, however, depend on a contradictory philosophical position, because the belief in "multiple constructed realities," rather than a "single tangible reality" (Lincoln & Guba, 1985, p. 295), which lies at the heart of the constructivist paradigm, is not consistent with the idea that criteria for judging the trustworthiness of an account are possible. Relativism does not sit well with attempts to establish "truth," even if the term is placed in inverted commas.

Acknowledging this problem, then, in later work (Guba & Lincoln, 1989, 1994), a fifth criterion, "authenticity," is proposed as being consistent with the relativist view that research accounts do no more than a represent a sophisticated but temporary consensus of views about what is to be considered true. In detailing the components of authenticity, Guba and Lincoln (1989, 1994) reveal a sympathy for political conceptions of the role of research that was already evident in their earlier commitment to the value of member checking. Authenticity, they say, is demonstrated if researchers can show that they have represented a range of different realities ("fairness"). Research should also help members develop "more sophisticated" understandings of the phenomenon being studied ("ontological authenticity"), be shown to have helped members appreciate the viewpoints of people other than themselves ("educative authenticity"), to have stimulated some form of action ("catalytic authenticity"), and to have empowered members to act ("tactical authenticity"). Of course, the view that fairness, sophistication, mutual understanding, and empowerment are generally desirable is itself a value-laden, culture-bound position that a Foucauldian deconstructionist might very well enjoy taking apart. It represents an attempt to pull back from the relativist abyss, but the substitution of political goals as foundations for research is problematic in a world where there is no fixed consensus on the desirability of particular goals (Hammersley, 1995). A softer version of political commitment might involve researchers simply offering readers a reflexive account of their politics and leaving it to the democratic process in wider society to resolve clashes of interests. Nevertheless, it is hard not to agree with Guba and Lincoln's (1994) following conclusion: "The issue of quality criteria in constructivism is . . . not well resolved, and further critique is needed" (p. 114).

These authors, then, along with many others in the qualitative social research community, have traveled on a path beginning with a rejection of positivist criteria and the substitution of interpretivist alternatives. Dissatisfied with the limitations of these, constructivism has been embraced, introducing an element of relativism. Political versions of the value of research have then been imported to save facing the logical implications of relativism, which seem to threaten a nihilistic vision and abandonment of the research enterprise. What is a practicing social researcher to make of all this? How can these inconclusive debates become a resource for researchers rather than a source of frustration and negativity? Before turning to this, I want to consider some more purely philosophical concerns.

PHILOSOPHICAL MOMENTS

At a philosophical level, discussion of the problem of foundations for knowledge are also inconclusive. Nevertheless, philosophical positions are sometimes claimed as being in another sense "foundational" for research practice by criteriologists. Thus, empiricism is claimed as foundational for modernist paradigms, antiempiricism is proposed as foundational for constructivist and postmodern views, and so on. I propose here to examine just one attempt to provide foundations for research practice in a philosophical position, the "subtle realist" conclusion of Hammersley (1992), together with some criticisms of this. I do not propose subtle realism as a solution (though it has attractive qualities as a pragmatic compromise between several extremes), but want to use it to illustrate the limits of any approach that expects research practice to conform precisely to a philosophical position.

Subtle realism involves maintaining a view of language as both constructing new worlds and as referring to a reality outside the text, a means of communicating past experience as well as imagining new experiences. Hammersly (1992, 1995) presents this as an adequately grounded place for social researchers seeking a middle way between the various paradigm positions that are nowadays available. Like analytic realism (Altheide & Johnson, 1994), Kantian soft or "transcendental" idealism, and critical realism (Bhaskar, 1989), it is a marker of an approach to social research that takes the view that, although we always perceive the world from a particular viewpoint, the world acts back on us to constrain the points of view that are possible. The researcher treading this middle way is continually aware of the somewhat con-

structed nature of research but avoids the wholesale application of constructivism to his other own practice, which would result in a descent into nihilism.
Research, then, constructs "transitive objects" such as the concepts of social
science, to represent the real (Williams & May, 1996, p. 85). Knowledge is always mediated by preexisting ideas and values, whether this is acknowledged
by researchers or not. Yet, some accounts are more plausible than others, and
human communities in practice have created reasonably firm grounds on
which plausibility can be judged, whether or not these grounds can be supported in some ultimate senses by means of philosophical reasoning. Judgments about he plausibility of research accounts inevitably involve a
temporary subscription to the view that language is referential to a reality outside the text. This is a long way from a simple correspondence theory of truth,
but it contains elements of this. Neither does it claim that truth solely lies in
the consistency of claims with some other set of claims, though this can legit-
imately be an element in judging truth claims. It involves opposition to the
pure constructivist view that states there is no possibility of knowing a real
world that exists separately from language.

   At the heart of the advocacy of subtle realism lies the idea of a research
community with agreed standards of judgment for the plausibility, credibility,
and relevance of research reports. Distinguishing claims from evidence, providing the strongest evidence for more important claims, and exposing the
judgments of the researcher for readers to scrutinize are all methods for addressing the standards applied by a community of critical peers. In arguing for
this, Hammersley (1992) pursues an argument similar to that of Popper
(1972), who claimed the authority of an imagined "third world" of objective
knowledge, humanly constructed but, by virtue of being a joint endeavor of a
community of scientists, having an existence independent of the biographies
of individual scientists. Hammersley (1992) is also similar to Popper (1963) in
advocating a fallibilistic approach, regarding "truths" as provisional until
there is good reason for contradictory versions to gain support. Hammersley
is therefore firmly in a postpositivist camp.

   As is well known from the criticisms of Popper that have emanated from
radical epistemological and political positions, reliance on norms of communal assessment has the potential to support a rather conservative approach.
We can observe that this community of researchers is not in fact an imagined
thing of the mind, but a reality. Particular people do concrete things in the

world and call them research. These people come from particular cultural backgrounds and bring specific, exclusive prejudices to bear in the standards that they maintain. In practice, the social research community is no different from the rest of society in its divisions of status and power, acting at times to oppress and silence particular groups who are unable to influence the discourses of social research (Harding, 1986). Hammersley's stress on whether findings are consistent with knowledge that is currently accepted in the relevant research community ("plausibility") initially looks rather dubious in this light. Against this, though, the advocate of subtle realism might point to the role of evidence in testing theories for both credibility and plausibility, which exerts a persuasive force on the research community and can result in revision of accepted wisdom and the eventual overthrow of dominant paradigms.

Yet, this is itself assailable, as it rests on assumptions about the evidentiary basis of what constitutes evidence. How should we make contact with an external reality that affirms or disaffirms claims? Is not all observation fundamentally driven by preexisting theoretical assumptions? To present subtle realism as a foundational basis for social research practice seems inadequate in light of these questions. Conventionally, there can be a turn to further philosophical work at this point, perhaps to constructivism or postmodernism, often claimed to be epistemologically nonfoundational, but nevertheless presented by some (for example, Denzin, 1997; Dickens & Fontana, 1994) as a new rationale for research practice, suggesting a foundationalist habit of thought with which I believe researchers should break.

The widespread appeal of postmodern, political, and constructivist conceptions of research is based on some fundamental dissatisfactions with the scientific world view. Quality does matter in qualitative research, but the modernist headings of *validity* and *reliability* no longer seem adequate to encapsulate the range of issues that a concern for quality must raise. The constructivist critique of criteriology has led us to see that "quality" is a somewhat elusive phenomenon that cannot be prespecified by methodological rules, though their reconstitution as "guidelines," to be followed with intelligence and knowledge of the particular research context, may assist us in moving toward good quality work. A major threat to quality is in fact the idea that research must be carried out under the burden of fulfilling some philosophical or methodological scheme. Practicing social researchers can learn to do good work from a variety of examples, done within different "moments," without needing to resolve methodological disputes before beginning their work. At the same time, the quality of qualitative research is enhanced if researchers engage with philosophical and methodological debate, so that the pursuit of quality becomes a "fertile obsession" as methodological awareness develops and feeds into practice (Lather, 1993).

The idea of a self-critical research community acting together to produce positive knowledge for the benefit of others retains its appeal for many researchers. The continuing desire to participate in a shared language, constructing and negotiating standards for judging quality, incorporating political and cultural differences, always involves an act of trust in the judgments of others, though this can be made easier by the application of certain methodological procedures. These procedures (discussed in more depth in Seale, 1999), are based on this view of a research community existing as a key audience for social researchers concerned about quality of their efforts. They include techniques such as the peer auditing described by Lincoln and Guba (1985). Acceptance of the researcher's case can then partly depend on the capacity of the researcher to expose to a critical readership the judgments and methodological decisions made in the course of a research study (Swanborn, 1996).

TRIANGULATION: A CASE STUDY OF A CRAFT SKILL

To illustrate an approach to research practice that cuts through inconclusive methodological disputes, retaining a conception of research as primarily a craft skill, I shall discuss a particular one of these skills. Triangulation describes a set of techniques that arose initially within a crudely realist paradigm. Attempts have been made to restrict its use to this paradigm by people who mistakenly believe in inevitable logical connections between paradigm positions and techniques. More enlightened methodologists have perceived that it has a place within a variety of paradigms. The next step in this logic, which I believe researchers should take, is to claim it as a valuable craft skill, relatively autonomous from any paradigm position.

The idea of triangulation derives from discussions of measurement validity by quantitative methodologists working with crudely realist and empiricist assumptions. Campbell and Fiske (1959) argued that "In contrast with the single *operationalism* now dominant in psychology, we are advocating . . . a *methodological triangulation*" (p. 101, emphasis in original), and proceeded to

outline their ideas for the convergent and discriminant validation of measurement instruments. Subsequently, Webb, Campbell, Schwartz, and Sechrest
(1966) used the idea to advocate multiple operationalism, the use of several
methods at once so that the biases of any one method might be canceled out
by those of others. Its use in qualitative research, though, was first advocated
and then popularized by Denzin (1970) whose textbook has been through
several editions (1978, 1989) in which the original concept was modified.
Other textbook definitions at times contain distant echoes of this background
in the quantitative research tradition, as where Hammersley and Atkinson
(1983) describe it as a method whereby "links between concepts and indicators are checked by recourse to other indicators" (p. 199). The term itself is designed to evoke an analogy with surveying or navigation, in which people
discover their position on a map by taking bearings on two landmarks, lines
from which will intersect at the observer's position. If only one landmark were
taken, the observer would only know that they were situated somewhere along
a line. Triangulation used in this way assumes a single fixed reality that can be
known objectively through the use of multiple methods of social research
(Blaikie, 1991). Many might feel that it is therefore a technique impossible to
employ without also taking on modernist philosophical commitments within
a positivist, or at least postpositivst, paradigm together with a commitment to
constructing a single true version.

Cicourel (1964, 1974) offers the most extreme vantage point from which to
view triangulation from a different paradigm position. His own critique of the
technique is typically paradoxical, in that he proceeds by enthusiastically advocating the advantages of "indefinite triangulation" (Cicourel, 1974, p. 124).
This rhetorical ploy (that I think could usefully be read now as a joke, though
this was probably not Cicourel's intention) proceeds by showing that what he
means by this is in fact the precise antithesis to the consensus on truth sought
in conventional triangulation. His illustration comes from his own practice.

The triangulation procedure varies with the research problem. When gathering
information on language acquisition in the home setting we left a tape recorder
for about one hour during lunch. A transcription of the tape was done by a typist who had been instructed to render a verbatim record. Then the transcript,
the first version of this scene, was read by the mother while she listened to the
tape; her comments produced another version of the interaction. The typist was

next asked to listen again to the tape and to describe what she thought was "going on," correcting her original transcript as she deemed necessary. In this elaboration and correction a different version of the scene was always produced. My phonetic transcription of the tapes created still another version. . . . The reader could now say that we should have simply combined the different versions to produce the "best" one possible, but the point is that different versions could have been produced indefinitely by simply hiring different typists and providing the mother with different transcripts. (Cicourel, 1974, p. 124)

This is an amusing little demonstration of the constructivist objection to realist tendencies in discussions of triangulation. As with postmodern views, it suggests that every reading of a text is likely to produce a new interpretation, with no version assuming privileged status. Cicourel's example leads Blaikie (1991) to claim that triangulation therefore only makes sense from within a positivist framework. Blaikie fails to see any irony in Cicourel's example ("But the question arises as to why it should be called triangulation' [Blaikie, 1991, p. 130]) and argues that the technique "has no relevance for genuine interpretivists and ethnomethodologists" (Blaikie, 1991, p. 131) because it necessarily involves subscription to inappropriate ontological and epistemological positions. I argue, by contrast, that researchers should question this claim that there is a necessary connection.

Bloor's (1997) objection to triangulation leads to a further questioning of its supposedly inevitable philosophical connotations, though it is also offers an opportunity to locate this skill within a subtle realist paradigm. Bloor (1997) says that even if all the different methods in a methodological triangulation exercise converge on the same thing, apparently agreeing with each other, how can we know that they are correct? Perhaps some hitherto unthought of method would reveal something different. In fact, this problem is analogous to that of induction: How can we reliably reason on the evidence of past experience that the sun will rise tomorrow? Logically of course, we cannot. Taken at this level, the objection to triangulation as a validation exercise is also unanswerable. Yet, we operate in the world all the time on the basis of what it is plausible to believe, and it will do us little good to assume that the sun will not rise tomorrow. A pragmatic, subtle realist might answer Bloor by saying that triangulation exercises can add to the credibility of a particular account as a part of a fallibilistic research strategy in which evidence is sought

for central claims. Thus, we can move from a crude to a subtle realist paradigm as a potential set of background assumptions for triangulation. Can we
go further toward Cicourel's view?

Silverman (1993) presents an argument that moves triangulation toward a
constructivist paradigm. At first, he makes the subtle realist point that triangulation exercises can deepen understanding, as a part of a fallibilistic approach to fieldwork, although being themselves no guarantee of validity. In a
similar vein, Cain and Finch (1981) argue that multiplication of methods can
help deepen understanding of different aspects of an issue. Dingwall (1997)
begins the move toward constructivism by saying that triangulation offers a
way of explaining how accounts and actions in one setting are influenced or
constrained by those in another. Silverman (1993) eventually has no problem
with this use of triangulation, finally saying that it can help "to address the situated work of accounts" rather than "using one account to undercut another"
(p.158). This version of triangulation then, which is now very close to Cicourel's view, gets away from the idea of convergence on a fixed point and accepts a view of research as revealing multiple constructed realities, something
that triangulation, now conceived as the revelation of difference, is well suited
to expose.

Flick (1992, 1998) completes this move toward what might be called a soft
constructivist version of triangulation, deriving this from a study in which a
conversation analytic study of psychological counseling was complemented
by interviews with counselors to elicit their accounts of what they tried to
achieve in their practices. Flick (1998) argues that, used in this spirit, "Triangulation is less a strategy for validating results and procedures than an alternative to validation . . . which increases scope, depth and consistency" (p. 230).

In Seale (1999) I show, further, the uses of triangulation exercises in generating material for discourse analytic studies, thereby improving their coherence and fruitfulness, suggesting that triangulation can be used for work that
is located within a poststructuralist, if not quite postmodern paradigm. It is
not hard, too, to conceive of triangulation exercises enhancing the quality of
politically driven research projects, whose emancipatory or enlightening effect
is enhanced by the elicitation of multiple perspectives on, or constructions of,
a phenomenon. That such shifts can occur in the discussion of just one of the
many techniques available to qualitative researchers supports the more general point that particular craft skills do not have to be linked inextricably to

particular philosophical or paradigm positions. I generalize this point in Seale (1999) to incorporate discussion of both established and newly formed qualitative research skills. These include member checking, accounting for negative instances, analytic induction, the uses of numbers, using low inference descriptors, the grounding of theory, deconstructive approaches, reflexive accounting, and new textual forms of reporting, as well as others.

CONCLUSION

Methodological writing is of limited use to practicing social researchers, who are pursuing a craft occupation, in large part learned "on the job," through apprenticeship, experience, trial, and error rather than by studying general accounts of method. Methodological discussion of the quality of research, if they have any use at all, benefit the quality of research by encouraging a degree of awareness about the methodological implications of particular decisions made during the course of a project. Intense methodological awareness, if engaged in too seriously, can create anxieties that hinder practice, but if taken in small doses can help to guard against more obvious errors. It may also give ideas for those running short on these during the course of a project. Reading and discussing such methodological ideas, then, is a sort of intellectual muscle-building exercise, time out in the brain gymnasium, before returning to the task at hand, hopefully a little stronger and more alert.

This is intended to be a rather pragmatic and skeptical orientation, reflecting the view that people learn how to do research through apprenticeship experiences, fortunately possible to have by reading others' work rather than actually going and sitting at their feet (although this also can be useful). Any contemplation of other people's research work, if it involves thinking seriously about its strengths and weaknesses, can be this kind of vicarious apprenticeship experience. But additionally, purely methodological writing may help to structure this experience a little more, focusing on particular themes that writers believe to be of importance when considering how to produce good quality research.

I have tried to show that people often make strong claims that philosophical, political, or theoretical positions ought to lie behind—indeed ought to determine—the decisions that social researchers make "on the ground" so that quality is underwritten by adherence to a particular position. This is even the case with postmodernism, though writers occupying this "moment" in qualitative work sometimes try to present themselves as being almost entirely permissive. I see things differently: Research practice, in fact, should be conceived as relatively autonomous from such abstract and general considerations.

In treading along this path, I hope carefully and with due consideration of the great variety of conflicting position that exist, it is possible to benefit from just about any of the key methodological discussion on how to ensure quality in social research. This includes so-called "positivist" methodology, neo-positivism, political perspectives, constructivism, postmodernism, and others I may not have listed. What I would like to see is some sense of there being a community of social researchers who have respect for the strengths of a variety of positions within that community, appreciating the need also to develop research skills taken from a number of genres (quantitative as well as qualitative, in fact), in much the same way as artists learn how to paint, draw, or sculpt in a number of different styles. Then, the development of one's own "style" can build on a series of principled decisions, rather than being the outcome of uninformed beliefs. Such are the ways in which a research community might work.

NOTE

Martyn Hammersley and David Silverman assisted me in the development of these ideas, both by the examples they set in their own methodological writings and by providing their time generously in commenting on related manuscripts. Norman Denzin, Paul Filmer, and Yvonna Lincoln also helped me improve the quality of this piece with some perceptive comments on earlier drafts.

REFERENCES

Altheide, D. L., & Johnson, J. M. (1994). Criteria for assessing interpretive validity in qualitative research. In N. K. Denzin & Y. S. Lincoln (eds.), *Handbook of qualitative research* (pp. 485–99). Thousands Oaks, CA: Sage.

Bhaskar, R. (1989). *Reclaiming reality*. London: Verso.

Blaikie, N. W. H. (1991). A critique of the use of triangulation in social research. *Quality and Quantity* 25, 115–36.

Bloor, M. (1997). Techniques of validation in qualitative research: A critical commentary. In G. Miller & R. Dingwall (eds.), *Context and method in qualitative research* (pp. 37–50). London: Sage.

Cain, M., & Finch, J. (1981). Towards a rehabilitation of data. In P. Abrams, R. Deem, J. Finch & P. Rock, (eds.), *Practice and progress: British sociology 1950–1980* (pp. 105–19). London: George Allen and Unwin.

Campbell, D. T., & Fiske, D. W. (1959). Convergent and discriminant validation by the multitrait-multimethod matrix. *Psychological Bulletin*, 56 (2), 81–105.

Campbell, D. T., & Stanley, J. C. (1966). *Experimental and quasi-experimental design for research.* Chicago: Rand McNally.

Cicourel, A. V. (1964). *Method and measurement in sociology.* New York: Free Press.

――――. (1974). *Cognitive sociology.* New York: Free Press.

Denzin, N. K. (1970). *The research act in sociology.* London: Butterworth.

――――. (1978). *The research act: A theoretical introduction to sociological methods* (2nd ed.). New York: McGraw-Hill.

――――. (1989). *The research act: A theoretical introduction to sociological methods* (3rd ed.). Englewood Cliffs, NJ: Prentice Hall.

――――. (1997). *Interpretive ethnography: Ethnographic practices for the 21st century.* Thousand Oaks, CA: Sage.

Denzin, N. K., & Lincoln, Y. S. (1994). Introduction: Entering the field of qualitative research. In N. K. Denzin & Y. S. Lincoln (eds.), *Handbook of qualitative research* (pp. 1–17). Thousand Oaks, CA: Sage.

Dickens, D. R., & Fontana, A. (eds.) (1994). *Postmodernism and social inquiry.* London: UCL Press.

Dingwall, M. (1997). Accounts, interviews and observations. In G. Miller & R. Dingwall (eds.), *Context and method in qualitative research* (pp. 51–65). London: Sage.

Flick, U. (1992). Triangulation revisited: Strategy of validation or alternative? *Journal for the Theory of Social Behaviour,* 22 (2), 175–197.

――――. (1998). *An introduction to qualitative research.* London: Sage.

Glaser, B. G., & Strauss, A. L. (1967). *The discovery of grounded theory: Strategies for qualitative research.* Chicago: Aldine.

Guba, E. G., & Lincoln, Y. S. (1989). *Fourth generation evaluation.* Newbury Park, CA: Sage.

———. (1994). Competing paradigms in qualitative research. In N. K. Denzin & Y. S. Lincoln (eds.), *Handbook of qualitative research* (pp. 105–17). Thousand Oaks, CA: Sage.

Hammersley, M. (1992). *What's wrong with ethnography: Methodological explorations.* London: Routledge.

———. (1995). *The politics of social research.* London: Sage.

Hammersley, M., & Atkinson, P. (1983). *Ethnography: Principles in practice.* London: Routledge.

Harding, S. (1986). *The science question in feminism.* Milton Keynes, UK: Open University Press.

Kirk, J., & Miller, M. (1986). *Reliability and validity in qualitative research.* Newbury Park, CA: Sage.

Lather, P. (1993). Fertile obsession: Validity after poststructuralism. *Sociological Quarterly,* 34 (4), 673–93.

LeCompte, M., & Goetz, J. (1982). Problems of reliability and validity in ethnographic research. *Review of Educational Research,* 52 (1), 31–60.

Lincoln, Y. S., & Guba, E. (1985). *Naturalistic inquiry.* Beverly Hills, CA: Sage.

Popper, K. R. (1963). *Conjectures and refutations.* London: Routledge and Kegan Paul.

———. (1972). *Objective knowledge.* Oxford: Clarendon Press.

Seale, C. F. (1999). *The quality of qualitative research.* London: Sage.

Silverman, D. (1993). *Interpreting qualitative data: Methods for analyzing talk, text and interaction.* London: Sage.

Swanborn, P. G. (1996). A common base for quality control criteria in quantitative and qualitative research. *Quality and Quantity,* 30, 19–35.

Webb, E. J., Campbell, D. T., Schwartz, R. D., & Sechrest, L. (1966). *Unobtrusive measures: Non-reactive research in the social sciences.* Chicago: Rand McNally.

Williams, M., & May, T. (1996). *Introduction to the philosophy of social research.* London: UCL Press.

9

Issues of Validity in Openly Ideological Research: Between a Rock and a Soft Place

Patti Lather

In this paper, I attempt to reconceptualize validity within the context of openly ideological research.[1] The usefulness of this reconceptualization is tested by applying it to examples from three explicitly value-based research programs: feminist research, neo-Marxist critical ethnography, and Freirian "empowering" research.[2] Finally, validity issues within research committed to a more equitable social order are discussed.

THE CONTEXT FROM WHICH I SPEAK

The attempt to produce value-neutral social science is increasingly being abandoned as at best unrealizable, and at worst self-deceptive, and is being replaced by social sciences based on explicit ideologies.

—*Mary Hesse (1980)*

To say that positivism remains the orthodox approach to doing empirical research in the human sciences is not to deny that we are in a postpositivist era.[3] Thomas Kuhn wrote that "rather than a single group conversion, what occurs

Reprinted from *Interchange* 17, no. 4 (winter 1986): 63–84.

[with a paradigm shift] is an increasing shift in the distribution of professional allegiances" as practitioners of the new paradigm "improve it, explore its possibilities, and show what it would be like to belong to the community guided by it" (1962, pp. 157–58).

The foundation of postpositivism is the cumulative, trenchant, and increasingly definitive critique of the inadequacies of positivist assumptions in the face of the complexities of human experience (Oppenheimer, 1956; Kaplan, 1964; Cronbach, 1975; Bernstein, 1976; Mishler, 1979; Giroux, 1981; Guba & Lincoln, 1981; Feinberg, 1983; Lincoln & Guba, 1985). As the orthodox paradigm for inquiry in the human sciences proves obsolete, new visions are required (Rose, 1979; Schwartz & Ogilvy, 1979; Hesse, 1980; Reason & Rowan, 1981). The result is a rich ferment in contemporary discourse regarding empirical research in the human sciences—a discourse spanning epistemological, theoretical, and to a much lesser degree, methodological issues.[4]

This paper is rooted in that rich ferment and has two basic premises. The first is that "since interest-free knowledge is logically impossible, we should feel free to substitute explicit interests for implicit ones" (Reinharz, 1985, p. 17). As the phrase "openly ideological research" implies, I take issue with the claims of positivism regarding objectivity and neutrality. Feminist research, neo-Marxist critical ethnography, and Freirian "empowering" research all stand in opposition to prevailing scientific norms through their "transformative agendas" and their concern with research as praxis (Rose, 1979). Each argues that scientific "neutrality" and "objectivity" serve to mystify the inherently ideological nature of research in the human sciences and to legitimate privilege based on class, race, and gender.

Within this frame of reference, research which is openly valued based is neither more nor less ideological than is mainstream positivist research. Rather, those committed to the development of research approaches that challenge the status quo and contribute to a more egalitarian social order have made an "epistemological break" from the positivist insistence upon researcher neutrality and objectivity (Hesse, 1980, p. 196).

The second premise in this paper is that for those exploring the possibilities of a postpositivist paradigm, the central challenge is to formulate approaches to empirical research which advance emancipatory theory-building through the development of interactive and action-inspiring research designs. There is a pioneering dimension to this task. Since the formation of the

Frankfurt School, critical theorists have been calling for such research while spinning obtuse webs of abstract "grand theory" (Mills, 1959; Kellner, 1975, p. 149; Stanley & Wise, 1983, p. 100).

Fifty years ago, the Italian neo-Marxist Antonio Gramsci urged intellectuals to adhere to a "praxis of the present" by aiding developing progressive groups in their effort to become increasingly conscious of their own actions and situations in the world (Salamini, 1981, p. 73). What are the implications of this advice from Gramsci for those seeking empirical approaches which can change, rather than merely describe, the world? The task of this paper is to explore the central questions in the effort to formulate an approach to empirical research which both advances emancipatory theory-building and empowers the researched.

Of the three openly value-based research programs discussed in this paper, neo-Marxist critical ethnography (Foley, 1979; Ogbu, 1981; Masseman, 1982) is the most advanced in terms of developing empirical approaches for the building of emancipatory social theory. All empirical work within this research program attempts to problematize what goes on in schools in terms of the reproduction of social inequality and the potential for social transformation. Such theoretical emphasis, however, brings to the fore the danger of conceptual overdeterminism: circular reinforcement of theory by experience conditioned by theory.

The recent empirical emphasis in neo-Marxism has been primarily interested in the creation of an empirically informed Marxism to meet the criticisms of those such as Bottomore (1978) and E. P. Thompson (178) who argue that too much of neo-Marxist social theory is "an immaculate conception which requires no gross empirical impregnation" (Thompson, 1978, p. 13; see also, Kellner, 1975, p. 149; Wright, 1978, p. 10; Krueger, 1981, p. 59; Comstock, 1982, p. 371). Theoretically guided empirical work exploring the mirror-image relationship between schools and the needs of corporate capitalism was the first to be produced (Bowles & Gintis, 1976; Apple, 1979b). More recently, given the extensive critique of an over-socialized conception of human nature as empirically inaccurate and politically suicidal (Apple, 1979a, 1980–81; Wrong, 1961; Giroux, 1981, 1983; Willis, 1977), empirical studies of human resistance to hegemonic forces are burgeoning (see, for example, Willis, 1977; McRobbie 1978; Everhart, 1983; Miller, 1983; Anyon, 1983).

Such research is a beginning, but the lack of clear strategies for linking theory and research is pervasive. Although some attention is beginning to be focused on

the need for an approach to research which advances egalitarian transformation (Apple, 1982; Fay, 1977; Comstock, 1982), the methodological implications of critical theory are relatively unexplored (Bredo & Feinberg, 1982,
p. 281). There is also a lack of self-reflexivity in the empirical work that exists
within critical inquiry. Sabia and Wallis point out that, too often, critical self-
awareness comes to mean "a negative attitude toward competing approaches
instead of its own self-critical perspective" (1983, p. 26).

Research within a postpositivist context mandates a self-corrective element to
prevent phenomena from being forced into preconceived interpretive schemes.
Postpositivism has cleared methodology of prescribed rules and boundaries and
has created a constructive turmoil as a result of successful challenges by philosophers of science during the past several decades (Polkinghorne, 1983, pp. 4–5).
Because we are not able to assume anything, we must take a self-critical stance regarding the assumptions we incorporate into our empirical approaches. No
longer does following the correct method guarantee "true" results: "Method does
not give truth; it corrects guesses" (Polkinghorne, 1983, p. 249). If critical theory
is to change the way social science is conceived of and practiced, it must become
genuinely reflexive (Moon, 1983, p. 30).

While the development of empowering approaches to empirical research
is at the heart of Freirian research and, increasingly, of feminist research,
they, too, by and large suffer from a lack of self-reflexivity. My central argument is that new paradigm researchers must begin to be more systematic
about establishing the trustworthiness of data. Reducing the ambiguity of
what we do does not mean we have to deny the essential indeterminacy
of human experience, "the irreducible disparity between the being of the
world and the knowledge we might have of it" (White, 1973). But if we want
illuminating and resonant theory grounded in trustworthy data, we must
formulate self-corrective techniques that will check the credibility of our
data and minimize the distorting effect of personal bias upon the logic of
evidence (Kamarovsky, 1981).

I offer the following reconceptualization of validity in the hope that it will
aid those of us who work within openly ideological research programs to focus more of our energies on how best to establish data credibility. Our task is
to create a body of research exemplars that will stand as testimony to the vigor
that comes, not from positivist retrenchment, but from viewing the move into
the postpositivist era with a sense of possibility.

BETWEEN A ROCK AND A SOFT PLACE

Relevance without rigor is no better than rigor without relevance.

—*Egon Guba (1981)*

To recast a familiar metaphor, the "rock" is the unquestionable need for trustworthiness in data generated by alternative paradigms (Guba, 1981) and the "soft place" is the positivist claim to neutrality and objectivity (Campbell, 1981).[5] Within newly emerging patterns of inquiry, approaches to validity must reach beyond the obfuscating claims of objectivity used by positivism to skirt the role played by researcher values in the human sciences.

Specific techniques of validity are tied to paradigmatic assumptions (Guba & Lincoln, 1981; Morgan, 1983). Positivists formulate tidy, quantifiable procedures based on "the first positivist assumption" that natural science methods are appropriate for the study of human beings (Westkott, 1977). The classic psychometric approach to establishing data trustworthiness focuses on the measurable. In spite of "validity coefficients" and "multitrait-multimethod matrices," however, validity remains elusive. Basic construct validity, so central to theory construction (Cronbach & Meehl, 1955), continues to defy quantification. Error-of-estimate formulae and multiple-regression equations are substituted for the much slipperier process of searching out and establishing independent, external validity criteria.

Within conventional, positivist research, the quantifiable concepts of discriminant and concurrent validity rise to the fore; factor analysis carries the weight of construct validity; and face validity, so inherently impressionistic, is defined as rapport and public relations and relegated to a distinctly second-class concern (Kidder, 1982). Statistical manipulations replace the logical grounding of constructs. Reliability, for example, held to be necessary but not sufficient in establishing validity, often stands alone in experimental and quasi-experimental research—mute testimony to the lack of attention paid to construct validity. At best, this leads to consistent subjectivity. At worst, it results in the reification of constructs that are the projections of social biases, masculinity-femininity being but one prime example (Constantinople, 1973; Lewin, 1984).

With the present epistemological and methodological ferment in the human sciences, however, paradigmatic uncertainty is leading to the reconceptualization of validity. Efforts to set subjective, tacit knowledge apart from the "context of verification" are seen as "naïve empiricism." The process of inquiry is increasingly viewed as a tapestry in which tacit knowledge is the "warp" and propositional knowledge the "woof" (Heron, 1981, p. 32). With no ready-made formulae to guarantee valid social knowledge, "we must operate simultaneously at epistemological, theoretical and empirical levels with self-awareness" (Sharp & Green, 1975, p. 234). What we are faced with is a lack of workable procedures or specific rules for analyzing and verifying data (Huberman & Miles, 1983, p. 282). Our best shot at present is to construct research designs that push us toward becoming vigorously self-aware.

Going beyond predisposition in our empirical efforts requires techniques that will give confidence in the trustworthiness of data. Reason (1981) wants "objectively subjective" inquiry (p. xiii). Guba and Lincoln (1981) argue, more systematically, for analogues to the major criteria of rigor within the orthodox paradigm. Guba (181) states that the least we should expect in establishing trustworthy data in new paradigm research is triangulation, reflexivity, and member checks. Reason and Rowan (1981) advise borrowing concepts of validity from traditional research but refining and expanding them in ways appropriate to "an interactive, dialogic logic" (p. 240). Building on all of this, what follows is a reconceptualization of validity appropriate for research openly committed to a more just social order.

RECONCEPTUALIZING VALIDITY

The job of validation is not to support an interpretation, but to find out what might be wrong with it. A proposition deserves some degree of trust only when it has survived serious attempts to falsify it.

—*Lee Cronbach (1980)*

Once we recognize that just as there is no neutral education there is no neutral research, we no longer need apologize for unabashedly ideological research and its open commitment to using research to criticize and change the status quo. The development of data credibility checks to protect our research and theory construction from our enthusiasms, however, is essential in our efforts to create a self-reflexive human science. To guard against researcher biases distorting the logic of evidence within openly ideological research, the following guidelines are offered.

Triangulation, expanded beyond the psychometric definition of multiple measures to include multiple *data sources, methods,* and *theoretical schemes,* is critical in establishing data trustworthiness. It is essential that the research design seek counterpatterns as well as convergences if data are to be credible.

Construct validity must be dealt with in ways that recognize its roots in theory construction (Cronbach & Meehl, 1955). Emancipatory social theory require a ceaseless confrontation with the experiences of people in their daily lives in order to stymie the tendency to theoretical imposition which is inherent in theoretically guided empirical work. *Asystematized reflexivity,* which gives some indication of how a priori theory has been changed by the logic of the data, becomes essential in establishing construct validity in ways that will contribute to the growth of illuminating and change-enhancing social theory.

Face validity needs to be seen as much more integral to the process of establishing data credibility. Guba and Lincoln (1981) refer to "member checks" which they consider to be "the backbone of satisfying the truth-value criterion" (p. 110). Reason and Rowan (1981) argue that such member checks (recycling analysis back through at least a subsample of respondents) need to become a standard part of emancipatory research designs: "Good research at the non-alienating end of the spectrum . . . goes back to the subject with the tentative results, and refines them in the light of the subjects' reactions" (p. 248).

Catalytic validity (Reason & Rowan, 1981, p. 240; Brown & Tandom, 1978) refers to the degree to which the research process re-orients, focuses, and energizes participants in what Freire (1973) terms "conscientization," knowing reality in order to better transform it. Of the guidelines proposed here, this is by far the most unorthodox as it flies directly in the face of the essential positivist tenet of researcher neutrality. My argument is premised not only on a recognition of the reality-altering impact of the research process itself, but also on the need to consciously channel this impact so that respondents gain self-understanding and, ideally, self-determination through research participation.

My concern is that efforts to produce social knowledge that is helpful in the struggle for a more equitable world pursue rigor as well as relevance. Otherwise, just as "pointless precision" (Kaplan, 1964) has proven to be the bane of the conventional paradigm, the rampant subjectivity inherent in the more phenomenologically based paradigms will prove to be the nemesis of new paradigm research.

Feminist Research

The overt ideological goal of feminist research is to correct both the *invisibility* and the *distortion* of female experience in ways relevant to ending women's unequal social position. This entails the substantive task of making gender a fundamental category for our understanding of the social order, "to see the world from women's place in it" (Callaway, 1981, p. 460). The methodological task becomes that of generating and refining interactive, contextualized methods which search for pattern and meaning rather than for prediction and control (Reinharz, 1983). While the first wave of feminist research operated largely within the conventional paradigm (Westkott, 1979), the second wave is more self-consciously methodologically innovative (Eichler, 1980; Reinharz, 1983; Stanley & Wise, 1983; Bowles & Duelli-Klein, 1983).

A few examples will illustrate how such an unabashedly ideological perspective works to frame research approaches and questions. Mies (1984) field-tested seven methodological guidelines for doing feminist research in an action-research project in Cologne, Germany, designed to respond to violence against women in the family. Highly visible street action drew people who were then interviewed regarding their views on wife beating. The resulting publicity led to the creation of Women's House to aid victims of domestic abuse. Principles of action and egalitarian participation, developed through life histories, guided consciousness-raising regarding the sociological and historical roots of male violence in the home. The purpose was to empower the oppressed to come to understand and change their own oppressive realities. Oakley (1981) studied the effects of motherhood on women's lives over an extended period of time through a series of interviews that focused on "interactive self-disclosure," a collaborative dialogue seeking for greater clarity. Carol Gilligan's work on female moral development (1977, 1982) and the highly contradictory body of work on female achievement motivation (Horner, 1969; Sassen, 1980) serve to counter interpretations that view women as deviants from male-established norms. Such work asks, "How do male-based constructs need to be reformulated from the vantage point of female experience?"[6]

Gilligan's work clarifies the distortion of Kolhberg's androcentric conception of moral development which values autonomy at the expense of interrelatedness. Her research suggests that the female conception of a moral problem may come from conflicting responsibilities rather than from competing rights and that resolution requires contextual thinking rather than formal abstraction. For women, morality seems defined in terms of interpersonal responsibilities rather than individualistic rights. Gilligan's findings challenge the assumed centrality of male experience in theories of development and expose the all-male samples underlying purportedly "universal theories." Hence, her work is an oft-cited exemplar in feminist research.

Gray (1982) writes that Gilligan's initial concern was the shakiness of construct validity based on hypothetical rather than real-life moral dilemmas. During the Viet Nam War, she intended to interview young men making draft-resistance choices, and she got an all-female sample quite by accident when the war ended (p. 52). Abortion had recently been legalized, and Gilligan soon recognized the moral dilemma of whether to carry a child to full term as a real-life situation with great potential for expanding the methodology of moral development research beyond hypothetical situations.

Twenty-nine women, diverse in age, race, and social class, were referred by abortion and pregnancy counseling services and interviewed. Three of Kolhberg's standardized hypothetical moral dilemmas were administered during the second half of the interview. By allowing categories to arise out of the language of respondents, Gilligan discovered a central tension in women's lives between selfishness and responsibility to self as well as others. In a culture that on the one hand equates feminine goodness with self-sacrifice and on the other hand equates adulthood with separation, individuation, and detachment, women were caught in a classic "double bind."

By structuring the research to focus first on the contextual particularity of a pressing real-life moral dilemma, Gilligan discovered that respondents refused to formulate an ethics abstracted from contextual complications. Their response to the hypothetical dilemmas was, "The wrong questions are being asked," and they insisted on information regarding the lives of the characters. This led Gilligan to surmise that decontextualized hypothetical dilemmas deny the central female experience of contextualized interrelationship and, hence, create Kolhberg's "objective principles of justice" *as a research artifact.* This is all very interesting as a critique of Kohlberg, but what corrective mechanisms did Gilligan use so that her interview data become scientific research rather than impressionistic journalism?

Triangulation of methods is apparent in the inclusion of both interview data and Kolhberg's standardized hypothetical moral dilemmas, but convergence seems to be sought rather than disconfirmation. Criteria for including/excluding data are not given, and there is no indication of a conscious search for counter-patterns. The triangulation of different data *sources* is not strong; especially at risk is the small (n = 29) all-female characterisitcs of the sample. How can one argue for gender-specific patterns based on a single-sex sample and a gender-specific situation? The triangulation of different *theories* is strong. Gilligan worked with Kohlberg for several years. Her work is, in essence, a critique and revision of his theory-building. The theoretical vitality of what she is doing comes largely out of her strong grounding in Kolhberg's notably different theoretical constructs: the universal, invariant sequence claims, the hierarchical nature of his theory with its relegation of relational concerns to a second-class status, and the assumption that valid data can be evoked on the basis of standardized, hypothetical moral dilemmas.

Construct validity is premised on the convergence of Gilligan's review of psychological and literary sources with the research data and the comparison of Kolhberg's categories with categories arising out of the language of respondents. Some degree of self-reflexivity can be ascertained from the development of theoretical insights, but this is by no means systematized.

Catalytic validity undergoes an interesting development. As respondents began to examine their own thinking, a pattern developed whereby they moved from a conventional feminine construction of the moral problem (equating feminine goodness with self-sacrifice) to a recognition of the conflict between the dependence and self-sacrifice of femininity and the choice and existential responsibility of adulthood. Hence, the research process provided an opportunity for respondents to grow through thoughtful assessment of their experiences. This seems to be an unexpected and relatively unnoted aspect of the research, however, and was in no way consciously invited through the research design. Also, no effort is made to triangulate this growth in self-understanding. This leaves the claims of growth wide open to both the limitations of self-reporting and the projection of the researcher's aspirations for respondents onto the data analysis.

Face validity is perhaps the most seriously lacking. The research design called for two interviews, approximately one year apart. Neither categories nor conclusions were recycled back through respondents. This would have been relatively easy, and the payoff in both construct and catalytic validity would likely have been worth the effort.

The intellectual power of Gilligan's work is such that concern about establishing the trustworthiness of here data is subsumed by the provocativenss of her theorizing. But issues of data trustworthiness concern her—one of her Ph.D. students worked on a coding system that allows reliable data aggregation across interviews in a sample selected to *refute* a sex differences hypothesis; another worked on self-constructed moral dilemmas that focus on the interaction between justice and caring in an effort to deepen construct validity; Gilligan moved into open-interviewing with adolescent females around self-identity and self-defined moral dilemmas. Additionally, Gilligan and her students work as a team to stress reflexivity.[7] As she and her students move from exploratory, hypothesis-generating work to theory construction and validation within a long-term, ongoing research program, validity issues grow increasingly important. That Gilligan is fully cognizant of this speaks hopefully for the continuing importance of her work.

Neo-Marxist Critical Ethnography

The overt ideological goal of neo-Marxist critical ethnography is to expose the contradictions and delusions of liberal democratic education in order to create less exploitative social and economic relations (Willis, 1977; Apple, 1980–81; Reynolds, 1980–81). The substantive task is the portrayal of the role of schooling in the reproduction of inequality in all of its content and specificity, its contradictions and complexities. The methodological task is the ethnographic revelation of participants' views of reality, where these views come from, and the social consequences of such views, all situated within a context of theory-building. The overriding goal, then, is to produce "an adequate theory of schooling in the context of cultural imperatives" (Ogbu, 1981, p. 9). The theory is to make clear "the order of structural transformation necessary to honor commitments to human rights and justice" (Pinar, 1981, p. 439).

Within this theoretically guided search for data, which is the dominant characteristic of critical ethnography, reality is held to be something more than negotiated accounts. Critical ethnographers hold that by limiting analysis to the actors' perceptions of their situations, non-Marxist ethnographies and phenomenological research reify interpretive procedures and reduce research to a collection of functionalist, subjective accounts that obscure the workings of false consciousness and ideological mystification (Foley, 1979). They argue that Marxism's profound skepticism of both appearance and common sense produces a more valid analysis than does phenomenological research. Such skepticism, however, is tempered by an opposition to reductive forms of determinism as the central theoretical inadequacy of orthodox Marxism: the economistic reduction of humanity to pawns in the great chessgame of capitalism (Apple, 1982; Giroux, 1981; Willis, 1977). Willis writes:

> Capital requires it, therefore schools do it! Humans become dummies, dupes, zombies.... This will not do theoretically. It will certainly not do politically. Pessimism reigns supreme in this, the most spectacular of secular relations of predeterminism. (1977, p. 205)

The following examples illustrate how this research program frames its questions. Do progressive, liberal primary schools focus more on liberation than on social control (Sharp & Green, 1975; Apple, 1979b)? How do young working-class males deal with their entrapment in the lower rungs of the hierarchical work world (Willis, 1977)? How do working-class females deal with the school's efforts to prepare them for their primary roles as wife, mother, and reserve labor force (McRobbie, 1978)? Where do teachers' "commonsense" views of student differences come from and how do these views affect kids' life chances (Carlson, 1980)? How do students react to curricular offerings sanitized of any sense of struggle and oppression (McNeil, 1981)?

Paul Wills's *Learning to Labor: How Working Class Kids Get Working Class Jobs* (1977) is the standard work in the critical ethnography of schooling (Apple, 1979a). A three-year participant observation study of 12 "disaffected" male teenagers in a working-class British industrial area, it focuses on the transition from school to work in order to shed light on the willing acceptance of restricted work opportunities on the part of working-class youth. Using informal interviewing, regular and recorded group discussion, diaries, and participant observation in and out of school, Willis collected data throughout "the lads'" last two years of schooling and into the first six months of work. Parents, teachers, and work supervisors were included in the interviews. Participant observation included attending classes as a student and working alongside the lads at their jobs. The research design included comparative case studies selected to be similar in sex, patterns of friendship grouping, and likelihood of leaving school at age 16.

Theory guided the search for oppositional, counter-school group members as the main research sample used to substantiate the concept of working-class resistance to official authority. Theory guided the search for contradictions: that between teachers' expressed goal of enabling working-class students to transcend their class-limited lives versus teachers' efforts to stymie the "self-disqualification" of disaffected students from the meritocratic merry-go-round (p. 148); that between the lads' "felt sense of cultural election" as they moved into the adult world of work and money versus the too-late recognition of the determinants that settled a major life decision to their disadvantage (p. 107). Theory guided the "plunge beneath the surface of ethnography in[to] a more interpretive mode" (p. 119) to transcend the limitations of the "ethnography of visible forms" (p. 121) which is as likely to conceal as reveal cultural dynamics. Theory guided the view of humans as active appropriators who reproduce existing structures of inequality only through struggle, contestation, and partial penetration: "Just because there are what we call structural and economic determinants, it does not mean that people will unproblematically obey them" (p. 171). Theory guided the interpretation that while the cultural freedoms of capitalism are essentially used for self-damnation, permanent struggle is the deeper reality.

Within research so theoretically top-heavy, what self-corrective mechanisms did Willis use?

Triangulation of methods is strong, especially the combination of interviewing and participant observation. The triangulation of different data sources is also quite strong. The comparative case studies are built into the research design, and the search for counter-patterns as well as convergences is documented. The wide array of subjects observed and interviewed over the course of this extended three-year study is notable. The triangulation of different theories is present in that Willis's theoretical advances are premised on reformulations of both the liberal theory of schooling with its espousal of equal opportunity through meritocracy and the overdeterminism of orthodox Marxism.

Construct validity is strengthened by collecting data at work and at home as well as at school. Especially powerful in establishing the meaninglessness of working-class jobs is the interview data with fathers and shopfloor supervisors. But there is no systematic self-reflexivity. Given the centrality of theory, it seems of paramount importance to document how researcher perspectives were altered by the logic of the data. With no account of this, one is left viewing the role of theory as nondialectical, unidirectional, an a priori imposition that subsumes counter-patterns.

Catalytic validity comes through in the following interview transcript:

> Something should have been done with us, I mean there was so much talent there that it was all fuckin' wasted. . . . We've just been thrust into society too soon, we've been brought up to be too selfish . . . we couldn't care less, you see on the tele so many people fuckin' affluent, you just want to try and do that, make it, get money, you don't care about others, the working class. (pp. 195–98)

But his was in no way an intended aspect of the research and the lad's continued sense of cultural election in the face of meaningless work comes through clearly, indicating that the catalytic validity was minimal.

Face validity was consciously built into the research design, but only at the end. Willis brought the lads to the university at the conclusion of the research to discuss how they saw his role as researcher and what the "results" of the research meant to them. Marxism has long been infamous for its alienating jargon. The methodological appendix makes clear that the lads had no inkling of what Willis was getting at in his text:

> "The bits about us were simple enough. . . . It's the bits in between. . . . Well, I started to read it . . . then I just packed it in." (p. 195)

Overall, this is a stellar exemplar of theoretically guided ethnography. The extended time spent in the field using a wide variety of methods and the invitation of disconfirmation through the use of comparative case studies are its methodological strengths. Notable weaknesses are twofold. One is the lack of systematic self-reflexivity; the other is the lack of attention to catalytic validity. Regarding the latter, while Willis acknowledges the general responsibility of the researcher to the researched, he views it in terms of enlightening those with the cultural authority to redirect policy rather than helping respondents gain understanding of and control over their own lives: "The progressive use and mobilization of the research on a wider political and pedagogic place must be the main form of return and repayment [to the researched]" (p. 221). There is a failure to use the research process itself to empower the researched.

Freirian "Empowering" Research

The last of the counter-research programs rooted in the search for a science "derived from the radical needs of the oppressed" (Rose, 1979, p. 280) is modeled after Paulo Freire's *Pedagogy of the Oppressed* (1973). The openly ideological goal is to blur the distinctions between research, learning, and action by providing conditions under which participants' self-determination is enhanced in the struggle toward social justice (Hall, 1975, p. 30; Heron, 1981, p. 35). The substantive task is to delineate collective identification of and solutions to local problems in ways that link this process to larger structural issues (Hall, 1981). The methodological task is to proceed in a reciprocal, dialogic manner, empowering subjects by turning them into co-researchers. Ideally, such research involves participants in the planning, execution, and dissemination of social research (Rowan, 1981, p. 97).

Historically, this research program is a descendent of Lewin's action research. But Lewin's goal was self-management within a society assumed to operate from a consensual value base (Sanford, 1981, p. 178), whereas Freirian research focuses on promoting liberation and growth within a society assumed to be class divided and, hence, inequitable. Two concepts characterize this body of research.

The first is the effort to democratize knowledge and power through the research process (Hall, 1981). Freire's concept of cultural imposition becomes a critique of subjects. Such a "cult of expertise" is part of the unequal relationships inherent in an oppressive social order. Mainstream researchers "live patronizingly in a delusion of relevance" (Maruyama, 1974). The researcher's role as a privileged possessor of expert knowledge must be reconceptualized as that of a catalyst who works with local participants to understand and solve local problems. The researched become as important as the researcher in formulating the problem, discussing solutions, and interpreting findings (Hall, 1975).

The second concept characterizing Freirian research is designed to have "an arousal effect," to reorient participants' perceptions of issues in ways that influence subsequent attitudes and behaviors (Brown & Tandon, 1978). The "vivification" of "ideas that open beyond themselves" (Torbert, 1981, p. 148) can energize the desire to do things differently *provided the issues are of central importance of the participants.* Self-determination, hence, require both the demystification of ideologies that distort dominant and oppressive social relationships and the empowerment of the oppressed so that they can take charge of improving their own situations.

Much of the empirical work within this research program is conducted with adult populations in Third World countries. Literacy work is where Freire began to formulate his pedagogical ideas. Others have used local participant-conducted surveys to guide development priorities in Africa (Swantz, 1975); to train inmates to study violence (Maruyama, 1969); to assist Norwegian bank employees to assess the effects of the installation of computer terminals (Elden, 1979); and to help impoverished farmers in India improve local agricultural practices (Tandon, 1981).

While there are no oft-cited exemplars in this research program, Swantz's work (1981) is typical. Working through the University of Norway and the government of Tanzania, Swantz's team conducted a four-year participatory research project to study the process of change in rural villages. Researchers lived in the village and took part in daily activities in order to become familiar with the context of acute problems. The researchers' role was to probe and stimulate the villagers' formulation and to search for solutions to their perceived problems. Theory was used dialectically to problematize the contradictions underlying daily difficulties so that policies and strategies could be formulated that would create long-term solutions (p. 286).

As well as day-to-day informal participant observation, various seminars involving all adult villagers were taped and reports were distributed to all participants (although no mention was made of how literacy rates affected hits); villagers were involved in the design of surveys; task groups worked on such projects as collecting local music and storytelling; villagers helped design and conduct training programs for agricultural, veterinary, and health care officers. All phases of the research were characterized by a continuing mutual feedback process.

The self-corrective mechanisms were:

Triangulation of methods is strong: extensive time in the field included participant observation, grounded surveys, and interviews. *Data sources* were extremely varied at both the local and national level. Theory triangulation is especially strong. In arriving at a sense of development that reflected villager needs and aspirations, theoretical constructs were triangulated from four sources: (1) concrete case material and the incorporation of the villagers' own thinking on issues; (2) the need for guidelines for national development policies; (3) the commitment to derive theory in ways that would directly benefit the villagers' own micro-level development process; and (4) a priori, loosely neo-Marxist theoretical constructs such a sexism and the contradictions inherent in social stratification. What is noteworthy in this process is how concrete situations influenced theory-building and proceeded in a manner that fostered the participants' awareness of their own resources and their right to influence decisions concerning themselves.

Construct validity was grounded in the dialectic between a priori theory, the villagers' own ways of thinking, and the researchers' long-term involvement in the productive work of the village.

Catalytic validity was consciously built into the research design and can be detected in the activism of pastoral women over the closure of the research, particularly in their growing insistence that they be given literacy skills (p. 286), and the changed behavior of the pastoralists as a group reflected in their insistence on their right to be part of local decision-making (p. 291).

Face validity permeated the research process in both systematic and informal ways. Analytical categories and emerging conclusions were continually recycled back through the respondents. As this was a report of research in progress, it remains to be seen what form the final report will take and whether there will be an effort to assess validity through participant reaction to the results of the research.

A reading of Swantz's earlier work (1975) recommends caution in celebrating the empowering dimensions of participatory research. The gap between intent and practice is noted, but subtle coercion and external imposition permeate her efforts to get villagers to perform a self-study of local resources. Her later work seems more authentically participatory, and one can surmise that important lessons were learned regarding the involvement of participants a co-researchers.

Given this caveat, the strengths of Swantz's research regarding validity are the continuous feedback system and the dialectical development of theory which strengthen construct validity and the changed behavior of villagers which bespeaks the high quality of the study's face and catalytic validity. Its central weakness is the lack of systematized self-reflexivity, but, given the dialectical approach to theory construction, such a lack is by no means as critical in this research program as it is in the theory-laden empirical work of critical ethnography. Additionally, this was a team effort so one can assume a degree of reflexivity, although Reason and Rowan warn against "consensus collusion" (1981, p. 244).

BEYOND PREDISPOSITION

The structures and procedures of [emancipatory] research are open to many questions and uncertainties; but it seems that social scientists concerned with the analysis of the societally shaped consciousness and subjectivity of various groups should engage in it experimentally, that is, with an open mind. Further exploration of the theoretical and methodological possibilities . . . should be . . . on the agenda.

—*Marlis Krueger (1981)*

These case studies of the treatment of validity in openly ideological research were chosen both for their typicality and in the case of Gilligan and Willis for their exemplary status. By looking at how the best examples of a research program deal with establishing data credibility, potential strengths and troublesome weaknesses become most evident. While by no means exhaustive, the following issues seem of pressing importance for openly ideological researchers.

Is the Method the Message?

The effort to create an emancipatory social science must confront the need for methods that are at least nonalienating, at best empowering. The classic quandry of ends over means can be seen most starkly in comparing the role of the researcher in Freirian and neo-Marxist research. The former works intentionally at thwarting the cult of expertise that has fostered what Reinharz terms the "rape model" of research: career advancement of social scientists built on alienating and exploitative methods (1979, p. 95). Within Freirian research, the inquiry process itself is committed to enhancing the personal power of participants. The neo-Marxist researcher, in contrast, is seen as "interpreter of the world," exposer of false consciousness (Reynolds, 1980–81, p. 87).

This nondialectical perception of the role of the researcher confounds the intent to demystify the world for the dispossessed. Respondents become objects, targets of research, rather than subjects who have been empowered to understand and change their situations. While there is at last some needed revision of the tendency to dismiss resistance to Marxist interpretations as "false consciousness" (Apple, 1980–81, p. 81; Fay, 1977), empirical and theoretical insights continue to be aimed at other intellectuals. Building a more just social order becomes a matter of "getting more people to talk the way they do" (Browning, 1983, p. 55). Only those with advanced education have a shot at piercing through the theory and the jargon and arriving at a greater understanding of social forces.

Neo-Marxist empirical inquiry is too often characterized by an attitude captured in the words of one research team: "We would not expect the teachers interviewed to either agree with or necessarily understand the inferences which were made from their responses" (Bullough, Goldstein & Holt, 1982, p. 133). Given the all-male research team and the largely female teacher subjects, one could make much of the gender politics involved in such a statement. What are at issue here, however, are the implications of such a stance for the purposes of emancipatory theory-building.[8] And what becomes apparent is that the neo-Marxist agenda for equalizing social power is stymied by tendencies to elitism and alienation engendered by its own research methods.

In contrast, participatory research and, increasingly, feminist research stress the use of the research process to empower participants through emphasis on both face and catalytic validity. Yet neo-Marxist theory makes it clear that establishing validity in the eyes of respondents is not enough to make data credible. Neo-Marxist assumptions regarding false consciousness and ideological mystification argue cogently that phenomenological, a structural, ahistorical perspectives stymie the development of emancipatory social theory. Given the reciprocally confirming nature of hegemony, analysis should not be limited to the actors' perceptions of their situation. Our common-sense ways of looking at the world are permeated with meanings that sustain our powerlessness. There are, hence, limits on the degree to which "member checks" (Guba & Lincoln, 1981) can help establish data validity. Perhaps, like reliability within positivism, building catalytic and face validity into our research designs is a necessary but not sufficient technique for establishing data credibility.

Must We Choose between Conceptual Vigor and Methodological Rigor?

I am not the first to note that leftists are better at criticizing existent research than at creating an empirically informed Marxism (Karabel & Halsey, 1977, p. 55; Dickens, 1983, p. 155). But if the ultimate goal of our work is transformative social praxis, theory is needed which explains lived experience. Such theory can only evolve through empirical grounding. Because of the lack of self-reflexivity in neo-Marxist empirical work, there is no way of assessing the degree to which this happens. On the contrary, one is left with the impression that the research conducted provides empirical specificities for more general, a priori theories.

Critical ethnography is an important perspective in the development of a human science that contributes to social change. But praxis is a two-way street produced in the interaction between theory and practice. While there may indeed be no theory-independent facts (Hesse, 1980, p. 172), moving beyond predisposition require systematizing procedures for minimizing and/or understanding the ways that the investigator's values enter into research. Empirical validation requires a critical stance regarding the inadequacies of our pet theories and an openness to counter-interpretations. In cautioning that conceptual validity precedes empirical accuracy, Michael Apple (1980–81) continues to not see the validity problems inherent in the largely undialectical role that theory plays in critical ethnography. Empirical evidence must begin to be viewed as a mediator for constant self- and theoretical interrogation if neo-Marxist theory is to prove any more useful in the struggle against privilege than has bourgeois liberalism.

Mitroff and Kilman (1978) argue that what makes theory provocative is how *interesting* it is, not how *true* it is. Truth becomes indeterminant at the theoretical level; theory exists precisely because of the need to take credible leaps into the unknown. But the issue is not theoretical vigor versus method-ological rigor. The vitality of postpositivist research programs necessitates the development of credibility checks that can be built into the design of openly ideological (and phenomenologically based) research. Both our theory and our empirical work will be the better for the increased attention to the trust-worthiness of our data.

I grant that few appropriate mechanisms exists. This is new territory. Though unassailable answers to questions of rigor are the illusion of naïve empiricists, making our data and analyses as public and as credible as possi-ble is essential. The present turmoil in the human sciences creates the freedom to construct new designs based on alternative tenets and epistemological commitments. As Polkinghorne notes:

> What is needed most is for practitioners to experiment with the new designs and to submit their attempts and results to examination by other participants in the debate. The new historians of science have made it clear that method-ological questions are decided in the practice of research by those committed to developing the best possible answers to their questions, not by armchair philosophers of research. (1983, p. xi)

The task is to get on with it.

What Minimal Standards Might We Begin to Move Toward?

What I have found over and over again in the methodological literature of openly value-based research is a fuzziness on the need for data credibility checks. Reason and Rowan argue for the researcher's self-actualization through engagement in personal and interpersonal development (1981, p. 246). Lacey (1977) and Rose (1979, p. 140) argue that an appeal to the reader's own experiences is at the base of perceptions of truth in research. Sharp and Green (1975, p. 228), Willis (1977), and Mies (1984) argue that the validity of emancipatory empirical work can be judged by its effects on social policy. What rises to the fore in this literature is that researchers recast the is-sue as the failure of mainstream research in its insistence upon neutrality and scientific objectivity. But to recognize the pervasiveness of ideology in the hu-man sciences and to acknowledge personal bias are not sufficient to foster a body of empirical work suitable for our theory-building. Haphazard consider-ations of the need for trustworthy data are not enough if openly ideological research is to be accepted as data rather than as metaphor by those who do not share its value premises.

Whether we can do research that appears valid from multiple points of view or whether Heron is correct that truth in research is a function of shared values (1981, p. 33) is presently a moot issue. Given the primitive state of validity issues within openly value-based research (Feinberg, 1983; Reason & Rowan, 1981; White, 1973; Dickens, 1983, p. 151; Moon, 1983, p. 171), we need to recognize that the "spectre of relativism" may be our inevitable companion as we reshape science and move away from its positivist incarnation (White, 1973, p. 170). We also need to recognize Lee Cronbach's point that "to call for value-free standards of validity is a contradiction in terms, a nostalgic longing for a world that never was" (1980, p. 105).

By arguing for a more systematic approach to triangulation and reflexivity, a new emphasis for face validity, and inclusion of the new concern of catalytic validity, I stand opposed to those who hold that empirical accountability is either impossible to achieve or able to be side-stepped in new paradigm research. At minimum, I argue that we must build the following into our research designs:

- triangulation of *methods, data sources,* and *theories*
- reflexive subjectivity (some documentation of how the researcher's assumptions have been affected by the logic of the data)
- face validity (established by recycling categories, emerging analysis, and conclusions back through at least a subsample of respondents)
- catalytic validity (some documentation that the research process has led to insight and, ideally, activism on the part of the respondents)

CONCLUSION

As the shakiness of validity within the positivist paradigm and the pervasiveness of ideology within the human sciences are increasingly acknowledged (Fay, 1975; Bernstein, 1976; Mishler, 1979; Nowotny & Rose, 1979; Hesse, 1980), we see that what is at first impression the "hard place" of validity coefficients and multirait-multimethod matrices is, in fact, a soft spot. The "rock" is not the unassailable validity of positivist research findings but rather the need to establish the trustworthiness of data which are "qualitative, fleeting, and, at times, frankly impressionist" (Reason, 1981, p. 185). For new paradigm researchers, the task becomes the confrontation of issues of empirical accountability in our methodological formulations, the need to offer grounds for accepting a researcher's description and analysis, and the search for novel, *workable* ways of gathering validity data.

Ignoring data credibility within openly value-based research programs will not improve the chances for the increased legitimacy of the knowledge they produce. Agreed-upon procedures are needed to make empirical decision-making public and, hence, subject to criticism. Most importantly, if we fail to develop these procedures, we will fail to protect our work from our own passions, and our theory-building will suffer.

Reason and Rowan's call for "a new rigor of softness" (1981, p. 490), a "validity of knowledge in process" (p. 250), an "objective subjectivity" (p. xiii) may be the best that we can do. But let us begin to move toward that.

NOTES

1. I use "ideology" in the expanded neo-Marxist sense of including the need to explore the social genesis, limitations, and transformative possibilities of points of view. This notion is opposed to orthodox Marxist usage which sees ideology as a distortion of reality, protective of existing power arrangements.

Apple's recent formulation of ideology reflects the revised neo-Marxist usage of the term based on Gramsci and Althusser. Gramsci theorizes that ideology comes in progressive as well as oppressive forms and Althusser distinguishes between practical and theoretical ideologies. The former posits ideology as the material and common-sense aspects of daily life rather than merely ideas. People *inhabit* ideologies which speak to both determinant and creative/autonomous qualities of culture (Apple, 1982, p. 112. See also Wexler, 1982; Giroux, 1983).

I am aware of the argument that, for analytic usefulness, the term must be bounded. Barrett (1980), for example, argues both against an "unacceptedly expansionist definition of ideology" (p. 253) and for a recognition that the concept is inadequately theorized in both Marxist and feminist theory (p. 84). While thoroughly agreeing with the latter, I would argue against the former if Marxism and feminism themselves are to be viewed as the social constructions that they inherently are. To do otherwise is to become dogmatic, thereby crippling the thrust toward a critical social theory.

2. While it is tempting to use the phrase "openly ideological research paradigms," I agree with Guba and Lincoln that *paradigm* should be reserved for "axiomatic

systems characterized essentially by their differing sets of assumptions about the phenomena into which they are designed to inquire" (1981). Neo-Marxism with its theory-generated search for data and its assumptions of a singular material reality of dominance and oppression and the historical inevitability of a more just social order (Ullrich calls this the "doctrine of eventual salvation" [1979, p. 132]) qualifies it as an inquiry paradigm. But Freirian research, although grounded in a dialectical, loose neo-Marxism, shares the assumptions of the naturalistic, interpretive paradigm (Lincoln & Guba, 1985). And feminist research operates out of both the conventional and naturalistic paradigms. Additionally, with the development of Marxist-feminist theory, there is a growing body of feminist empirical work that shares the assumptions of the inquiry paradigm of neo-Marxism (e.g., McRobbie, 1978; Sacks, 1984).

3. In an appendix to his *Methodology for the Human Sciences* (1983), Polkinghorne traces the history of the term "human science." He argues that "behavioral sciences" retain the spectre of behaviorism and the prohibition against consciousness as a part of scientific study. "Social science" carries connotations of natural science in its nomothetic or law-seeking mode of inquiry. "Human science," he argues, is more inclusive, using multiple systems of inquiry, "a science which approaches questions about the human realm with an openness to its special characteristics and a willingness to let the questions inform which methods are appropriate" (p. 289).

4. Exceptions to this lack of attention to the methodological implications of the postpositivist era are: Guba and Lincoln, 1981; Reason and Rowan, 1981; Comstock, 1982; Reinharz, 1983; Polkinghorne, 1983; Lincoln and Guba, 1985.

5. Brofenbrenner originally recast the metaphor in terms of rigor vs. relevance (quoted in Guba, 1980, p. 13).

6. An encouraging example of the impact of feminist criticism on more mainstream behavioral researchers is David McClellan's *Power: The Inner Experience* (Irving Press, 1975). Unlike his earlier work on achievement motivation, McClellan looked at both sexes and discovered that power works differently for men and women: "Power motivation apparently helps women develop into higher stages of maturity, just as it hinders men" (p. 96).

A far less encouraging example is Elizabeth Dodson Gray's discussion of Kolhberg's recent *The Philosophy of Moral Development* (Harper & Row, 1981), with its "Six Universal Stages." Gilligan's work is consigned to one paragraph and dismissed: "The gender implications of her work are never acknowledged, and the limitations they imply for the 'universal stages' are never even raised! . . . How long will male scholars in patriarchy . . . refuse to acknowledge the relativity of their own gender standing point? How long can they ignore the sociology of their own knowledge?" (Gray, 1982, p. 56).

7. Talk delivered by Carol Gilligan at the American Educational Researchers' Association Special Interest Group/Research on Women in Education, mid-year conference, Philadelphia, November, 1982.

8. I explore the methodological implications of critical theory, especially the need to create research designs that empower the researched, in Lather (1986).

REFERENCES

Anyon, J. (1983). Accommodation, resistance, and female gender. In S. Walker & L. Barton (eds.), *Gender and education*. Sussex, England: Falmer Press.

Apple, M. (1979a). What correspondence theories of the hidden curriculum miss. *Review of Education*, 5(2), 101–12.

———. (1979b). *Ideology and curriculum*. London: Routledge & Kegan Paul.

———. (1980–81). The other side of the hidden curriculum: Correspondence theories and the labor process. *Interchange*, 11(3), 5–22.

———. (1982). *Education and power*. Boston: Routledge & Kegan Paul.

Barrett, M. (1980). *Women's oppression today: Problems in Marxist-feminist analysis*. London: Verso.

Bernstein, R. (1976). *The restructuring of social and political theory*. New York: Harcourt, Brace & Jovanovich.

———. (1983). *Beyond objectivism and relativism: Science, hermeneutics, and praxis*. Philadelphia: University of Pennsylvania Press.

Bottomore, T. (1978). Marxism and sociology. In T. Bottomore & R. Nisbet (eds.), *A history of sociological analysis*. London: Hunemann.

Bowles, S., & Gintis, H. (1976). *Schooling in capitalist America*. New York: Basic Books.

Bowles, G., & Duelli-Klein, R. (1983). *Theories of women's studies*. Boston: Routledge & Kegan Paul.

Bredo, E., & Feinberg, W. (eds.) (1982). *Knowledge and values in social and educational research*. Philadelphia: Temple University Press.

Brown, D., & Tandon, R. (1978). Interview as catalysts. *Journal of Applied Psychology*, 63(2), 197–205.

Browning, F. (Jan. 1983). Neoradicals rethink Marxism. *Mother Jones*, 55–56.

Bullough, R., Goldstein, S., & Holt, L. (1982). Rational curriculum: Teachers and alienation. *Journal of Curriculum Theorizing*, 4(2), 132–43.

Callaway, H. (1981). Women's perspectives: Research as re-vision. In P. Reason & J. Rowan (eds.), *Human inquiry* (pp. 457–72). New York: John Wiley.

Campbell, P. (1981). *The impact of societal biases on research methods*. Washington, DC: U.S. Department of Education monograph.

Carlson, D. (1980). Making student "types": The links between professional and common-sense knowledge systems and educational practice. *Interchange*, 11(2), 11–29.

Comstock, D. (1982). A method for critical research. In E. Bredo & W. Feinberg (eds.), *Knowledge and values in social and educational research* (pp. 370–90). Philadelphia: Temple University Press.

Constantinople, A. (1973). Masculinity-femininity: An exception to a famous dictum. *Psychological Bulletin*, 80(5), 389–407.

Cronbach, L., & Meehl, P. (1955). Construct validity in psychological tests. *Psychological Bulletin*, 52, 281–302.

Cronbach, L. (1975, Feb). Beyond the two disciplines of scientific psychology. *American Psychologist*, 116–127.

———. (1980). Validity on parole: Can we go straight? *New Directions for Testing and Measurement*, 5, 99–108.

Dickens, D. R. (1983). The critical project of Jurgen Habermas. In D. Sabia & J. Wallis (eds.), *Changing social science* (pp. 131–55). Albany: University of New York Press.

Eichler, M. (1980). *The double standard*. New York: St. Martin's Press.

Elden, M. (1979). Bank employees begin to participate in studying and changing their organization. In M. Nijhoff (ed.), *Working and the quality of working life: Developments in Europe*. The Hague.

Everhart, R. (1983). *Reading, writing and resistance: Adolescence and labor in a junior high school*. Boston: Routledge & Kegan Paul.

Fay, B. (1975). *Social theory and political practice*. London: George Allen & Unwin.

Fay, B. (1977). How people change themselves: The relationship between critical theory and its audience. In T. Ball (ed.), *Political theory and praxis* (pp. 200–233). Minneapolis: University of Minnesota Press.

Feinberg, W. (1983). *Understanding education: Toward a reconstruction of educational inquiry.* New York: Cambridge University Press.

Foley, D. (1979). Labor and legitimization in schools: Notes on doing critical ethnography. Unpublished paper.

Freire, P. (1973). *Pedagogy of the oppressed.* New York: Seabury Press.

Gilligan, C. (1977). In a different voice: Women's conceptions of self and morality. *Harvard Education Review,* 47(4), 481–517.

——. (1982). *In a different voice.* Cambridge, MA: Harvard University Press.

Giroux, H. (1981). *Ideology, culture and the process of schooling.* Philadelphia: Temple University Press.

——. (1983). *Theory and resistance in education: A pedagogy for the opposition.* South Hadley, MA: Bergin & Garvey.

Glaser, B., & Strauss, A. (1967). *The discovery of grounded theory: Strategies for qualitative research.* Chicago: Aldine.

Gray, E. D. (1982). *Patriarchy as a conceptual trap.* Wellesley, MA: Roundtable Press.

Guba, E. (1980). Naturalistic and conventional inquiry. Paper presented at the American Educational Research Association annual conference.

——. (1981). Criteria for assessing the trustworthiness of naturalist inquiries. *Educational Communications and Technology,* 29, 75–81.

Guba, E., & Lincoln, Y. (1981). *Effective evaluation.* San Francisco: Jossey-Bass.

Hall, B. (1975). Participatory research: An approach for change. *Convergence,* 8(2), 24–31.

——. (1979). Knowledge as a commodity and participatory research. *Prospects,* 9(4), 393–408.

——. (1981). The democratization of research in adult and non-formal education. In P. Reason & J. Rowan (eds.), *Human inquiry* (pp. 447–56) New York: John Wiley.

Heron, J. (1981). Experiential research methods. In P. Reason & J. Rowan (eds.), *Human inquiry* (pp. 153–66). New York: John Wiley.

Hesse, M. (1980). *Revolution and reconstruction in the philosophy of science.* Bloomington: Indiana University Press.

Horner, M. (1969). Fail: Bright women. *Psychology Today,* 3(6), 36–38.

Huberman, A. M., & Miles, M. (1983). Drawing valid meaning from qualitative data: Some techniques of data reduction and display. *Quality and Quantity,* 17, 281–339.

Kamarovsky, M. (1981). Women then and now: A journey of detachment and engagement. *Women's Studies Quarterly,* 10(2), 5–9.

Kaplan, A. (1964). *The conduct of inquiry: Methodology for behavioral science.* San Francisco: Chandler.

Karabel, J., & Halsey, A. H. (eds.) (1977). *Power and ideology in education.* New York: Oxford University Press.

Kellner, D. (1975). The Frankfurt School revisited. *New German Critique,* 4, 131–52.

———. (1978). Ideology, Marxism and advanced capitalism. *Socialist Review,* 42, 37–65.

Kidder, L. (June 1982). Face validity from multiple perspectives. In D. Brinberg & L. Kidder (eds.), *New directions for methodology of social and behavioral science: Forms of validity in research, #12* (pp. 41–57). San Francisco: Jossey-Bass.

Krueger, M. (1981). In search of the "subjects" in social theory and research. *Psychology and Social Theory,* 1(2), 54–61.

Kuhn, T. (1962) *The structure of scientific revolutions.* Chicago: The University of Chicago Press.

Lacey, C. (1977). *The socialization of teachers.* London: Methuen.

Lather, P. (1986). Research as praxis. *Harvard Educational Review,* 56(3), 257–77.

Lewin, M. (ed.) (1984). *In the Shadow of the Past.* New York: Columbia University Press.

Lincoln, Y., & Guba, E. (1985). *Naturalistic inquiry.* Beverly Hills, CA: Sage.

Malya, S. (spring 1975). Tanzania's literacy experience. *Literacy Discussion,* 45–68.

Maruyama, M. (1969). Epistemology of social science research: Exploration in culture researchers. *Dialectica,* 23, 229–80.

———. (Oct. 1974). Endogenous research vs. "experts" from outside. *Futures,* 389–94.

Maseman, V. (1982). Critical ethnography in the study of comparative education. *Comparative Education Review*, 26(1), 1–15.

McNeil, L. (1981). Negotiating classroom knowledge: Beyond achievement and socialization. *Curriculum Studies*, 13(4), 313–28.

McRobbie, A. (1978). Working class girls and the culture of femininity. In Women's Studies Group, *Women take issue: Aspects of women's subordination* (pp. 96–108). London: Hutchinson.

Mies, M. (1984). Towards a methodology for feminist research. In E. Altbach et al. (ed.), *German feminism: Readings in politics and literature* (pp. 357–66). Albany: State University of New York Press.

Miller, J. (1983). The resistance of women academics: An autobiographical account. *The Journal of Educational Equity and Leadership*, 3(2), 101–9.

Mills, C. W. (1959). *The sociological imagination*. New York: Oxford University Press.

Mishler, E. (1979). Meaning in context: Is there any other kind? *Harvard Educational Review*, 49(1), 1–19.

Mitroff, I., & Kilman, R. (1978). *Methodological approaches to social science*. San Francisco: Jossey-Bass.

Moon, J. D. (1983). Political ethics and critical theory. In D. Sabia & J. Wallis (eds.), *Changing social science* (pp. 171–88). Albany: State University of New York Press.

Morgan, G. (ed.) (1983). *Beyond method: Strategies for social research*. Beverly Hills, CA: Sage.

Nowotny, H. (1979). Science and its critics: Reflections on anti-science. In Nowotny & Rose (eds.), *Counter-movements in the sciences: The sociology of the alternatives to big science* (pp. 1–26). Boston: D. Reidel.

Oakley, A. (1981). Interviewing women: A contradiction in terms. In H. Roberts (ed.), *Doing feminist research* (pp. 30–61). Boston: Routledge & Kegan Paul.

Ogbu, J. (1981). School ethnography: A multilevel approach. *Anthropology and Education Quarterly*, 12(1), 3–29.

Oppenheimer, R. (1956). Analogy in science. *American Psychologist*, 11, 127–35.

Pinar, W. (1981). The abstract and the concrete in curriculum theorizing. In H. Giroux, A. Penna, & W. Pinar (eds.), *Curriculum and instruction: Alternatives in education* (pp. 431–54). Berkeley, CA: McCutchan.

Polkinghorne, D. (1983). *Methodology for the human sciences: Systems of inquiry.* Albany: State University of New York Press.

Reason, P., & Rowan, J. (1981). Issues of validity in new paradigm research. In P. Reason & J. Rowan (eds.), *Human inquiry: A sourcebook of new paradigm research* (pp. 239–62). New York: John Wiley.

Reinharz, S. (1979). *On becoming a social scientist.* San Francisco: Jossey-Bass.

———. (1983). Experiential analysis: A contribution to feminist research. In G. Bowles & R. Duelli-Klein (Eds.), *Theories of women's studies.* Boston: Routledge & Kegan Paul.

———. (1985). Feminist distrust: A response to misogyny and gynopia in sociological work. Unpublished paper, 1985. Expanded version. Feminist distrust: Problems of context and content in sociological work. In D. Berg & K. Smith (Eds.), *Clinical demands of social research.* Beverly Hills, CA.: Sage.

Reynolds, D. (1980–81). The naturalistic method and education and social research: A Marxist critique. *Interchange,* 11(4), 77–89.

Roberts, H. (1981). *Doing feminist research.* London: Routledge & Kegan Paul.

Rose, H. (1979). Hyper-reflexivity—A new danger for the counter-movements. In Nowotny & Rose (eds.), *Counter-movements in the sciences* (pp. 277–89). Boston: D. Reidel.

Sabia, D., & Wallis, J. (eds.) (1983). *Changing social science: Critical theory and other critical perspectives.* Albany: State University of New York Press.

Sacks, K. B. (1984). *My troubles are going to have trouble with me: Everyday trials and triumphs of women workers.* New Brunswick, NJ: Rutgers University Press.

Salamini, L. (1981). *The sociology of political praxis: An introduction to Gramsci's theory.* London: Routledge & Kegan Paul.

Sanford, N. (1981). A model for action research. In P. Reason & J. Rowan (eds.), *Human inquiry* (pp. 173–82). New York: John Wiley.

Sassen, G. (1980). Success anxiety in women. *Harvard Educational Review,* 50(1), 13–24.

Schwartz, P., & Ogilvy, J. (1979). *The emergent paradigm: Changing patterns of thought and belief.* Analytical report: Values and lifestyles program. Menlo Park, CA: S. R. I. International.

Sharp, R., & Green, A. (1975). *Education and social control: A study in progressive primary education.* Boston: Routledge & Kegan Paul.

Stanley, L., & Wise, S. (1983). *Breaking out: Feminist consciousness and feminist research*. Boston: Routledge & Kegan Paul.

Swantz, M. L. (1975). Research as an educational tool for development. *Convergence: An International Journal of Adult Education*, 8(2), 44–53.

————. (1981). Culture and development in the bazamoyo district of Tanzania. In P. Reason & J. Rowan (eds.), *Human inquiry* (pp. 283–91). New York: John Wiley.

Tandon, R. (1981). Dialogue as inquiry and intervention. In P. Reason & J. Rowan (eds.). *Human inquiry* (pp. 293–302). New York: John Wiley.

Thompson, E. P. (1978). *The poverty of theory and other essays*. New York: Monthly Review Press.

Torbert, W. (1981). Why educational research has been so uneducational: The case for a new model of social science research based on collaborative inquiry. In P. Reason & J. Rowan (eds.), *Human inquiry* (pp. 141–52). New York: John Wiley.

Ullrich, O. (1979). Counter-movements in the sciences. In H. Nowotny & Rose (eds.), *Counter-movements in the sciences* (pp. 127–46) Boston: D. Reidel.

Wexler, P. (1982). Ideology and education: From critique to class action. *Interchange*, 13(1), 53–78.

Westkott, M. (1977). Conservative method. *Philosophy of Social Science*, 7, 67–76.

————. (1979). Feminist criticism of the social sciences. *Harvard Educational Review*, 49(4), 422–30.

White, H. (1973). Foucault decoded: Notes from underground. *History and Theory*, 12, 23–54.

Willis, P. (1977). *Learning to labor: How working class kids get working class jobs*. New York: Columbia University Press.

Wright, E. O. (1978), *Class, crisis and the state*. London: National Labor Board.

Wrong, D. (1961). The oversocialized conception of man in modern sociology. *American Sociological Review*, 26(2), 183–93.

The Ethical Revolution

Clearly, all qualitative researchers must immediately confront the ethics and politics of empirical inquiry. Qualitative researchers continue to struggle with ethical standards that will guide their research; there is, as yet, no common agreement on what such standards should be, although there are many proposals from various researchers. The only thing that is clear is that the conventional standards, embodied in federal regulations regarding protection of data and human subjects, is inadequate to the deep investigation of social life and lived experience in which the ethnographer and qualitative researcher engage. Social science work often affects the lives of those studied. This can lead persons to see themselves in ways which they feel are disrespectful or in ways they do not like. Indeed, social science may portray groups or individuals in ways that ultimately disadvantage them socially or economically.

Some social scientists hold to a deception model of inquiry, a model that endorses investigative voyeurism in the name of science, truth, and understanding. While deception of research participants would generally be eschewed by the contemporary generation of postmodern social scientists, it is still an approved practice in some circles, and regulations that govern the use of systematic deception in the name of social science belong to the canon of social scientific practices so well accepted that there are federal guidelines for conducting such research.

Lincoln and Guba review the traditional arguments supporting the codes of ethics endorsed by scholarly societies. Professional scholarly societies and federal law mandate four areas of ethical concern, three of which are the protection of subjects from harm (physical and psychological), deception, and loss of privacy. Informed consent, the fourth area, is presumed to protect the researcher from charges that harm, deception, or invasions of privacy have occurred. Lincoln and Guba analyze the weaknesses of each of these claims, challenging the warrant of science to create conditions that invade private spaces, dupe subjects, and challenge a subject's sense of moral worth and dignity. Lincoln and Guba call for an empowering, educative ethic that joins researchers and subjects together in an open, collegial relationship. In such a model, deception is removed, and threats of harm and loss of privacy operate as barriers that cannot be crossed.

A new set of ethical criteria is emerging (Lincoln 1995). They stress the importance of community, voice, reciprocity, and the building of collaborative, trusting, nonoppressive relationships based on a concept of the sacred. These criteria complement Christians's (2000) call for an ethics based on the values of a feminist communitarianism. We endorse this position. It is time to tie a new knot.

REFERENCES

Christians, Clifford. 2000. "Ethics and Politics in Qualitative Research." In Norman K. Denzin and Yvonna S. Lincoln, eds., *Handbook of Qualitative Research* (2nd ed., pp. 133–55). Thousand Oaks, Calif.: Sage.

Lincoln, Yvonna. 1995. "Emerging Criteria for Quality in Qualitative and Interpretive Inquiry." *Qualitative Inquiry* 1: 275–89.

10

Ethics: The Failure of Positivist Science

Yvonna S. Lincoln and Egon G. Guba

Despite the widespread proliferation of professional ethical standards such as those of the American Psychological Association (Ad Hoc 1973, 1982), ethical concerns continue to plague social research. The maturing of social science over the past fifty years has not been accompanied by a concomitant maturing of ethical standards. Rather, increasing social complexity has provoked new questions and suggested new issues not covered even by the more recently developed standards. As Bulmer has noted,

> the moral implications for society of natural, medical, and social science research have become sharper. Ethical and related concerns about nuclear physics, genetic engineering, organ transplants, and real-world social experiments have become major public issues. The public scrutiny of scientific work, including social science, is correspondingly keener. . . . Regulation of research is increasing, and social scientists are increasingly likely to find their research activities circumscribed in various ways. Apart from the intrinsic importance of such issues, they are a test of the social relevance, responsibility, usefulness, and moral stature of social science, as well as a challenge to us to explain and justify our activities to the wider society. (1980, 124)

Reprinted from *Review of Higher Education* 12, no. 3 (spring 1989): 221–40.

We feel that a major cause of the ethical dilemmas that continue to plague social science inquiry is the set of metaphysical assumptions that undergirds conventional methodologies. These assumptions provide a warrant for near-unethical decisions, raising highly justified concerns on moral grounds. We shall review the present status of ethical guidelines for inquiry and show how the ontological and epistemological belief system on which conventional inquiry rests abets their circumvention. However, these difficulties may be resolved by a shift from a realist ontology and toward an interactive epistemology, as found, for example, in our earlier work in naturalistic inquiry (Lincoln and Guba, 1985) and also shared to a greater or lesser degree by constructivist, hermeneutic, and phenomenological alternatives to positivism (including post-positivism). But of course the shift to another metaphysical system does not remove all ethical dilemmas and, while relieving some, may introduce others of which positivism is relatively free. We shall review the disadvantages as well as the advantages of the proposed shift.

CONVENTIONAL RESPONSES TO ETHICAL DILEMMAS

Social scientists concerned with ethical problems have tried to deal in different ways with the question of what constitutes ethical behavior and how it can be achieved. Some unethical behavior is directed by individual scientists against members of their peer group—for example, concocted data or plagiarism. However, most discussions of ethical behavior focus on the inequities and insults that can be inflicted on hapless research participants, conventionally termed *subjects,* a word reflecting the concept that research participants have things done to them. We prefer "respondent." Needless to say, participants are relatively powerless compared to the inquirers themselves, especially when the inquirers have the warrant of a university, government, or foundation sponsor. This power disparity led professional groups like the American Psychological Association to devise "rules of the game" since, without the influence of some external controlling mechanism, subjects may be exploited by unprincipled inquirers. Typically, such discussions focus on one of three different concerns: *ethical levels,* the means for taking *moral responsibility,* and *legal definitions.*

Ethical Levels

Edward Diener and Rick Crandall suggest three levels of ethical guidelines: *wisdom ethics,* which are expressions of "ideal practice" as found, for example, in the *APA Standards* (Ad Hoc 1973, 1980) and which may be thought of as guidelines for anticipating and avoiding ethical problems; *content ethics*, which "state which acts are right and which are wrong" (1978, 4) and which represent a more operational definition of ethical behavior; and *ethical decisions*, which "emphasize the process by which decisions are made as well as the final choice" (1978, 4). Wisdom and content ethics can at best be markers along a treacherous road, they aver. Ultimately the inquirer must make individual judgments reflecting his or her value structure, the internalized ethical codes of mentors and trainers, and the situation in which the inquiry is conducted. Thus, ethical decisions are basically left to the individual inquirer. Since as Webb et al. (1966) have noted, the "individual moral boiling points" of inquirers differ, so will the ethical decisions they reach, even under similar circumstances.

Moral Responsibility

Moral philosopher Sisella Bok, who has written extensively on the moral dilemmas of lying, concealment, and revelation (1978, 1982), suggests three criteria for judging the ethicality of some inquirer decision or proposed decision. First is the criterion of *publicity*. That is, the dilemma must be "capable of public statement and defense" (1978, 97). Further, this public scrutiny must be carried out with a public of *reasonable persons*, preferably "those who share the perspective of those affected by our choices" (1978, 98). Finally, much depends on the criterion of *discretion*, that is, "the intuitive ability to discern what is and what is not intrusive and injurious" (1982, 41). But the prudent and cautious reserve implied by the criterion of discretion is, like Diener and Crandall's concept of ethical decisions, an individual matter. Again, the problem of nonequivalent "boiling points" must be faced.

Legal Responsibilities

It seems apparent from the long, sorry, and well-documented history of ethical abuses that leaving ethical matters to the virtue and/or discretion of individual inquirers is not sufficient. Nothing intrinsic in the conventional processes of inquiry either mandates or rewards the ethical behavior. That fact is well recognized in the many legal restraints imposed upon social science inquiry. Here are the most commonly used:

1. *No harm.* Generally accepted principles dictate that respondents not be harmed or placed at risk, including the "lawful" harm that may result when

subjects lose, or are cajoled or deceived into giving up, their rights. Of course, harm can also be inflicted if respondents are denied what might have been an auspicious or gainful intervention of "treatment," or when the values of inquirers (or of their sponsors or funders) are served to the detriment of or at the expense of the values of the subjects themselves. These last two conditions are frequently overlooked in defining what constitutes physical or psychic harm.

2. *Fully informed consent.* Federal guidelines and regulations now specify what may constitute legitimate informed consent for participating in an inquiry project, including a series of prescriptions and proscriptions that govern inquirer/subject interactions. But the inquirer's definition of "full information" may be far different from the subject's. Inquirers frequently argue that subjects are too unsophisticated about either the content or the process of a given inquiry to make full information possible. We consider this argument mere rationalization, insufficient to override this requirement. Subjects cannot make informed decisions about participation if they are misled about the purposes or procedures of the inquiry.

3. *Protection of privacy and confidentiality.* As in the case of informed consent, federal guidelines and regulations stabilize boundaries around some of the more glaring violations. As a general rule, individuals are entitled by law to privacy for their persons and confidentiality of information about themselves. Such records as medical claims, school grades, test scores, and financial statements, by law, must be treated as privileged documents, released only with the person's specific permission. Nevertheless, computer access to networked data banks across the country had made this requirement difficult or impossible to enforce. The temptation to access data that are available even though "protected" may be too great to resist.

4. *No deception.* The issue of deception is the most difficult to cope with. Bok (1978) identifies several arguments inquirers use who do feel it necessary to deceive subjects. Sometimes they deceive to "avoid" greater harm, as when physicians lie to a patient with a terminal illness to spare him or her mental anguish and suffering. Others argue that deception is justified in the interest of fairness: to redress a wrong, to right an injustice, or to protect someone's privacy. It is difficult to imagine how a lie might ultimately redress a wrong or right an injustice, but it is easy to see how some lies might protect the privacy of individuals. The minor alteration of names, place descriptions, and the like is virtually de rigueur in social science research. Some inquirers urge that de-

ception is justified in the larger end of maintaining or protecting the truth, although once again, it is hard to see how a lie can protect the truth.

But Bok's fourth justification for deception is simultaneously the most perverse and the most frequently cited, implicitly or explicitly, in the interest of defending what might otherwise be deemed morally reprehensible: the lie allows some larger benefit or social good. This argument is often phrased as "serving the interests of science," "the search for truth," or the "public's right to know."

It is precisely in the putative interests of science that deceptions such as those proscribed under the "no harm," "fully informed consent," and "protection of privacy and confidentiality" provisions are so often perpetrated, as eloquently documented by such researchers as Diener and Crandall (1978). Treatments *are* withheld to meet scientific criteria of controlled experimentation. Respondents' values *are* systematically disregarded as mere opinions with no basis in scientific knowledge. Purposes of research *are* systematically withheld from subjects on the ground that were they to know them, the "technical adequacy" of the study would be compromised, as for example, through reactivity. Protected personal information is accessed when the researcher deems it useful to his or her larger search for truth. Finally, the public's right to know is at best an Ockham's Razor, seemingly justifying the abuse of respondents' rights to gain some putative good for the population as a whole.

What can we learn from this brief look at the status of inquiry ethics? First, it seems clear that much depends on the "moral boiling point" of the individual inquirer; different inquirers will make different decisions even when confronted with similar circumstances. Second, it seems clear that nothing inherent in conventional modes of social science research either mandates or rewards ethical behavior. Third, inquirers have managed to find many apparently sound reasons for avoiding "wisdom ethics"—the ideal ethical practices—in conducting their research. How can we account for this state-of-affairs? And is there no way to resolve this problem?

THE TILT OF THE CONVENTIONAL PARADIGM
The difficulty, as we see it, stems from the metaphysics undergirding conventional (positivist) inquiry, viz., a realist ontology and an objectivist epistemology (Lincoln and Guba 1985). Positivism's fundamental ontological premise

is that there exists an *actual reality*, a "way things really are," that can be discovered (converged on) by the methods of science. This actual reality operates according to a series of natural laws, the "way things really work," which it is also the business of science to determine. If that reality can be discovered and its governing laws determined, then it is possible for science to predict and control future events, to exploit nature for the putative advantage of personkind. Given this ontological position, it follows that scientists, in their work of discovery and determination, must be *objective*, that is, assume a detached stance so that they will not influence the outcome of the inquiry nor allow their values (or those of the client or sponsor) to affect the results. To find out "how things really are" and "how things really work," the inquirer must be in a position to put questions directly to nature and get nature's answers directly back.

With such a metaphysical warrant for the search for truth in hand, the social scientist is free to argue convincingly that his or her research requires and justifies deception. A scientist needs a higher order of "truth"—a "reality" that is described as precisely as possible with its rules and laws plainly understood, so that, ultimately, prediction and control are possible. So long as prediction and control are seen as contributing to some "higher order social good," the warrant becomes complete. Thus, to use the terminology of Diener and Crandall (1978), *wisdom ethics* (ideals) operate to undermine *ethical process decisions* in the conduct of research.

Presumptions about the nature of reality reinforce—and indeed require—treating human research subjects as though they were objects. Objectifying human beings in the process of searching for "truth" has led, as feminist Evelyn Fox Keller (1983) has argued, to the depersonalization and devaluing of human life. The posture on reality assumed by conventional scientific inquirers rests, as Diane Baumrind puts it, on "the logical positivist presupposition that laboratory observations *could* provide unassailable knowledge if only we were able to produce a uniform psychological reality and do away with error variance . . . in the hope that the experimenter can . . . infer unambiguously the existence and direction of causal relations by ruling out alternative causal explanations" (1985, 170). Of course, the flaw in such reasoning lies in assuming the possibility that such "unassailable knowledge" can be obtained or even approximated. Baumrind points out that "the claim that observations can provide value-free, objective knowledge has been challenged by philosophers and scientists at least since Heisenberg's [indeterminacy] principle was enunciated" (1985, 170).

Even if such unassailable knowledge *could* be obtained (an assertion we flatly deny), the costs of obtaining it might be too high. For one thing, conducting research in a way that fully meets the ontological and epistemological requirements of the conventional paradigm may lead to false findings—at least false in the sense of not representing the "way things really are" or the "way things really work." Carefully controlled studies lead to findings generalizable in conventional terms only to other similar carefully controlled settings (e.g., laboratories). Furthermore, even traditional inquirers like Baumrind are now admitting that the price of deceptive research practices is not worth the game. H. W. Reese and W. J. Fremouw posit that "the ethics of *science* deal with the integrity of data; unethical practices undermine science as a body of knowledge. . . . The ethics of *research* deal with the protection of human rights; unethical practices do not undermine science as a body of knowledge, but they undermine society at large through the implications of the research findings or society as embodied in human research participants through the methods used" (1984, 963). Society attempts to bring normal ethics and normative ethics into conformity by the institution of peer review boards, institutional committees to oversee the protection of human subjects, and federal and state regulation of the human research process; but they challenge "the assumption that ethical conduct has been adequately legislated through peer review or federal regulation" (Reese and Fremouw 1984, 863), since "legislated review boards are more concerned with legalistic due-process compliance that with ethical behavior; they confuse accounting with responsibility, and religion with faith. They are concerned with form rather than substance, and by legislation they are barely qualified to determine whether proposed research is good science" (p. 871). Thus normative societal ethics rarely get translated into the normal ethics of science.

The implications of this disjunction are serious. When researchers deceive in the name of science, respondents' "rights to autonomy, dignity and privacy are necessarily violated" (Baumrind 1985, 71). In this violation, Baumrind argues, there are three types of costs, each of which is onerous, dangerous, and too high to be borne: costs to the respondents themselves, costs to the profession, and costs to the society as a whole.

Costs to the respondents include an undermining of their trust in their own judgment; a loss of trust in fiduciaries; and the psychological stresses of having been duped, including admitting to having been duped and engaging in destructive obedience. Costs to respondents also include the loss of self-determination and the loss of individual locus of control.

Costs to the profession include: "(a) exhausting the pool of naive subjects, (b) jeopardizing community support for the research enterprise, and (c) undermining the commitment to truth of the researchers themselves" (Baumrind 1985, 169).

Costs to society include a loss of "trust in expert authorities . . . , increased self-consciousness in public places, broadening the aura of mistrust and suspicion that pervades daily life, inconveniencing and irritating persons by contrived situations, and desensitizing individuals to the needs of others" (Baumrind 1985, 169–70). Taken together, these costs not only destroy the credibility of social science but also subvert the social principles upon which societies rest and which permit international and civil public action.

In sum, the mandate imposed on social scientists to search for a putative truth allows the traditional or conventional scientist to objectify research participants and to deceive respondents in the pursuit of that truth. But social scientists themselves are slowly rejecting the costs of such public deceit as too high and ultimately counterproductive to the research enterprise itself. As a consequence of the criticism, social scientists are asking whether those costs might not be avoided. Such a critique from within the confines of the conventional paradigm itself signals a fundamental reappraisal of how science ought to proceed in the future.

A POSSIBLE SOLUTION: THE NATURALISTIC PARADIGM

Given legal boundaries, moral principles, and the social costs of engaging in traditional science, how can we avoid unethical behavior and confront or side-step the problems engendered by positivist social science? The simplest answer to this question is to move to an alternative paradigm, one based on fundamentally different ontological and epistemological assumptions and hence not subject to the critique leveled against positivism. Rather than using a realist ontology and an objective, dualistic epistemology, we propose using a naturalistic paradigm founded on a relativist (constructivist) ontology and a subjective, monistic epistemology. The ontological shift precludes citing a "higher order" or "ultimate" truth as a warrant for unethical behavior, while the latter shift mandates an openness with respondents that precludes deceiving and objectifying them.

Recall the hidden promises of positivism: deception is justified if it leads to greater knowledge, at least so long as it "protects" human subjects, who may, within these parameters, be treated in whole or in part as "objects" of the scientist's investigation. Naturalistic inquiry avoids both of these pitfalls and, in the process, responds to criticism from both the social science community itself and from social scientists who wish to work within another paradigm of inquiry (for example, see Reason and Rowan, 1981, among others).

Naturalistic inquirers respond to the twin problems of positivism in two ways. First, naturalism has no underlying premise that there is a "way things really are" or a "way things really work." Instead, social realities are social constructions, selected, built, and embellished by social actors (individuals) from among the situations, stimuli, and events of their experience. As a result, the naturalist is not interested in pursuing some single "truth," but rather in uncovering the various constructions held by individuals and often shared among the members of socially, culturally, familiarly, or professionally similar groups in some social context. These constructions represent (we would argue, they are) the meanings that human beings attach to events, situations, and persons in their effort to impose order on social interaction. In that sense, constructions are intensely personal and idiosyncratic and, consequently, as plentiful and diverse as the people who hold them.

In confronting the proposition that there is not a single, ultimate truth but rather multiple, divergent, and whole-cloth constructions, the naturalist is ill-served by engaging in deception; indeed, deception is absolutely counterproductive to his or her research purpose. Deception merely confuses the participants, who are at a loss to know what kinds of responses the naturalist wants and needs. (Of course it may not be counterproductive for the participant to engage in deception, for example, in the interest of putting his or her best foot forward. But that is not the matter at issue here, and is, in any event, a problem in all paradigms.) Since it is the constructions themselves which are of interest to the naturalistic inquirer and since deception serves only to obfuscate the naturalist's search, the naturalist is reinforced, even rewarded, for avoiding deception. Suddenly, deception ceases to eliminate bias and contribute to validity, as it presumably does in conventional inquiry, but actually frustrates the very search which it was intended to aid. If the inquirer is interested in constructions, then it is pointless to lie to or deceive respondents. A researcher cannot uncover individual and group [emic] constructions by deliberately misleading individuals and groups about the purpose of the research.

The second way in which naturalistic inquiry guards against deception is through the special relationship implied by the interaction between researcher and respondent. Naturalists reject the idea that the researcher-researched relationship ought to be objective and distanced. It is, furthermore, a relationship between equals, built on mutual respect, dignity, and trust. Reinharz (1978) characterizes it as a "lover model" (mutual exchange and respect) rather than a "rape model" (researcher takes what's wanted and leaves).

If scientists have no license to treat others as "objects," then they must build a wholly new relationship on the basis of mutual exchange, the preservation of human dignity, privacy, and confidentiality, and the joint negotiation of research purposes, strategies, and interpretations. This means nothing less than a form of inquiry which is increasingly collaborative or joint (Reason and Rowan 1981), with the researched being equal partners with an equal voice in collecting and interpreting the data and in distributing the "results." The power of agency and the locus of control never leave the province of the respondents, and their decisions regarding information about them—including evaluating the possible harm they may suffer—remain theirs to negotiate in the present and in the future.

Because of the shifts in the metaphysical assumptions—that reality is a multiple entity socially constructed and that respondents cannot be treated as objects but must be accepted as viable partners at every step in the inquiry— naturalistic inquiry demands that *no deception ever be employed in the service of social science research.*

THE ETHICAL PROBLEMS OF THE NATURALISTIC PARADIGM

Of course the naturalistic paradigm, while it may redress certain failings of positivism, has problems of its own. The relativism of naturalism suggests that it is impossible (and always will be) to specify any ultimately true methodology for coming to know. The best we can hope for is for a more sophisticated and informed paradigm than that which guided the giants on whose shoulders we stand. Further, because new paradigms are often constructed, at least initially, to address weaknesses or incompleteness in earlier forms, we need be alert to the strong possibility that the new paradigm has problems. Such is, in fact, the case with naturalistic inquiry, although we prefer its dilemmas to those posed by conventional inquiry.

Among the dilemmas peculiar to naturalistic inquiry (and we do not pretend that our list is complete) are the special nature of intense, face-to-face contacts with participants; the difficulties with maintaining or preserving confidentiality and anonymity; the relationships of trust required which must be constructed in very short periods; the powerful pressure for completely open negotiations in light of the need to honor respondents' emic constructions; and the framing of the resulting case studies (which we believe are the appropriate "product" of any naturalistic inquiry) themselves—what should be included and what excluded, and how should the "self" of the researcher be finally represented? Each of these deserves mention, although our treatment here must necessarily be brief.

Face-to-Face Contacts

Since naturalistic inquiry depends on re-creating respondents' realities, gathering and testing those realities necessitates person-to-person data collection with a human being, the inquirer, as instrument (Guba and Lincoln, 1981). Dobbert believes that "humans are polyphasic learners who absorb information both coded and uncoded, implicit and explicit, intended and unintended, through simultaneous multiple modalities—the olfactory, auditory, visual, kinesthetic, tactile, positional, cognitive, and emotional ones; and with the ethologist . . . that humans are primates who learn through (I believe) exploration, manipulation, *activity*, and *interaction* (1982, 14–15, italics added). This activity and interaction, however, place both researcher and respondent in jeopardy. That jeopardy revolves about the highly personal relationships which are built as each gives, takes, shares, and teaches the other. Such highly personal interactions create vulnerability as knower and known exchange roles, barter trust, and reconstruct identities.

The inquirer faced with conventional questionnaires never confronts the frightening risk of knowing and being known, nor do his or her research participants need to provide slices of their lives. The instrument buffers the conventional inquirer from research participants, but there is little protection when the instrument is the inquirer. The unarmed and inaccessible human in touch with the unarmed and inaccessible participant is an encounter fraught with every possibility that can emerge from human interaction.

Anonymity, Confidentiality, and Privacy

Although the naturalist operates under the same legal rules and regulations as the conventional scientist, he or she may find particular difficulties in maintaining research participants' anonymity or privacy. Tom Skrtic, Egon Guba, and Earle Knowlton found this to be exactly the case:

> It is the nature of naturalistic research and the case study reporting method that both are more susceptible to breaches of confidentiality and anonymity than conventional inquiry. Most naturalists are therefore very sensitive to the ethics involved and may go to extraordinary lengths to protect respondents and sites from discovery. . . . It seems to be well established that respondents have a right to privacy, and, if they give up that right in the spirit of cooperation with the researcher, they at least deserve as much protection as the researcher can provide. *As we have seen, such protection may be difficult to extend and impossible to guarantee.* Even if all the names and places and dates are changed "to protect the innocent," it is quite likely that other locals will be able to pinpoint the agencies and parties involved. And *that* breach of confidence may have the most serious consequences of all, for it is these other locals who may be in positions of authority or influence with respect to the research participants, and *thus may have the most powerful sanctions to apply.* (1985, 111; italics added)

As we have made clear earlier (Lincoln and Guba 1985), one of the procedures for establishing trustworthiness is the member check. Research personnel continuously test data and interpretations with members of the groups from which data are solicited. While researchers can be scrupulous in not revealing actual data sources (those data may have been collected from other members of the same audience), nevertheless, expressions or particular views may be recognizable as those of only one or two possible sources. Confidentiality and anonymity obviously cannot be guaranteed. Consequently, the trust relationships which are built must necessarily be negotiated with full disclosure of the risks which respondents are taking.

Trust

Trust between mature adults is built over time, a process complicated by the very human need to present the self at its best. Achieving trust demands forthrightness, clear and fair explication of the purposes of the research, and authentic presentation of the researcher's self—conditions which require time to fulfill. Some projects, however, operate on short time schedules, producing intra- and interpsychic stresses in researcher and researched alike. It is not impossible to establish good rapport in a short time; it is, however, costly (in psychological terms) to both parties. Researchers cannot, in short time frames, afford the repeated casual contacts which permit trust to build; and participants cannot afford to be misled about the intents and purposes of the research. The normal constraints on fieldwork that relies on the human instrument intensify as the time available shortens—hence the need for powerful self-awareness before entering the field.

Negotiation

Negotiation is a characteristic of naturalist inquiry which expresses itself most strongly in the relations between respondents and researchers. The presumption of agency on the part of respondents and the assumption that respondents' constructions are the stuff of which research is made require the researcher to engage in participative modes of inquiry which may seem unfamiliar and initially uncomfortable. The researcher may feel an irresistible desire to "take control," legitimated by the argument that it is necessary to protect the "technical adequacy" of the study. But negotiation—for data, for constructions, for interpretations, for respondents' cooperation—is the best and only way to proceed in an inquiry marked by face-to-face contact, by relationships which must be re-formed at every stage of the inquiry process, and by the intense need to have respondents be the ultimate arbiters of credibility and plausibility.

FRAMING CASE STUDIES

Two ethical problems emerge in framing a case study, particularly in deciding what to include and to exclude. First, how much of the researcher's "self" should be introduced into the case report? To what extent does the researcher speak with an "authorial voice," taking the role of the "professional stranger"? To what extent may the researcher be "informed and transformed" in the process? If we abandon the conventional requirement of objectivity, permitting research findings to emerge from the subjective interaction of researcher and researched, must not the self become an intimate part of the process?

The ethical dilemma here is not an unwillingness to give up the objective perspective, but the possibility that the self will be allowed greater weight in determining the outcome than it ought to be. The traditional power relationship between researcher and researched is tipped in favor of the researcher, who has both institutional sanctions and superior substantive background to support his or her personal conclusions. How can we protect the joint participants against disenfranchisement?

The second problem has to do with choices about what material to include and exclude from the case report. These choices are not solely the investigator's. The case report in its final form represents the joint construction to which all concerned parties have come as a result of negotiation. That process sets a context for the report and legitimizes the interpretations made in it. When interpretations are negotiated and settled, then data and incidents supporting those interpretations are chosen. Features of the context which call forth behaviors, activities, and value will need to be presented to ground them in that particular context. Of course, items of information cannot be left out of the report willy-nilly; the negotiation process ought to require confrontation of all data items and to make some reasonable disposition of them. If they are not to be included in the construction that emerges, there ought to be good reasons for their exclusion. The choices, whether of the researcher or the respondents, cannot be arbitrary.

WHOSE AGENDA?

This list of problems by no means exhausts the ethical dilemmas arising from the naturalistic paradigm. The notion of "cooperative" or "participative" inquiry embraces other problems, one of the most acute of which is, "Whose agenda?"

Both Diener and Crandall (1978) and Dobbert (1982) make clear that all social research has some agenda. The former caution, as part of their general guidelines, that "when a study is supported by a funding agency, the scientist must determine whether the research will be used for beneficial purposes. He [or she] should examine the possible applications of social scientific findings and endeavor to make these uses constructive. Before conducting a study the researcher must consider how the information will affect the people being studied" (p. 217).

If the researcher does not undertake the study alone, then he or she has some obligation to discover why the funder wants the study done at all and to what ends the results will (may be) turned. Dobbert is quite clear that this process of sorting out different stakeholders' agendas is part and parcel of the ethical responsibility of any social scientist (1982, 76–85). She describes two situations but says that there are "just as bad or worse" to be had for the listening at any professional meeting:

> A field worker hired by an agency of any sort to do research and provide recommendations for future policy and actions to the agency has, automatically, two clients—the agency utilizing the research and the study's subjects, for whom the policy or actions are intended. Often the situation is even more complex and five-party situations are not at all rare. A government may, for example, hire a research company to study schools in a certain problem area and make recommendations for their improvement. The agency in turn hires a fieldworker who goes out to study the local situation, only to discover that there are two very strongly opposed factions attempting to control the schools in question and that each has a different philosophy, which leads to incompatible plans for their schools. Ethically, the fieldworker in this situation is responsible to both hiring agencies . . . ; to himself or herself personally; and to both of the studied groups, who have given time and effort to provide data, with the hopes of having their side of the issue heard. (1982, 82–83)

Our own experience verifies that such a situation is not unusual.

The ethical concern is exacerbated when the agendas to be served are compared to the maze of reality constructions. Whose reality gets presented? The respondents'? Which of the respondent subgroups? The investigators'? The funder's? The contracting agency's? The complexity of the problem can be appreciated from Figure 10.1.

We raised the issue earlier of the appropriateness of moving toward a more cooperative paradigm of research, one in which both investigators and participants negotiated interpretations of the data gathered (Lincoln and Guba 1985). We are now prepared to state unequivocally that, as an ethical concern, cooperation and negotiation between researcher and respondents/participants are essential both to maintain research authenticity and to fulfill the criterion of safeguarding human dignity. When participants do not "own" the data they have furnished about themselves, they have been robbed of some essential element of dignity, in addition to having been abandoned in harm's way. If they are accorded the dignity of ownership, they have the right to shape that information's use and to assist in formulating the purposes to which they will lend

FIGURE 10.1
Agenda Conflicts in Applied Fieldwork

Whose Reality?	Whose Agenda?*					
	Funder	Investigator	Respondent Groups			Some Combination**
			1	2	...	N	
Insider (Emic construction; subjective)						
Outsider (Etic construction; intersubjective)						

*Agenda implies values, design, control, and uses of knowledge.
**Combination implies a negotiated, participative, or cooperative research paradigm, in which respondents become participants and maintain some or all control over all agenda items.

their names and information. To do less is to violate, to intrude, and to condemn to indignity.

CONCLUSION

We have argued that a central failure of conventional or positivistic inquiry is its inability to acknowledge and correct the socially and morally repugnant fact of deception in research and its violation of such societal ethics as dignity, self-determination, and individual human agency. Deception and the warrant to deceive that investigators inherit in the conventional paradigm have personal, social, and professional costs so high that even conventional inquirers reject them, as do those using a different paradigm (Lincoln and Guba 1985) and those debating the intersection of feminism and science (Keller 1983) or Marxism and science (Reynolds 1980–81).

The ethical concerns embodied in this failure may be seen as moral, legal, or social, although these three dimensions are not exclusive. Moral dimensions include tests for whether reasonable persons would approve the research, whether it would pass the test of publicity, and whether it would afford discretion in restraining intrusiveness and injuriousness. Legal tests revolve about whether the research sufficiently protects individuals from harm, from lapses in informed consent, from deception, and finally, from violations of privacy and confidentiality. Social tests include determining the costs of a cynical public disenchanted with the arrogance of a deceptive social science community.

Conventional inquiry acquires the warrant to engage in deceptive and even injurious research by virtue of its focus on a supposed single "reality." Convergence upon this reality as the single most important focus of research has justified deception as a way of preventing ambiguity of research results. This dubious means, of course, has failed to prevent ambiguity; furthermore, the costs of deception are added to the research, and the research results might not be deemed sufficient compensation.

The costs to research enterprises resulting from real or possible deception can be avoided if the research is conducted with the emergent paradigm of naturalistic inquiry. This paradigm's focus on the multiple realities of divergent social constructions eliminates the search for a single "reality." The emphasis on using rather than compensating for the interactivity of researcher and respondents allows participants to retain their individual loci of control, to make informed decisions about their participation, and to have substantial agency in shaping the processes and results of the inquiry into their lives.

Avoiding the necessity to deceive and the reliance on dominant-subordinate relationships in the research process does not, unfortunately, eliminate all problems associated with ethical social research. The naturalistic paradigm brings a new set of problems—fostering intense, face-to-face contact with participants, maintaining privacy and confidentiality, building and maintaining trust, negotiating joint responsibility and control, and constructing a case report that controls the intrusiveness of the researcher's self and makes decisions about inclusion and exclusion on the basis of the jointly devised construction.

Nevertheless, although each paradigm resolves one set of problems while raising another, we believe that the warrant to deceive in positivist inquiry raises serious ethical difficulties in social research; the rescinding of that warrant is another powerful reason for seriously considering a paradigm shift.

BIBLIOGRAPHY

Ad Hoc Committee on Ethical Standards in Psychological Research. *Ethical Principles in the Conduct of Research with Human Participants.* Washington, D.C.: American Psychological Association, 1973.

———. *Ethical Principles in the Conduct of Research with Human Participants.* Washington, D.C.: American Psychological Association, 1982.

Baumrind, Diane. "IRBs and Social Science Research: The Costs of Deception." *IRB: A Review of Human Subjects Research* 1, no. 6 (1979): 1–4.

———. "Research Using International Deception: Ethical Issues Revisited." *American Psychologist* 40 (1985); 165–74.

Bok, Sisella. *Lying: Moral Choice in Public and Private Life.* New York: Random House, 1978.

———. *Secrets: On the Ethics of Concealment and Revelation.* New York: Pantheon, 1982.

Bulmer, Martin. "The Impact of Ethical Concerns upon Sociological Research." *Sociology: The Journal of the British Sociological Association* 40 (1980): 125–30.

Diener, Edward, and Rick Crandall. *Ethics in Social and Behavioral Research.* Chicago: University of Chicago Press, 1978.

ETHICS: THE FAILURE OF POSITIVIST SCIENCE

Dobbert, Marion Lundy. *Ethnographic Research: Theory and Application for Modern Schools and Societies.* New York: Praeger, 1982.

Guba, Egon G., and Yvonna S. Lincoln. *Effective Evaluation.* San Francisco: Jossey-Bass, 1981.

Keller, Evelyn Fox. "Feminism as an Analytic Tool for the Study of Science." *Academe* 69 (1983): 15–22.

Lincoln, Yvonna S., and Egon G. Guba. *Naturalistic Inquiry.* Beverly Hills, Calif.: Sage Publications, 1985.

———. "Ethics: The Failure of Positivist Science." Paper presented at the annual meeting of the American Educational Research Association, Washington, D.C., April 1987.

Reason, Peter, and John Rowan. *Human Inquiry: A Sourcebook of New Paradigm Research.* San Francisco: Jossey-Bass, 1981.

Reese, Hayne Waring, and William J. Fremouw. "Normal and Normative Ethics in Behavioral Sciences." *American Psychologist* 39 (1984): 863–76.

Reinharz, Shulamit. *On Becoming a Social Scientist.* San Francisco: Jossey-Bass, 1978.

Reynolds, David. "The Naturalistic Method of Educational and Social Research." *Interchange* 11 (1980–81): 77–89.

Skrtic, T., Egon G. Guba, and H. E. Knowlton. "Interorganizational Special Education Programming in Rural Areas: Technical Report on the Multi-site Naturalistic Field Study." Washington, D.C.: National Institute of Education, 1985.

Webb, Eugene J., Donald T. Campbell, Richard D. Schwartz, and Lee Sechrest. *Unobtrusive Measures: Nonreactive Research in the Social Sciences.* Chicago: Rand-McNally, 1966.

The Methodological
Revolution

The methodological revolution unties old knots concerning understandings
and acceptable strategies for describing and representing the social world. We
start with the interview, a favorite social science methodology. We live in an
interview society, one whose members seem to believe that interviews generate useful information about lived experience and its meanings. The interview
is no longer the province of social scientists; rather, it is used by newscasters,
marketing consultants, and others, many of whom have no formal training in
its use or analysis. The interview has become a taken-for-granted feature of
our mediated, mass culture.

THE INTERVIEW
But the interview is a negotiated text, a site where power, gender, race, and
class intersect. The British sociologist Ann Oakley identifies a major contradiction between positivistic research, which requires objectivity and detachment, and feminist-based interviewing, which requires openness, emotional
engagement, and the development of a potentially long-term, trusting relationship between the interviewer and the subject. A feminist interviewing
ethic redefines the interview situation. It creates the context for the active interview. In the active interview, interviewers and respondents carry on a conversation about mutually relevant, often biographically critical issues.

239

THE CAMERA

Twentieth-century social scientists were defined, in part, by their voyeurism. Sociologists were obsessed with looking and gazing at culture and its processes. Visual sociologists and anthropologists use photography, motion pictures, the Web, interactive CDs, CD-ROMs, and virtual reality as ways of making the social world visible. Often called "the mirror with a memory," photography takes the researcher into the everyday world, where the issues of observer identity, the subject's point of view, and what to photograph become problematic.

No technology is neutral ideologically. The camera is an ideological tool. It represents reality in a particular way, including a way that hides the observer's presence. The short contribution from Margaret Mead and Gregory Bateson vividly dramatizes these issues. Bateson thought that the photographic record should be an art form, and Mead thought that it should be an objective record of social life. It is, of course, both and neither. While some social science photography is artistic, art is not necessarily its first purpose. And we now understand far more fully that there is no such thing as an objective record of social life. This knot continues to be tied and untied.

NARRATIVE

We live in narrative's moment. The linguistic and textual basis of knowledge about society is now privileged. Everything we study is contained within a storied, or narrative, representation. The self itself is a narrative production. There is no dualism between self and society. Material social conditions, discourses, and narrative practices interweave to shape the self and its many identities. Narrative's double duty is complex; self and society are storied productions. This is why narrative is a prime concern of social science today.

Narrative is a telling, a performance event, the process of making or telling a story. A story is an account involving the narration of a series of events in a plotted sequence that unfolds in time. (A story and a narrative are nearly equivalent terms.) A story has a beginning, a middle, and an ending. Stories have certain basic structural features, including narrators, plots, settings, characters, crises, and resolutions. Experience, if it is to be remembered and represented, must be contained in a story that is narrated. We have no direct access to experience as such. We can study experience only through its representations, through the ways in which stories are told.

The biographical, interpretive method rests on the collection, analysis, and performance of stories, accounts, and narratives that speak to turning-point (liminal, epiphanic) moments in people's lives. Narratives are temporal productions. The content of a narrative exists independent of its telling, although many narratives can be told only by the person who experienced the events reported on. Significant biographical experiences are recorded, told, and retold in narrative form.

What we take narrative (and story) to be determines how it will be collected and studied. If stories are defined as a form of narrative, then stories can be obtained through structured, semistructured, and unstructured (as well as oral history) interviews, free association methods, and collectively produced autobiographies. Methodologically, narratives as stories can be subjected to content, discourse, cultural, literary, psychoanalytic, formal, structural, semiotic, and feminist analyses. Of course, preexisting narratives (myths) can also be examined. In the same way, stories can be connected to larger narrative structures.

Chase takes narrative seriously and wants to use the turn to narrative as a way of reconceptualizing method and theory in interview studies. More specifically, she wants to use in-depth interviews as occasions for asking for life stories. Asking for stories rather than reports is a radical move. Chase's essay is filled with examples where researchers did just this: asked for stories. In her discussion of the problems with this approach, Chase shows how stories take us back to culture and the gendered and class-based meanings that circulate in everyday life.

Mishler shows how the transcription of an interview is an interpretive act. The essential indeterminacy of meaning sets the context for viewing transcription as an interpretive practice. Thus, an interview is not an open window into the mind of another. Nor is the "writing down" of interview data free of engagement and interpretation.

11

Interviewing Women:
A Contradiction in Terms

Ann Oakley

Interviewing is rather like marriage: everybody knows what it is, an awful lot of people do it, and yet behind each closed front door there is a world of secrets. Despite the fact that much of modern sociology could justifiably be considered "the science of the interview" (Benney and Hughes, 1970, p. 190), very few sociologists who employ interview data actually bother to describe in detail the process of interviewing itself. The conventions of research reporting require them to offer such information as how many interviews were done and how many were not done; the length of time the interviews lasted; whether the questions were asked following some standardised format or not; and how the information was recorded. Some issues on which research reports do not usually comment are: social/personal characteristics of those doing the interviewing; interviewees' feelings about being interviewed and about the interview; interviewers' feelings about interviewees; and quality of interviewer-interviewee interaction; hospitality offered by interviewees to interviewers; attempts by interviewees to use interviewers as sources of information; and the extension of interviewer-interviewee encounters into more broadly-based social relationships.

Reprinted from *Doing Feminist Research*, ed. Helen Roberts (Boston: Routledge, 1981).

I shall argue in this chapter that social science researchers' awareness of those aspects of interviewing which are "legitimate" and "illegitimate" from the viewpoint of inclusion in research reports reflect their embededness in a particular research protocol. This protocol assumes a predominantly masculine model of sociology and society. The relative undervaluation of women's models has led to an unreal theoretical characterisation of the interview as a means of gathering sociological data which cannot and does not work in practice. This lack of fit between the theory and practice of interviewing is especially likely to come to the fore when a feminist interviewer is interviewing women (who may or may not be feminists).

INTERVIEWING: A MASCULINE PARADIGM?

Let us consider first what the methodology textbooks say about interviewing. First, and most obviously, an interview is a way of finding out about people. "If you want an answer, ask a question. . . . The asking of questions is the main source of social scientific information about everyday behaviour" (Shipman, 1972, p. 76). According to Johan Galtung (1967, p. 149):

> The survey method . . . has been indispensable in gaining information about the human condition and new insights in social theory.
>   The reasons for the success of the survey method seem to be two:
> (1) *theoretically relevant* data are obtained (2) they are amenable to *statistical treatment*, which means (a) the use of the powerful tools of correlation analysis and multi-variate analysis to test substantive relationships, and (b) the tools of statistical tests of hypotheses about generalizability from samples to universes.

Interviewing, which is one[1] means of conducting a survey is essentially a conversation, "merely one of the many ways in which two people talk to one another" (Benney and Hughes, 1970, p. 191), but it is also, significantly, an *instrument* of data collection: "the interviewer is really a tool or an instrument"[2] (Goode and Hatt, 1952, p. 185). As Benny and Hughes express it, (1970, pp. 196–97):

> Regarded as an information-gathering tool, the interview is designed to minimise the local, concrete, immediate circumstances of the particular encounter—including the respective personalities of the participants—and to emphasise only those aspects that can be kept general enough and demonstra-

ble enough to be counted. As an encounter between these two particular people the typical interview has no meaning; it is conceived in a framework of other, comparable meetings between other couples, each recorded in such fashion that elements of communication in common can be easily isolated from more idiosyncratic qualities.

Thus an interview is "not simply a conversation. It is, rather, a pseudoconversation. In order to be successful, it must have all the warmth and personality exchange of a conversation with the clarity and guidelines of scientific searching" (Goode and Hatt, 1952, p. 191). This requirement means that the interview must be seen as "a specialised pattern of verbal interaction—initiated for a specific purpose, and focussed on some specific content areas, with consequent, elimination of extraneous material" (Kahn and Cannell, 1957, p. 16).

The motif of successful interviewing is "be friendly but not too friendly." For the contradiction at the heart of the textbook paradigm is that interviewing necessitates the manipulation of interviewees as objects of study/sources of data, but this can only be achieved via a certain amount of humane treatment. If the interviewee doesn't believe he/she is being kindly and sympathetically treated by the interviewer, then he/she will not consent to be studied and will not come up with the desired information. A balance must then be struck between the warmth required to generate "rapport" and the detachment necessary to see the interviewee as an object under surveillance; walking this tightrope means, not surprisingly, that "interviewing is not easy" (Denzin, 1970, p. 186), although mostly the textbooks do support the idea that it is possible to be a perfect interviewer and both to get reliable and valid data and make interviewees believe they are not simple statistics-to-be. It is just a mater of following the rules.

A major preoccupation in the spelling out of the rules is to counsel potential interviewers about where necessary friendliness ends and unwarranted involvement begins. Goode and Hatt's statement on this topic quoted earlier, for example, continues (1952, p. 191):

Consequently, the interviewer cannot merely lose himself[3] in being friendly. He must introduce himself as though beginning a conversation but from the beginning the additional element of respect, of professional competence, should be maintained. Even the beginning student will make this attempt, else he will find himself merely "maintaining rapport," while failing to penetrate the clichés

of contradictions of the respondent. Further he will find that his own confidence is lessened, if his only goal is to maintain friendliness. He is a professional
researcher in this situation and he must demand and obtain respect for the task
he is trying to perform.

Claire Selltiz and her colleagues give a more explicit recipe. They say (1965,
p. 576):

> The interviewer's manner should be friendly, courteous, conversational and un-
> biased. He should be neither too grim nor too effusive; neither too talkative nor
> too timid. The idea should be to put the respondent at ease, so that he[4] will talk
> freely and fully. . . . [Hence,] A brief remark about the weather, the family pets,
> flowers or children will often serve to break the ice. Above all, an informal, con-
> versational interview is dependent upon a thorough mastery by the interviewer
> of the actual questions in his schedule. He should be familiar enough with them
> to ask them conversationally, rather than read them stiffly; and he should know
> what questions are coming next, so there will be no awkward pauses while he
> studies the questionnaire.

C. A. Moser, in an earlier text, (1958, pp. 187–8, 195) advises of the dangers of
"overrapport."

> Some interviewers are no doubt better than others at establishing what the psy-
> chologists call "rapport" and some may even be too good at it—the National
> Opinion Research Centre Studies[5] found slightly less satisfactory results from
> the . . . sociable interviewers who are "fascinated by people" . . . there is some-
> thing to be said for the interviewer who, while friendly and interested does not
> get too emotionally involved with the respondent and his problems. Interview-
> ing on most surveys is a fairly straightforward job, not one calling for excep-
> tional industry, charm or tact. What one asks is that the interviewer's
> personality should be neither over-aggressive nor over-sociable. Pleasantness
> and a business-like nature is the ideal combination.

"Rapport," a commonly used but ill-defined term, does not mean in this context what the dictionary says it does ("a sympathetic relationship" O.E.D.) but
the acceptance by the interviewee of the interviewer's research goals and the
interviewee's active search to help the interviewer in providing the relevant information. The person who is interviewed has a passive role in adapting to the

definition of the situation offered by the person doing the interviewing. The person doing the interviewing must actively and continually construct the "respondent" (a telling name) as passive. Another way to phrase this is to say that both interviewer and interviewee must be "socialised" into the correct interviewing behaviour (Sjoberg and Nett, 1968, p. 210):

> it is essential not only to train scientists to construct carefully worded questions and draw representative samples but also to educate the public to respond to questions on matters of interest to scientists and to do so in a manner advantageous for scientific analysis. To the extent that such is achieved, a common bond is established between interviewer and interviewee. [However,] It is not enough for the scientist to understand the world of meaning of his informants; if he is to secure valid data via the structured interview, respondents must be socialised into answering questions in proper fashion.

One piece of behaviour that properly socialised respondents do not engage in is asking questions back. Although the textbooks do not present any evidence about the extent to which interviewers do find in practice that this happens, they warn of its dangers and in the process suggest some possible strategies of avoidance: "Never provide the interviewee with any formal indication of the interviewer's beliefs and values. If the informant[6] poses a question . . . parry it" (Sjoberg and Nett, 1968, p. 212). "When asked what you mean and think, tell them you are here to learn, not to pass any judgment, that the situation is very complex" (Galtung 1967, p. 161). "If he (the interviewer) should be asked for his views, he should laugh off the request with the remark that his job at the moment is to get opinions, not to have them" (Selltiz et al., 1965, p. 576), and so on. Goode and Hatt (1952, p. 198) offer the most detailed advice on this issue:

> What is the interviewer to do, however, if the respondent really wants information? Suppose the interviewee does answer the question but than asks for the opinions of the interviewer. Should he give his honest opinion, or an opinion which he thinks the interviewee wants? In most cases, the rule remains that he is there to obtain information and to focus on the respondent, not himself. Usually, a few simple phrases will shift the emphasis back to the respondent. Some which have been fairly successful are "I guess I haven't thought enough about it to give a good answer right now," "Well, right now, your opinions are more important

than mine," and "If you really want to know what I think, I'll be honest and tell you in a moment, after we've finished the interview." Sometimes the diversion can be accomplished by a headshaking gesture which suggests "That's a hard one!" while continuing with the interview. In short, the interviewer must avoid the temptation to express his own views, even if given the opportunity.

Of course the reason why the interviewer must pretend not to have opinions (or to be possessed of information the interviewee wants) is because behaving otherwise might "bias" the interview. "Bias" occurs when there are systematic differences between interviewers in the way interviews are conducted, with resulting differences in the data produced. Such bias clearly invalidate the scientific claims of the research, since the question of which information might be coloured by interviewees' responses to interviewers' attitudinal stances and which is independent of this "contamination" cannot be settled in any decisive way.

The paradigm of the social research interview prompted in the methodology textbooks does, then, emphasise (a) its status as a mechanical instrument of data-collection; (b) its function as a specialised form of conversation in which one person asks the questions and another gives the answers; (c) its characterisation of interviewees as essentially passive individuals, and (d) its reduction of interviewers to a question asking and rapport-promoting role. Actually, two separate typifications of the interviewer are prominent in the literature, though the disjunction between the two is never commented on. In one the interviewer is "a combined phonograph and recording system" (Rose, 1945, p. 143); the job of the interviewer "is fundamentally that of a reporter, not an evangelist, a curiosity-seeker, or a debater" (Selltiz et al., 1965, p. 576). It is important to note that while the interviewer must treat the interviewee as an object or data-producing machine which, when handled correctly will function properly, the interviewer herself/himself has the same status from the point of view of the person/people, institution or corporation conduction the research. Both interviewer and interviewee are thus depersonalised participants in the research process.

The second typification of interviewers in the methodology literature is that of the interviewer as psychoanalyst. The interviewer's relationship to the interviewee is hierarchical and it is the body of expertise possessed by the interviewer that allows the interview to be successfully conducted. Most crucial in this exercise is the interviewer's use of non-directive comments and probes to encourage a free association of ideas which reveals whatever truth the research has been set up to uncover. Indeed, the term "nondirective interview" is derived directly from the language of psychotherapy and carries the logic of interviewer-impersonality to its extreme (Selltiz et al., 1965, p. 268):

> Perhaps the most typical remarks made by the interviewer in a nondirective interview are: "You feel that ..." or "Tell me more" or "Why?" or "Isn't that interesting?" or simply "Uh huh." The nondirective interviewer's function is primarily to serve as a catalyst to a comprehensive expression of the subject's feelings and beliefs and of the frame of reference within which his feelings and beliefs take on personal significance. To achieve this result, the interviewer must create a completely permissive atmosphere, in which the subject is free to express himself without fear of disapproval, admonition or dispute and without advice from the interviewer.

Sjoberg and Nett spell out the premises of the free association method (1968, p. 211):

> the actor's (interviewee's) mental condition (is) ... confused and difficult to grasp. Frequently the actor himself does not know what he believes; he may be so "immature" that he cannot perceive or cope with his own subconscious thought patterns ... the interviewer must be prepared to follow the interviewee through a jungle of meandering thought ways if he is to arrive at the person's true self.

It seems clear that both psychoanalytic and mechanical typifications of the interviewer and, indeed, the entire paradigmatic representation of "proper" interviews in the methodology textbooks, owe a great deal more to a masculine social and sociological vantage point than to a feminine one. For example, the paradigm of the "proper" interview appeals to such values as objectivity, detachment, hierarchy and "science" as an important cultural activity which takes priority over people's more individualised concerns. Thus the errors of poor interviewing comprise subjectivity, involvement, the "fiction"[7] of equality and an undue concern with the ways in which people are not statistically comparable. This polarity of "proper" and "improper" interviewing is an almost classical representation of the widespread gender stereotyping which has been shown, in countless studies, to occur in modern industrial civilisations (see for example Bernard, 1975, part I; Fransella and Frost, 1977; Griffiths and Saraga, 1979; Oakley, 1972; Sayers, 1979). Women are characterised as sensitive, intuitive, incapable of objectivity and emotional detachment and as immersed in the business of making and sustaining personal relationships. Men are thought superior through their capacity for rationality and scientific objectivity and are thus seen to be possessed of an instrumental orientation in their relationships with others. Women are the exploited, the abused; they are unable to exploit others through the "natural" weakness of altruism—a quality which is also their strength as wives, mothers and housewives. Conversely, men find it easy to exploit, although it is most important that any exploitation be justified in the name of some broad political or economic ideology ("the end justifies the means").

Feminine and masculine psychology in patriarchal societies is the psychology of subordinate and dominant social groups. The tie between women's irrationality and heightened sensibility on the one hand and their materially disadvantaged position on the other is, for example, also to be found in the case of ethnic minorities. The psychological characteristics of subordinates "form a certain familiar cluster: submissiveness, passivity, docility, dependency, lack of initiative, inability to act, to decide, to think and the like. In general, this cluster includes qualities more characteristic of children than adults—immaturity, weakness and helplessness. If subordinates adopt these characteristics, they are considered well adjusted" (Miller, 1976, p. 7). It is no accident that the methodology textbooks (with one notable exception) (Moser, 1958)[8] refer to the interviewer as male. Although not all interviewees are referred to as female, there are a number of references to "housewives" as the kind of people interviewers are most likely to meet in the course of their work (for example Goode and Hatt, 1952, p. 189). Some of what Jean Baker Miller has to say about the relationship between dominant and subordinate groups would appear to be relevant to this paradigmatic interviewer-interviewee relationship (Miller, 1976, pp. 6–8):

> A dominant group, inevitably, has the greatest influence in determining a culture's overall outlook—its philosophy, morality, social theory and even its science. The dominant group, thus, legitimizes the unequal relationship and incorporates it into society's guiding concepts. . . .

Inevitably the dominant group is the model for "normal human relationships." It then becomes "normal" to treat others destructively and to derogate them, to obscure the truth of what you are doing by creating false explanations and to oppose actions toward equality. In short, if one's identification is with the dominant group, it is "normal" to continue in this pattern. . . .

It follows from this that dominant groups generally do not like to be told about or even quietly reminded of the existence of inequality. "Normally" they can avoid awareness because their explanation of the relationship becomes so well integrated in *other terms*, they can even believe that both they and the subordinate group share the same interests and, to some extent, a common experience. . . .

Clearly, inequality has created a state of conflict. Yet dominant groups will tend to suppress conflict. They will see any questioning of the "normal" situation as threatening; activities by subordinates in this direction will be perceived with alarm. Dominants are usually convinced that they way things are is right and good, not only for them but especially for the subordinates. All morality confirms this view and all social structure sustains it.

To paraphrase the relevance of this to the interviewer-interviewee relationship we could say that: interviewers define the role of interviewees as subordinates; extracting information is more to be valued than yielding it; the convention of interviewer-interviewee hierarchy is a rationalisation of inequality; what is good for interviewers is not necessarily good for interviewees.

Another way to approach this question of the masculinity of the "proper" interview is to observe that a sociology of feelings and emotion does not exist. Sociology mirrors society in not looking at social interaction from the viewpoint of women (Smith, 1979; Oakley, 1974, chapter 1). While everyone has feelings, "Our society defines being cognitive, intellectual or rational dimensions of experience as superior to being emotional or sentimental. (Significantly, the terms 'emotional' and 'sentimental' have come to connote excessive or degenerate forms of feeling). Through the prism of our technological and rationalistic culture, we are led to perceive and feel emotions as some irrelevancy or impediment to getting things done." Hence their role in interviewing. But "Another reason for sociologists' neglect of emotions may be the discipline's attempt to be recognised as a 'real science' and the consequent need to focus on the most objective and measurable features of social life. This coincides with the values of the traditional 'male culture'" (Hochschild, 1975, p. 281).

Getting involved with the people you interview is doubly bad: it jeopardises the hard-won status of sociology as a science and is indicative of a form of personal degeneracy.

WOMEN INTERVIEWING WOMEN: OR OBJECTIFYING YOUR SISTER

Before I became an interviewer I had read what the textbooks said interviewing ought to be. However, I found it very difficult to realise the prescription in practice, in a number of ways which I describe below. It was these practical difficulties which led me to take a new look at the textbook paradigm. In the rest of this chapter the case I want to make is that when a feminist interviews women: (1) use of prescribed interviewing practice is morally indefensible; (2) general and irreconcilable contradictions at the heart of the textbook paradigm are exposed; and (3) it becomes clear that, in most cases, the goal of finding out about people through interviewing is best achieved when the relationship of interviewer and interviewee is non-hierarchical and when the interviewer is prepared to invest his or her own personal identity in the relationship.

[. . .]

Dissecting my practice of interviewing further, there were three principal reasons why I decided not to follow the textbook code of ethics with regard to interviewing women. First, I did not regard it as reasonable to adopt a purely exploitative attitude to interviewees as sources of data. My involvement in the women's movement in the early 1970s and the rebirth of feminism in an academic context had led me, along with many others, to re-assess society and sociology as masculine paradigms and to want to bring about change in the traditional cultural and academic treatment of women. "Sisterhood," a somewhat nebulous and problematic, but nevertheless important, concept,[9] certainly demanded that women re-evaluate the basis of their relationships with one another.

The dilemma of a feminist interviewer interviewing women could be summarised by considering the practical application of some of the strategies recommended in the textbooks for meeting interviewee's questions. For example, these advise that such questions as "Which hole does the baby come out of?" "Does an epidural ever paralyse women?" and "Why is it dangerous to leave a small baby alone in the house?" should be met with such responses from the interviewer as "I guess I haven't thought enough about it to give a good answer right now," or "a head-shaking gesture which suggests 'that's a hard one'" (Goode and Hatt, quoted above). Also recommended is laughing off the request with the remark that "my job at the moment is to get opinions, not to have them" (Selltiz et al., quoted above).

A second reason for departing from conventional interviewing ethics was that I regarded sociological research as an essential way of giving the subjective situation of women greater visibility not only in sociology, but, more importantly, in society, than it has traditionally had. Interviewing women was, then, a strategy for documenting women's own accounts of their lives. What was important was not taken-for-granted sociological assumptions about the role of the interviewer but a new awareness of the interviewer as an instrument for promoting a sociology for women[10]—that is, as a tool for making possible the articulated and recorded commentary of women on the very personal business of being female in a patriarchal capitalist society. Note that the formulation of the interviewer role has changed dramatically from being a data-collecting instrument for researchers to being a data-collecting instrument for those whose lives are being researched. Such a reformulation is enhanced where the interviewer is also the researcher. It is not coincidental that in the methodological literature the paradigm of the research process is essentially disjunctive, i.e. researcher and interviewer functions are typically performed by different individuals.

A third reason why I undertook the childbirth research with a degree of scepticism about how far traditional percepts of interviewing could, or should, be applied in practice was because I had found, in my previous interviewing experiences, that an attitude of refusing to answer questions or offer any kind of personal feedback was not helpful in terms of the traditional goal of promoting "rapport." A different role, that could be termed "no intimacy without reciprocity," seemed especially important in longitudinal in-depth interviewing. Without feeling that the interviewing process offered some personal satisfaction to them, interviewees would not be prepared to continue after the first interview. This involves being sensitive not only to those questions that are asked (by either party) but to those that are not asked. The interviewee's definition of the interview is important.

The success of this method cannot, of course, be judged from the evidence I have given so far. On the question of the rapport established in the Transition to Motherhood research I offer the following cameo:

A.O.: "Did you have any questions you wanted to ask but didn't when you last went to the hospital?"

M.C.: "Er, I don't know how to put this really. After sexual intercourse I had some bleeding, three times, only a few drops and I didn't tell the hospital because I didn't know how to put it to them. It worried me first off, as soon as I saw it I cried. I don't know if I'd be able to tell them. You see, I've also got a sore down there and a discharge and you know I wash there lots of times a day. You think I should tell the hospital; I could never speak to my own doctor about it. You see I feel like this but I can talk to you about it and I can talk to my sister about it."

More generally the quality and depth of the information given to me by the women I interviewed can be assessed in *Becoming a Mother* (Oakley, 1979), the book arising out of the research which is based almost exclusively on interviewee accounts.

So far as interviewees' reactions to being interviewed are concerned, I asked them at the end of the last interview the question, "Do you feel that being involved in this research—my coming to see you—has affected your experience of becoming a mother in any way?" Table 11.1 shows the answers. Nearly three-quarters of the women said that being interviewed had affected them and the three most common forms this influence took were in leading them to reflect on their experiences more than they would otherwise have done; in reducing the level of the anxiety and/or in reassuring them of their normality; and in giving a valuable outlet for the verbalisation of feelings. None of those who thought being interviewed had affected them regarded this affect as negative. There were many references to the "therapeutic" effect of talking: "getting it out of your system." (It was generally felt that husbands, mothers, friends, etc., did not provide a sufficiently sympathetic or interested audience for a detailed recounting of the experiences and difficulties of becoming a

Table 11.1. 'Has the Research Affected Your Experience of Becoming a Mother?' (percentages)

No	27
Yes:	73
Thought about it more	30
Found it reassuring	25
A relief to talk	25
Changed attitudes/behaviour	7

*Percentages do not add up to 100% because some women gave more than one answer.

mother.) It is perhaps important to note here that one of the main conclusions of the research was that there is a considerable discrepancy between the expectations and the reality of the different aspects of motherhood—pregnancy, childbirth, the emotional relationship of mother and child, the work of childbearing. A dominant metaphor used by interviewees to describe their reactions to this hiatus was "shock." In this sense, a process of emotional recovery is endemic in the normal transition to motherhood and there is a general need for some kind of "therapeutic listener" that is not met within the usual circle of family and friends.

On the issue of co-operation, only 2 out of 82 women contacted initially about the research actually refused to take part in it,[11] making a refusal rate of 2 per cent which is extremely low. Once the interviewing was under way only one woman voluntarily dropped out (because of marital problems); an attrition from 66 at interview 1 to 55 interview 4 was otherwise accounted for by miscarriage, moves, etc. All the women who were asked if they would mind me attending the birth said they didn't mind and all got in touch either directly or indirectly through their husbands when they started labour. The postcards left after interview 2 for interviewees to return after the birth were all completed and returned.

IS A "PROPER" INTERVIEW EVER POSSIBLE?

Hidden amongst the admonitions on how to be a perfect interviewer in the social research methods manuals is the covert recognition that the goal of perfection is actually unattainable: the contradiction between the need for "rapport" and the requirement of between-interview comparability cannot be solved. For example, Dexter (1956, p. 156) following Paul (1954), observes that the pretence of neutrality on the interviewer's part is counterproductive: participation demands alignment. Selltiz et al. (1965, p. 583) says that

> Much of what we call interviewer bias can more correctly be described as interviewer *differences*, which are inherent in the fact that interviewers are human beings and not machines and that they do not work identically.

Richardson and his colleagues in their popular textbook on interviewing (1965, p. 129) note that

> Although gaining and maintaining satisfactory participation is never the primary objective of the interviewer, it is so intimately related to the quality and

quantity of the information sought that the interviewer must always maintain a dual concern: for the quality of his respondents' participation and for the quality of the information being sought. Often . . . these qualities are independent of each other and occasionally they may be mutually exclusive.

It is not hard to find echoes of this point of view in the few accounts of the actual process of interviewing that do exist. For example, Zweig, in his study of *Labour, Life and Poverty*, (1949, pp. 1–2)

> dropped the idea of a questionnaire or formal verbal questions . . . instead I had casual talks with working-class men on an absolutely equal footing. . . .
> I made many friends and some of them paid me a visit afterwards or expressed a wish to keep in touch with me. Some of them confided their troubles to me and I often heard the remark: "Strangely enough, I have never talked about that to anybody else." They regarded my interest in their way of life as a sign of sympathy and understanding rarely shown to them even in the inner circle of their family. I never posed as somebody superior to them, or as a judge of their actions but as one of them.

Zweig defended his method on the grounds that telling people they were objects of study met with "an icy reception" and that finding out about other peoples' lives is much more readily done on a basis of friendship than in a formal interview.

More typically and recently, Marie Corbin, the interviewer for the Pahls' study of *Managers and their Wives*, commented in an Appendix to the book of that name (Corbin, 1971, pp. 303–5):

> Obviously the exact type of relationship that is formed between an interviewer and the people being interviewed is something that the interviewer cannot control entirely, even though the nature of this relationship and how the interviewees classify the interviewer will affect the kinds of information given . . . simply because I am a woman and a wife I shared interests with the other wives and this helped to make the relationship a relaxed one.

Corbin goes on:

> In these particular interviews I was conscious of the need to establish some kind of confidence with the couples if the sorts of information required were to be forthcoming. . . . In theory it should be possible to establish confidence simply

by courtesy towards and interest in the interviewees. In practice it can be difficult to spend eight hours in a person's home, share their meals and listen to their
problems and at the same time remain polite, detached and largely uncommu-
nicative. I found the balance between prejudicing the answers to questions
which covered almost every aspect of the couples' lives, establishing a relationship that would allow the interviews to be successful and holding a civilised
conversation over dinner to be a very precarious one.

Discussing research on copper mining on Bougainville Island, Papua New
Guinea, Alexander Mamak describes his growing consciousness of the political context in which research is done (1978, p. 176):

as I became increasingly aware of the unequal relationship existing between
management and the union, I found myself becoming more and more emotionally involved in the proceedings. I do not believe this reaction is unusual
since, in the words of the wellknown black sociologist Nathan Hare, "If one is
truly cognizant of adverse circumstances, he would be expected, through the
process of reason, to experience some emotional response."

And, a third illustration of this point, Dorothy Hobson's account of her research on housewives' experiences of social isolation contains the following
remarks (1978, pp. 80–1):

The method of interviewing in a one-to-one situation requires some comment. What I find most difficult is to resist commenting in a way which may
direct the answers which the women give to my questions. However, when
the taped interview ends we usually talk and then the women ask me questions about my life and family. These questions often reflect areas where they
have experienced ambivalent feelings in their own replies. For example, one
woman who said during the interview that she did not like being married,
asked me how long I had been married and if I liked it. When I told her how
long I had been married she said, "Well I suppose you get used to it in time,
I suppose I will." In fact the informal talk after the interview often continues
what the women have said during the interview.
    It is impossible to tell exactly how the women perceive me but I do not think
they see me as too far removed from themselves. This may partly be because I
have to arrange the interviews when my own son is at school and leave in time
to collect him.[12]

As Bell and Newby (1977, pp. 9–10) note "accounts of doing sociological research are at least as valuable, both to students of sociology and its practitioners, as the exhortations to be found in the much more common textbooks on
methodology." All research is political, "from the micropolitics of interpersonal
relationships, through the politics of research units, institutions and universities, to those of government departments and finally to the state"—which is
one reason why social research is not "like it is presented and prescribed in
those texts. It is infinitely more complex, messy, various and much more interesting" (Bell and Encel, 1978, p. 4). The "cookbooks" of research methods
largely ignore the political context of research, although some make asides
about its "ethical dilemmas": "Since we are all human we are all involved in
what we are studying when we try to study any aspect of social relations"
(Stacey, 1969, p. 2); "frequently researchers, in the course of their interviewing, establish rapport not as scientists but as human beings; yet they proceed
to use this humanistically gained knowledge for scientific ends, usually without the informants' knowledge" (Sjoberg and Nett, 1968, pp. 215–16).

These ethical dilemmas are generic to all research involving interviewing
for reasons I have already discussed. But they are greatest where there is least
social distance between the interviewer and interviewee. Where both share the
same gender socialisation and critical life-experiences, social distance can be
minimal. Where both interviewer and interviewee share membership of the
same minority group, the basis for equality may impress itself even more ur-
gently on the interviewer's consciousness. Mamak's comments apply equally
to a feminist interviewing women (1978, p. 168):

> I found that my academic training in the methodological views of Western so-
> cial science and its emphasis on 'scientific objectivity' conflicted with the expe-
> riences of my colonial past. The traditional way in which social science research
> is conducted proved inadequate for an understanding of the reality, needs and
> desires of the people I was researching.

[. . .]

Interviewees are people with considerable potential for sabotaging the attempt to research them. Where, as in the case of anthropology or repeated interviewing in sociology, the research cannot proceed without a relationship of
mutual trust being established between interviewer and interviewee the
prospects are particularly dismal. This inevitably changes the interviewer/

anthropologist's attitude to the people he/she is studying. A poignant example is the incident related in Elenore Smith Bowen's[13] *Return to Laughter* when
the anthropologist witnesses one of her most trusted informants dying in
childbirth (1956, p. 163):

> I stood over Amara. She tried to smile at me. She was very ill. I was convinced
> these women could not help her. She would die. She was my friend but my epi-
> taph for her would be impersonal observations scribbled in my notebook, her
> memory preserved in an anthropologist's file: "Death (in childbirth)/Cause:
> witchcraft/Case of Amara." A lecture from the past reproached me: "The anthro-
> pologist cannot, like the chemist or biologist, arrange controlled experiments.
> Like the astronomer, his mere presence produce changes in the data he is trying
> to observe. He himself is a disturbing influence which he must endeavour to keep
> to the minimum. His claim to science must therefore rest on a meticulous accu-
> racy of observations and to a cool, objective approach to his data."
> A cool, objective approach to Amara's death?
> One can, perhaps, be cool when dealing with questionnaires or when inter-
> viewing strangers. But what is one to do when one can collect one's data only by
> forming personal friendships? It is hard enough to think of a friend as a case
> history. Was I to stand aloof, observing the course of events?

Professional hesitation meant that Bowen might never see the ceremonies
connected with death in childbirth. But, on the other hand, she would see her
friend die. Bowen's difficult decision to plead with Amara's kin and the midwives in charge of her case to allow her access to Western medicine did not pay
off and Amara did eventually die.

An anthropologist has to "get inside the culture"; participant observation
means "that . . . the observer participates in the daily life of the people under
study, either openly in the role of researcher or covertly in some disguised role"
(Becker and Geer, 1957, p. 28). A feminist interviewing women is by definition
both "inside" the culture and participating in that which she is observing.
However, in these respects the behaviour of a feminist interviewer/researcher is
not extraordinary. Although (Stanley and Wise, 1979, pp. 359–61)

> Descriptions of the research process in the social sciences often suggest that the
> motivation for carrying out substantive work lies in theoretical concerns . . . the re-
> search process appears a very orderly and coherent process indeed. . . . The personal
> tends to be carefully removed from public statements; these are full of rational

argument [and] careful discussion of academic points. [It can equally easily be seen that] all research is "grounded," because no researcher can separate herself from personhood and thus from deriving second order constructs from experience.

A feminist methodology of social science requires that this rationale of research be described and discussed not only in feminist research but in social science research in general. It requires, further, that the mythology of "hygienic" research with its accompanying mystification of the researcher and the researched as objective instruments of data production be replaced by the recognition that personal involvement is more than dangerous bias—it is the condition under which people come to know each other and to admit others into their lives.

NOTES

1. I am not dealing with others, such as self-administered questionnaires, here since not quite the same framework applies.

2. For Galtung (1967, p. 138) the appropriate metaphor is a thermometer.

3. Most interviewers are, of course, female.

4. Many "respondents" are, of course, female.

5. See Hyman et al. (1955).

6. This label suggests that the interviewer's role is to get the interviewee to "inform" (somewhat against his/her will) on closely guarded and dangerous secrets.

7. Benney and Hughes (1970) discuss interviewing in terms of the dual conventions or "fictions" of equality and comparability.

8. Moser (1958, p. 185) says, "since most interviewers are women I shall refer to them throughout as of the female sex."

9. See Mitchell and Oakley (1976) and Oakley (1981a) on the idea of sisterhood.

10. See Smith (1979).

11. Both these were telephone contacts only. See Oakley (1980), chapter 4, for more on the research methods used.

12. Hobson observes that her approach to interviewing women yielded no refusals to co-operate.

13. Elenore Smith Bowen is a pseudonym for a well-known anthropologist.

REFERENCES

Becker, H. S. and Geer, B. (1957), "Participant Observation and Interviewing: A Comparison?" *Human Organisation*, vol. XVI, pp. 28–32.

Bell, C. and Encel, S. (eds) (1978), *Inside the Whale*, Pergamon Press, Oxford, U.K.

Bell, C. and Newby, H. (1977), *Doing Sociological Research*, Allen & Unwin, London.

Benney, M. and Hughes, E. C. (1970), "Of Sociology and the Interview" in N. K. Denzin (ed.), *Sociological Methods: A Source Book*, Butterworth, London.

Bernard, J. (1975), *Women, Wives, Mothers*, Aldine, Chicago.

Bowen, E. S. (1956), *Return to Laughter*, Gollancz, London.

Corbin, M. (1971), "Appendix 3" in J. M. and R. E. Pahl, *Managers and their Wives*, Allen Lane, London.

Denzin, N. K. (1970) (ed.), *Sociological Methods: A Source Book*, Butterworth, London.

———. (1970) "Introduction: Part V" in N. K. Denzin (ed.), *Sociological Methods: A Source Book*, Butterworth, London.

Dexter, L. A. (1956), "Role Relationships and Conceptions of Neutrality in Interviewing," *American Journal of Sociology*, vol. LX14, p. 153–7.

Evans-Pritchard, E. E. (1940), *The Nuer*, Oxford University Press, London.

Fransella, F. and Frost, K. (1977), *On Being a Woman*, Tavistock, London.

Galtung, J. (1967), *Theory and Methods of Social Research*, Allen & Unwin, London.

Goode, W. J. and Hatt, P. K. (1952), *Methods in Social Research*, McGraw Hill, New York.

Griffiths, D. and Saraga, E. (1979), "Sex Differences and Cognitive Abilities: A Sterile Field of Enquiry" in O. Hartnett et al. (eds), *Sex Role Stereotyping*, Tavistock, London.

Hartnett, O., Boden, G. and Fuller, M. (eds) (1979) *Sex-Role Stereotyping*, Tavistock, London.

Hobson, D. (1978), "Housewives: Isolation as Oppression" in Women's Studies Group, Centre for Contemporary Cultural Studies, *Women Take Issue*, Hutchinson, London.

Hochschild, A. R. (1975), "The Sociology of Feeling and Emotion: Selected Possibilities" in M. Milman and R. M. Kanter (eds), *Another Voice: Feminist Perspectives on Social Life and Social Science*, Anchor Books, New York.

Hyman, H. H. et al. (1955), *Interviewing in Social Research*, University of Chicago Press, Chicago.

Kahn, R. L. and Cannell, L. F. (1957), *The Dynamics of Interviewing*, John Wiley, New York.

Laslett, B. and Rapoport, R. (1975), "Collaborative Interviewing and Interactive Research," *Journal of Marriage and the Family*, November, pp. 968–77.

Mamak, A. F. (1978), Nationalism, Race-Class Consciousness and Social Research on Bougainville Island, Papua, New Guinea, in C. Bell and S. Encel (eds), *Inside the Whale*, Pergamon Press, Oxford, U.K.

Miller, J. B. (1976), *Toward a New Psychology of Women*, Beacon Press, Boston.

Mitchell, J. and Oakley A. (1976), "Introduction" in J. Mitchell and A. Oakley (eds), *The Rights and Wrongs of Women*, Penguin, Harmondsworth, U.K.

Moser, C. A. (1958), *Survey Methods in Social Investigation*, Heinemann, London.

Oakley, A. (1972), *Sex, Gender and Society*, Maurice Temple Smith, London.

———. (1974), *The Sociology of Housework*, Martin Robertson, London.

———. (1979), *Becoming a Mother*, Martin Robertson, Oxford.

———. (1980), *Women Confined: Towards a Sociology of Childbirth*, Martin Robertson, Oxford.

———. (1981a), *Subject Women*, Martin Robertson, Oxford.

———. (1981b), "Normal Motherhood: An Exercise in Self-Control," in B. Hutter and G. Williams (eds), *Controlling Women*, Croom Helm, London.

Paul, B. (1954), "Interview Techniques and Field Relationships" in A. C. Kroeber (ed.), *Anthropology Today*, University of Chicago Press, Chicago.

Rapoport, R. and Rapoport, R. (1976), *Dual Career Families Re-examined*, Martin Robertson, London.

Richardson, S. A. et al. (1965), *Interviewing: its Forms and Functions*, Basic Books, New York.

Rose, A. M. (1945), "A Research Note on Experimentation in Interviewing," *American Journal of Sociology*, vol. 51 pp. 143–4.

Sayers, J. (1979), *On the Description of Psychological Sex Differences* in O. Hartnett et al. (eds), *Sex Role Stereotyping*, Tavistock, London.

Selltiz, C., Jahoda, M., Deutsch, M. and Cook, S. W. (1965), *Research Methods in Social Relations*, Methuen, London.

Shipman, M. D. (1972), *The Limitations of Social Research*, Longman, London.

Sjoberg, G. and Nett, R. (1968), *A Methodology for Social Research*, Harper & Row, New York.

Smith, D. E. (1979), "A Sociology for Women" in J. A. Sherman and E. T. Beck (eds), *The Prism of Sex*, University of Wisconsin Press, Madison.

Stacey, M. (1969), *Methods of Social Research*, Pergamon, Oxford.

Stanley, L. and Wise, S. (1979), "Feminist Research, Feminist Consciousness and Experiences of Sexism," *Women's Studies International Quarterly*, vol. 2, no. 3, pp. 359–79.

Zweig, F. (1949), *Labour, Life and Poverty*, Gollancz, London.

12

On the Use of the
Camera in Anthropology

Margaret Mead and Gregory Bateson

Bateson: I was wondering about looking through, for example, a camera.

Mead: Remember Clara Lambert and when you were trying to teach her? That woman who was making photographic studies of play schools, but she was using the camera as telescope instead of as a camera. You said, "She'll never be a photographer. She keeps using the camera to look at things." But you didn't. You always used a camera to take a picture, which is a different activity.

Bateson: Yes. By the way, I don't like cameras on tripods, just grinding. In the latter part of the schizophrenic project, we had cameras on tripods just grinding.

Mead: And you don't like that?

Bateson: Disastrous.

Mead: Why?

Bateson: Because I think the photographic record should be an art form.

Mead: Oh why? Why shouldn't you have some records that aren't art forms? Because if it's an art form, it has been altered.

Bateson: It's undoubtedly been altered. I don't think it exists unaltered.

Mead: I think it's very important, if you're going to be scientific about behavior, to give other people access to the material, as comparable as possible to

Reprinted from *Studies in the Anthropology of Visual Communication* vol. 12, no. 2: 78–80.

the access you had. You don't, then, alter the material. There's a bunch of filmmakers now that are saying, "It should be art," and wrecking everything that we're trying to do. Why the hell should it be art?

Bateson: Well, it should be off the tripod.

Mead: So you run around.

Bateson: Yes.

Mead: And therefore you've introduced a variation into it that is unnecessary.

Bateson: I therefore got the information out that I thought was relevant at the time.

Mead: That's right. And therefore what do you see later?

Bateson: If you put the damn thing on a tripod, you don't get any relevance.

Mead: No, you get what happened.

Bateson: It isn't what happened.

Mead: I don't want people leaping around thinking that a profile at this moment would be beautiful.

Bateson: I wouldn't want beautiful.

Mead: Well, what's the leaping around for?

Bateson: To get what's happening.

Mead: What you think is happening.

Bateson: If Stuart reached behind his back to scratch himself, I would like to be over there at that moment.

Mead: If you were over there at that moment you wouldn't see him kicking the cat under the table. So that just doesn't hold as an argument.

Bateson: Of the things that happen, the camera is only going to record one percent anyway.

Mead: That's right.

Bateson: I want that one percent on the whole to tell.

Mead: Look, I've worked with these things that were done by artistic filmmakers, and the result is you can't do anything with them.

Bateson: They're bad artists, then.

Mead: No, they're not. I mean, an artistic filmmaker can make a beautiful notion of what he thinks is there, and you can't do any subsequent analysis with it of any kind. That's been the trouble with anthropology, because they had to trust us. If we were good enough instruments, and we said the people in this culture did something more than the ones in that, if they trusted us, they used it. But there was no way of probing further into the material. So we gradually developed the idea of film and tapes.

Bateson: There's never going to be any way of probing further into the material.

Mead: What are you talking about, Gregory? I don't know what you're talking about. Certainly, when we showed that Balinese stuff that first summer there were different things that people identified—the limpness that Marion Strahahan identified, the place on the chest and its point in child development that Erik Erikson identified. I can go back over it, and show you what they got out of those films. They didn't get it out of your head, and they didn't get it out of the way you were pointing the camera. They got it because it was a long enough run so they could see what was happening.

SB: What about something like that Navajo film, *Intrepid Shadows*? [see Worth and Adair 1972].

Mead: Well, that is a beautiful, an artistic production that tells you something about a Navajo artist.

Bateson: This is different, it's a native work of art.

Mead: Yes, and a beautiful native work of art. But the only thing you can do more with that is analyze the filmmaker, which I did. I figured out how he got the animation into the trees.

Bateson: Oh yes? What do you get out of that one?

Mead: He picked windy days, he walked as he photographed, and he moved the camera independently of the movement of his own body. And that gives you that effect. Well, are you going to say, following what all those other people have been able to get out of those films of yours, that you should have just been artistic?

SB: He's saying he was artistic.

Mead: No, he wasn't. I mean, he's a good filmmaker, and Balinese can pose very nicely, but his effort was to hold the camera steady enough long enough to get a sequence of behavior.

Bateson: To find out what's happening, yes.

Mead: When you're jumping around taking pictures . . .

Bateson: Nobody's talking about that, Margaret, for God's sake.

Mead: Well.

Bateson: I'm talking about having control of a camera. You're talking about putting a dead camera on top of a bloody tripod. It sees nothing.

Mead: Well, I think it sees a great deal. I've worked with these pictures taken by artists, and really good ones . . .

Bateson: I'm sorry I said artists; all I meant was artists. I mean, artists is not a term of abuse in my vocabulary.

Mead: It isn't in mine either, but I . . .

Bateson: Well, in this conversation, it's become one.

Mead: Well, I'm sorry. It just produces something different. I've tried to use *Dead Birds*, for instances . . . [see Gardner 1963].

Bateson: I don't understand *Dead Birds* at all. I've looked at *Dead Birds*, and it makes no sense.

Mead: I think it makes plenty of sense.

Bateson: But how it was made I have no idea at all.

Mead: Well, there is never a long enough sequence of anything, and you said absolutely that what was needed was long, long sequences from one position in the direction of two people. You've said that in print. Are you going to take it back?

Bateson: Yes, well, a long sequence in my vocabulary is twenty seconds.

Mead: Well, it wasn't when you were writing about Balinese films. It was three minutes. It was the longest that you could wind the camera at that point.

Bateson: A very few sequences ran to the length of the winding of the camera.

Mead: But if at that point you had had a camera that would run twelve hundred feet, you'd have run it.

Bateson: I would have and I'd have been wrong.

Mead: I don't think so for one minute.

Bateson: The Balinese film wouldn't be worth one quarter.

Mead: All right. That's a point where I totally disagree. It's not science.

Bateson: I don't know what science is, I don't know what art is.

Mead: That's all right. If you don't, that's quite simple. I do, (To Stuart:) With the films that Gregory's now repudiating that he took, we have had twenty-five years of re-examination and re-examination of the material.

Bateson: It's pretty rich material.

Mead: It is rich, because they're long sequences, and that's what you need.

Bateson: There are no long sequences.

Mead: Oh, compared with anything anybody else does, Gregory.

Bateson: But they're trained not to.

Mead: There are sequences that are long enough to analyze . . .

Bateson: Taken from the right place!

Mead: Taken from one place.

Bateson: Taken from the place that averaged better than other places.

Mead: Well, you put your camera there.

Bateson: You can't do that with a tripod. You're stuck. The thing grinds for twelve hundred feet. It's a bore.

Mead: Well, you prefer twenty seconds to twelve hundred feet.

Bateson: Indeed, I do.

Mead: Which shows you get bored very easily.

Bateson: Yes, I do.

Mead: Well, there are other people who don't, you know? Take the films that Betty Thompson studied [see Thompson 1970]. That Karbo sequence—it's beautiful—she was willing to work on it for six months. You've never been willing to work on things that length of time, but you shouldn't object to other people who can do it, and giving them the material to do it.

There were times in the field when I worked with people without filming, and therefore have not been able to subject the material to changing theory, as we were able to do with the Balinese stuff. So when I went back to Bali I didn't see new things. When I went back to Manus, I did, where I had only still photographs. If you have film, as your own perception develops, you can re-examine it in the light of the material to some extent. One of the things, Gregory, that we examined in the stills, was the extent to which people, if they leaned against other people, let their mouths fall slack. We got that out of the examining lots and lots of stills. It's the same principle. It's quite different if you have a thesis and have the camera in your hand, the chances of influencing the material are greater. When you don't have the camera in your hand, you can look at the things that happen in the background.

Bateson: There are three ends to this discussion. There's the sort of film I want to make, there's the sort of film that they want to make in New Mexico (which is *Dead Birds*, substantially), and there is the sort of film that is made by leaving the camera on a tripod and not paying attention to it.

SB: Who does that?

Bateson: Oh, psychiatrists do that. Albert Scheflen [1973] leaves a video camera in somebody's house and goes home. It's stuck in the wall.

Mead: Well, I thoroughly disapprove of the people that want video so they won't have to look. They hand it over to an unfortunate student who then does the rest of the work and adds up the figures, and they write a book. We both object to this. But I do think if you look at your long sequences of stills, leave out the film for a minute, that those long, very rapid sequences, Koewat Raoeh, those stills, they're magnificent, and you can do a great deal with them. And if you hadn't stayed in the same place, you wouldn't have those sequences.

SB: Has anyone else done that since?

Mead: Nobody has been as good a photographer as Gregory at this sort of thing. People are very unwilling to do it, very unwilling.

SB: I haven't seen any books that come even close to *Balinese Character* [see Mead and Bateson 1942].

Mead: That's right, they never have. And now Gregory is saying it was wrong to do what he did in Bali. Gregory was the only person who was ever successful at taking stills and film at the same time, which you did by putting one on a tripod, and having both at the same focal length.

Bateson: It was having one in my hand and the other round my neck.

Mead: Some of the time, and some not.

Bateson: We used the tripod occasionally when we were using long telephoto lenses.

Mead: We use it for the bathing babies. I think the difference between art and science is that each artistic event is unique, whereas in science sooner or later once you get some kind of theory going somebody or other will make the same discovery [see Mead 1976]. The principal point is access, so that other people can look at your material and come to understand it and share it. The only real information that *Dead Birds* gives anybody are things like the thing that my imagination had never really encompassed, and that's the effect of cutting off joints of fingers. You remember? The women cut off a joint for every death that they mourn for, and they start when they're little girls, so that by the time they're grown women, they have no fingers. All the fine work is done by the men in that society, the crocheting and what not, because the men have fingers to do it with and the women have these stumps of hands. I knew about it, I had read about it, it had no meaning to me until I saw those pictures. There are lots of thngs that can be conveyed by this quasi-artistic film, but when we want to suggest to people that it's a good idea to know what goes on between people, which is what you've always stressed, we still have to show your films, because there aren't any others that are anything like as good.

SB: Isn't that a little shocking? It's been, what, years?

Mead: Very shocking.

Bateson: It's because people are getting good at putting cameras on tripods. It isn't what happens between people.

Mead: Nobody's put any cameras on tripods in those twenty-five years that looked at anything that mattered.

Bateson: They haven't looked at anything that mattered, anyway. All right.

REFERENCES CITED

Gardner, Robert, Director
1964 *Dead Birds.* Peabody Museum, Harvard University. Color, 83 minutes. Available through New York Public Library.

Mead, Margaret
1976 "Towards a Human Science." Science 1919: 903–900.

Mead, M., and G. Bateson
1942 *Balinese Character: A Photographic Analysis.* New York Academy of Sciences; Special Publications, II. (Reissued 1962.)

Schanman, Albert E.
1973 *Body Language and the Social Order: Communication as Behavioral Central.* Englewood Cliffs, N.J.: Prentice-Hill.

Thompson, Betty
1970 "Development and Trial Applications of Method for Identifying Non-Vocal Parent-Child Communications in Research Film," Ph.D. thesis, Teachers College.

Worth, Sol, and John Adair
1972 *Through Navajo Eyes.* Bloomington: Indiana University Press. (*Intrepid Shadows* was made by Al Clah, a 19-year-old Navajo painter and sculptor.)

13

Taking Narrative Seriously: Consequences for Method and Theory in Interview Studies

Susan E. Chase

For years, humanities and social science scholars have debated the nature and significance of narrative in literature, historical writings, the popular media, personal documents such as diaries and letters, oral stories of various kinds, as well as in the academic disciplines themselves.[1] Although they disagree about what constitutes narrative and develop divergent approaches to the relation between narrative and life, narrative and subjectivity, narrative and culture, and narrative and fiction or truth, most scholars point to the ubiquity of narrative in Western societies and concur that all forms of narrative share the fundamental interest in making sense of experience, the interest in constructing and communicating meaning.

Despite the significance of narrative, qualitative researchers rarely focus specifically on eliciting narratives in the interview context and pay little attention to the narrative character of talk produced during interviews. Among others, Elliot Mishler (1986) argues that conventional methods of sociological interviewing tend to suppress respondents' stories, and that conventional methods of interpretation ignore the import of stories that they manage to tell despite our attempts to make them.[2] Mishler suggests that the impulse to narrate

Reprinted from *Interpreting Experience: The Narrative Study of Lives*, ed. Ruthellen Josselson and Amia Lieblich (Thousand Oaks, Calif.: Sage, 1995), 1–26. Copyright © 1995 by Sage Publications Inc.

is such an integral part of human experience that interviewees will tell stories even if we don't encourage them to do so.

I have found, however, that asking for and attending to another's story in the interview context is not a simple matter and that it requires an altered conception of what interviews are and how we should conduct them. If we take seriously the idea that people make sense of experience and communicate meaning through narration, *then in depth interviews should become occasions in which we ask for life stories.* By life stories, I mean narratives about some life experience that is of deep and abiding interest to the interviewee. Furthermore, taking narrative seriously has consequences for how we use those life stories to pursue our sociological interests. As many have argued, narration is a complex social process, a form of social action that embodies the relation between narrator and culture. Taking narrative seriously means directing our attention to that process of embodiment, to what narrators accomplish as they tell their stories, and how that accomplishment is culturally shaped. A major contribution of narrative analysis is the study of general social phenomena through a focus on their embodiment in specific life stories.[3]

INVITING STORIES RATHER THAN REPORTS DURING INTERVIEWS
Livia Polanyi's (1985) distinction between stories and reports provides a good starting point for articulating how and why interviews should become occasions to ask for life stories. She writes that "*stories* are told to make a point, to transmit a message ... about the world the teller shares with other people:" (p. 12). In telling a story, the narrator takes responsibility for "making the relevance of the telling clear" (p. 13). By contrast, a report is "typically elicited by the recipient," and "the burden of assigning differential weighting to the various narrated propositions thus falls to the receiver of the report" (p. 13). To illustrate this distinction, Polanyi offers the familiar example of a parent asking her child what happened at school today. We all recognize the difference between an obligatory chronicle and an animated story of the day's events.

In the interview context, whether we hear stories or reports has to do with who takes responsibility for the import of the talk. If we want to hear stories rather than reports then our task as interviewers is to invite others to tell their stories, to encourage them to take responsibility for the meaning of their talk. A successful interviewer manages to shift the weight of responsibility to the other in such a way that he or she willingly embraces it.

But how does this shifting of responsibility happen (or fail to happen) in the course of actual interviews? How do we go about inviting others to tell their stories? The answer lies in the questions we ask, and more deeply, in the orientation to others embedded in our questions. Qualitative researchers certainly agree that the questions we ask make a difference to the quality of the information we collect; that our questions should be phrased in everyday rather than sociological language; that we need to ask about participants' experiences, thoughts, and feelings to gather data thick enough to shed light on our sociological problems; and that the relationships we construct with interviewees affect the quality of their responses to our questions. Nevertheless, even when interviewers put these widely accepted ideas into practice, they may end up inviting reports rather than stories. Shifting responsibility to the participant requires something more. By way of illustration, I present examples from three different interview studies.

Karen Sacks's Study of Working-Class Women's Workplace Militancy

In her research on the union drives by service and clerical workers at Duke Medical Center, Karen Sacks (1988, 1989) sought to understand, among other things, working-class women's militancy and leadership in the workplace. She suspected that there was a strong connection between what women learned from their families and their resistance to oppression at work. When her participant observation produced no evidence of this link, she began to interview women about their families.

> In the spirit of feminist collectivity, though naively, I put my problem to as many of the women as I knew who were willing to discuss it: I had a strong hunch that women learned the values and skills to resist oppression at work from their families. Did they share that feeling? If so, could they figure out what they learned and how they learned it?
>
> The questions I posed to the women were sociological, and women responded in that mode, giving me answers that linked sociological variables to personal militance. At first there was no definitive pattern: maybe birth order was important, maybe race, or working mothers, marital status, and so on. Their answers were as abstract and uninformative as my own thinking. (1989, p. 88)

By sharing her thoughts and interests—her sociological questions—Sacks treated research participants as equals, as persons as capable as she was of analyzing the social factors that have shaped their lives.[4] Indeed, Sacks got what she asked for, but not what she was looking for. Because her questions were sociological, the women offered sociological responses. Together, they speculated on significant factors that might have shaped their family lives and thus their actions at work. But the abstraction of such talk—its disconnectedness from their actual lives—made it hollow. Sacks concluded that the idea of putting sociological questions on the table is naïve—even when done in a collective, feminist spirit—because such questions produce answers that have little to do with how people live their lives. The problem lay not in the wording of her questions but in their orientation; they directed others to her research interest rather than to their own life experiences.

Sacks dropped her sociological questions and began to ask for life stories—something she had no intention of doing when she started the study—when she realized that the general processes she sought to understand were embedded in women's lives.

> There were a few women whose constructions of their life narratives and analyses became exemplars of how family learning empowered women to rebel, and whose experiences became central for developing that model. *This happened when I finally asked them how they learned about work and what it meant to them.* That question generated narratives about work—childhood chores, and a progress report about the kinds of tasks and responsibilities each woman had at different ages. (1989, p. 88, emphasis added)

Sacks finally stumbled on the specific questions that *invited* women to tell stories about growing up, taking on increasing responsibilities at home, developing self-respect as a result of the work done at home, and recognizing the importance of demanding respect from others. She learned from these stories that the sense of responsibility and self-respect developed at home conflicted with the poor treatment working-class women encountered at work; as she listened to these stories, she realized that conflict was at least one important source of working-class women's workplace militancy.

My Study of Women's Experiences in the White- and Male-Dominated Profession of the Public School Superintendency

In our interviews with women of various racial and ethnic backgrounds who are public school superintendents in rural, small town, and urban districts across the United States, my coresearcher, Colleen Bell, and I asked about the work they do, the professional and interpersonal contexts in which they work, their work histories, and the relationship between their personal and professional lives. At certain points in the interviews, we also asked about the inequalities these educational leaders have faced in their profession, which is 95 percent white and 96 percent male (Bell & Chase, 1993). Generally speaking, our interest lay in hearing about their work experiences in this white- and male-dominated leadership occupation. Nonetheless, in the course of our early interviews, we learned about the difference between questions that invite stories and those that invite reports.

In our earliest interviews, which were with white women in rural and small-town districts, we included a set of questions about what it is like to be one of a few women in a male-dominated context: Are you treated as a representative of women in general? As an exception? Do other women look to you as a role mode? What are the effects of your visibility? Do you experience social awkwardness with male colleagues? Was there any particular point in your career when you began to think that being a woman might make some kind of a difference? We presented these questions much like Sacks presented here, in the spirit of asking women to help us check out sociological understandings through the reality of their own experiences. We introduced these questions by giving a brief overview of what sociologists say about the experiences of women in male-dominated professions. This introduction was important, or so we thought, because it allowed the women to hear where the questions came from. By offering this background, we attempted to make the questions less abstract and to make the research relationship collaborative. Like Sacks, we thought we were inviting others to speak "in the spirit of feminist collectively." Listen, for example, to the following exchange between me and Laura Stuart, a white superintendent from a working-class background.[5] This exchange came near the end of a three-hour interview. Notice that I state in five different ways that I'm interested in hearing "your experience."[6]

SC: OK Now *this* is a set of questions about um [p]
    experiences that women have who work in male-dominated professions
    so what I—what we've done is read the sociology
    what the sociologists *say* about these things
    and what *I'd* like to do is ask for *your experience* of them

like *you're* the informant
you know the sociologists have theories and they say these things and
I'd like to ask you *whether* you have experienced them
whether you think they are true or not
so I really want your opinions abut them
the one thing they say happens is that a woman who's in a male-dominated
profession gets treated as a representative of women in general
because she's the only *woman* up there as a leader
that other people don't really know what to do with her
and and they might do things like
if she does the job poorly then they'll say
"oh women can't do that job"
if she does the job well then they'll say
"oh yeah I guess women can do that job."
Have you experienced anything like that?

I'm clearly doing my best to invite Laura Stuart to share with us whatever she has to say about these sociological formulations of women's experiences. Here is her response:

LS: No I really haven't.

I have every reason to believe that Laura Stuart answered my question honestly and in the collaborative spirit in which I asked it. In effect, she communicated something like this: "If you want to know whether my experiences fit with sociologists' ideas about women's experiences in male-dominated professions, I'm happy to help you out." In other words, she heard my question as requesting a report, which meant that the burden of interpreting the significance of her response rested with me, the one who asked for it in the first place. Despite my repeated statements of interest in her experience, she heard that my primary interest lay in the connection between her experience and sociological ideas. In the case of this question she felt no such connection, and so she had nothing to say but "No I really haven't." Our exchange continued:

SC: What about other women treating you as a role model
looking up to you
you've talked a bit about that

LS: Well [sigh] um I hope that I have been
    and I've I've had two people call me since I've been here
    to ask uh *my* advice *my* help with them applying for a superintendency
    I've given them a copy of my resume
    things I have prepared
    shared with them the black book I prepared for my interview and this sort of
    thing.
    So I always hope to be a *helping* for someone and not ever a hindrance you
    know.
    I don't have any [p]
    I've read articles you know
    in some journals on women on how hard when a woman is the boss
    but I haven't experienced that
SC: you mean when they say it's hard to work II for a woman II
LS: II uh huh yes II
SC: you haven't had that problem with men or women?
LS: no

After reporting on my question about others treating her as a role model, Laura Stuart anticipates and answers a third sociological question. Interestingly, I articulated that question—"you mean when they say it's harder to work for a woman . . . you haven't had that problem with men or women?"—only after she answered it.

Not every woman had so little to say in response to these sociological questions. And even Laura Stuart had more to say as we went along; she began to supplement her reports with stories about her workplace relationships. But the excerpts offered here capture the problematic character of these questions in any case: They *invite* reports. They do not invite the other to take responsibility for the import of her response because the weight of the question lies in the sociological ideas. Although some women did tell stories in response to these questions, they did so in spite of rather than because of the questions. In fact, when Stuart added stories to her answers, she apologized for doing so, stating, "Go on with your question. I got way off base." And later, "I get off on the wrong stories."

The exchange surrounding my sociological questions stands in sharp contrast to the lively, lengthy, and engrossing story Laura Stuart told earlier in the interview about her upward mobility from secretary to superintendent. Indeed, my brief request for her work history allowed her to launch into a story that continued with little interruption from us for more than an hour.

> SC: So [p] the story of your work life [small laugh]
> LS: OK I started [p] some 15–16 years ago as secretary to to the superintendent.
> I was a *nurse* at the time.
> CB: ‖ Oooh ‖
> LS: ‖ I was ‖ working for a doctor and the superintendent of schools called me
> at Libertyville and said "would you be interested in going to work for me?"
> And I had had a little secretarial training course that was manpower
> they don't even have that I think they call it something else now (CB: hm
> hmm)
> but back at that time it was a manpower program
> and so I went to that for 6 months and and got *re* [p]
> oh uh *trained* myself.
> But I didn't use the secretarial training at that time.
> The hospital called and said "would you be interested in coming back to work?"
> I had worked there previously till the kids were born
> as a nurse and then went back and did private duty
> and I said "well I just finished school
> I'm really interested in getting into another line of work"
> and I said you know "besides you don't pay enough."
> "Well we will pay you."
> So they *upped* the salary to what I I felt like I could get as a secretary.
> So I I really *liked* nursing and uh so I went back to work at the hospital.
> I didn't have my license but I had had RN training.
> I I just quite did not finish uh and in a little small rural town like that well
> that you know if you have any training at all that was a plus.

My request for Laura Stuart's work history was brief and required no explanation in part because we had begun the interview by telling her about the kinds of questions we would ask, including this one. More importantly, my request required no explanation because *this was the story she most wanted to tell during the interview.* In this excerpt, her story tumbles out, with different events toppling over each other as if each event is so tied to all the others that she can't talk about one without immediately bringing up the rest.

Like Karen Sacks, my coresearcher and I eventually dropped our sociological questions because they were too external to women's experiences; they encouraged reports rather than stories.[7] The problem with those questions did not lie in their wording—the excerpts show that I used everyday language—but in the way they pulled women away from their experiences. When we asked the sociological questions, we got what we asked for, but not what we were most interested in hearing. Those questions distracted us from the deeper and broader life story the interviewee had to tell.

My Own Experience as a Subject in a Study of Academic Women

Rose Jones, a student in another social science department at my university, asked whether she could interview me as part of her study of women in academe. I agreed, thinking it would be fun to be the interviewee for a change. During the interview, I noticed that some of her questions invited me or at the very least allowed me to tell the story of my own experiences. For example, her first question was "What were the motivating factors that got you into the academic profession?" Rather than listing motivating factors, I chose to talk about how I ended up in graduate school, what graduate school was like for me, and how I made the transition from graduate school to an academic job. Interestingly, my answer suggests that I was not actually motivated to get into the profession because I did not orient to the profession even as I worked my way toward it. I began graduate school with an interest in getting a better education, never imagining that I would come out of it with a Ph.D. and that I would end up as a full-fledged academic with a real job in the profession.[8] Although Rose asked for motivating factors, I answered a broader life story question: "How did you end up in academe?" Nonetheless, her question was close enough to the one I wanted to answer that it did not inhibit my story. She asked a number of other questions that permitted me to tell my own stories, such as: How do you manage teaching versus research? What is keeping you in the profession?

By contrast, some of the questions she asked were not about my experiences at all, but about my opinion concerning the difference gender makes in the profession. For example, What do you think about the issue of tenure for women in academe? How do you think women are represented in institutions of higher education? How do you think your male colleagues manage teaching versus research? I felt impatient with these questions but not because I had nothing to say bout them. Indeed, I have plenty to say about the differences gender makes in this and other occupations, difference that I talk about in my courses as well as during everyday conversations with friends, colleagues, and students. I was impatient because this was neither a classroom interaction nor a casual conversational context; this was supposed to be an interview about *my* experiences. I did not want the focus to shift away from me and my stories. These questions asked me to speak as a sociologist, something I am perfectly capable of doing but which I didn't want to do here. In short, these questions felt like work. Not surprisingly, I offered sociological responses to her sociological questions. Listen, for example, to part of my answer to her question about women and tenure.[9]

> SC: Women tend to do more service activities because of the low representation of women on campuses, but when it comes to tenure that doesn't count. It's not intentional discrimination, it's institutional discrimination.

This is not a description of my own experiences but a summary of what I assume to be many women's experiences. Rose Jones's sociological questions invited me to report my observations of what women in general do rather than to recount what I in particular have done.

In sum, all three examples suggest that sociological questions fail to invite the other's story because they orient the interviewee to the researcher's interests. Even when the researcher phrases such questions in everyday speech and intends to produce a collaborative research relationship, sociological questions direct the other to the researcher's concerns and away from her own life experiences. In some cases, of course, participants willingly enter such a conversation to help the researcher with his or her questions. But even in those cases, the researcher invites a report rather than a story because the weight or import of the question remains on the researcher's side, with the interviewee acting at best as a willing reporter or informant.

What, then, does it mean to invite the other's story and how do we articulate a good life story question? Unlike sociological questions, questions that invite the other's story encourage a shift of responsibility for the import of the talk. Our task as interviewers is to provide the interactional and discursive conditions that will arouse her desire to embrace that responsibility. We are most likely to succeed when we orient our questions directly and simply to life experiences that the other seeks to make sense of and to communicate.

But even if we aim to invite the other to tell her story, it's not always clear in advance which question will serve as an invitation. Sacks did not know she

had asked a good question until she started to hear stories about how childhood chores produced a sense of responsibility and self-respect. In her case,
the good questions were: How did you learn about work? And what did work
mean to you? In my study of women educational leaders, the request for work
histories invited them to take responsibility for determining the direction and
significance of their talk. But even though my coresearcher and I asked that
question from the beginning of the project, I did not recognize it as the pivotal question until later.

Our work as interviewers, then, includes careful formulation of questions
that will invite the other's story. Before we start interviewing, we need to begin with, or at least work our way toward, some sense of the broad parameters
of the other's story, the life experience he or she seeks to make sense of and to
communicate. And we do this by articulating what makes this group of people's life experiences interesting in the first place.

In the case of my study, the anomaly of women holding positions of power
makes their experiences interesting, not only to themselves, but to researchers,
journalists, and the public at large. As public school superintendents, these educators occupy influential positions in their communities. As white women
and women of color, they are continuously subject to gender and racial inequalities in a male- and white-dominated profession. It is the coexistence of
power and subjection in their worklives that makes their experiences interesting within the context of contemporary American society. Although we did
not articulate it at the time, my coresearcher and I, as well as the women we
interviewed, *assumed* that as highly successful professional women, they
would have stories to tell that others want and need to hear, stories about how
they rose to such influential leadership positions despite the anomaly of their
gender or race, stories about what is like to work in such positions, stories
about the inequalities they face and how they handle them. These assumptions reveal the broad parameters of the life stories women educational leaders have to tell. Hence the appropriateness of the request for their work
histories.

ENCOUNTERING NARRATIVE DIFFICULTIES
AND REITERATING THE INVITATION

Knowing the broad parameters of the other's story prepares us to ask a
good question. However, the very thing that makes any group of people's

life experiences interesting may also produce narrative difficulties. For example, as women educational leaders recounted their work histories, they told stories about themselves *both* as highly accomplished, successful professionals *and* as women who are subject to sexism and racism in the profession. As I analyzed their narratives, I discovered that women often have difficulty bringing together these two distinct experiences of self. That difficulty is not psychological or personal (although it might have psychological or personal consequences). Rather it is cultural and discursive. In narrating their work experiences, successful professional women work at integrating two kinds of talk—two discursive realms—that do not usually belong together in American culture: talk about individual achievement and success, and talk about gender and racial inequality.[10]

In articulating the general parameters of the other's story, then, we need to attend to what may be culturally problematic about that story and what may produce narrative difficulties or complexities. In listening to the other tell her story, we need to remain attentive to the ways in which its culturally problematic character may produce silences, gaps, disruptions, or contradictions. Thus, inviting the other's story requires more than a good life story question, it also requires reiterating the invitation throughout the interview. This means that we may need to ask questions that will encourage her to fill in what she has left out or to articulate more fully her contradictory feelings.

I return to Laura Stuart's work history to illustrate how a narrative difficulty arose that my coresearcher and I should have explored in more depth. In recounting her career story, Stuart emphasized her hard work and determination in her upward mobility from the humble position of secretary to the powerful position of superintendent of schools. Throughout that story she wove the theme of her growing self-confidence through mastery of new responsibilities and recognition of how much she had accomplished with so few resources. Yet a less obvious theme bubbled to the surface at certain points: her nagging feeling of inadequacy. The gap or contradiction between her growing self-confidence and her persistent lack of self-confidence indicates a narrative difficulty.

In the following excerpt, Laura Stuart concludes her discussion of how she managed to finish her bachelor's, master's, specialist's, and administrative degrees while working full-time in jobs with increasing responsibility: secretary, secretary-teacher, business manager, and administrative assistant to the superintendent.

LS: And I graduated from [university] [p]
    same weekend I became a grandmother.
    It was a *very* exciting weekend.
CB and SC: [laugh] yeah
LS: But anyway it's been a very uh [p] uh *exciting* period. (CB: hm hmm)
    People *anyone* could have what I have attained
    if they had the determination and willing to make the sacrifices that I had to do
    because I haven't been blessed with
    I mean I'm not *super* intelligent like I think Ruth Porter is
    like Adrienne like Mary [other women superintendents]
    I feel like they're just head and shoulders above me
    you know I feel so *inadequate* sometimes when I'm in their presence because
    I think they have so much.
    I guess because I've come up that way that my you know a lot of mine has
    been *practical* experience. (CB: hm hmm)
    But I *honestly* do not feel like I could have handled this job here had I not had
    the background of that secretarial you know training and coming up . . .
    it has been a *great* benefit to me
    I think if you interviewed any one of my employees here from the cooks to
    the custodians
    they will tell you you know that uh I've made them feel important . . .
    this belongs to them too
    and I think that comes from my background.

In terms of narrative process, Laura Stuart sandwiches her statements
about her inadequacy between more convincing and fully developed descriptions of her strengths. At the beginning of this excerpt, as she summarizes a
busy, exciting period in her life—one filled with many accomplishments—
Stuart points to her own determination and willingness to make sacrifices as
the source of her success. And at the end of the excerpt, she articulates the
strengths she has gained form her practical experience. Virtually all superintendents enter the educational system as teachers (a professional occupation);
Stuart's beginning as a secretary (a working-class job) is unusual. She claims
that her unique background has provided her with the insight and skills to
make all school employees feel a part of the educational community.
    It is unclear from this passage why Laura Stuart thinks she is not as in-
telligent as the women superintendents she names; indeed, she provides no

evidence of that claim. The disjunction between her feelings of inadequacy and her descriptions of her strengths points to a narrative difficulty.[11] How can a professional woman who occupies one of the most influential positions in her community make sense of her recurrent lack of self-confidence? Cultural discourse about professional work makes it easy for Laura Stuart to tell a story about increasing responsibilities and thus increasing self-confidence. In other words, that is an intelligible, recognizable story in our society. In contrast, it is difficult to narrate her feelings of inadequacy because they do not make sense within conventional discourse about professional work. Thus her lack of self-confidence surfaces in her narrative without becoming integrated into it. My point is not that it is impossible to imagine her feelings of inadequacy—what professional has not felt inadequate at times in comparison to peers?—but that the undeveloped description of those feelings indicates the limited character of professional discourse within which she has been telling her story.

Interestingly, neither my coresearcher nor I pick up on Laura Stuart's feelings of inadequacy at this point. Here is how we continue:

> SC: I'm I'm missing a little piece of the story.
>> How did you decide when you were administrative assistant to the super-
>> intendent
>> how did you decide that you would start applying for superintendencies
>> yourself?
> LS: OK the superintendent was going to retire
>> and uh I felt like I was next in line for the job there...
>> BUT guess who he recommended
> CB: the high school principal
> LS: and I said "I'm not going to train another high school principal.
>> This is it.
>> I have carried the ball for you." ...
>> That last superintendent had [emphatically] the *best* job of any of my super-
>> intendent
>> because I had *grown* and matured *professionally*
>> had assumed more responsibility you know as time went on. . . .
>> [emphatically] He *never* filled out a report.
>> Not one.
>> I did *all* the agendas.

We discussed what was but I did I was responsible for the *agenda*
I was responsible for the *budget.*
I was the district *treasurer.* . . .
So he was you know he *really* had it made.
Consequently I *always really* worked with him before he went into a board meeting on Monday
I spent the *day with him going tutoring* him on what
because I didn't want him to have to turn to me and say
you know I was still [deep sigh] [p]
trying to make him look good
and willing to take the back seat . . .
I didn't begrudge him [the high school principal] applying for the job.
What I *REALLY* detested was that this superintendent *knew*
and if he had stayed neutral and said
"either one of them is an *excellent* candidate"
because he knew
but he did not feel like I could handle the job the people.
But *I KNEW* I had the people skills to do it.
SC: So he didn't—you were ready but he didn't he didn't know you were ready
or he didn't—
LS: *He* didn't *he* went with the good old boy.
He went with [p] because he was a man.

Laura Stuart's confidence in her readiness for the title and full responsibility of the superintendency comes through loud and clear. Through a series of first-person, declarative statements, she convinces us of her competence and that she had already taken on much of the superintendent's work. She also expresses outrage at her superior's blatant sexism in failing to recommend her as his successor. As listeners, we sense that this discriminatory episode was a turning point, the moment at which she decisively rejected her previous pattern of doing male superiors' work for them. At the same time, she acknowledges her collusion in the superintendent's facade, and her deep sigh indicates her understanding that something was terribly amiss in that arrangement. What remains unstated, however, is how she got herself into such a situation in the first place and how she felt about it at the time. We need more emotional details to understand the transition fully. Again, the point is not that such a situation is unimaginable; indeed, it is all too familiar in professional

women's stories. Rather, the point is that Laura Stuart hints at a story that remains untold—the story about taking a back seat while working hard to make
the superintendent look good. As interviewers we need to attend to submerged
stories like this one and invite their telling. This story appears to be more difficult to tell than a story about growing professional confidence, which is the
dominant frame Stuart uses in her work history, including in this excerpt.
From my retrospective, analytic standpoint, I begin to wonder whether this
submerged story is related to the earlier one about feelings of inadequacy.

Toward the end of her long work history, Laura Stuart described a situation
in which a colleague in another school district had invited Stuart rather than
others to apply for a certain prestigious job. She expressed genuine pleasure at
being singled out in this way. At this point her feelings of inadequacy suddenly
resurfaced:

LS: [sigh] I think *some*body is going to tap me on the shoulder one of these days
    and tell me to get back down where I belong (CB: hmmm)
    you know I have those feelings sometimes
    I don't know if you all ever experience it or not
    and my daughter sent me a book titled *The Imposter* || *Feeling* ||
CB: || hm hmmm ||
    so that's || what you're thinking about ||
LS: || and I read it || you know I get it out every once in a while and go back and
    read a chapter or two because [p]
    I didn't have any self-confidence uh for a number of years.
    But now I feel like I can do it
    you know I feel in*adequate* sometimes
    I feel like Ruth and they are are so much *smarter* than I am
    but I *still* feel like I can hold my own
    I'm running this school system too
    maybe not as *big* as what they are doing but I still
    I'm making things work for me. (CB: hm hmm)
    I I'm proud of myself I really am.
SC: What changed there/
    You said you used to not have self-confidence and now you do even though
    sometimes—
LS: I I went back to school.
    I went back to college and made straight As.
    M first report card my first grades I could not *believe* it

I was so amazed.
I thought "*I* can do *this.*"
CB: So actually doing things
LS: I guess
CB: you've convinced || yourself ||
LS: || yeah || and along about that time after I got out of college I lost some
weight
and um it made a difference in my appearance.
I'm not beautiful but I like myself better now.
And I don't know just all of it added together maybe.

Here my coresearcher and I finally attend to Laura Stuart's feelings of inadequacy, perhaps because she dwells on the topic for a while, or because feeling like an imposter is more extreme than feeling inadequate, or because she includes us as professional women who may have felt similarly. Notice that once again she counters these negative feelings with her confidence and even pride in her accomplishments. When I ask "What changed there?" I am finally trying to bring the submerged story to the surface. Although my question asks for her process of self-development on this issue, my interrupted phrase "even though sometimes—" only hints at the more problematic features of her narrative: Her lack of self-confidence *recurs* even now that she has achieved a prominent leadership position. The nagging persistence of these feelings needs more illumination. The best way to tap that would have been to ask about specific recent incidents when she felt inadequate or like an imposter.[12]

In sum, Laura Stuart experienced our request for her work history as an invitation to tell her story about her upward mobility from secretary to superintendent, and about her hard work, determination, and growing confidence in confronting obstacles—including sex discrimination—that she encountered along the way. In taking up that invitation, she eagerly embraced responsibility for the import of her talk. However, the excerpts I have examined from her work history reveal narrative difficulties in the form of hinted at but unarticulated aspects of her experience, narrative difficulties that call for reiteration of the invitation to tell her story. Our task as interviewers, then, includes listening for gaps, silences, or contradictions, and reiterating the invitation through questions that encourage fuller narration of the complexities of her story. By reiterating the invitation, we work at continually shifting narrative responsibility to the other.

NARRATIVE ANALYSIS: STUDYING THE
RELATION BETWEEN THE GENERAL AND THE PARTICULAR

Many researchers who study narratives produced during interviews assert that we learn about general social processes through analysis of specific narratives.[13] From this standpoint, narrative analysis is grounded in a particular theoretical commitment: Understanding general social processes *requires* a focus on their embodiment in actual practices, that is, in actual narratives. In other words, life stories themselves embody what we need to study: the relation between *this* instance of social action (*this* particular life story) and the social world the narrator shares with others; the ways in which culture marks, shapes, and/or constrains this narrative; and the ways in which *this* narrator makes use of cultural resources and struggles with cultural constraints. By analyzing the complex process of narration in specific instances, we learn about the kinds of narratives that are possible for certain groups of people, and we learn about the cultural world that makes their particular narratives possible—and problematic—in certain ways. The significant point here is that the general (cultural and discursive resources and constraints) is not fully evident to use in advance; we know the general fully only through its embodiments.

My discussion of narrative difficulties in the previous section illustrates this theoretical commitment. By attending to the problematic content of Laura Stuart's narrative (the gap between her self-confidence and her feelings of inadequacy) as well as to disjointedness in her narrative process (the sudden surfacing and submerging of her feelings of inadequacy), we can begin to analyze the boundaries of cultural discourse about professional work. Similarly, the smoothly narrated parts of her work history—for example, about growing self-confidence through increasing responsibilities—point not only to her personal comfort with that aspect of her experience but also to the kind of cultural discourse that is readily accessible for describing one's professional development.

Laura Stuart's work history also illustrates how general social processes related to gender and social class are embedded in her narrative. She speaks directly about her working-class background and the unusual pattern of her upward mobility. Furthermore, she suggests that her background and atypical career path have enabled her to develop specific skills that are useful in her work as superintendent. She also explicitly acknowledges sexist treatment she encountered as she worked her way from secretary to educational administrator. Notice that we did not have to ask directly about gender issues to hear about them; I asked the fruitless series of questions that produced her reports about gender-related experiences *after*. She gave us her work history. Her sex discrimination story, which she told as part of her work history, is much more fully developed than those reports.[14] Laura Stuart's direct references to gender and class hint at the impact of general social processes on her work experiences; more precisely, they tell us how she interprets the relationship between the general and the particular in her own life.

However, what is more interesting to me, and much more difficult to decipher, is how general social processes related to gender and class are embedded in Stuart's submerged stories. To address this question, we would need to identify all of the places where submerged stories surface, such as those about inadequacy, impostership, and taking a back seat to men while doing their work for them. Then we would need to examine the relationship between those submerged stories and her larger, more fully developed narrative about growing self-confidence. Are there any patterns in the way she mentions and then drops the subject of inadequacy? What aspects of her work experience does she use to push these feelings aside? What is it about these submerged experiences and feelings that inhibits their fuller expression in her work history? By contrast, what is it about her larger story of hard work, determination, and growing self-confidence that makes those aspects of experience easy to narrate?

It is reasonable to consider that there might be gender and class underpinnings to the narrative difficulties in Laura Stuart's work history. After all, women from working backgrounds receive little cultural encouragement to be ambitious and plenty of encouragement to work selflessly for others and to think of themselves as inadequate. But the task of narrative analysis is to find out how she embeds those general social processes in her narrative. We might continue our analysis by examining the places where she easily acknowledges how class and gender shape her experiences and comparing them to the places where she could have pointed to gender and class influences but didn't. What in the submerged stories keeps her from making similar connections? Could it be that she attaches shame or self-blame to the experiences hinted at in those stories? For example, might she be ashamed of herself for colluding with a man's exploitation of her, thinking that as a professional woman she should have known better? If so, a sense of responsibility for her own predicament may make it difficult for her to identify gender and class influences in the experiences described in these submerged stories. By contrast, it might be easier to identify blatant sex discrimination and material obstacles related to her working-class background (such as having to work full-time while pursuing her education) as problems not of her own making.

The excerpts I have examined from Laura Stuart's work history are not sufficient to demonstrate any particular argument; I have simply suggested possibilities for further inquiry. In any case, analyzing specific narratives to answer questions like these allows us to develop fuller knowledge about how cultural discourses simultaneously provide us with resources for articulating experience and constrain us when we do so. Such analysis also educates us about the range of ways in which narrators reproduce those discourses and struggle with those constraints as they make sense of their life experiences. However, this kind of narrative analysis depends on our ability to invite others to recount their life stories in rich detail and on our sensitivity to narrative difficulties that signal our need to reiterate the invitation again and again throughout our interviews. The more fully particular are the stories we hear, the stronger our analyses will be of the relationship between the general and the particular. We serve our theoretical interest in general social processes when we take seriously the idea that people make sense of life experiences by narrating them.

NOTES

1. See, for example, Blum and McHugh (1984), Brown (1987), Bruner (1986), Hunter (1990), Maines and Ulmer (1993), Martin (1986), Mishler (1986), Mitchell (1980), Richardson (1990), and Rosenwald and Ochberg (1992).

2. See also Riessman (1990), especially the appendix, "A Narrative about Methods."

3. The idea of studying the general through the particular continues to be more widely accepted in anthropology and psychology than in sociology. Nonetheless, several sociological traditions—symbolic interaction, phenomenology, ethnomethodology—advance the idea that individuals' practices embody what is general to the group or society of which they are members. For full discussions see Blum and McHugh (1984), Garfinkel (1967), and Chase (1995), especially chapter 1. Rosenwald (1986) articulates similar ideas from the standpoint of psychology.

4. For discussions of the influence of feminism on research methods see Cancian (1992), Harding (1987), and Reinharz (1992).

5. "Laura Stuart" is a pseudonym as are all of the names of people and places mentioned in the interview excerpts. I have also given a pseudonym to "Rose Jones," the student who interviewed me, as discussed in the next section.

6. Sociologists and others who base their research on interviews typically edit interview talk when they present excepts. They exclude what appears to be extraneous, distracting material: stutters, repetitions, asides, pauses, the interviewer's questions, interruptions, and nonlexical responses such as "hm hmm." The intention of such editing, of course, is to provide readers with the content of speech. Yet as many others have argued, such editing ignores that meaning is communicated through the complex practices of speech as well as through words (Mishler, 1986; Stromberg, 1993). Thus my interview transcripts include material that some deem distracting. By listening carefully to how speakers express themselves, I can interpret more fully what they are saying. My transcribing procedures highlight the flow and intensity of speech. Each line of a transcript represents what Chafe (1980, pp. 14–15) calls a "spurt of language." I determine the boundaries of a "spurt" by listing to intonation, a rise or fall in pitch. When a "spurt" is longer than a line of text, I indent the subsequent lines to show that speech is continuous. Italics indicate emphasis; capital letters signify extra emphasis or loudness; and dashes show a break-off of speech or interruption. When speakers talk simultaneously, their overlapping words are placed within double lines. Noticeable pauses of less than 3 seconds are identified by [p] and pauses of more than three seconds by [P]. Laughter and other nonlexicals are noted in brackets. I use punctuation sparingly, only when intonation clearly indicates a full stop or question. Quotation marks show that a speaker is reporting someone else's (or her own) speech. Ellipses (. . .) mark places where I have deleted material. My method of transcription is closest to that developed by Riessman (1990). For a discussion of how theories of language are embodied in transcribing practices, see Mishler (1991) and Ochs (1979).

7. For an analysis of awkward moments produced by these questions in one of our earliest interviews, see Chase and Bell (1994).

8. This may be a gendered story. See Aisenberg and Harrington (1988), especially chapter 2, "Transformation."

9. During the interview Rose Jones agreed to give me a copy of the interview tape; unfortunately, she accidentally erased the tape after making a rough transcript. I quote here from the transcript she gave me.

10. I develop this idea in chapters 1 and 2 of Chase (1995).

11. Stuart's statement of her inadequacy could also be interpreted as a marker, "a passing reference . . . to an important event or feeling state," a hint thrown out for the interviewer to pick up on (Weiss, 1994, p. 77).

12. Weiss (1994) provides the best discussion I have read of how to elicit full, detailed stories from interviewees (especially pp. 71–73). Interestingly, he does not relate his discussion specifically to narrative research.

13. Within this general idea of narration as a complex social process, narrative analysts have various interests and purposes. For example, some focus on how narratives embody, reproduce, and/or alter cultural scripts or disjunctive discursive realms (Chase, 1995; Walkover, 1992). Others examine the ways that narratives push at the boundaries of what is unsayable and untellable in particular contexts (Greenspan, 1992; Stromberg, 1993). And some are interested in how narration shapes identity and in the formative and deformative effects of narration (Rosenwald & Ochberg, 1992).

14. Some women superintendents did not talk about discrimination as they narrated their work histories. In those cases we asked a direct question about sex and/or race discrimination at the end of her work history. Unlike the series of questions we asked Laura Stuart and a few other women at the beginning of the study, this question was intended to reiterate the invitation to tell her story. In other words, we were asking about what we assumed was being left out. Indeed, all of the women acknowledge that they are subject to some form of gender and/or racial inequality. If we wanted to hear the full story of women's work experiences, then, sometimes we needed to ask directly about those experiences of inequality that the professional world discourages them from talking about. See Chase (1995), especially chapters 3, 4, and 5.

REFERENCES

Aisenberg, N., & Harrington, M. (1988). *Women of academe: Outsiders in the sacred grove.* Amherst: University of Massachusetts Press.

Bell, C., & Chase, S. (1993). The underrepresentation of women in school leadership. In C. Marshall (ed.), *The new politics of race and gender* (pp. 144–54). London: Falmer Press.

Blum, A., & McHugh, P. (1984). *Self-reflection the arts and sciences.* Atlantic Highlands, NJ: Humanities Press.

Brown, R. H. (1987). *Society as text: Essays on rhetoric, reason, and reality.* Chicago: University of Chicago Press.

Brunner, E. M. (1986). Ethnography as narrative. In V. W. Turner & E. M. Bruner (eds.), *The anthropology of experience.* Urbana, IL: University of Chicago Press.

Cancian, F. M. (1992). Feminist science: Methodologies that challenge inequality. *Gender & Society,* 6, 623–42.

Chafe, W. L. (1980). The deployment of consciousness in the production of a narrative. In W. L. Chafe (ed.), *The pear stories: Cognitive, cultural, and linguistic aspects of narrative production* (pp. 9–50). Norwood, NJ: Ablex.

Chase, S. E. (1995). *Ambiguous empowerment: The work narratives of women school superintendents.* Amherst: University of Massachusetts Press.

Chase, S. E., & Bell, C. S. (1994). Interpreting the complexity of women's subjectivity. In F. M. McMahan & K. L. Rogers (eds.), *Interactive oral history interviewing* (pp. 63–81). Hillsdale, NJ: Lawrence Erlbaum.

Garfinkel, H. (1967). *Studies in ethnomethodology.* Englewood Cliffs, NJ: Prentice Hall.

Greenspan, H. (1992). Lives as texts: Symptoms as modes of recounting in the life histories of holocaust survivors. In G. C. Rosenwald & R. L. Ochberg (eds.), *Storied lives: The cultural politics of self-understanding* (pp. 145–64). New Haven, CT: Yale University Press.

Harding, S. (ed.) (1987). *Feminism and methodology: Social science issues.* Bloomington: Indiana University Press.

Hunter, A. (ed.) (1990). *The rhetoric of social science research: Understood and believed.* New Brunswick, NJ: Rutgers University Press.

Maines, D. R., & Ulmer, J. T. (1993). The relevance of narrative for interactionist thought. *Studies in Symbolic Interaction,* 14, 109–24.

Martin, W. (1986). *Recent theories of narrative.* Ithaca, NY: Cornell University Press.

Mishler, E. G. (1986). *Research interviewing: Context and narrative.* Cambridge, MA: Harvard University Press.

———. (1991). Representing discourse: The rhetoric of transcription. *Journal of Narrative and Life History,* 1, 255–80.

Mitchell, W. J. T. (ed.) (1980). *On narrative.* Chicago: University of Chicago Press.

Ochs, E. (1979). Transcription as theory. In E. Ochs & B. B. Schieffelin (eds.), *Developmental pragmatics* (pp. 43–72). New York: Academic Press.

Polanyi, L. (1985). *Telling the American story: A structural and cultural analysis of conversational storytelling.* Norwood, NJ: Ablex.

Reinharz, S. (1992). *Feminist methods in social research.* New York: Oxford University Press.

Richardson, L. (1990). Narrative and sociology. *Journal of Contemporary Ethnography,* 19, 116–35.

Riessman, C. K. (1990). *Divorce talk: Women and men make sense of personal relationships.* New Brunswick, NJ: Rutgers University Press.

Rosenwald, G. C. (1986). A theory of multiple-case research. *Journal of Personality,* 56, 239–65.

Rosenwald, G. C., & Ochberg, R. L. (eds.) (1992). *Storied lives: The cultural politics of self-understanding.* New Haven, CT: Yale University Press.

Sacks, K. B. (1988). *Caring by the hour: Women, work, and organizing at Duke Medical Center.* Urbana: University of Illinois Press.

———. (1989). What's a life story got to do with it? In Personal Narratives Group (ed.), *Interpreting women's lives: Feminists theory and personal narratives* (pp. 85–95). Bloomington: Indiana University Press.

Stromberg, P. G. (1993). *Language and self-transformation: A study of the Christian conversion narrative.* Cambridge, NY: Cambridge University Press.

Walkover, B. C. (1992). The family as an overwrought object of desire. In G. C. Rosenwald & R. L. Ochberg (eds.), *Storied lives: The cultural politics of self-understanding* (pp. 178–91). New Haven, CT: Yale University Press.

Weiss, R. S. (1994). *Learning from strangers: The art and method of qualitative interview studies.* New York: Free Press.

14

Representing Discourse:
The Rhetoric of Transcription

Elliot G. Mishler

INTRODUCTION

Photography might be considered the prototypical method for representing reality, or at the least a point of reference and comparison for other claimants. Certainly, this was the source of the awe and wonder with which its invention was greeted 150 years ago. "Nature paints itself" and the "mirror with a memory" were early characterizations. And, although "the camera never lies" may be a worn-out cliché, it remains a popular truism that resists disconfirmation despite certain anomalies that were present right from the beginning.

As a way of understanding what a photograph means—what it represents—this perspective of naïve realism retains its hold. Nonetheless, alternative views of representation have gained strength in the last few decades and resistance to the earlier conception is growing. The "contest of meaning" (Bolton, 1989a) that has surfaced in recent critical studies of photography parallels discussion of the problem of representation in science (e.g., Clifford & Marcus, 1986; Lynch & Woolgar, 1988a/1990a; Young, 1991). A brief review of these issues in photography may help sensitize us to problems in the transcription of speech, a form of representation that is central to discourse studies, which is the specific focus of this article.

Reprinted from *Journal of Narrative and Life History* 1, no. 4 (1991): 255–80.

One puzzling question, retrospectively present at the birth of photography, is how it was possible to see different images, produced by different processes, as equivalent and true representations of the same reality. Two separate inventions were formally announced to the general public in 1839—now the conventionally agreed-upon date for the invention. The daguerreotype—a one-of-a-kind positive image on a metal plate with a sharpness of detail comparable to an etching—was the produce of the French partnership of Niepce and Daguerre. The Talbotype—a negative paper image with a reversal of black and white values, with less sharpness—was developed by Talbot in England.

Despite obvious differences between the two types of images, they were both treated as pictures of reality and credit was given equally to Niepce, Daguerre, and Talbot for their independent and simultaneous invention of photography. From recent historical research (Simcock, 1991), credit for being the first person to develop a process to preserve images made by exposure to light on chemically coated paper belongs properly to Elizabeth Fulhame, a British chemist who first published an account of her experiments in 1794. However, Fulhame's pictures, and those of later investigators, either faded with the passage of time or darkened with exposure to light. The signal, collective contribution of Niepce, Daguerre, and Talbot was their discovery of a way to fix such images permanently.[1]

Further developments followed rapidly, including ways of making multiple positive prints from negatives, and photography soon achieved widespread popularity.[2] By 1855, there were so many different processes and types of prints, with different names and much attendant confusion, that a proposal to call them all photography—etymologically "writing with light"—was quickly adopted (Trachtenberg, 1989).[3] Clearly, placing all these types of images (i.e., representations) into the same category and giving it a name was a significant act of interpretation with important consequences for how they were to be understood. These diverse procedures all produced images in black and white, or more precisely in a range of grays along the achromatic scale of tonal values—a significant departure from the chromatic spectrum of reality. (Early Talbotypes were sepia-toned, but the point still applies.) Yet, in the face of this obvious disparity, these different-looking achromatic images were treated as equivalent representations of the one and only reality.[4]

The range of parameters among which choices must be made in making a photograph has increased rather than diminished over the years. Different cameras vary in height-to-width ratios of the image frame, lenses are wide-angle and telephoto, films vary in speed and resolution, printing papers vary in contrast and tone, and darkroom practices of "dodging" and "burning in" offer endless possibilities for altering the original image. And all these differences now apply to color as well. Rather than the development of a standard way to represent reality by a photograph, there is now an extraordinary diversity of possible images of the same object.

The different ways in which we can take, develop, and print images, that is, the technical practices that collectively constitute the craft of photography, are only one part of the problem in how we interpret what reality photographs represent. Issues of context are critical to how we interpret photographs. What we assume to have been "really" there, and how the photographer selected and framed the event, and how the photograph is presented and located within the flow of other information, including other images in either museums or newspapers, along with the text that serves as its caption, all influence our understanding. Thus, our sense of what happened depends on an unreflective view of an innocent relationship between photographer and scene—that, for example, the object or event was not tampered with but is shown as it was. Cultural values and political ideologies provide additional interpretive vantage points to locate the social, cognitive, or affective relevance of, for example, unfamiliar-looking persons or activities as exotic, sympathetic, or dangerous.[5]

In sum, I argue that the meaning of a representation is problematic and dependent on variations in craft and context. The connection between image and reality is not simply "here," even when we might naïvely expect it to be as in the case of a photograph. It must be made (i.e., constructed) and in this sense photography is a "thoroughly cultural formation" (Bolton, 1989b, p. xiii).

Science, of course, has made the same claim as photography to represent reality. And, as we know, one or another form of naïve realism also served for a long period of time as the way of understanding the tasks and achievements of scientific research. The modern critique of this traditional view, in conjunction with studies of scientific practice (Mishler, 1990), has led to a different understanding of science; it too is a "thoroughly cultural formation." In this article, I explore some of the implications of this perspective for our understanding of transcription—the ways we re-present speech as written text. I compare three instances where alternative transcripts, that is, different representations, have been made of the same stretch of speech. Through this comparison, I hope to show that transcription is not merely a technical procedure but an interpretive practice.

RE-PRESENTING SPEECH: PROBLEMATIZING TRANSCRIPTION

Rather than the progressive development of a standard set of methods, analytic procedures, and even a universal language of science as envisaged by the logical positivists, the actual course of scientific research in all fields has been toward diversification, as it has seen in photography. And as was the case in the latter, there is a strong tendency to deny or ignore the implications of this diversity. Different methods are conflated as if they were variants of the same one, the contextualized and pragmatic practices of scientists that make the methods work are omitted from reports of findings, and adherents of one or another approach argue for their own to be accepted as standard (Mishler, 1990).

Transcription—the entextualization of speech—has only recently been taken seriously.[6] The casual approach characterizing earlier research practices assumed a nonproblematic relation between spoken and written language. Viewing language and meaning as transparent to each other, researchers apparently believed that what was said could be represented adequately in the form of paraphrases or summaries. Differences between speech and written text were not seen as significant, and details of the flow of talk were neither described nor analyzed. But this status has all changed through the work of conversation analysts, enthomethodologists, sociolinguists, and others. Although many researchers do not seem to have heard the news, the traditional ways have lost their hegemony, if not their legitimacy, both theoretically and methodologically.

The widespread critique of a realist philosophy of the relations between language and meaning has been a significant backdrop to, stimulus for, and resource in these developments. Our modern (or postmodern) understanding of this relationship as contextually grounded, unstable, ambiguous, and subject to endless reinterpretation both underpins and penetrates changes in our research practices.[7] As transcription has become both more routine and precise, however, emphasis on it as a technical procedure has tended to detach the process from its deeper moorings in this critical reflection on the intractable uncertainties of meaning—language relationships. The accuracy of transcripts is used as a criterion for assessing the value of studies, and claims are made for objectivity as it is revealed in increasingly microscopic levels of detail. That is, researchers strive for more precision, detail, and comprehensiveness—pauses to be counted (by proper instruments) in hundreds rather than tenths of a second, the inclusion of intonation contours—as if that would permit us (finally) to truly represent speech. In accord with this aim, proposals are made to standardize listening practices and notation systems (Psathas & Anderson, 1990).[8]

Treating transcription as primarily (if not solely) a technical procedure is a regression to the stance of naïve realism with which the first photographs were viewed. Videocameras with microphones have replaced the camera with its lens, and "nature records itself" on magnetic tape. And then, as if we were printing positives from negatives, we inscribe the sounds in writing. Each of these steps of re-presentation is a transformation and each may be made in many different ways. Again, as in the case of photography, we seem to be able to treat the variants as equivalent representations of the original reality.[9]

The problem is no different than the general problem of data representation, or inscription, by natural and biological scientists that sociologists of science have examine (Latour & Woolgar, 1979; Lynch & Woolgar, 1988a/1990a). How discourse researchers assemble and display speech as transcripts is a critical step in the social production of scientific knowledge (Mishler, 1984, 1990). It has a similar function and requires analogous skills and competences to understand, as do the graphs, diagrams, charts, and tables of numbers produced and referred to by other scientists as representations of the "real-world" phenomena in which they are interested.

There are an endless number of decisions that must be made about the re-presentation of speech as text, that is, as a transcript, which, although apparently mundane, have serious implications for how we might understand the discourse. For example, do we define our fundamental analytic unit as a clause or tone group as linguists do, or as an utterance which psychologists seem to prefer, or as a speaker turn in the way of conversation analysis? And having chosen a unit, do we use it to define separate lines in the transcript or run the text across the page to the standard margin, noting the units with slash marks? How do we decide where to locate pauses between speakers' turns—at the end of the first speaker's utterance, the beginning of the second speaker's, or between them? These procedural and methodological decisions reflect implicit and explicit theoretical assumptions, and as I argue later, also serve rhetorical functions.[10]

THE POETIC STRUCTURE OF CONVERSATION

Table 14.1 includes a pair of contrasting transcripts of the same stretch of talk, as presented by Tannen (1990). Their source is a dinner-table conversation that served as the focus of her earlier monograph on conversational style, where she examined a variety of linguistic devices, such as pacing and rate of speech, as dimensions of an individual speaker's style (Tannen, 1984). This brief fragment was not included in that report of her study, but the first version (Transcript #1) follows the form of transcription used there. The second versions (Transcript #2) is oriented toward and framed by a different research interest, namely, the relations between conversation and literary discourse.

In her new analysis, Tannen (1990) argued that both conversation and literary discourse rely on forms of "linguistic patterning which are part of a system of coherence constraints" (p. 20). Her aim was to demonstrate that there is an aesthetics of conversation, which "implies that form and meaning are inseparable; understanding grows out of form as much as—or more than—it grows out of propositional or referential meaning" (p. 16). Further, she suggested that "conversation works much like literary language" in that "hearers experience an aesthetic response to the coherence of form and meaning in the discourse" (p. 17). Specifically, the "means to meaning in interaction," that is, recognition and understanding by participants of what is being said, reflects the use of such conventionalized devices as: "patterns of sound, intonation, pitch, prosody, lexicon, and syntax" (p. 17), as well as the content expressed (see also Tannen, 1989).

The first version bears a family resemblance to transcripts typically presented by conversation analysts and sociolinguists. Though there is variation in level of detail and transcription conventions, they tend to include such features of interaction as emphasis, pauses, and overlapping speech. The second version is a vehicle for Tannen's thesis about the literary nature of conversation. It is arranged in lines that represent the rhythmic dynamics of spoken discourse—the "chunks segmented by prosody, intonation, pausing, and discourse markers such as *and*, *but*, and *y'know*" (p. 19), which have been proposed as characteristic of oral narratives and resemble transcripts produced within that research tradition (Chafe, 1980; Gee, 1985; Hymes, 1981; Scollon & Scollon, 1981). The text is also segmented into three stanzas: lines 1–3, 4–14, and 15–19.

Table 14.1   The Poetic Structure of Conversation

Transcript #1.

CHAD: I go out a lot.
DEBORAH: I go out and eat.
PETER: You go out? The trouble with ME is if I don't prepare and eat well. I eat a LOT. . . .
  Because it's not satisfying. And so if I'm just eating like cheese and crackers, I'll
  just STUFF myself on cheese and [fast — — — — — — — crackers.   But if I fix
  myself something nice. I — — — — — — —]
  don't have to each that much. I've noticed that, yeah.
DEBORAH: Hmmm . . . Well then it works, then it's a good idea.
PETER: It's a good idea in terms of eating, it's not a good idea in terms of time.

Transcript #2

1	CHAD:	I	go out a lot.
2	DEBORAH:	I	go out and eat.
3	PETER:	You go out?	

4		The	trouble with ME is
5		if	I don't prepare.
6		and	eat well.
7			I eat a LOT. . . .
8		Because	it's not satisfying.
9		And so if	I'm just eating like cheese and crackers.
10			I'll just STUFF myself on cheese and crackers.
11		But if I	fix myself something nice.
12			I don't have to eat that much.
13	DEBORAH:		Oh yeah?
14	PETER:	I've noticed that.	yeah.
15	DEBORAH:	Hmmm . . .	
16		Well then it works.	
17		then it's	a good idea.
18	PETER:	It's	a good idea in terms of eating,
19		it's not	a good idea in terms of time.

Note. From "Ordinary Conversation and Literary Discourse: Coherence and the Poetics of Repetition" by
D. Tannen, 1990, *Annals of New York Academy of Sciences, 583*, p. 21. Copyright 1990 by the New York
Academy of Sciences. Reprinted by permission of the author.

Further, because Tannen wanted to examine one type of linguistic patterning in this analysis, namely, repetition, she reported "moving around bits of
the lines" to make "more of the repetition stand out" (p. 21). Examples of lexical repetition that become prominent in this display are the phrase *"go out"*
in lines 1, 2, and 3; *"cheese and crackers"* in 9 and 10; *"it's a good idea"* in 17,
18, and 19.

Clearly, Tannen's retranscription is theory driven, as she is well aware. But
this is unavoidable and as true of her first transcript as of those presented by
other investigators. She is, however, unusually explicit in showing us how she

produced a transcript to correspond to her theoretical position. The "poetic line structure," division of lines into stanzas, and the spacing of words on lines display the discourse in order to document, make visible, and warrant her claim that conversations are poetic forms.

This textual display, a re-presentation of speech, is in itself a rhetorical device. By highlighting repetitions, she is showing us that they can be discerned and located within the stream of conversation—if one knows how to construct the right kind of text. This empirical demonstration supports her interpretation of the essential function of repetitions and other literary forms in conversation, as "textbuilding strategies" that play a "significant role in establishing the shared universe of discourse created by conversational interaction in that language" (p. 24). Finally, she suggested that the general effect of poetic forms is to move an audience emotionally, and that the creation of these patterns of form and meaning in conversation "moves it participants to understanding and rapport—or their opposites—in either case, an emotional process" (p. 30).

It seems likely from her approach that had she chosen to study some other literary device, such as intonation, her transcript would have taken a different form. It is also important to note the some features of the first version, which were included for the theoretical and interpretive aims of that study, are excluded in the second version, presumably because they do not bear on the new aims. Thus, the pacing of speech, which was marked between lines of text in the first version by musical notation and dashes enclosed in brackets, is not marked in the new line and stanza version.

Neither of Tannen's transcripts is more accurate or objective than the other. They are each tailored to suit particular theoretical aims, as are the others that I examine later.

NARRATIVIZATION IN THE ORAL STYLE

Table 14.2 includes three transcript versions of a story. For reasons of space only a few parallel segments are shown for the first two, but the third is presented in full. It was told by a seven-year-old Black girl in response to her teacher's request during a "sharing time" period in a second grade class. This classroom exercise is organized to encourage and privilege a literate style of communication, prompting students to tell a story that has a single topic and temporally connected episodes—in short, a beginning, middle, and end with

Table 14.2. Narrativization in the Oral Style

Transcript #1[a]

LEONA'S PUPPY

\#

L: 1 L:a:st / la:st / yesteray / when / uh/m'my father / in the morning /
2 and he / there was a hó:ok / on the 'top of the staiŕway /
3 and my •father was •pickin' me up / and I •got •stuck on the hook /
4 'up thére / and I •hadn't had breakfast / he 'wouldn't 'take me •down =
5 until I finished ⌈'a:ll 'my (breakfast) cause I didn't 'like •oatmeal either //
6 and then my puppy cá:me / he was aslée:p / and he was — he was /
7 he tried to get úp / and he •ripped my pa:nts / and he •dropped the oatmeal=
8 'all over hím / and / and my father cáme / and he said

. . .

18 and he 'always be •followin' me when I go •everywhere //
19 he wants to go to the store / and only he •could •not •go to pla:ces /
20 whe:re / 'we •could go / like / to: / like / t' the store /
21 he could go but he have to be• chained 'up //

. . .

25 and / he's still in the ho:spital / and th-- the doctor said that/he 'hasta
26 he got a •shot be •cause hĕ: / 'he was / 'he was ne:rvous /
27 about my v́home that 'I had / and •he / and he could still stay but /
28 he thought he wasn't gonna be a-/ he thought he wasn't gonna be able =
29 to let him go: //

Transcript #2[b]   Puppy—1

1. L:a:st
2. last
3. yesterday
4. when
5. uh
6. m' my father
7. in the morning
8. an' he
9. there was a ho:ok
10. on the top o' the stairway
11. an' my father was pickin'; me up
12. an' I got stuck on the hook
13. up there
14. an' I hadn't had breakfast
15. he wouldn't take me down =
16. until I finished a:ll my breakfast =
17. cause I didn't like oatmeal either //
18. an' then my puppy came
19. he was asleep
20. an' he was—he was
21. he tried to get up
22. an' he ripped my pa:nts
23. an' he dropped the oatmeal 'all over hi:m
24. an'

continued

Table 14.2. *continued.*

. . .
48. an' he always be followin' me =
49. when I go anywhere
50. he wants to go to the store
51. an' only he could not go t' pla:ces
52. whe:re
53. we could go
54. like
55. to:
56. like
57. t' the stores
58. he could go =
59. but he have t' be chained up
. . .
70. he's still in 'e ho:spital
71. an' the doctor said that he hasta
72. he got a shot because he:
73. he was
74. he was ne:rvous
75. about my home that I had
76. an' he
77. an' he could still stay but
78. he thought he wasn't gonna be a
79. he thought he wasn't gonna be able =
80. t' let him go: / /

Transcript #3[b]

Puppy–2

Part 1: INTRODUCTION
Part 1A: SETTING
1. Last yesterday in the morning
2. there was a hook on the top of the stairway
3. an' my father was pickin' me up
4. an I got stuck on the hook up there
5. an' I hadn't had breakfast
6. he wouldn't take me down =
7. until I finished all my breakfast =
8. cause I din't like oatmeal either / /

Part 1B: CATALYST
9. an' then my puppy came
10. he was asleep
11. he tried to get up
12. an' he ripped my pants
13. an' he dropped the oatmeal all over him

14. an' my father came
15. an he said "did you eat all the oatmeal?"
16. he said "where's the bowl?" / /

Table 14.2. *continued.*

17. I said "I think the dog took it" //
18. "Well I think I'll have t'make another bowl" //

Part 2: CRISIS
Part 2A: COMPLICATING ACTIONS
19. an' so I didn't leave till seven
20. an' I took the bus
21. an' my uppy he always be following me
22. my father said "he—you can't go" //
23. an' he followed me all the way to the bus stop
24. an' I hadda go all the way back
    (25. by that time it was seven thirty) //
26. an' then he kept followin' me back and forth =
27. an' I hadda keep comin' back //

Part 2B: NON-NARRATIVE SECTION (EVALUATION)
28. an' he always be followin' me = when I go anywhere
29. he wants to go to the store
30. an' only he could not go to places where we could go
31. like to the stores he could go = but he have to be chained up

Part 3: RESOLUTION
Part 3A: CONCLUDING EPISODES
32. an' we took him to he emergency
33. an' see what was wrong with him
34. an' he got a shot
35. an' then he was crying
36. an' last yesterday, an' now they put him asleep
37. an' he's still in the hospital
38. (an' the doctor said . . .) he got a shot because
39. he was nervous about my home that I had

Part 3B: CODA
41. an' he could still stay but
42. he thought he wasn't gonna be able to let him go //

a. From "Leona's Puppy" (a previously unpublished draft transcript, dated November 13, 1981) originally transcribed by research assistant C. New, with prosodic information added by S. Michaels (1991). Published with permission from S. Michaels.
b. From "The Narrativization of Experience in the Oral Style" by J. P. Gee, 1985, *Journal of Education, 167*, 32–35. Copyright 1985 by the Trustees of Boston University. Reprinted by permission of the author.

a point. The story is one of a number collected in a study of cultural differences in children's narrative styles (Michaels, 1981). The first version is a previously unpublished draft transcript (Michaels, 1991). The second and third versions are from Gee's (1985) retranscription and reanalysis.

This child's story does not have the preferred well-formed structure and was not understood by her teacher, who found it hard to follow, inconsistent, unclear, and perhaps not true. Gee made a counter argument, namely, that the story is coherent, well-organized, and meaningful, but that it achieves these criteria through linguistic strategies of the oral rather than the literate narrative tradition. He attempted to demonstrate this by how he re-presented its structure and in his interpretation of how the linguistic strategies of the oral tradition do their work.

Michaels (1981) used a form of prosodic analysis to analyze children's stories and her draft transcript (Transcript #1) marks features of intonation, such as rising and falling pitch and points of stress. The units into which she separated the flow of talk are tone group units: segments of speech with a continuous intonation contour and further distinguished as minor or major depending on whether they indicate closure—here marked, respectively, by single slashes ("/") or double slashes ("//"). She was particularly interested in whether or not children told stories that met the teacher's criteria for coherence and well-formedness. From her analyses, she concluded that White, middle-class children's stories matched teachers" expectations and she referred to their stories as *topic centered*. Black children's stories has a different form that she called *topic associating*.

Gee also used prosodic features as the basis for his retranscription and re-analysis. In addition, he divided the text into lines and stanzas as basic structural units, much as Tannen did in her transcriptions (Transcript #2). Finally, as a further step, he clustered the stanzas into larger episodes that have narrative or discourse functions that he named introduction, crisis, and resolution (Transcript #3).

In Michaels' work, the topic associating narrative style tends to be characterized by its differences from the standard topic-centered style, although she also points to the former as deriving from an alternative narrative tradition with different adult standards of adequacy. Gee's intents is a more general critique of mainstream educational practices that emphasize the Western literate style—the teacher's standard—and thereby penalize children from non-Western cultural and linguistic groups that use an oral style (see also Gee, 1990). His task is to show that there is an alternative style of narrativization that has its own tradition as a set of linguistic practices and is, therefore, an equally legitimate and viable form. If he can demonstrate that his child is able to organize her experience through language in a meaningful though different way, he will be able to provide grounds for his argument that she is linguistically competent.

How does he do this? His first retranscription (Transcript #2) displays all
the child's speech as a series of elemental building blocks, that is, units having
single intentional contours—the tone groups or idea units. These are essentially the same as Michael's units, but now they are given separate lines and the
transcript has a different appearance. These are relatively short sequences of
words, most of which end on a non-falling pitch glide and are the minor tone
groups of a standard prosodic analysis. After a number of these, a sequence
appears with the contour of a falling pitch glide at the end; these are indicated
by double slashes in the transcript and are the major tone groups.

The importance of this, as Gee pointed out, is how it differs from standard
literate speech where falling contours tend to mark the ends of sentences,
thereby serving a syntactic function. For this child, they have a "discourse-
level function" appearing "to mark the ends of episodes, not the ends of sentences" (p. 14). This functional interpretation of major tone groups differs
from Michaels' topic-coherence characterization of narrative styles.

Gee referred to his final transcript (Transcript #3), as "an ideal realization of
the text" (p. 14). On the assumption that "it appears that L is aiming at a series
of short clauses as her ideal idea units" (p. 14), he removed "obvious false starts
and repairs . . . and collapse(s) the few subject nouns or noun phrases that are
idea units by themselves into the clauses they belong to" (p. 14). Examples of
these changes include the deletion of nonlexicals like "*uh*" (lines 5 and 39 in
Transcript #2), false starts like "*an' he was # he was*" (line 20), and repetitions,
such as "an" (line 24), and the complex compression of lines 54–57 in Transcript #2 to the phrase "like to the stores" (line 31 in Transcript #3).

From his detailed analysis, Gee concluded that this child made sense of her
world through a story that is "in fact, from start to finish, a tour de force . . . a
remarkable narrative" (p. 24). Though her teacher found it "incoherent . . . inconsistent, disconnected, and rambling," he finds, instead, that she carried out
the task of narrativizing her experience in "a quite sophisticated way" (p. 24).
Using linguistic "technical devices that . . . are hallmarks of spoken language in
its most oral mode, reaching its peak in the poetry, narratives, and epics of oral
cultures" (p. 26), she "uses language full tilt, with prosody, parallelism, rhetoric,
and audience participation all contributing, together with lexical choice and
syntax, to the communication of message, emotion, and entertainment" (p. 25).

Tannen's and Gee's final transcripts are no more complete, accurate, or
valid than their earlier ones. We have seen that both delete features found in

earlier versions, which, needless to say, does not make the earlier ones more complete, accurate, or valid.[11] Their analyses should help put to rest any notion that there is one standard, ideal, and comprehensive mode of transcription—a singular and true re-presentation of spoken discourse. Transcriptions of speech, like other forms of representation in science, reflexively document and affirm theoretical positions about relations between language and meaning. Different transcripts are constructions of different worlds, each designed to fit our particular theoretical assumptions and to allow us to explore their implications. And, as is made particularly clear in Gee's analysis, they have a rhetorical function that locates them within a larger political and ideological context.

VOICES OF THE LIFEWORLD AND OF MEDICINE

The pair of transcripts in table 14.3 is from my studies of medical discourse (Mishler, 1984). They are alternative representations of a stretch of talk—about one and three quarters of a minute in length—between a patient and a physician during a clinical interview. The two texts are identical in the sense that both include the same words and notations for other features of spoken discourse, such as speech overlaps and interruptions, the location and length of silences, false starts, and so forth.

However, they are not identical at the level of lines. This is evident from the beginning, in the second and third lines, and continues throughout so that by the end there are more lines that are different than the same. In contrast to Tannen's and Gee's analyses, lines served no analytic purpose in any approach and it did not matter whether they were the same or different in the two versions. The appearance of lines was left to the printers who adjusted line lengths within their constraints of page margins and type size, while retaining the locations I specified for interruptions, overlaps, pauses, and turn beginnings. The latter were of analytic significance within the theoretical framework I was applying, in which speaker turns rather than lines were the primary discourse unit. Whereas lines require systematic definition in terms of tone groups or clauses, turns are defined by speaker, and how turns begin, end, and are related to each other is of analytic significance. Therefore, it was important for such features as interruptions and overlaps to be represented exactly as I specified. As can be seen, this rule was adhered to even though the lines vary.

Table 14.3. Voices of Medicine and the Lifeworld

Transcript #1

```
I       001   D    Hm hm . . . . Now what do you mean by a sour stomach?
        002   P    . . . . . . . . . . . . . . . . What's a sour stomach? A heartburn
        003        like a heartburn or something.
                                              [
        004   D                     Does it burn over here?
II      005   P                                        Yea:h
        006        It li- I think—I think it like—If you take a needle
        007        and stick ya right . . . . there's a pain right here . .
                           [        [                            [
        008   D                Hm hm  Hm hm              Hm hm
        009   P    and and then it goes from here on this side to this side.
        010   D    Hm hm Does it go into the back?
III                                     [
        011   P              It's a:ll up here. No. It's all right
        012        up here in the front.
                   [
        013   D    Yeah              And when do you get that?
IV      014   P                                . . . . . . . .
        015        . . . . . . . . .Wel:l when I eat something wrong.
        016   D                                  How- How
V       017        soon after you eat it?
VI      018   P                      . . . . . . . . . . . . . . . . . Wel:l
        019        . . . . . . probably an hour . . . . maybe less.
                                              [
        020   D                           About an hour?
VII     021   P    Maybe less . . . . . . . . . . . . I've cheated and I've been
        022        drinking which I shouldn't have done.
        023   D                      . . . . . . . . .
        024        Does drinking making it worse?
                   [
VI      025   P    (. . .)                      Ho ho uh ooh Yes. . . . .
        026        . . . . . . Especially the carbonation and the alcohol.
        027   D    . . . . . . . . Hm hm . . . . . . . . How much do you drink?
VII     028   P                                      . . . . . .
VII*    029        . . . . . . . . . . . . . . I don't know . . . Enough to make me
        030        go to sleep at night . . . . . . . . . . and that's quite a bit.
        031   D    One or two drinks a day?
VII**   032   P                         O:h no no no humph it's (more
        033        like) ten. . . . . . at night.
                        [
        034   D         How many drinks- a night.
        035   P                         At night.
        036   D                      . . . . .
        037        . . . . . Whaddya ta- What type of drinks? . . . . I (. . .)-
VIII                                              [
        038   P                              Oh vodka
        039        . . yeah vodka and ginger ale.
        040   D                         . . . . . . . . . . . . . . . . . . . .
        041        . . . . . . How long have you been drinking that heavily?
IX      042   P    . . . . . . . . . . . . . . Since I've been married.
IX*     043   D                      . . . . . .
        044        . . How long is that?
```

continued

Table 14.3. *continued.*

IX**	045	P (giggle. .) Four years. (giggle)
	046	huh Well I started out with before then I was drinkin
	047	beer but u:m I had a job and I was . . . . ya know . . . . . .
	048	had more things on my mind and ya know I like- but
	049	since I got married I been in and out of jobs and
	050	everything so . . . . I- I have ta have something to
	051	go to sleep.
	052	D . . . . . . Hm:m.
	053	P . . . . I mean I'm not
	054	gonna- . . . . . . It's either gonna be pills or it's
	055	gonna be . . alcohol . . . . and uh alcohol seems
	056	to satisfy me moren than pills do . . . . They don't
	057	seem to get strong enough . . . . pills that I have
	058	got I had- I do have Valium . . . . but they're two
	059	milligrams . . . . and that's supposed to
	060	quiet me down during the day but it doesn't.
	061	D . . . . . .
	062	How often do you take them?
X		(1'47")

Transcript #2

	130	D Hm hm
		[
M7	131	D . . . . . Now what do you mean by a sour stomach?
	132	P . . . . .What's a sour stomach? A heartburn like a
	133	heartburn or somethin.
		[
	134	D Does it burn over here?
	135	P Yea:h. It li- I think-
	136	I think it like- If you take a needle and stick ya right . . . .
		[[
	137	D Hm hm Hm hm
	138	P there's a pain right here . . and then it goes from here on this
		[
	139	D Hm hm
	140	P =side to this side.
	141	D Hm hm Does it go into the back?
		[
	142	P It's a:ll up here. No. It's
	143	all right up here in front.
		[
	144	D Yeah. And when do you get this?
	145	P . . . . . .
	146	. . . . Wel:l when I eat something wrong.
	147	D How- How soon
	148	after you eat it?
	149	P . . . . Wel:l . . . . . . probably
	150	an hour . . . . maybe less.
		[
	151	D About an hour?
	152	P Maybe less.
		[
L7	153	P . . . . I've
	154	cheated and I've been drinking which I shouldn't have done.

Table 14.3. *continued.*

M8	155	D	
	156		.... Does drinking make it worse?
			[
	157	P	(. . .) Ho ho uh ooh Yes..........
	158		Especially the carbonation and the alcohol.
	159	D	.... Hm hm
	160		.... How much do you drink?
	161	P	.... I don't
	162		know.
			[
L8	163	P	.. Enough to make me go to sleep at night .... and that's
	164		quite a bit.
			[
M9	165	D	One or two drinks a day?
	166	P	O:h no no no humpf it's
	167		(more like) ten ...... at night.
			[
	168	D	How many drinks- a night.
	169	P	At night.
	170	D	....
	171		Whaddya ta- what type of drinks? .... 1 (. . .)
			[
	172	P	Oh vodka . . . yeah
	173		vodka and ginger ale.
	174	D	.... How long
	175		have you been drinking that heavily?
			[
L9	176	P	.... Since
	177		I've been married.
			[
M10	178	D	.... How long is that?
	179	P	(giggle.) Four
	180		years.
			[
L10	181	P	(giggle) huh Well I started out with before then I was
	182		drinkin beer but u:m I had a job and I was .... ya know ......
	183		had more things on my mind an ya know I like- but since I
	184		got married I been in and out of jobs and everything so ....
	185		I- I have ta have somethin to go to sleep.
	186	D	...... Hmmm
	187	P	....
	188		.... I mean I'm not gonna- ...... It's either gonna be pills
	189		or it's gonna be . . alcohol .... and uh alcohol seems
	190		to satisfy me moren pills do .... They don't seem to get
	191		strong enough .... pills that I have got I had- I do have
	192		Valium .... but they're two milligrams .... and
	193		that's supposed to quiet me down during the day but it doesn't
			[
M11	194	D	
	195		.... How often do you take them?

Note. From *The Discourse of Medicine: Dialectics of Medical Interviews* (pp. 84–85 and 133–135) by E. G. Mishler, 1984, Norwood, NJ: Ablex. Copyright 1984 by Ablex Publishing Corporation. Reprinted by permission of the author.

The two transcripts also differ in how sequences of turns are partitioned into larger discourse units that are analogues to Gee's and Tannen's stanzas. This distinction between the two transcripts is of critical analytic significance. The alternative ways that turns are grouped together reflect different theoretical conceptions of the clinical encounter. The two re-presentations lead to and support different interpretations of what is going on between the patient and physician that is important to our understanding of such encounters.

In the first version, the discourse units are based on the sequence of questions and answers that is typical of medical interviews. The criterion for defining a turn as relevant to the analysis is whether it serves one of these discourse functions: as either a question from the physician or a response from the patient. Each unit represents three successive turns: the physician's first question, the patient's response, and the physician's next question with an optional assessment of the patient's answer to the prior question. These units are marked by brackets in the left-hand margin and numbered sequentially with Roman numerals. In my analysis, I referred to this as the basic structural unit of the interview. The physician's second question in one unit is, simultaneously, his first question in the succeeding unit, thus serving a dual discourse function. In brief, the discourse structure of the interview is represented in the first transcript as a connected sequence of three-turn units, where the physician's question is the critical link—terminating one unit and initiating the next.

It should be noted that some expressions are not treated as relevant turns; for example, the physician's nonlexical interjections like "hm" in lines 008 and 052, and the exchange in 034–035, which was viewed as a redundant clarification (although in retrospect it could as well have been defined as a separate unit). Other uncertainties on unit specification are indicated as dashed brackets with subunit markers, as in V and V, VII and VII, and IX and IX.

This form of representation reflected my initial view of the medical interview, and of clinical work in general, as dominated by physicians pursuing their agenda—their clinical tasks of eliciting and assembling medically relevant information from patients to arrive at a specific diagnosis and appropriate treatment plan. This view was based on earlier research showing that such interviews were organized, that is, structured, primarily by physicians' questions. These findings were reconfirmed in my study. Some of the empirical questions that were opened up by this conception of a discourse dominated by physician questions were: How patients' responses were constrained by the questions and which types of questions were more or less constraining, the degree to which next questions selectively attended to different types of information in patients' responses, how questions served to initiate and continue topics, and how patients conformed to or resisted the demands and constraints of questions.

Findings from these analyses led me to elaborate on how physicians controlled the interview, how this control reaffirmed the asymmetry of power in clinical relationships, and how a struggle for power between patients and physicians was manifested and managed. I referred to this as a struggle between two voices, of medicine and the lifeworld, each representing a different conception and logic of illness. the first expressed the bioscience model of modern medicine and focused on symptoms and disease; the second expressed the significance of discomforts and difficulties in functioning in the patient's social world.

Despite my recognition of the two voices and the struggle between them, my analysis relied on a characterization of the structure of the interview that assumed, a priori, the dominant role of the physician. This assumption determined how I transcribed the discourse, for example, by my treating the physician's question as the first turn in each discourse unit and by assigning it a dual function, thus making it the basis for the organization and coherence of the encounter. Interpreting the physician as dominant was, in a sense, already preordained by my initial conception and supported by the mode of transcription that provided a re-presentation of speech that conformed with that conception.

This insight came only after completing the first analysis. It led me to see that analysis as inconsistent with my general critique of medical practice, particularly with my aim of providing a formulation of and guidelines for a more humane clinical practice, in which the empowerment of patients is a central value. Clearly, this is an ideological position. Reflecting back on my analysis, it appeared to me that rather than supporting this value my methods and the findings they generated tended to contradict it. Thus, although I had shown how physicians controlled the interview and, thus assured the dominance of the voice of medicine and neglect of the voice of the lifeworld, I continued to rely on the physician's perspective. For example, treating is questions as both starting and ending points for basic discourse units, easily led to characterizing patients' responses in terms of their adequacy as answers to his questions.

Giving the physician the coherence-structuring role in the discourse resulted in my interpreting the patient's efforts to say more than what was asked for and to speak in lifeworld terms as interruptions in the smooth flow of a question-based discourse.

To address this problem, I reexamined the interviews from the patient's perspective. I reformulated the structure of the discourse in terms of the two voices, rather than in terms of questions and responses. This led to a different re-presentation in the form of the second transcript in this pair. The lines of text are now differentiated from each other by whether they express either the voice of the lifeworld or of medicine. The structural units, marked in the left-hand margin by M and L for the two voices, now display the sequences of lines within each of these categories. Speaker turns and questions and answers no longer define the form and boundaries of the structural units. Rather, since both patients and physicians may speak in either voice, and in both voices within one turn, the same turn can be divided with part of it falling into one unit and the other part into the next unit.

For example, in the first transcript, lines 020–024 are shown as a sub-unit V with the physician's question "*About an hour?*" beginning it, and his next question, "*Does drinking make it worse?*" ending it and beginning unit VI. The patient's response to the first question is contained within the unit. In the second transcript, the same sequence of lines—now numbered 151–156, are distributed through three structural units. The physician's first question and the first part of the patient's answer, "*Maybe less,*" are in the voice of medicine—in unit M7; the second part of the patient's answer, "*I've cheated and I've been drinking which I shouldn't have done,*" is a tag comment in the voice of the lifeworld—in unit L7; and the physician's next question, in Line 156, returns the interview to the voice of the medicine. There is the same type of change from unit VII, lines 027–031 in the first transcript, to lines 160–165 in the second transcript.

Clearly, these two transcripts are quite different representations of the same interview. By focusing on how the discourse was structured through voices, rather than through physicians' questions, I could break away from my earlier reliance on the physician's perspective. Giving both voices equal weight in the analysis, allowed me to reformulate the interview as a struggle between them rather than as a medically directed discourse interrupted by the patient's medically irrelevant responses (e.g., her tag comments). Locating utterances within these categories of voices gave me a way to describe their underlying structures of logic and meaning. I could also suggest a deeper understanding of the physician's dominance in terms of his persistent return to the voice of medicine, rather than simply in terms of his control of turns through questions. And finally, I could relate the structure and dynamics of these particular interviews to larger social conflicts, in particular to the struggle between a technical-instrumental mode of reasoning and action, that is, the dominance in the modern world of a technocratic consciousness, and the practical-symbolic mode of everyday life.

CONCLUSION

I have examined three instances in which alternative transcripts were produced as representations of the same piece of discourse. My intent was neither to reify transcripts nor to fault investigators for their inability to develop a standard procedure.[12] Rather, the aim of this exercise was to show through concrete examples how transcription is problematic in a fundamental way. Although criteria of accuracy and precision are not irrelevant, technical advances in recording equipment and detailed notation systems do not address the analytic and theoretical issues that are inherent in any form of re-presentation.

In research on discourse, the decisions concerning how to produce a transcript—what we include as relevant features of speech and how we arrange and display the text—are among the many decisions we make in the course of doing our work. All of them reflect theoretical assumptions abut relations between language and meaning, and between method and theory, and are consequential for what we report as findings as well as how we interpret and generalize from those findings. Furthermore, and most importantly, there is no way not to make such decisions. The search for a standard system that might be applied to any form of talk for any purpose is a misguided effort. Transcripts are our constructions and making them is one of our central research practices.

Situating transcription within its general research context, with its complex array of social, cultural, and linguistic traditions and practices (Mishler, 1990), and, at the same time, resisting the tendency to reify transcripts, does not diminish their importance. From my own experience and that of others I have worked with, the dual process of close and repeated listening with the methical transcribing of details of speech—whatever system is used—leads to the discovery of features and patterns in the talk that were not evident either on its first hearing, or on later rehearings not specifically intended to produce a transcript. How we arrange and rearrange the text in light of our discoveries is a process of testing, clarifying, and deepening our understanding of what is happening in the discourse.

The form of representation we use serves theoretical and rhetorical functions, and perhaps aesthetic ones as well. The transcripts developed by Tannen, Gee, and myself are no different in this respect from the paired split-screen format of micro photographs and schematic diagrams used in biology (Lynch, 1988/1990). Their significance, however, does not end at the boundaries of the academic disciplines. Rather, as is the case with photography, where styles and forms of such genres as portraiture and landscape photography embody dominant social, economic, and political positions and perspectives (Krauss, 1982/1989; Rosler, 1981/1989; Sekula, 1986/1989; and other papers in Bolton, 1989a; Trachtenberg, 1989), what features of speech we consider important enough to re-present as text are also influenced by our stance in the larger world of conflicting claims and contested meanings. This was evident, for example, in Gee's emphasis on the significance of linguistic strategies of the oral tradition for creating coherence and meaning in order to counter the dominant reliance in education on the literate tradition; and in my effort to show the struggle between the voices of the life-world and of medicine in a clinical encounter and to link it to the power of the technocratic consciousness in the modern world.

By locating researchers' transcription practices within the context of the philosophical and programmatic critique of naïve realism that I referred to earlier, I hoped to stimulate further discussion of the implications of that critique for studies of discourse. The problematic relation between reality and representation, and between meaning and language, is not simply an abstract philosophical position but an inescapable feature of our work as empirical scientists. Not being able to rely on a conception of a stable, universal, noncontextual, and transparent relation between representation and reality, and between language and meaning, confronts researchers with serious and difficult theoretical and methodological problems. And, as I observed earlier, these problems are not isolated within the ivory tower; how they are formulated and solved is shaped by events beyond the walls.

As a final word, I want to highlight an important implication of the perspective adopted in this article, namely, that it brings the analyst/interpreter into the field of study. That is, it is not only the discourse of our respondents and subjects that must be located within the framework of culturally constrained linguistic practices and conflicts among discursive formations, but the methods, theories, and analytic practices of researchers as well. Examining the assumptions and aims of different forms of transcription, that is, of the representation of speech as text—as well as other methods and practices—may help us move toward more reflective and critical studies of the multiple ways by which we construct meaning through our discourses.

ACKNOWLEDGMENTS

An early version of this article was presented in March 1991 at a course on "Subjectivity and the Production of Knowledge" sponsored by the Danish Research Academy, and at a colloquium at the University of Aarhus Institute of Psychology.

I am grateful for those opportunities to explore problems of representation with investigators from Denmark and other Scandanavian countries, to the course organizers: Klaus Bruhn Jensen, University of Copenhagen; Steinar Kvale, University of Aarhus Centre for Qualitative Research; Jan-Helge Larsen, Copenhagen Institute of General Practice; and, Grethe Skylv, Copenhagen Rehabilitation Centre for Torture Victims.

Vicky Steinitz' close readings of earlier drafts led to many improvements. The article also benefited from the suggestions of Jane Attanucci, Darlene Douglas-Steele, and Catherine Riessman. James Gee, Sarah Michaels, and Deborah Tannen graciously granted me permission to reprint transcripts from their studies.

NOTES

1. Agreements on the date of photography's invention and the names of is inventors are convenient fictions, giving us persona and occasions to celebrate; for example, the worldwide exhibits and coffee-table picture books on its 150th anniversary in 1989. However, the story is more complicated. Reflected images, for example, had been produced for more than 300 years by the *camera obscura*, a dark room or box with a small aperture fitted with a lens through which a scene projected itself. And, as noted, Elizabeth Fulhame published her findings in 1794. From Niepce's letters, he appears to have made negatives as early as 1816, and one of his positive prints from 1826 still exists. In 1827, he requested permission to report on his experiments to the

British Royal Society, which "refused to receive his communication because it was against its rules to discuss secret processes and Niepce declined to reveal his technique" (Newhall, 1949/1964, p. 16). For surveys of the background, history, and development of the early stages of photography, see Goldberg, 1981; Newhall, 1949/1964; Simcock, 1991; and Trachtenberg, 1989.

2. Although daguerreotypes could be turned into etchings for publication, no direct copies could be made—each was a unique original. Despite this limitation, they initially caught on more quickly and the process spread throughout the world, particularly for portraits. In the United State, for example, almost 1,000 commercial daguerreotypists were listed in the 1850 census and 2 million daguerreotypes were being produced annually by 1853. By 1860, these numbers had jumped, respectively, to over 3,000 and 3 million (Trachtenberg, 1989, p. 294). Another different form of photographic image, the stereograph, also diffused widely, reaching its peak of popularity between the 1850s and 1880s. For example, by 1857—less than 20 years after photography's invention—a London company had sold 500,000 stereoscopes and its 1859 catalogue listed more than "a hundred thousand different stereo views" (Krauss, 1982/1989, p. 291).

3. Simcock, however, suggests an earlier date for the term—perhaps 1839–1840—and states that the process was named photography by Herschel, a British chemist and scientist, who first demonstrated the photosensitivity of platinum salts to Talbot and others in 1831 (Simcock, 1991, pp. 84–85).

4. Bourdieu's (1965/1990) insightful analysis of the social functions of photographic practice focused directly on the problem of representation. He observed that because the primary social function of photographs is to record significant family events, all that is required is a "recognizable souvenir" (p. 58). "Photographic representations only really appear 'lifelike' and 'objective' because they obey laws of representation which were produced before the media for creating them mechanically existed. . . . Photography was predisposed to become the standard of 'realism' because it supplied the mechanical means for realizing the '*vision of the world*' invented several centuries earlier, with perspective" (pp. 191–192). "But, at a deeper level, only in the name of a naïve realism can one see a realistic a representation of the real world which owes it objective appearance not to its agreement with the very reality of things (since this is only ever conveyed through socially conditioned forms of perception) but rather to conformity with rules which define its syntax within its social use, to the social definition of the objective vision of the world; in conferring upon photography a guarantee of realism, society is merely confirming itself in tautological certainty

that an image of the real which is true to its representation of objectivity is really objective" (p. 77).

5. The influence on our assessment of the reality represented by a photograph of how it is framed and contextualized may be suggested by the impact of three famous, emblematic, and powerful images of war. The first, Robert Capa's 1936 photograph, entitled *Soldier at the Moment of Death, Spanish Civil War*, shows a single Loyalist soldier falling backwards, his rifle falling from his hand, and a tuft of hair flying away from his head, presumably where he has been hit by a bullet. Reproduced widely in numerous mass media magazines as well as collections of famous photographs, it is likely to be found in any photography exhibit about war. The second, and the most publicized photograph of World War II, is Joe Rosenthal's photograph of four U.S. Marines raising the American flag on a small hill, thus marking the U.S. victory in the Battle of Iwo Jima. The third is Eddie Adams' picture, taken during the Vietnam War, of a South Vietnamese police chief in uniform holding a gun to the head of a Vietcong prisoner. The far side of the prisoner's head is being blown outward, so we know the gun has just been fired.

These picture serve as metaphors for the different wars they represent: Capa's dying soldier represents the defeat of the Loyalist cause, an omen for the rise of fascism; Rosenthal's image was the model for our national monument to American victory in World War II, now on the mall in Washington, D.C.; and Adams's picture of the public killing of an unarmed prisoner resonated with the growing sense within the U.S. of the brutality and cynicism of the war. The interesting question, for the problems addressed in this paper, is whether and how our interpretations of the meaning of each of these pictures—our understanding of the realities they represented—might have been different if we had further information about their context that only became available some time after their publication. For example, Capa took his picture by accident; afraid of being shot, he held his camera over the edge of the trench he was in, snapped the shutter, and discovered the picture only later when the film was developed. Rosenthal saw the marines raising the flag but missed the shot. Afterwards, he asked them to re-enact what they had done and took the picture—a retrospective simulation of the event. And Adams discovered after the picture was published that the innocent, unarmed victim had just murdered the police chief's best friend and knifed to death his entire family. Within these new contexts—of accident and luck, of simulation, and of possibly adequate reason for an apparent act of wanton murder—what realities do these pictures represent?

For discussion of these issues in photography: of framing, contextualization, and the role of interpretive practices, see the papers reprinted in Bolton

(1980), particularly those by Krauss (1982), Rosler (1981), Sekula (1986), and Trachtenberg (1989).

6. Until 20 to 25 years ago, what people actually said was treated quite casually by social scientists. Survey researchers, presumably engaged in the task of asking respondents to express their personal opinions and attitudes, did not bother to tape-record their interviews. Thus, they avoided the problem by ignoring it. Having nothing to transcribe, they relied instead on interviewers' online summaries and paraphrases for their data (Mishler, 1986). Ethnographers, for their part, wrote their field notes back in their tents at night, basing their analyses and their claims for authoritative interpretations (Clifford, 1988) on their recollections of what had been said, and how, and to whom and when. Clinicians' notes served as representations patients' accounts of their illnesses and were dutifully recorded in charts and records, serving as the official realities of illnesses for the studies of medical sociologists and epidemiologists.

7. This is not the place for a review of this complex and diverse critique. The usual litany of names of the seminal figure would include Bakhtin, Barthes, Derrida, Foucault, Garfinkel, Levi-Strauss, Wittgenstein, and others of each reader's choice whose work led into the various streams of ethnomethodology, hermeneutic interpretation, structuralism, poststructuralism, deconstruction, and postmodernism.

8. Psathas and Anderson (1990) were cautious about their claims for the objectivity of transcripts and their functions in research—noting, for example, that no particular transcription system is neutral and that each reflects theoretical and analytic aims. They also stress the point "that the status of the transcript remains that of 'merely' being a representation of the actual interaction" (p. 77). But it is the phrase *actual interaction* that is fundamental to their proposals. It leads them to suggest a decontextualized approach to reliability, namely, *relistenings* through which we would come to agree about what was really there. And although they recognize that "seemingly 'innocent' decisions of format and presentation can and do have substantial implications for the analysis" (p. 85), their view of transcripts as mere and feasible versions of a hearable interactional reality leads them to downplay the rhetorical and theoretical functions of different transcription practices that are the focus of this article.

9. A wide range of speech features may be transcribed, as can be seen in some of the prominent variants of transcript notation systems: conversation analysts display the location and duration of pauses, overlaps, and interruptions among speakers; false

starts and repetitions; and other paralinguistic markers (Psathas & Anderson, 1990; Schenkein, 1978); Labov and Fanshel (1977) showed pitch frequency distributions as indicators of affective intensity; intonation contours are used to define idea units (Chafe, 1980; Gumperz, 1982) or lines and stanzas (Gee, 1985, 1991; Hymes, 1981); and Ochs (1979) includes observed gestures and actions in her transcripts of children's speech.

10. Ochs (1979) discussed a number of these and other transcription problems that are particularly significant for representing children's speech whose ways of communicating include a strong nonverbal component. She pointed, for example, to "top to bottom" and "left to right" biases in page layouts of transcripts, and to problems in displaying the sequential and simultaneous occurrence of nonverbal actions and speech for one or more speakers. Her emphasis on the theoretical basis and implications of different transcription practices accords with my position.

11. Lynch and Woolgar's (1988b/1990b) observations on the significance of studies of "representational practice in science are relevant to this point: "To claim that our investigations reveal deficiencies in representational practice in science would be to assume a correspondence between argument and object as our ideal representational aim. . . . The very idea of deficiency implies the availability of 'objects' which are somehow free of representation. On the contrary, our position is that representations and objects are inextricably interconnected; that objects can only be 'known' through representation" (p. 13).

12. In conversation analysis (CA), transcription has been accorded a particularly central role in both training and research. Although CA investigators are cautioned not to reify transcripts and to be aware of the selective and theoretical bases of any transcription system, and there is recognition of the craft in use of the method (Psathas & Anderson, 1990), emphasis on the fidelity of the transcript to the actual speech tends to overwhelm these cautions. Thus, Pathas and Anderson remarked: "However, the final arbiter of the fidelity of the transcription is not the skill or 'artfulness' of the transcriber, but rather the adequacy of the transcription when compared with a direct listening/viewing of the original data" (p. 77). And Schenkein (1978), in one of the early presentations of the widely used Jefferson transcript-notation system, noted that the intention of a system of notation and transcript design is to "produce a reader's transcript—one that will look to the eye how it sounds to the ear" (p. xi). Thus, recorded speech is given place of honor as objective reality—as the original data—a position that contrasts with the perspective information this article, and with Lynch and Woolgar's (1988b/1990b) point that "representations and objects are inextricably interconnected; that objects can only be

'known' through representation" (p. 13), and with Bourdieu 91965/1990), just cited in footnote 4.

REFERENCES

Bolton, R. (ed.) (1989a). *The contest of meaning: Critical histories of photography.* Cambridge, MA: MIT Press.

Bolton, R. (1989b). Introduction. In R. Bolton (ed.), *The contest of meaning: Critical histories of photography* (pp. ix–xix). Cambridge, MA: MIT Press.

Bourdieu, P. (1990). *Photography: A middle-brow art.* Stanford CA: Stanford University Press. (Original work published 1965).

Chafe, W. L. (1980). The deployment of consciousness in the production of a narrative. In W. L. Chafe (ed.), *The pear stories: Cognitive, cultural, and linguistic aspects of story production* (pp. 9–50). Norwood, NJ: Ablex.

Clifford, J. (1988). On ethnographic authority. *The predicament of culture: Twentieth-century ethnography, literature, and art* (pp. 21–54). Cambridge, MA: Harvard University Press.

Clifford, J., & Marcus, G. (eds.) (1986). *Writing culture: The poetics and politics of ethnography.* Berkeley: University of California Press.

Gee, J. P. (1985). The narrativization of experience in the oral style. *Journal of Education,* 167, 9–35.

———. (1990). *Social linguistics and literacies: Ideology in discourses.* London: Falmer.

———. (1991). A linguistic approach to narrative. *Journal of Narrative and Life History,* 1, 15–39.

Goldberg, V. (ed.) (1981). *Photography in print: Writings from 1816 to the present.* New York: Simon & Schuster.

Gumperz, J. J. (1982). *Discourse strategies.* Cambridge, U.K.: Cambridge University Press.

Hymes, D. (1981). *"In vain I tried to tell you": Essays in Native American ethnopoetics.* Philadelphia: University of Pennsylvania Press.

Krauss, R. (1989). Photography's discursive spaces. In R. Bolton (ed.), *The contest of meaning: Critical histories of photography* (pp. 287–301). Cambridge MA: MIT Press. (Original work published 1982).

Labov, W., & Fanshel, D. (1977). *Therapeutic discourse: Psychotherapy as conversation.* New York: Academic.

Latour, B., & Woolgar, S. (1979). *Laboratory life: The construction of scientific facts.* Princeton, NJ: Princeton University Press.

Lynch, M. (1990). The externalized retina: Selection and mathematization in the visual documentation of objects in the life sciences. In M. Lynch & S. Woolgar (eds.), *Representation in scientific practice* (pp. 153–86). Cambridge, MA: MIT Press. (Original work published 1988).

Lynch, M., & Woolgar S. (eds.) (1990a). *Representation in scientific practice.* Cambridge, MA: MIT Press. (Original work published 1988).

———. (1990b). Introduction: Sociological orientations to representational practice in science. In M. Lynch & S. Woolgar (eds.), *Representation in scientific practice* (pp. 1–18). Cambridge, MA: MIT Press. (Original work published 1988).

Michaels, S. (1981). "Sharing time": Children's narrative styles and differential access to literacy. *Language in Society,* 10, 423–42.

———. (1991). *Leona's puppy* (Draft transcript: 11/13/81). Unpublished manuscript.

Mishler, E. G. (1984). *The discourse of medicine: Dialectics of medical interviews.* Norwood, NJ: Ablex.

———. (1986). *Research interviewing: Context and narrative.* Cambridge MA: Harvard University Press.

———. (1990). Validation in inquiry-guided research: The role of exemplars in narrative studies. *Harvard Educational Review,* 60, 415–42.

Newhall, B. (1964). *The history of photography: From 1839 to the present day* (rev. ed.) New York: Museum of Modern Art. (Original work published 1949).

Ochs, E. (1979). Transcription as theory. In E. Ochs & B. B. Schieffelin (eds.), *Developmental pragmatics* (pp. 43–73). New York: Academic.

Psathas, G., & Anderson, T. (1990). The "practices" of transcription in conversation analysis. *Semiotica,* 78, 75–99.

Rosler, M. (1989). In, around, and afterthoughts (on documentary photography). In R. Bolton (ed.), *The contest of meaning: Critical histories of photography* (pp. 303–40). Cambridge, MA: MIT Press. (Original work published 1981).

Schenkein, J. (1978). *Studies in the organization of conversational interaction.* New York: Academic.

Scollon, R., & Scollon, S. (1981). *Narrative, literacy, and face in interethnic communication.* Norwood, NJ: Ablex.

Sekula, A. (1989). The body and the archive. In R. Bolton (ed.), *The contest of meaning: Critical histories of photography* (pp. 343–89). Cambridge MA: MIT Press. (Original work published 1986).

Simcock, A. V. (1991). Essay review: 195 years of photochemical imaging 1794–1989. *Annals of Science,* 48(1), 69–86.

Tannen, D. (1984). *Conversational style: Analyzing talk among friends.* Norwood, NJ: Ablex.

———. (1989). *Talking voices: Repetition, dialogue, and imagery in conversational discourse.* Cambridge: Cambridge University Press.

———. (1990). Ordinary conversation and literary discourse: Coherence and the poetics of repetition. *Annals of the New York Academy of Sciences,* 583, 15–32.

Trachtenberg, A. (1989). *Reading American photographs: Images as history—Mathew Brady to Walker Evans.* New York: Hill & Wang.

Young, K. (1991). Perspectives on embodiment: The uses of narrative in ethnographic writing. *Journal of Narrative and Life History,* 1, 213–43.

VI

The Crisis in Purpose: What Is Ethnography for, and Whom Should It Serve?

Whom do we serve in our qualitative research? Patti Lather wants a politically engaged social science, one that empowers people and changes the world for the better. Savage contends that ethnographic narrative can be used in an empowering, neighborly manner. Using insights taken from the practice of teachers and pastoral workers in the liberation movements of Latin America, she shows how ethnographers can assist teachers in resisting structures of segregation and domination.

Conquergood (1991, 190; 1998) calls for a critical cultural politics. He raises five questions concerning the future of performance studies, performance ethnography, cultural politics, and the performance paradigm. These questions are fitted to the problems surrounding critical pedagogy, politics, text, context, performance and praxis. They cluster around five intersecting planes of analysis. Each cluster, or plane, is predicated on the proposition that if the world is a performance, not a text, then today we need a critical performative cultural politics, a radical performative social science that confronts the problems surrounding democracy and the color line in the twenty-first century. Accordingly, Conquergood argues, it is necessary to rethink the relationship between

• performance and cultural process;
• performance and ethnographic praxis;
• performance and hermeneutics;
• performance and the act of scholarly representation and
• performance and the politics of culture (Conquergood 1991, 190).

A brief discussion of each cluster, or question, is proffered.

The first cluster treats culture as a verb, a process, or an ongoing performance, not a noun, a product, or a static thing. Culture is an unfolding production, thereby placing performances and their representations at the center of lived experience. Contemporary geopolitics place all of us in an "interdependent . . . world marked by borrowing and lending across porous national and cultural boundaries . . . border-crossings [are] emblematic of our postmodern world" (Rosaldo 1989, 217; see also Conquergood 1991, 184). We inhabit a federation of diasporas, postnational social formations marked by violence, and ethnic and cultural genocide (Appadurai 1993, 424). This complex, troubled, fluid, but culturally rich space is defined by improvisation, blurring, confusion, contingency, multiple identities, and hybridity.

In this contested world, experience cannot be studied directly. It is studied through and in its performative representations, including improvised acts, drama, and ritual. Every identity becomes a cultural performance (Conquergood 1991, 185). There are no originals against which a performance or an identity can be judged. Every performance, every identity, is an original, a new representation of meaning and experience.

Every performance is likewise political, an act involving potential struggles and negotiations over meaning, identity, and power, a site where the performance of possibilities occurs (Madison 1998, 277). The performance of possibilities "functions as a politically engaged pedagogy . . . [it] centers on the principles of transformation and transgression, dialogue and interrogation" (277–86). Culture so conceived turns performance into a site where memory, fantasy, and desire fuel one another (277).

There is an unbreakable link between hermeneutics, politics, pedagogy, ethics, and scholarly representation. Conquergood (1991, 190) is quite firm on this point. Performances should be treated as a complementary form of research publication. Performance is an alternative method, venue, or way of interpreting and presenting the results of one's ethnographic work. In turn, performance events allow audience members to enter critically into the world of another.

In the performance disciplines of art, theater, music, dance, and cinema, performers have showings, exhibits, performances, recitals, and screenings. These performance events are evidence of scholarly and artistic productivity and are part of a performer's artistic portfolio. This is how autoethnographic and ethnographic performances should also be treated, that is, as if they were scholarly publications.

This means that performances become a critical site of power and politics, the fifth cluster. A radical pedagogy underlies this notion of cultural politics.

The performative becomes an act of doing, an act of resistance, a way of connecting the biographical, the pedagogical, and the political. Foucault reminds us that where there is power, there is always resistance. In performances, racial, gender, and political ideologies are reproduced, sustained, challenged, subverted, naturalized, and subjected to criticism (Conquergood 1991, 190).

15

Can Ethnographic Narrative Be a Neighborly Act?

Mary C. Savage

Nicaragua changes you. Even a short time spent there steeps you in the passionate Nicaraguan faith that people can transform their country so the poor and marginalized become centers of national concern. The tropical atmosphere of this faith opens your pores and warms the membranes of your nose and lungs as you breathe in its astounding vitality. Nicaragua changes you because this vision gives you a way of sensing alternatives to the prevailing atmosphere in North America, where even the prophets are alienated and depressed. The fierce resolve of the Nicaraguans to carry out their revolution helps you taste what it is like to live beyond despair.

I changed. The example of the Nicaraguan people abides with me, encouraging me to ask what we can do to bring their revolution home to our teachers and students. How can we release the creative energies of our teachers? How can we educators take into our hearts the fate of the most marginalized of our citizens? How can we teach so we foster critical awareness of the structures that limit our freedom?

I have a hunch about ethnography and this kind of change. I have visited the neighborhood of ethnography for only a short time, in efforts to enhance

Reprinted from *Anthropology & Education Quarterly* 19 (1988): 3–19.

work in faculty development with college teachers, but I have been struck by how much in the effectiveness of ethnographic narrative can be accounted for by the principles of emotionally convincing representations of reality drawn out by Aristotle in the *Rhetoric* and the *Poetics*. So my "home" disciplines of classical rhetoric and literary criticism have prompted me to wonder about the effects of ethnographic narrative on their authors and audiences. My hunch is that critical ethnography may be one way of transforming a spirit-crushing educational structure that limits relations between universities and schools and universities and civic communities.

Our educational system is segregated and hierarchical. At the top are research institutions in which advanced students and privileged practitioners make esoteric knowledge, understandable only to a few initiates, which is carefully separated from the world of the mundane and the commonplace. So insulated is university knowledge that even different kinds of specialized knowledge are separated from one another. Philosophical and ethical reflection, moreover, are almost always separated from the disciplines they should inform. At the next level of the system are less privileged practitioners and student-initiates who carry on the business of taking new members into the guild that controls dissemination of knowledge. At the third level are teachers who do not practice a discipline, but who tell students about a discipline that students will never themselves practice.

Advancement in this hierarchy depends on review by those slightly higher up. Less privileged practitioners can become privileged by gaining approval or displacing those already privileged, generally by publishing the results of research. Teachers who are not practitioners will most likely never advance.

Elementary and secondary teachers are segregated at even lower levels of this system. While elementary and secondary teachers sometimes become university professors, the opposite is rarely true.

Because these hierarchies exist within disciplines and professional associations that interact with, but are not the same as, the structure of colleges and universities, one's advancement frequently depends on the discipline as much or more than on service to the institution where one works, and certainly much more than on service to the wider civic community of which one is a part. Advancement is arduous, requiring as it does the investment of a great deal of time and a considerable portion of one's identity and emotional stability. Consequently, the energies of large numbers of highly educated people are drawn off from domestic and public life. Rites of passage in this system—dissertations, for example—are notoriously hard on relationships, and persons going up for tenure rarely hold public office. In this way, disciplinary knowledge is also insulated from action and from public scrutiny (Bernstein 1971).

As is the case in all hierarchies, higher-ups in the system project onto lower-downs those aspects of the business of living that higher-ups find tedious, troublesome, or messy. Dominants in the educational system also project onto subordinates qualities that make them seem unsuitable agents for purer, more real, or more central work. Lower-downs on the hierarchy are thought of as essentially weaker, lacking in initiative, or unable to decide for themselves, and, consequently, as incapable of change or development. In actuality, the system of unequal relations between dominants and subordinates blocks subordinates from freedom of expression and action and militates against dominants forming alliances with them (Baker Miller 1976).

One very unfortunate characterization of persons who are at subordinate levels of the educational system is that they are less capable of theoretical and critical work. In the disciplinary sense, knowledge is made at the top and repeated or applied lower down. In the professional sense, discretion and some degree of autonomy are reserved for those who are higher up. Those who are lower down live professional lives prescribed and routinized by others.

In the following pages I inquire whether educational ethnographic research can become an integral part of ongoing transformative action to overcome the segregation of teachers at various levels of the system. Such action would claim an integrated critical consciousness as the right of all persons in the system and would try to heal the split between theory, critical reflection, and mundane work. I carry this inquiry out in three parts: the first part describes research in the empirical and postpositivist traditions; the second describes *neighborliness* as a characteristic that integrates research, critical reflection, and action in liberation pedagogy and theology as these have developed in Latin America; the third describes what the practice of ethnographic research as a neighborly act might look like.

RESEARCH

A friend of mine now working in Nicaragua likes to tell the story of a science librarian at Yale who, although very taken with the revolution, constantly lamented that Nicaragua was just not producing research any more. My friend likes to tell this story because if allows him to talk about the renewal of research now taking place in Managua and Leon. The lakes are being cleaned up; native plants are being studied for their medicinal potential; ways to preserve and market fish are being explored. But this research is not published in the journals collected in the Yale science libraries. Instead it is published and used locally to solve environmental and social problems.

This is especially true of educational research. Students and teachers work together on actual national problems, both in the disciplines students will teach (biology, chemistry, etc.) and in education. For example, students at the College of Education are designing flexible pedagogical methods for the college preparatory schools established for the daughters and sons of the poor. So, research there is aplenty, but whether one sees it or counts it as such depends on what one thinks research is, what it is for, and how it is evaluated.

After I had returned from Nicaragua to New Haven, much of the research done at Yale looked very strange. Yale University takes up much of center city New Haven. From the top floor cafeteria of Kline Biology Tower, a major research facility on the east side of the center city, a researcher on her lunch break can see the sluggish Mill River. The Mill forms one leg of the isosceles triangle that is the working-class neighborhood of Fair Haven where I live. The other leg of the triangle is formed by the Quinnipiac River, and its wide end is open to Long Island Sound. One third of my neighbors live below the poverty line. Many cannot read or write.

The Quinnipiac, once site of a thriving oyster industry, now supports little activity except boating, although long-time Fair Haveners can remember swimming at a public beach on what is now the rundown playground of a public housing project.

It seems strange to me that, although on a clear day I can see the smoke rising from Kline Tower, researchers there are not working on projects to make the Mill and Quinnipiac vital sources for life for New Haven. It seems strange to me that Yale can exist in a city where the rate of illiteracy is over 20 percent. On days when I am cynical, I think the researcher looking out of the window at the top of Kline sees not the Mill River but another laboratory in another city where someone she went to graduate school with is working on similar research. As a researcher, the questions she asks, the methods she uses, the standards by which she and other judge her work, and the pattern of life she will lead (Geertz 1983) are profoundly influenced by the empirical paradigms of her discipline. In these, there is relatively little room for the problems of my neighborhood. Her research is alien and alienating. It is alien to the neighborhood and it alienates the researcher from her surroundings for the sake of aligning her with a community of practitioners. There is little in the researcher's training and almost nothing in her professional work that will encourage her to look at Fair Haven and to publish locally work that will help us clean up our rivers, teach our people to read, find jobs for our workers.

This positivist tradition of research is often supported by conventions that border on "scientism" and that obscure the fact that research, like all social life, is a kind of praxis, action with a political-moral dimension. "Scientism," the idea that the formal and natural sciences are the only or most important measure of what counts as knowledge (Bernstein 1983) is supported by discourse conventions giving the impression that method yields truth or verifiable fact, that reality may be described objectively, that the most important audience for research is the disciplinary community. In the social sciences, such conventions, no matter what information they produce, insulate researchers from their own alienation. They ratify the reduction of human agency and the abstraction of human action to things that can be measured and held constant. They obscure the intersubjective connections of researcher and researched as well as the fact that research itself is a social action with social consequences.

Both ethnography and the critical social sciences have responded to the limitations of scientism by affirming that reality is socially constructed, that all researchers are more or less objective, and that qualitative as well as quantitative methods are valid. As a profession, ethnography has been attentive to such ethical issues as whether a study might violate the rights of a research population or misuses its resources (Dobbert 1982). Ethnographers, moreover, adopt perspectives that resist the tendency to be reductive. Educational ethnographers working in most ethnographic traditions formulate complex questions about education and frame these within a broad cultural context. These traditions hold promise for seeing the problems of my Fair Haven neighborhood, even if the topic of research is a high school in another section of the city. This promise is especially rich for the study of segregated and hierarchical systems, when ethnographers see culture itself as composed of multiple discourses in conflicting relationships (Clark and Holquist 1984).

The potential of ethnography for transforming education is even richer when the ethnographer sees ethnography as a social action that can influence the way communities change. Shirley Brice Heath draws out some of this potential in the preface to *Ways with Words* when she describes how her work helped children and teachers articulate relations between cultural patterns, knowledge, and rational choice (Brice Heath 1983). Patti Lather, a theorist working in the tradition of emancipatory social science, suggests some principles for deciding what counts as valid knowledge in research done from this perspective, that is, from the perspective of researchers committed to changes that will make the distribution of the world's goods, including knowledge and power, more equitable (1986). A primary aim of such sciences is to create knowledge that will increase awareness of the contradictions and distortions of our present unjust arrangements, because such knowledge can also direct attention to powerful possibilities for social transformation that are equally present. The aim of this research is to empower persons to transform the limitations of their circumstances. Consequently, one criterion for validity is "catalytic validity," that is, research is judged by "the degree to which the research process reorients, focuses, energizes participants toward knowing reality in order to transform it" (Lather 1986, 272).

Within this liberatory tradition, educational ethnographers could look at schools and universities marked by multiple and conflicting discourses reflecting unequal distribution of the world's goods in order to focus the energy of teachers and students on changing the limits imposed on education by its segregated and hierarchical structure.

At this point I wish to introduce the concept of *neighborliness* as a way of enhancing ethnography's potential for transforming education. Neighborliness is a concept I have drawn from liberatory educational and pastoral work being done in Latin America. In its own context neighborliness has healed splits between research, critical reflection, and action in the service of greater equality. Once I have illustrated and "unpacked" the concept, I will offer a fantasy of how the profession of ethnography might change if carried out in a spirit of neighborliness.

NEIGHBORLINESS
Neighborliness is Praxis

Neighborliness is what educational and pastoral workers have been doing in poor villages and neighborhoods in Latin America. It is a kind of praxis, practical activity (like teaching people to read, preaching, helping women provide better nutrition for infants, accompanying a grieving family at a wake). This activity also has an intellectual dimension. Aristotle describes praxis both as the kind of *thinking* and the kind of action that is characteristic of a free person in the polis or civic community. In praxis, theory and practice are both active and together constitute two dimensions of life that is human and free (Bernstein 1971). So praxis is work that includes research, practical and ethical judgments, reflection, and contemplation.

Historical Background

Neighborliness is part of historic changes going on in educational and church circles in Latin America. This change is most emphatic in the Roman Catholic Church. Historically, most church officials, theologians, and pastoral workers, whether they themselves had origins among the poor or not, had become aligned with the interests of the middle and upper classes. In the last twenty years, however, church workers, women and men, lay people and vowed religious, foreign- and native-born, have broken with this identification and have gone to live among the poor and work in solidarity with them. As a result, church workers have undergone radical changes in consciousness and have experienced vitality arising from faith that the future is open even if the present is marked by almost unendurable hardship.

Liberation theologian Gustavo Gutierrez often uses the parable of the Good Samaritan to explain this change in consciousness (1973). In that story a lawyer challenges Jesus to define exactly who is neighbor is, that is, exactly whom he is supposed to love as himself. The secular equivalent would be to ask with whom one was to identify. In the story of the Samaritan who turned aside from a journey he was on because he heard the cry of a person who had been robbed, beaten, and left for dead, the lawyer learns how to reframe his question. The question is not who has a legitimate claim on me, but whose cry do I hear, toward whom do I move, whose interests do I serve. Pastoral workers have come to identify with the interests of those who have been beaten down and marginalized by unjust social and political structures.

Another way to understand the dynamics of this change is to consider the biographies of the pastoral workers, especially those from North America. The journey of Maryknoll missionary Nancy Donovan from suburban Connecticut to a small village in the north of Nicaragua is one illustration of the process by which consciousness changes.

Donovan was born in 1932 into a middle-class family in Waterbury, Connecticut. Friends attribute her reckless courage to the enthusiasm with which she appropriated the motorcycles her father sold to test them on the back roads of the Connecticut countryside. Donovan joined Maryknoll soon after graduating from Sacred Heart High School. One of her first missions was teaching in a school for very wealthy students in Guatemala. She describes this as a period of rather conservative beliefs exemplified by her great disappointment that the opening up of vowed religious life after the Second Vatican Council meant she would not wear the traditional Maryknoll habit on her first mission. Her missionary experience changed Donovan's outlook considerably. Working on cooperative projects with Indians in Guatemala initiated a period of coming closer to the poor and learning to see the world from their perspective. She remembers vividly a shift in perspective that happened when some young Guatemalan friends visit her in New York. When she went with them to the grocery store, she suddenly saw the rows of various brands of cat and dog food through the eyes of those who knew how many Indian children were dying of hunger.

Donovan also came to understand that the location of the poor in a social context affects their lives considerably. As Oscar Romero said, "Nowadays an authentic Christian conversion must lead to an unmasking of the social mechanism that turns the worker and the peasant into marginalized persons. Why do the rural poor become part of society only in the coffee- and cotton-picking seasons?" (Guitierrez 1984, 98).

Another turning point came as a result of Donovan's organizing cooperatives in small towns in Mexico. "The idea was to help rural people get a fair price in selling their products and make it easier to buy the things they needed. There was a lot of enthusiasm: when the people got together to talk about the problems of doing business, the organizing efforts just flowed from their talks. But eventually we realized we had gone as far as we could because of the whole capitalistic arrangement. Ultimately, the government stepped in and set up distribution centers and undermined our cooperative" (Everett 1986, 142). As Guitierrez says, it is precisely this awareness of the structural causes of poverty that has changed the mission of the church in Latin America (1973).

Soon after the overthrow of Somoza, Donovan volunteered to go to Nicaragua for four months. She has remained for seven years, serving the people of Ocotol and San Juan de Limay. Nicaragua, she says, is exciting: "You can feel the hope and the excitement of the people." And she is deeply touched by the religious spirit and intelligence of the people.

Donovan's life in San Juan de Limay is punctuated by experiences that keep her oriented and connect her to the world outside the village. She visits Managua to see other pastoral workers, attends regional gatherings of small Christian communities, and once or twice has returned to Maryknoll in New York. In many ways, moreover, she remains an Irish Catholic nun from New England. Anyone from Connecticut or Massachusetts would recognize her by her accent and her wit. Although Donovan lives with the poor, she will never be poor. As Guitierrez says, "Being poor is also a way of feeling, knowing, reasoning, making friends, loving, believing, suffering, celebrating, and praying. The poor constitute a world of their own" (1973). Donovan is in that world but not of it. In the difference between these two—the poor in their world and Donovan who comes as a neighbor—there is a dynamic that produces change—in Donovan, in her peasant friends, in their circumstances.

Philosophical and Theological Dimensions

Paulo Freire's educational work seeks to produce such changes in consciousness. In fact, much of liberation pastoral practice is based on Freire's concept of *conscientizaçao*, or critical consciousness (Berryman 1987).

The theological dimensions of neighborliness can be found in the documents produced by the Latin American bishops (CELAM) at their meetings in Medellin (1968) and Puebla (1979). These meetings elaborated the idea that the gospel calls Christians to exercise a preferential option for the poor. A 1979 letter issued by the Guatemalan bishops in the face of death squads that had murdered and abducted hundreds of citizens illustrates the conditions that moved the Church to place itself at the side of the poor. The bishops assert that each human being is called to be free and to live in community because each is made in the image of God who has given to human persons intelligence and will. On the basis of this vision and in the face of the suffering of their people, the bishops conclude that "the most humble of Guatemalans, the most exploited and outcast, the sickest and most unschooled, is worth more than all the wealth of the country, and is sacred and untouchable" (Berryman 1987, 112).

In Latin America, the philosophical and theological dimensions of neighborliness have sustained work that attempts to narrow the great gulf between the rich and the poor. It is a vision that empowers those who were once aligned with the rich to see truly how their actions have affected the lives of the poor and it is a vision that endows the poor with their true capacity for rational action and change. My hope is that the concept of neighborliness will help us in North America to remember our rich tradition of common life (from New England town meetings, to fraternal organizations in Chicago, to barn raising on the plains of Nebraska).

Freire's educational work is imbued with the philosophical position that persons are rational, called to common or political life, and having the capacity for transforming acts of knowing (Berryman 1987). Freire says that from the beginning he sought to design a literacy program that was itself an act of creation, an act that was capable of "releasing other creative acts, one in which students would develop the impatience and vivacity which characterize search and invention" (1981). Such a program rests on a vision of human persons as agents, and as agents in relationship. "We began with the conviction that the role of [the person] was not only to be in the world, but to engage in relations with the world— that through acts of creation and re-creation, [the human person] makes cultural reality and thereby adds to the natural world" (1981, 43). This view, which has a long history in philosophy—from Aristotle to Marx—is really radical only in its application. The radical act is to envision this possibility as a realistic possibility for the poor of Latin America and to revitalize our faith in truly democratic education. Some such vision might prompt us to transform an educational system that limits the potential of teachers from growth and change at all levels by segregating critical reflection and mundane action at different levels.

Analytical Dimensions

The philosophical and theological dimensions of neighborliness are informed by the use of critical social science theory and analysis to inquire into the causes of present social conditions. In this sense, educational and pastoral work also includes "a clear and critical attitude regarding economic and sociocultural issues" (Gutierrez 1973, 11). According to Gutierrez, to regard social and cultural issues in the light of faith that works through "real charity, action, and commitment to the service" of people is to engage in the kind of reflection that leads to action that transforms the present.

Characteristic of neighborly practice is that such analysis is exercised for the sake of another who has been marginalized and is sustained by the hope that "death and injustice are not the final words of history" (Guitierrez 1984, 118).

Interpretive and Pedagogical Dimensions

As practice in literacy education, this vision of the human capacity for critical consciousness and transformative action is enacted as an interpretive process. Reconceptualizing ethnographic narrative along the lines of this process could enhance ethnography's liberatory potential considerably. The pedagogical methods of liberating education are rooted in the notion that interpretation is a circular activity. A group of knowers "reads" some re-presentation of their circumstances. This interpretive act produces a critical distance which, in turn, leads to the capacity to envision possibilities for greater freedom and community in present circumstances and to the capacity for change. These changes lead yet again to the reading of another re-presentation, and so on, so that knowing and acting become an ongoing hermeneutic or gnostological circle (Freire 1981).

Freire's pedagogical method uses "codes" to re-present the daily life of the people in such a way that description and analysis of the codes produces critical consciousness about limitations and possibilities for change. The codes are drawings or pictures of daily life made on the basis of research conducted to discover the ways people in the educational program think about their experience. On the basis of this research, certain themes are selected to be encoded in the drawings. They are then organized and discussed so as to make the limitations of the people's worldview more problematic. Freire, early in his career, worked with peasants who had almost no idea of the human capacity for agency, Brazilian women and men who distinguished almost not at all between the human ways of being in the world and the ways of animals and plants. As a result, many of the themes he selected from field research related to the differences between nature and culture. These themes provoked discussion of the human capacity to make and to act. The codes reproduced in *Education for Critical Consciousness* are pictures showing people farming, taking care of children, and reading. With the help of an educator, people in the literacy program would discuss a man making a pot, for example. In the course of the discussion, many would come to realize that peasants can make things; that they are artists capable of transforming the clay around them into useful and beautiful things; that their previous understanding that they were animal-like and worthless was part of a way of thinking that kept them from changing their circumstances. It is in this context that the peasants learned to read, and that learning to read the word became a way of learning to read the world.

The philosophy of liberation pedagogy that emphasizes the ability of persons to reach new understanding that can lead them to change the circumstances of their lives is thus lived out in educational practice that relies on a circle of interpretation in which a "picture" of the situation is presented, discussed, acted upon, and then a new picture drawn up. In this process the dialogical relationship of the educator or pastoral worker (in part a result of her or his difference) is a catalyst for learners' being able to be critical of their circumstances and to generate alternatives. Ethnographic research could also become catalytic in this sense.

Summary

Neighborliness, then, is a kind of praxis, a practical activity having a complex intellectual dimension, exercised for the sake of assisting the marginalized on a journey toward greater freedom and participation in common life. Into the practical activity of neighborliness (teaching, organizing cooperatives) are integrated a number of intellectual activities: researching the concrete circumstances in which "the others" live; analyzing the social, cultural, and economic causes of these conditions; envisioning new possibilities; making judgments; transcending the limitations of one's prior loyalties and prior understandings. As an interpretive or educational activity, neighborliness takes the form of describing, representing, or mirroring a group's understanding of its own circumstances and discussing these so that the group comes to consciousness about the problematic character of their circumstances in ways that assist them in becoming more able to transform these. Changes in consciousness take place, in part, because the "difference" of the neighborly educator and the abstracting possibilities of the representations assist people both in coming near to the circumstances of their lives and in gaining a critical distance in relation to them. This dual movement assists understanding the causes of oppression without, however, leaving people with consciousness so alienated they are incapable of action. Energy, not cynicism, results.

Neighborly activity is supported by a philosophical view of human persons as "worth more than all the wealth of the country," called to freedom and community, and capable of transforming their circumstances through critical action.

ETHNOGRAPHY AS A NEIGHBORLY ACT

Could the exercise of ethnography as a neighborly act actualize and freshen the potential of ethnography for transforming the spirit-crushing limitations placed on the relationships between universities, schools, and civic life? Since these limits arise from the segregation and hierarchical arrangement of teachers at various levels of the system and since they are reinforced by the insulation of specialized knowledge, especially the separation of philosophical and ethical reflection from "professional" knowledge, the transformative potential of neighborly ethnography may be great.

Ethnography already threatens "scientism." The notion that cultures are complex and whole and that they can be represented in their mundane density confronts the tendency of scientism to reduce human agency and to decontextualize action. As Paul Willis says, "The only satisfying way to achieve *reliability* as 'representativeness,' 'generalizability'—the survey and questionnaire—simply does not have the depth to report and show the creative life of cultures. The question is not so much one of quantitative proof or accuracy (though I certainly would not dismiss these), but more one of whether the culture, or form of life, is reported correctly and presented in a way that really reproduces something of the original" (1977, 218). Willis goes on to suggest that "the truth or not" of the report is, in part, rhetorical, that is, it is to be judged by how the report "touches others' experience in its reception" (1977, 218). Ethnography also resists "scientism" by its recognition that the observer is also a participant and that there are ethical relations and moral obligations between the researcher and researched.

I think the concept of neighborliness can extend these qualities by highlighting the fact that research is action with social and political dimensions. Given the hierarchical positions of universities and schools, relations between university researchers and school teachers are unequal. Knowledge, prestige, and the power of the profession belong to the researcher, not the researched. Further, publishing what is learned from the researched for a disciplinary community is an action that has the possibility of advancing the career of the researcher who uses the research as a marketable commodity. This action has the consequent possibility of separating and alienating the researcher even more from "ordinary" teachers. It is revulsion against what has been called this "rape model of research" in which career advancement is built on "alienating and exploitative inquiry methods" that prompts ethnographers to share their findings with their subjects and has suggested to Patti Lather that research findings should be jointly negotiated with those who are researched.

If, however, we follow Willis's hint that ethnographies ought to be rhetorically efficacious, that one ought to "give life" to what is reported "as a conscious and political device," we can also see ethnography as a powerful device of neighborly activity.

Fantasy of an Ethnographer as Neighbor

One day, not long after she was awarded tenure, an up-and-coming ethnographer at a major research institution, say—for the sake of argument—Yale University, attends a film on educational reform in Nicaragua. Along with the history of the literacy campaign and of special college preparatory schools established for the poor, she hears how UNAN (the national university in Leon) has changed since the Revolution. With great pride, the director explains that a major transformation at the university has been in orientation. "No longer," he says, "do we produce professionals who look on their degrees as licenses to exploit people who are less learned. We teach professionals to serve the people." The ethnographer—call her Nancy Donovan—becomes increasingly uneasy. She remembers the two years she spent as an elementary school teacher before she left for graduate school. She remembers how much she enjoyed working with the children and how much she liked the camaraderie she experienced with other teachers. She also remembers the crushing burden of the routinized day and curriculum, the frustration of working without enough supplies, the burnout. Now, however, she is on the fast track. Life is exhilarating. She has just published a theoretical work that is getting a great deal of attention and a number of frenzied attacks. She must be doing something right.

But she is lonely. Her relationships with her colleagues are guarded. She no longer has time to see her old friends from the elementary school. Nor does she want to. There is a gulf there now. They cannot share her enthusiasm for theory; she finds the pettiness of their days and (to tell the truth) their minds oppressive and limiting.

After seeing the film she begins to think that her loneliness and isolation and their limited, routinized days are related.

With two of her graduate students who, because they are entering upper levels of the hierarchy are able to make knowledge, she goes to St. Rose's grammar school in the Fair Haven section of New Haven to practice her profession. With her graduate students she intends to publish an ethnography of St. Rose's that will extend her theoretical work. But she also intends to be a neighbor to the teachers there. She will publish the results of this research locally, first at St. Rose's, then at other schools in New Haven.

Neighborly Research

What will this neighborly research be like? It will include participant observation, negotiated meanings with teachers and students, social analysis, and ethical reflection. In all of this work, Nancy's presence as a neighbor in the school will have been crucial. Her presence as a person working in the interests of the teachers will have lent them a new self-confidence, will have helped them reflect on "the complexity and promise" of their lives, will have gathered energy and support for the task of envisioning liberating alternatives. The attentiveness an ethnographer brings a community is a great gift. As one of Willis's "lads" says, "The main difference is, you listen to us, you want to know what we've got to say, they don't, none of them" (Willis 1977, 197).

Her attentiveness matters—and so does her difference. Shirley Brice Heath found that the teachers she worked with experienced the positive force of her presence as rooted in the fact that she was both an "insider and outsider." She identified with them (and was identified by them) as a teacher, but she was an outsider to the political structure of the school system. Teachers described her as

> someone outside the "system" to talk to—not an administrator, teacher, or parent of a child in my classroom; I knew I could blow off steam and you would listen.
> ... a fellow teacher. Because you once were a public school teacher, I never felt I had to hide those "little problems" of daily life in the classroom. [Brice Heath 1983, 357]

Nancy is an anomaly in the system. She is a university researcher engaged in a neighborly relationship with a group of elementary school teachers. She is dedicated to understanding their understandings, to helping them reflect on their experience, to joining them in discovering alternatives that would make their lives less routinized and more autonomous, less restricted and more open to possibilities of communal life both inside and outside the school.

During the two years she works at St. Rose's, moreover, Nancy changes. What began as a hunch (a memory, really) that elementary teachers are every bit as capable of theoretical reflection as university professors has become a daily reality. She is frequently awed by the insight and energy of the teachers around her. Just as frequently she is furious at the structures that work to keep teachers routinized and at her own stupidity for not having come to these realizations sooner. Her loyalties begin to slip. These teachers and their interests become more important. The professional journals seem dull in comparison to their insights. By contrast her university colleagues seem to lack energy. They are bright, but delicate and attenuated, rather like tropical birds. Her attentiveness to the teachers turns into the kind of affection and respect that can only truly transpire among equals.

What began as a hunch becomes a stubborn resolve. People can change. She has seen it. She has changed. Her work is more integrated. Professional research, critical reflection, social action are bound together. She is no longer isolated. Her energies no longer drawn off like "top milk" from the daily lives of "ordinary" teachers.

Neighborly Publication

At the end of her second year at St. Rose's, Nancy decides it is time "to publish" her research. She knows there are few models for what she wants to do and has heeded Willis's warning that "we cannot invent a form out of its time." But she also knows that the time has come for her and the teachers to become more critical of their circumstances, to place them in various contexts, to interrogate their causes and consequences. She knows that some abstracting medium would help this work considerably. So she plunges on, assured by Willis that "it is necessary above all to approach the real now in one way or another." She looks at the models she has. She likes the density and humanity of *Ways with Words*. She also admires the dialogical character of *Learning to Labor*. The last few chapters of this book are respectful conversations with "the lads," Willis's critics, his American readers, and they draw out some of the implications of this theory for practitioners needing to face what happens on Monday morning.

Nancy decides to write a school pageant with several of the teachers and to present it in a series of workshops the last week of the school year. At the center of the pageant is an ethnography written for exactly the reason Willis suspects them: "The ethnographic account is a supremely ex post facto product of the actual uncertainty of life. There develops, unwilled, a false unity which asks, 'What follows next?' 'How does it end?' 'What makes sense of it?'" (Willis 1977, 194).

The tendency of ethnographic narrative to ask "What follows next?" "How did it end?" "What makes sense of it?" recommends it to Nancy as a consciousness-raising genre. Good narrative tends to form plots, sequences in which the character of agents, the causes and consequences of events, the emotional responses of audiences are woven into a coherence. Plot, Aristotle tells us, is the soul of tragedy and it is what makes the poet like the philosopher. Plot makes narrative more coherent and general than the confused and concrete reality of daily life. In this scene, a plot is very similar to a Freirean code. It is a mechanism for abstracting and re-presenting understandings of daily life so people can come to see it as more problematic and more open to the future. Whatever else there may be in the pageant, there will be good story theater.

Nancy is also interested in dialogue. She wants to replay the multiple and conflicting discourses she has observed. And she wants to stimulate dialogue. So she sets the story theater in the context of several discussions of the usefulness of the ethnography. The teachers discuss it and they also play the parts of students, parents, administrators, university researchers, public officials, and others whose responses might be illuminating. All week this ongoing pageant is punctuated by workshops that make plans for next year, plans that will increase autonomy and community participation. Nancy begins to think her research will have a high degree of catalytic validity.

She also has a plan of her own. She plans to take up Willis's challenge—"Is it possible to imagine the ethnographic account upwards in a class society?" She is arranging for the two graduate students to take over her work at the elementary school and for two teachers at St. Rose's to join her in an ethnographic study of the effect of the tenure system on the autonomy and community participation of university professors.

Yesterday she met a colleague who had moved away to take a better position in another city. He remarks she has more energy now, that she is less bitter and cynical. But he warns her to be careful. He predicts her work will be looked at with suspicion. Ethnography is already under attack as being "unscientific." What if the dean uses her study as a chance to close out the department? How could she ever continue the work at St. Rose's? How could she support her work in Fair Haven then?

Nancy smiles but doesn't reply. She is remembering the fierce dedication she saw in the face of Francisco Limas, the director of adult literacy in the Nicaragua film. He had just described how his faith in the people was constantly renewed, even under the terrible conditions in the north where contra attacks were frequent. Two days ago, he said, a literacy teacher had been taken off a bus and executed. The very next evening his relatives took his books from their hiding place and continued his class. This courage gives him joy and increases his dedication. But, the interviewer wanted to know, what if contra attacks become so severe that you can't get books and supplies to the literacy volunteers? "We will write in the mud," he said, "That is our calling and our dedication. Our people deserve no less."

We will write in the mud, she thought. That is what it is like to live beyond despair.

The practice of ethnography as a neighborly act—even by a few ethnographers—could begin to realign the profession with schools and civic communities in ways that weaken the segregated and hierarchical structure of our educational systems. Neighborly ethnographers could gather energies for building critical consciousness in teachers and encouraging them toward liberating action. In so doing, ethnography could slowly change the systematic relations that separate teaching practice from theoretical and ethical reflection and could encourage integrated and liberating teaching practice at all levels. Conversely, the practice of ethnography as a neighborly act could build neighborly sensibilities in ethnographers, helping them become more conscious of the social consequences of their research and of their participation in a hierarchically organized structure. Instead of leading merely to a deadening and deadly critique of such structures, however, neighborly acts should develop in ethnographers noses for the vital and the possible.

Neighborliness could seep into ethnography wherever possible: as one kind of research, as part of discussions about the ethics of the profession, as a necessary part of graduate training, as one way to publish the results of research, as a critique of what now "counts" as professional activity, as actually "counting" for tenure. This kind of change could come about wherever people acted in a neighborly way, although its results would remain fragile and unstable, like all new life. And some people would be able to risk doing more of it than others. Nevertheless, the heart of the profession could be enriched wonderfully by neighborliness.

On clear fall days when I see the smoke from Kline Biology Tower rise to float over Fair Haven, I sometimes catch a gleam in the eye of the researcher in the cafeteria as she begins for the first time to see the possibilities the Mill River holds for research.

REFERENCES CITED

Baker Miller, Jean
1976 *Toward a New Psychology of Women.* Boston: Beacon Press.

Bernstein, Richard
1971 *Praxis and Action: Contemporary Philosophies of Human Activity.* Philadelphia: University of Pennsylvania Press.

1983 *Beyond Objectivity and Relativism: Science, Hermeneutics and Praxis.* Philadelphia: University of Pennsylvania Press.

Berryman, Philip
1987 *Liberation Theology.* New York: Pantheon Books.

Brice Heath, Shirley
1983 *Ways with Words: Language, Life, and Work in Communities and Classrooms.* Cambridge: Cambridge University Press.

Clark, Katerina, and Michael Holquist
1984 *Mikhail Bakhtin.* Cambridge: Harvard University Press.

Dobbert, Marion Lundy
1982 *Ethnographic Research: Theory and Application for Modern Schools and Societies.* New York: Praeger.

Everett, Melissa
1986 *Bearing Witness, Building Bridges: Interviews with North Americans Living and Working in Nicaragua.* Philadelphia: New Society.

Freire, Paulo
1981 *Education for Critical Consciousness.* New York: Continuum.

Geertz, Clifford
1983 "The Way We Think Now: Toward an Ethnography of Modern Thought." In *Local Knowledge.* (147–63). New York: Basic Books.

Guitierrez, Gustavo
1973 *A Theology of Liberation: History, Politics and Salvation.* Maryknoll, N.Y.: Orbis Books.

1984 *We Drink from Our Own Wells: The Spiritual Journey of a People.* Maryknoll, N.Y.: Orbis Books.

Lather, Patti
1986 "Research as Praxis." *Harvard Educational Review* 46 (3):257–77.

Willis, Paul
1977 *Learning to Labor: How Working Class Kids Get Working Class Jobs.* New York: Columbia University Press.

16

Rethinking Ethnography: Towards a Critical Cultural Politics

Dwight Conquergood

Critical theory is not a unitary concept. It resembles a loose coalition of interests more than a united front. But whatever it is or is not, one thing seems clear: Critical theory is committed to unveiling the political stakes that anchor cultural practices—research and scholarly practices no less than the everyday. On this point the participants in this forum agree. Yes, critical theory politicizes science and knowledge. Our disagreements arise from how we view (and value) the tension between science/knowledge and politics. Logical empiricists are dedicated to the *eviction* of politics from science. Critical theorists, on the other hand, are committed to the *excavation* of the political underpinnings of all modes of representation, including the scientific.

Ethnography, with its ambivalent meanings as both a method of social science research and a genre of social science text (see Clifford & Marcus, 1986; Van Maanen, 1988), has been the most amenable of the social sciences to poststructuralist critique. It presents a particularly sensitive site for registering the aftershocks of critical theory. No group of scholars is struggling more acutely and productively with the political tensions of research than ethnographers.

Reprinted from *Communication Monographs* 58 (June 1991):179–94. Used by permission of the National Communication Association.

For ethnography, the undermining of objectivist science came roughly at the same time as the collapse of colonialism. Since then, post-colonial critics have set about unmasking the imperialist underpinnings of anthropology (Asad, 1973; Ashcroft, Griffiths, & Tiffin, 1989; Miller, 1990), the discipline with which ethnography has been closely but not exclusively associated. Clifford Geertz explains (1988, pp. 131–32):

> The end of colonialism altered radically the nature of the social relationship between those who ask and look and those who are asked and looked at. The decline of faith in brute fact, set procedures, and unsituated knowledge in the human sciences, and indeed in scholarship generally, altered no less radically the askers' and lookers' conception of what it was they were trying to do. Imperialism in its classical form, metropoles and possessions, and Scientism in its, impulsions and billiard balls, fell at more or less the same time.

The double fall of scientism and imperialism has been, for progressive ethnographers, a *felix culpa*, a fortunate fall. The ensuing "crisis of representation" (Marcus & Fischer, 1986, p. 7) has induced deep epistemological, methodological, and ethical self-questioning.

Though some assume defensive or nostalgic postures, most ethnographers would agree with Renato Rosaldo's current assessment of the field (1989, p. 37): "The once dominant ideal of a detached observer using neutral language to explain 'raw' data has been displaced by an alternative project that attempts to understand human conduct as it unfolds through time and in relation to its meanings for the actors." Moreover, a vanguard of critical and socially committed ethnographers argues that there is no way out short of a radical rethinking of the research enterprise. I will chart four intersecting themes in the crucial rethinking of ethnography: (1) The Return of the Body, (2) Boundaries and Borderlands, (3) The Rise of Performance, and (4) Rhetorical Reflexivity.

RETURN OF THE BODY

Ethnography's distinctive research method, participant-observation fieldwork, privileges the body as a site of knowing. In contrast, most academic disciplines, following Augustine and the Church Fathers, have constructed a Mind/Body hierarchy of knowledge corresponding to the Spirit/Flesh opposition so that mental abstractions and rational thought are taken as both epistemologically and morally superior to sensual experience, bodily sensations, and the passions. Indeed, the body and the flesh are linked with the irrational, unruly, and dangerous—certainly an inferior realm of experience to be controlled by the higher powers of reason and logic. Further, patriarchal constructions that align women with the body, and men with mental faculties, help keep the mind-body, reason-emotion, objective-subjective, as well as masculine-feminine hierarchies stable.

Nevertheless, the obligatory rite-of-passage for all ethnographers—doing fieldwork—requires getting one's body immersed in the field for a period of time sufficient to enable one to participate inside that culture. Ethnography is an *embodied practice*; it is an intensely sensuous way of knowing. The embodied researcher is the instrument. James Clifford acknowledges (1988, 24): "Participant-observation obliges its practitioners to experience, at a bodily as well as an intellectual level, the vicissitudes of translation." In a posthumously published essay, "On Fieldwork," the late Erving Goffman emphasized the corporeal nature of fieldwork (1989, p. 125):

> It's one of getting data, it seems to me, by subjecting yourself, your body and your own personality, and your own social situation, to the set of contingencies that play upon a set of individuals, . . . so that you are close to them while they are responding to what life does to them.

This active, participatory nature of fieldwork is celebrated by ethnographers when they contrast their "open air" research with the "arm chair" research of more sedentary and cerebral methods.

Ethnographic rigor, disciplinary authority, and professional reputation are established by the length of time, depth of commitment, and risks (bodily, physical, emotional) taken in order to acquire cultural understanding. Letters of recommendation often refer approvingly to bodily hardships suffered by the dedicated ethnographer—malarial fevers, scarcity of food, long periods of isolation, material discomforts, and so forth, endured in the field.

Bronislaw Malinowski, credited with establishing modern standards of ethnographic fieldwork—whose own practice remains unsurpassed—recommended bodily participation, in addition to observation, as a mode of intensifying cultural understanding (1922/1961, pp. 21–22):

> [I]t is good for the Ethnographer sometimes to put aside camera, notebook and pencil, and to join in himself in what is going on. He can take part in the

354 DWIGHT CONQUERGOOD

natives' games, he can follow them on their visits and walks, sit down and listen and share in their conversations.

Fifty years later Geertz still affirms that corporeal nature and necessity of fieldwork (1973, p. 23):

It is with the kind of material produced by long-term, mainly (though not exclusively) qualitative, highly participative, and almost obsessively fine-comb field study in confined contexts that the mega concepts with which contemporary social science is afflicted . . . can be given the sort of sensible actuality that makes it possible to think not only realistically and concretely *about* them, but, what is more important, creatively and imaginatively *with* them.

Although ethnographic fieldwork privileges the body, published ethnographies typically have repressed bodily experience in favor of abstracted theory and analysis. In this shift from ethnographic method (fieldwork) to ethnographic rhetoric (published monograph), named individuals with distinct personalities and complex life histories are inscribed as "the Bororo" or "the Tikopia." Finely detailed speech and nuanced gesture are summarized flatly: "All the voices of the field have been smoothed into the expository prose of more-or-less interchangeable 'informants'" (Clifford, 1988, p. 49). The interpersonal contingencies and experiential give-and-take of fieldwork process congeal on the page into authoritative statement, table, and graph. According to post-colonial feminist critic Trinh T. Minh-ha (1989, p. 56): "It is as if, unvaryingly, every single look, gesture, or utterance has been stained with anthropological discourse."

Recognition of the bodily nature of fieldwork privileges the processes of communication that constitute the "doing" of ethnography: speaking, listening, and acting together. According to Stephen Tyler (1987, p. 172), the postmodern recovery of the body in fieldwork means the return of speaking, communicating bodies, a "return to the commonsense, plurivocal world of the speaking subject." He pushed this point (1987, p. 171): "Postmodern anthropology is the study of [wo]man—'talking.' Discourse is its object and means." Trinh reminds us that interpersonal communication is grounded in sensual experience (1989, p. 121): "[S]peaking and listening refer to realities that do not involve just the imagination. The speech is seen, heard, smelled, tasted, and touched." When modernist ethnographers systematically record their *observations*, they forget that "seeing is mediated by saying" (Tyler, 1987, p. 171).

Michael Jackson wants to recuperate the body in ethnographic discourse (1989, p. 18), to reestablish "the intimate connection between our bodily experience in the everyday world and our conceptual life." He argues (1989, p. 11): "If we are to find common ground with them [the people we study], we have to open ourselves to modes of sensory and bodily life which, while meaningful to us in our personal lives, tend to get suppressed in our academic discourse." Jackson wants to restore the epistemological and methodological, as well as etymological, connection between experience and empiricism. He names his project "radical empiricism" and positions it within and against "traditional empiricism." What traditional empiricism attempts to control, suspend, or bracket out—"the empirical reality of our personal engagement with and attitude to those others" (1989, p. 34)—radical empiricism privileges as "the intersubjective grounds on which our understanding is constituted" (1989, p. 34):

> The importance of this view for anthropology is that it stresses the ethnographer's *interactions* with those he or she lives with and studies, while urging us to clarify the ways in which our knowledge is grounded in our practical, personal, and participatory experience in the field as much as our detached observations. Unlike traditional empiricism, which draws a definite boundary between observer and observed, between method and object, radical empiricism denies the validity of such cuts and makes the *interplay* between these domains the focus of its interest. (1989, p. 3)

The project of radical empiricism changes ethnography's traditional approach from Other-as-theme to Other-as-interlocutor (Theunissen, 1984), and represents a shift from monologue to dialogue, from information to communication. Jackson provocatively argues that traditional ethnographic "pretenses" about detached observation and scientific method reveal anxiety about the uncontrollable messiness of any truly interesting fieldwork situation (1989, p. 3):

> Indeed, given the arduous conditions of fieldwork, the ambiguity of conversations in a foreign tongue, differences of temperament, age, and gender between ourselves and our informants, an the changing theoretical models we are heir to, it is likely that "objectivity" serves more as a magical token, bolstering our sense of self in disorienting situations, than as a scientific method for describing those situations as they really are.

The radical empiricist's response to the vulnerabilities and vicissitudes of fieldwork is honesty, humility, self-reflexivity, and an acknowledgement of the interdependence and reciprocal role-playing between knower and known.

In this process we put ourselves on the line; we run the risk of having our sense of ourselves as different and distanced from the people we study dissolve, and with it all our pretensions to a supraempirical position, a knowledge that gets us above and beyond the temporality of human existence. (Jackson, 1989, p. 4)

Johannes Fabian focuses on temporality as a strategy for bringing back the body-in-time in ethnographic discourse, and with it the body politic. In a trenchant rhetorical critique of ethnographic texts (1983, p. 148), he identifies the "denial of coevalness" as a strategy for "keeping Anthropology's Other in another time" and thereby keeping "others" in their marginal place. Coevalness is the experience of contemporarily, the recognition of actively sharing the same time, the acknowledgment of others as contemporaries. Fabian argue forcefully that enthnography manifests "schizochronic tendencies" (1983, p. 37). On the one hand, the discipline insists on the coeval experience of fieldwork as the source of ethnographic knowledge, and on the other hand, this coevalness is denied in professional discourse that temporally distances others through labels such as "tribal," "traditional," "ancient," "animistic," "primitive," "preliterate," "neolithic," "underdeveloped," or the slightly more polite, "developing," and so forth. Clifford (1988, p. 16) calls this tactic a "temporal setup." In a deeply contradictory way, ethnographers go to great lengths to become cotemporal with others during fieldwork but then deny in writing that these others with whom they lived are their contemporaries. Fabian warns (1983, p. 33): "These disjunctions between experience and science, research and writing, will continue to be a festering epistemological sore."

More problematically, he reveals (Fabian, 1983, p. 144) how the expansionist campaigns of colonialist-imperialist policies "required Time to accommodate the schemes of a one-way history: progress, development, modernity (and their negative mirror images: stagnation, underdevelopment, tradition). In short, *geopolitics* has its ideological foundations in *chronopolitics.*" Anthropology is complicit with imperialism and the ideology of progress when it rhetorically distances the Other in Time.

For Fabian, the way to prevent temporal reifications of other cultures is for ethnographers to rethink themselves as communicators, not scientists. He states this fundamental point in strong terms (1983, p. 71): "only as communicative praxis does ethnography carry the promise of yielding new knowledge about another culture." Ethnographers must recognize "that fieldwork is a form of communicative interaction with an Other, one that must be carried out coevally, on the basis of shared intersubjective Time and intersocietal contemporaneity" (1983, pp. 148). He privileges communication because "for human communication to occur, coevalness has to be *created*. Communication is, ultimately, about creating shared Time" (1983, pp. 30–31). Whereas Paul Ricoeur (1971) wanted to fix the temporal flow and leakage of speaking, to rescue "the said" from "the saying," the contemporary ethnographers struggle to recuperate "the saying from the said," to shift their enterprise from nouns to verbs, from mimesis to kinesis, from textualized space to co-experienced time.

This rethinking of ethnography as primarily about speaking and listening, instead of observing, has challenged the visualist bias of positivism with talk about voices, utterances, intonations, multivocality. Sight and observation go with space, and the spatial practices of division, separation, compartmentalization, and surveillance. According to Rosaldo (1989, p. 41), "the eye of ethnography" is connected to "the I of imperialism." Sight and surveillance depend on detachment and distance. Getting perspective on something entails withdrawal from intimacy. Everyday parlance equates objectivity with aloofness. Being "too close" is akin to losing perspective and lacking judgment.

Metaphors of sound, on the other hand, privilege temporal process, proximity, and incorporation. Listening is an interiorizing experience, a gathering together, a drawing in, whereas observation sizes up exteriors. The communicative praxis of speaking and listening, conversation, demands copresence even as it decenters the categories of knower and known. Vulnerability and self disclosure are enabled through conversations. Closure, on the other hand, is constituted by the gaze. The return of the body as a recognized method for attaining "vividly felt insight into the life of other people" (Trinh, 1989, p. 123) shifts the emphasis from space to time, from sight and vision to sound and voice, from text to performance, from authority to vulnerability.

BOUNDARIES AND BORDERLANDS

Geertz's well-known "Blurred Genres" essay (1983, pp. 19–35) charts ethnography's ambivalent participation in the postmodern redistribution of analytical foci from center to periphery, delimitation to dispersal, whole to fragment, metropole to margin. To be sure, ethnographers for a long time have been situated more characteristically in the peripheral village than in the metropolitan center. They have been predisposed professionally to seek out the frontier and hinterlands, the colony rather than the capital. But this preoccupation with marginal cultures that obliged them figuratively and literally to live on the boundary did not present them from still seeing identity and culture, self and other, as discrete, singular, integral, and stable concepts. Once they crossed the border and pitched their tent on the edge of the encampment, they confidently set about describing "the Trobrianders," or the "the Nuer," or "the ghetto," interpreting these cultures as distinct, coherent, whole ways of life. In so doing, they centralized the peripheral instead of de-centering the "metropolitan typifications" that they carried inside their heads (Rosaldo, 1989, p. 207).

All that confidence in continuous traditions and innocent encounters with pristine cultures has been shattered in our post-colonial epoch. Borders bleed, as much as they contain. Instead of dividing lines to be patrolled or transgressed boundaries are now understood as criss-crossing sites inside the postmodern subject. Difference is resituated within, instead of beyond, the self. Inside and outside distinctions, like genres, blur and wobble. Nothing seems truer now than Trinh's pithy insight (1989, p. 94): "Despite our desperate, eternal attempt to separate, contain, and mend, categories always leak."

Rosaldo believes that contemporary geo-politics, including decolonization and multinational corporations, requires thinking about boundaries not simply as barriers but as bridges and membranes (1989, p. 217): "All of us inhabit an interdependent late-twentieth-century world marked by borrowing and lending across porous national and cultural boundaries that are saturated with inequality, power, and domination." Further, the border-crossings emblematic of our postmodern world challenge ethnography to rethink its project: "If ethnography once imagined it could describe discrete cultures, it now contends with boundaries that crisscross over a field at once fluid and saturated with power. In a world where 'open borders' appear more salient than 'closed communities,' one wonders how to define a project for cultural studies" (Rosaldo, 1989, p. 45). Rosaldo argues that the research agenda needs to move from centers to "borderlands," "zones of difference," and "busy intersections" where many identities and interests articulate with multiple others (1989, pp. 17, 28).

The major epistemological consequence of displacing the idea of solid centers and unified wholes with borderlands and zones of contest is a rethinking of identity and culture as constructed and relational, instead of ontologically given and essential. This rethinking privileges metonym, "reasoning part-to-part" over synecdoche, "'reasoning part-to-whole" (Tyler, 1987, p. 151); it features syntax over semantics. Meaning is contested and struggled for in the interstices, in between structures. Identity is invented and contingent, not autonomous: "'I' is, therefore, not a unified subject, a fixed identity, or that solid mass covered with layers of superficialities one has gradually to peel off before one can see its true face. 'I' is, itself, *infinite layers*" (Trinh, 1989, p. 94).

Clifford argues (1988, p. 10) that much of non-western historical experience has been "hemmed in by concepts of continuous tradition and the unified self." The presuppositions of pattern, continuity, coherence, and unity characteristic of classic ethnography may have had more to do with the West's ideological commitment to individualism than with on-the-ground cultural practices. "I argue," says Clifford (1988, 10), "that identity, ethnographically considered, must always be mixed, relational, and inventive." The idea of the person shifts from that of a fixed, autonomous self to a polysemic site of articulation for multiple identities and voices.

From the boundary perspective, identity is more like a performance in process than a postulate, premise, or originary principle. From his historical study of the "colonial assault" on Melanesia, and his 1977 fieldwork study of a courtroom trial in Massachusetts where land ownership by Mashpee Native Americans was contingent upon "proof" of tribal identity, Clifford (1988, p. 9) came to understand identity as provisional, "not as an archaic survival but as an ongoing process, politically contested and historically unfinished." In our postmodern world the refugee, exile, has become an increasingly visible sign of geopolitical turbulence as well as the emblematic figure for a more general feeling of displacement, dispersal, what Clifford describes (1988, p. 9) as "a pervasive condition of off-centeredness."

Betwixt and between worlds, suspended between a shattered past and insecure future, refuges and other displaced people must create an "inventive poetics of reality" (Clifford, 1988, p. 6) for recollecting, recontextualizing, and refashioning their identities. The refugee condition epitomizes a postmodern existence of border-crossings and life on the margins. With displacement, upheaval, unmooring, come the terror and potentiality of flux, improvisation,

and creative recombinations. Refugees, exiles, homeless people, and other no-
mads enact the post-structuralist idea of "putting culture into motion" (Rosaldo, 1989, p. 91) through experiences that are both violent and regenerative.
Taking the Carribean as an illuminating example, Clifford notes (1988, p. 15)
that its history is one of "degradation, mimicry, violence, and blocked possibilities," but it is also "rebellious, syncretic, and creative."

In *The Practice of Everyday Life*, Michel de Certeau (1984, p. 30) celebrates
the interventions of marginal people whose creativity, "the art of making do,"
gets finely honed from living on the edge, a borderlands life:

> Thus a North African living in Paris or Boubaix (France) insinuates *into* the sys-
> tem imposed on him by the construction of a low-income housing develop-
> ment or of the French language the ways of 'dwelling' (in a house or a language)
> peculiar to his native Kabylia. He superimposes them and, by that combination,
> creates for himself a space in which he can find *ways of using* the constraining
> order of the place or of the language. Without leaving the place where he has no
> choice but to live and which lays down its law for him, he established within it
> a degree of *plurality* and creativity. By an art of being in between, he draws un-
> expected results from his situation.

My own fieldwork with refugees and migrants in Thailand, the Gaza Strip,
and inner-city Chicago resonates deeply with Clifford's observations (1988,
p.16): "Many traditions, languages, cosmologies, and values are lost, some literally murdered; but much has simultaneously been invented and revived in
complex, oppositional contexts. If the victims of progress and empire are
weak, they are seldom passive."

There are implications of rhetoric and communication studies from
ethnography's current interest in boundary phenomena and border negotiations. Communication becomes even more urgent and necessary in situation
of displacement, exile, and erasure. Trinh, a Vietnamese-American woman,
speaking as an exile to other exiles, articulates the difficulty and urgency of expression for all refugees and displaced people (1989, p. 80):

> You who understand the dehumanization of forced removal-relocation-
> reeducation-redefinition, the humiliation of having to falsify your own reality,
> your voice—you know. And often cannot say it. You try and keep on trying to
> unsay it, for if you don't, they will not fail to fill in the blanks on your behalf,
> and you will be said.

The *discourse of displacement* is a project that beckons rhetorical and communication scholars.

And if the increasingly pervasive feeling of discontinuity and finding oneself "off center among scattered traditions" (Clifford, 1988, p. 3) incites us to speak, then we must draw on *topoi* from among multiple discursive styles and traditions. Jackson notes the intertextual and heteroglossic nature of discourse (1989, p. 176): "reviewing the historical mutability of discourse, I am also mindful that no one episteme ever completely supercedes another. The historical matrix in which our present discourse is embedded contains other discursive styles and strategies, and makes use of them." Never has the rhetorical canon of *inventio* taken on more emphatic meaning than in the current rethinking of culture and ethos (see Wagner, 1980).

Cities throughout the United States have become sites of extraordinary diversity as refugees and immigrants, increasingly from the hemispheres of the South and the East, pour into inner-city neighborhoods. Rosaldo makes the point that one does not have to go to the "Third World" to encounter culture in the borderlands (1989, p. 28): "Cities throughout the world today increasingly include minorities defined by race, ethnicity, language, class, religion, and sexual orientation. Encounters with 'difference' now pervade modern everyday life in urban settings." For more than three years I have been conducting ethnographic research in one of these polyglot immigrant neighborhoods in inner-city Chicago. More than fifty languages and dialects are spoken by students at the local high school. The "Bilingual Student Roster" displays an exotic array of languages that in addition to Spanish, Korean, and Arabic, includes Assyrian, Tagalog, Vietnamese, Khmer, Hmong, Malayalam, Gujarati, Lao, Urdu, Cantonese, Greek, Pashto, Thai, Punjabi, Italian, Armenian, Dutch, Turkish, Ibo, Amharic, Slovenian, Farsi, and others. For the first twenty months of fieldwork I lived in an apartment alongside refugee and immigrant neighbors from Mexico, Puerto Rico, Iraq, Laos, Cambodia, Poland, Lebanon, as well as African-American, Appalachian White, and elderly Jews all living cheek-by-jowl in the same crowded, dilapidated tenement building. The local street gang with which I work reflects the same polyglot texture of the neighborhood. It is called the Latin Kings, originally a Puerto Rican gang, but the current members include Assyrian, African-American, Puerto Rican, Guatemalan, Salvadoran, Vietnamese, Lao, Korean, Palestinian, Filipino, Mexican, White, and others (Conquergood, Friesma, Hunter & Mansbridge, 1990).

Few phrases have more resonance in contemporary ethnography—and with my own fieldwork—than Bakhin's powerful affirmation (1986, p. 2) that "the most intense and productive life of culture takes place on the boundaries."

THE RISK OF PERFORMANCE

With renewed appreciation for boundaries, border-crossings, process, improvisation, contingency, multiplex identities, and the embodied nature of fieldwork practice, many ethnographers have turned to a performance-inflected vocabulary. "In the social sciences," Geertz observes (1983, p. 22), "the analogies are coming more and more from the contrivances of cultural performance than from those of physical manipulation." No one has done more than Victor Turner to open up space in ethnography for performance, to move the field away from preoccupations with universal system, structure, form, and towards particular practices, people, and performances. A dedicated ethnographer, Turner wanted the professional discourse of cultural studies to capture the struggle, passion, and praxis of village life that he so relished in the field. The language of drama and performance gave him a way of thinking and talking about people as actors who creatively play, improvise, interpret, and represent roles and scripts. In a rhetorical masterstroke, Turner (1986, p. 81) subversively redefined the fundamental terms of discussion in ethnography by defining humankind as *homo performans*, humanity as performer, a culture-inventing, social-performing, self-making and self-transforming creature. Turner was drawn to the conceptual lens of performance because it focused on humankind alive, the creative, playful, provisional, imaginative, articulate expressions of ordinary people grounded in the challenge to making a life in this village, that valley, and inspired by the struggle for meaning.

Distinguishing characteristics of performance-sensitive research emerge from Turner's detailed and elaborated work on social drama an cultural performance. The performance paradigm privileges particular, participatory, dynamic, intimate, precarious, embodied experience grounded in historical process, contingency, and ideology. Another way of saying it is that performance-centered research takes as both its subject matter and method the experiencing body situated in time, place, and history. The performance paradigm insists on face-to-face encounters instead of abstractions and reductions. It situates ethnographers within the delicately negotiated and frag-

ile "face-work" that is part of the intricate and nuanced dramaturgy of everyday life (see Goffman, 1967).

Turner appreciated the heuristics of embodied experience because he
understood how social drama must be acted out and rituals performed in
order to be meaningful, and he realized how the ethnographer must be a
co-performer in order to understand those embodied meanings. In one of his
earlier works (1975, pp. 28–29) he enuciated the role of the performing body
as a hermeneutical agency both for the researcher as well as the researched:

> The religious ideas and processes I have just mentioned belong to the domain
> of performance, their power derived from the participation of the living people
> who use them. My counsel, therefore, to investigators of ritual processes would
> be to learn them in the first place "on their pulses," in coactivity with their en-
> actors, having beforehand shared for a considerable time much of the people's
> daily life and gotten to know them not only as players of social roles, but as
> unique individuals, each with a style and a soul of his or her own. Only by these
> means will the investigator become aware.

The bodily image of learning something "on the pulses" captures the distinctive method of performance-sensitive ethnography. The power dynamic of
the research situation changes when the ethnographer moves from the gaze of
the distanced and detached observer to the intimate involvement and engagement of "coactivity" or co-performance with historically situated, named,
"unique individuals."

The performance paradigm can help ethnographers recognize "the limitations of literacy" and critique the textualist bias of western civilization (Jackson, 1989). Geertz (1973, p. 452) enunciates the textual paradigm in his
famous phrase: "The culture of a people is an ensemble of texts, themselves
ensembles, which the anthropologist strains to read over the shoulders of
those to whom they properly belong." In other words, the ethnographer is
construed as a displaced, somewhat awkward reader of texts. Jackson vigorously critiques this ethnographic textualism (1989, p. 184):

> By fetishizing texts, it divides—as the advent of literacy itself did—readers from
> authors, and separates both from the world. The idea that "there is nothing out-
> side the text" may be congenial to someone whose life is confined to academe,
> but it sounds absurd in the village worlds where anthropologists carry out their

work, where people negotiate meaning in face-to-face interactions, not as individual minds but as embodied social beings. In other words, textualism tends to ignore the flux of human relationships, the ways meanings are created intersubjectively as well as "intertextually," embodied in gestures as well as in words, and connected to political, moral, and aesthetic interests.

Though possessed of a long historical commitment to the spoken word, rhetoric and communication suffer from this same valorizing of inscribed texts. A recent essay in the *Quarterly Journal of Speech* (Brummett, 1990, p. 71; emphasis mine) provides a stunning example of the field's extreme textualism: "Such a [disciplinary] grounding can only come about in the moment of methodological commitment *when someone sits down with a transcript of discourse* and attempts to explain it to students or colleagues—*in that moment we become scholars of communication.*" In the quest for intellectual respectability through disciplinary rigor, some communication and rhetorical scholars have narrowed their focus to language, particularly those aspects of language that can be spatialized on the page, or measured and counted, to the exclusion of embodied meanings that are accessible through ethnographic methods of "radical empiricism" (Jackson, 1989).

The linguistic and textualist bias of speech communication has blinded many scholars to the preeminently rhetorical nature of cultural performance—ritual, ceremony, celebration, festival, parade, pageant, feast, and so forth. It is not just in non-western cultures, but in many so-called modern communities that cultural performance functions as a special form of public address, rhetorical agency:

> [C]ultural performances are not simple reflectors or expressions of culture or even of changing culture but may themselves be active agencies of change, representing the eye by which culture sees itself and the drawing board on which creative actors sketch out what they believe to be more apt or interesting "designs for living." ... Performative reflexivity is a condition in which a sociocultural group, or its most perceptive members acting representatively, turn, bend or reflect back upon themselves, upon the relations, actions, symbols, meanings, codes, roles, statuses, social structures, ethical and legal rules, and other sociocultural components which make up their public "selves." (Turner, 1986, p. 24)

Through cultural performances many people both construct and participate in "public" life. Particularly for poor and marginalized people denied access to middle-class "public" forums, cultural performance becomes the venue for "public discussion" of vital issues central to their communities, as well as an arena for gaining visibility and staging their identity. Nancy Fraser's (1990, p. 67) concept of "subaltern counterpublics" is very useful: "arenas where members of subordinated social groups invent and circulate counterdiscourses, which in turn permit them to formulate oppositional interpretations of their identities, interests, and needs."

What every ethnographer understands, however, is that the mode of "discussion," the discourse, is not always and exclusively verbal: Issues and attitudes are expressed and contested in dance, music, gesture, food, ritual, artifact, symbolic action, as well as words. Cultural performances are not simply epideictic spectacles: Investigated historically within their political contexts they are profoundly deliberative occasions (see Fernandez, 1986).

Although cultural performances often frame a great deal of speech-making—formal oratory, stylized recitation and chant, as well as backstage talk and informal conversation—it would be a great mistake for a communication researcher simply "to sit down with a transcript of discourse" and privilege words over other channels of meaning. Turner (1986, p. 23) emphatically resists valorizing language or studying any of the multiple codes of performed meaning extricated from their complex interactions: "This is an important point—rituals, dramas, and other performative genres are often orchestrations of media, not expression in a single medium." There is a complex interplay, for example, between song, gesture, facial expressions, and the burning of incense, and even incense has different meanings when it is burned at different times, and there are different kinds of incense. "The master-of-ceremonies, priest, producer, director creates art from the ensemble of media and codes, just as a conductor in the single genre of classical music blends and opposes the sounds of the different instruments to produce an often unrepeatable effect" (Turner, 1986, p. 23).

Turner encourages ethnographers to study the interplay of performance codes, focusing on their syntactic relationships rather than their semantics (1986, pp. 23–24):

> It is worth pointing out, too, that it is not, as some structuralists have argued, a matter of emitting the *same* message in different media and codes, the better to underline it by redundancy. The "same" message in different media is really a set of subtly variant messages, each medium contributing its own generic message

to the message conveyed through it. The result is something like a hall of mirrors—magic mirrors, each interpreting as well as reflecting the images beamed to it, and flashed from one to the others.

The polysemic nature of cultural performances "makes of these genres flexible and nuanced instruments capable of carrying and communicating many messages at once, even of subverting on one level what it appears to be 'saying' on another" (Turner, 1986, p.24). The performance paradigm is an alternative to the atemporal, decontextualized, flattening approach of text-positivism.

Rethinking the "world as text" to the "world as performance" opens up new questions that can be clustered around five intersecting planes of analyses:

1. *Performance and Cultural Process.* What are the conceptual consequences of thinking about culture as a *verb* instead of a *noun*, process instead of product? Culture as unfolding performative invention instead of reified system, structure, or variable? What happens to our thinking about performance when we move it outside of Aesthetics and situate it at the center of lived experience?

2. *Performance and Ethnographic Praxis.* What are the methodological implications of thinking about fieldwork as the collaborative performance of an enabling fiction between observer and observed, knower and known? How does thinking about fieldwork as performance differ from thinking about fieldwork as the collection of data? Reading of texts? How does the performance model shape the conduct of fieldwork? Relationship with the people? Choices made in the field? Positionality of the researcher?

3. *Performance and Hermeneutics.* What kinds of knowledge are privileged or displaced when performed experience becomes a way of knowing, a method of crucial inquiry, a mode of understanding? What are the epistemological and ethical entailments of performing ethnographic texts and fieldnotes? What are the range and varieties of performance modes and styles that can enable interpretation and understanding?

4. *Performance and Scholarly Representation.* What are the rhetorical problematics of performance as a complementary or alternative form of "publishing" research? What are the differences between reading an analysis of fieldwork data, and hearing the voices from the field interpretively filtered

through the voice of the researcher? For the listening audience of peers? For the performing ethnographer? For the people whose lived experience is the subject matter of the ethnography? What about enabling the people themselves to perform their own experience? What are the epistemological underpinnings and institutional practices that would legitimate performance as a complementary form of research publication?

5. *The Politics of Performance.* What is the relationship between performance and power? How does performance reproduce, enable, sustain, challenge, subvert, critique, and naturalize ideology? How do performances simultaneously reproduce and resist hegemony? How does performance accommodate and contest domination?

The most work has been done in Numbers One, Two, and Five, particularly One. Although we still need to think more deeply and radically about the performative nature of culture, Erving Goffman, Kenneth Burke, Dell Hymes, and a host of other social theorists have already set the stage. The expansive reach of conceptualizing performance as the agency for constituting and reconstituting culture, leads from performance as Agency to performance as ultimate Scene: "All the world's a stage." The popularity of Shakespeare's adage notwithstanding, we scarcely have begun to unpack and understand the radical potential of that idea.

Number Three and especially Four are the most deeply subversive and threatening to the text-bound structure of the academy. It is one thing to talk about performance as a model for cultural process, as a heuristic for understanding social life, as long as that performance-sensitive talk eventually gets "written up." The intensely performative and bodily experience of fieldwork is redeemed through writing. The hegemony of inscribed texts is never challenged by fieldwork because, after all is said and done, the final word is on paper. Print publication is the telos of fieldwork. It is interesting to note that even the most radical deconstructions still take place on the page. "Performance as a Form of Scholarly Representation" challenges the domination of textualism.

Turner (1986, pp. 139–55) advocated, practiced, and wrote about performance as a critical method for interpreting and intensifying fieldwork data. It is quite another thing, politically, to move performance from hermeneutics to a form of scholarly representation. That moves strikes at the heart of academic politics and issues of scholarly authority. Talal Asad points in this direction (1986, p. 159):

> If Benjamin was right in proposing that translation may require not a mechanical reproduction of the original but a harmonization with its *intentio*, it follows that there is no reason why this should be done only in the same mode. Indeed, it could be argues that "translating" an alien form of life, another culture, is not always done best through the representational discourse of ethnography, that under certain conditions a dramatic performance, the execution of a dance, or the playing of a piece of music might be more apt.

If post-structuralist thought and the postmodern moment continue to open up received categories and established canons, more of this experimentation with scholarly form might happen. If the Performance Paradigm simply is pitted against the Textual Paradigm, then its radical force will be coopted by yet another either/or binary construction that ultimately reproduces modernist thinking. The Performance Paradigm will be most useful if it decenters, without discarding, texts. I do not imagine life in a university without books, nor do I have any wish to stop writing myself. But I do want to keep thinking about what gets lost and muted in texts. And I want to think about performance as a complement, alternative, supplement, and critique of inscribed texts. Following Turner and others, I want to keep opening up space for nondiscursive forms, and encouraging research and writing practices that are performance-sensitive.

RHETORICAL REFLEXIVITY

Far from displacing texts, contemporary ethnography is extremely interested in and self-conscious about its own text-making practices. There is widespread recognition of "the fact that ethnography is, from beginning to end, enmeshed in writing" (Clifford, 1988, p. 25). These writings are not innocent descriptions through which the other is transparently revealed. "It is more than ever crucial for different peoples to form complex concrete images of one another," Clifford affirms (1988, p. 23), "as well as of the relationships of knowledge and power that connect them; but no sovereign scientific method or ethical stance can guarantee the truth of such images. They are constitutes—the critique of colonial modes of representation has shown at least this much—in specific historical relations of dominance and dialogue." Geertz

(1988, p. 141) argues that even "the pretense of looking at the world directly, as though through a one-way screen, seeing others as they really are when only God is looking . . . is itself a rhetorical strategy, a mode of persuasion."

Ethnography is being rethought in fundamentally rhetorical terms. Many of the most influential books recently published in ethnography are meta-rhetorical critiques. It seems that everyone in ethnography nowadays is a rhetorical critic. Many ethnographers now believe that disciplinary authority is a matter of rhetorical strategy not scientific method. Geertz is perhaps most blunt about the essentially rhetorical nature of ethnography (1988, pp. 143–44):

> The capacity to persuade readers . . . that what they are reading is an authentic account by someone personally acquainted with how life proceeds in some place, at some time, among some group, is the basis upon which anything else ethnography seeks to do . . . finally rests. The textual connection of the Being Here and the Being There sides of anthropology, the imaginative construction of a common ground between the Written At and the Written About . . . is the *fons et origo* of whatever power and anthropology has to convince anyone of anything—not theory, not method, not even the aura of the professorial chair, consequential as these last may be.

Much of the current rethinking of ethnography has been sobered and empowered by vigorous rhetorical critique of anthropological discourse.

Geertz is foremost among ethnography's practicing rhetorical critics. His rhetorical criticism of E. E. Evans-Pritchard's (E-P) ethnographic texts is exemplary (1988). He identifies E-P's stylistic token as "drastic clarity" (1988, p. 68) that translates onto the page as "a sting of clean, well-lighted judgments, unconditional statements so perspicuously presented that only the invincibly uninformed will think to resist them," a sort of "first-strike assertiveness" (1988, p. 63). The rhetorical questions Geertz (1988, p. 64) puts to E-P's texts are: "How (Why? In what way? Of what?) does all this resolute informing inform?" His "deep reading" of E-P yields these insights (1988, p. 64):

> *How he does it*: The outstanding characteristic of E-P's approach to ethnographic exposition and the main source of his persuasive power is his enormous capacity to construct visualizable representation of cultural phenomena—anthropological transparencies. *What he does*: The main effect,

and the main intent, of this magic lantern ethnography is to demonstrate that
the established frames of social perception, those upon which we ourselves in-
stinctively rely, are fully adequate to whatever oddities the transparencies may
turn out to picture.

According to Geertz (1988, p. 66) E-P produces a "see-er's rhetoric." With
E-P's texts, like all rhetorical practice, "the way of saying is the what of saying"
(1988, p. 68).

At a deep level, Geertz insightfully notes (1998, p. 70), E-P's discussion of
the Nuer and the Azande underwrite his own cultural ethos as much as they
illuminate the other:

> it validates the ethnographer's form of life at the same time as it justifies those
> of his subjects—and that it does the one by doing the other. The adequacy of
> the cultural categories of, in this case, university England, to provide a frame of
> intelligible reasonings, creditable values, and familiar motivations for such odd-
> ities as poison oracles, ghost marriages, blood feuds, and cucumber sacrifices
> recommends those categories as of somehow more than parochial importance.
> Whatever personal reason E-P may have had for being so extraordinarily anx-
> ious to picture Africa as a logical and prudential place—orderly, straightforward
> and levelheaded, firmly modeled and open to view—in doing so he constructed
> a forceful argument for the general authority of a certain conception of life. If it
> could undarken Africa, it could undarken anything.

By bringing "Africans into a world conceived in deeply English terms" he
thereby confirmed "the dominion of those terms" (1988, p. 70).

Geertz as rhetorical critic moves beyond formalist analysis and situates
ethnographic texts within their distinctive institutional constraints and en-
gendering professional practices (1988, pp. 129–30):

> However far from the groves of academe anthropologists seek out their subjects—
> a shelved beach in Polynesia, a charred plateau in Amazonia; Akobo, Meknes, Pan-
> ther Burn—they write their accounts with the world of lecterns, libraries,
> blackboards, and seminars all about them. This is the world that produces anthro-
> pologists, that licenses them to do the kind of work they do must find a place if it
> is to count as worth attention. In itself, Being There is a postcard experience ("I've
> been to Katmandu—have you?"). It is Being Here, a scholar among scholars, that
> gets your anthropology read..published, reviewed, cited, taught.

Geertz weights the Being Here writing it down side of the axis. To be sure, ethnography on the page constrains and shapes performance in the field. But it is also true, I believe, that experiential performance sometimes resists, exceeds, and overwhelms the constraints and strictures of writing. It is the task of rhetorical critics to seek out these sites of tension, displacement, and contradiction between the Being There of performed experience and the Being Here of the written texts.

This rhetorical self-reflexivity has helped politicize ethnography: "The gap between engaging others where they are and representing them where they aren't, always immense but not much noticed, has suddenly become extremely visible. What once seemed only technically difficult, getting 'their' lives into 'our' works, has turned morally, politically, even epistemologically, delicate" (Geertz, 1988, p. 130). Ethnographic authority is the empowering alignment between rhetorical strategy and political ideology. Once shielded by the mask of science, ethnographers now have become acutely aware of the sources of their persuasive power (Geertz, 1988, pp. 148–49):

> What it hasn't been, and, propelled by the moral and intellectual self-confidence of Western Civilization, hasn't so much had to be, is aware of the sources of its power. If it is now to prosper, with the confidence shaken, it must become aware. Attention to how it gets its effects and what those are, to anthropology on the page, is no longer a side issue, dwarfed by problems of method and issues of theory. It . . . is rather close to the heart of the matter. (148–49).

Trinh (1989, p. 43) enacts this struggle towards self-reflexive awareness of textual power in her book subtitled "Writing Postcoloniality and Feminism": "what is exposed in this text is the inscription and de-scription of a non-unitary female subject of color through her engagement, therefore also disengagement, with master discourses."

It is ironic that the discipline of communication has been relatively unreflexive about the rhetorical construction of its own disciplinary authority. It would be illuminating to critique the rhetorical expectations and constraints on articles published in the *Quarterly Journal of Speech*, or *Communication Monographs*. What kinds of knowledge, and their attendant discursive styles, get privileged, legitimated, or displaced? How does knowledge about communication get constructed? What counts as an interesting question about human communication? What are the tacitly observed boundaries—the range of appropriateness—regarding the substance, methods, and discursive styles of communication scholarship? And, most importantly for critical theorists, what configuration of socio-political interests does communication scholarship serve? How does professionally authorized knowledge about communication articulate with relations of power? About the connection between a field of knowledge and relations of power, Michel Foucault (1979, p. 27) offers this sobering insight: "power produces knowledge . . . ; power and knowledge directly imply one another; . . . there is no power relation without the correlative constitution of a field of knowledge, nor any knowledge that does not presuppose and constitute at the same time power relations."

REFERENCES

Asad, T. (ed.) (1973). *Anthropology and the colonial encounter.* London: Ithaca Press.

———. (1986). The concept of cultural translation in British social anthropology. In J. Clifford & G. Marcus (eds.), *Writing culture: The poetics and politics of ethnography* (pp. 141–64). Berkeley: University of California Press.

Ashcroft, B., Griffiths, G., & Tiffin, H. (1989). *The empire writes back: Theory and practice in post-colonial literatures.* New York: Routledge.

Bakhtin, M. (1986). *Speech genres.* (C. Emerson and M. Holquist, eds.; V. McGee, trans.) Austin: University of Texas Press.

Brummett, B. (1990). A eulogy for epistemic rhetoric. *Quarterly Journal of Speech,* 7, 69–72.

Clifford, J. (1988). *Predicament of culture.* Cambridge: Harvard University Press.

Clifford, J., & Marcus G. (eds.) (1986). *Writing culture: The poetics and politics of ethnography.* Berkeley: University of California Press.

Conquergood, D., Friesema, P., Hunter, A., & Mansbridge, J. (1990). *Dispersed ethnicity and community integration: Newcomers and established residents in the Albany Park area of Chicago.* Evanston, IL: Center for Urban Affairs and Policy Research, Northwestern University.

De Certeau, M. (1984). *The practice of everyday life.* (S. Randall, trans.) Berkeley: University of California Press.

Fabian, J. (1983). *Time and the other: How anthropology makes its object.* New York: Columbia University Press.

Fernandez, J. (1986). *Persuasions and performances: The play of tropes in culture.* Bloomington: Indiana University Press.

Fraser, N. (1990). Rethinking the public sphere: A contribution to the critique of actually existing democracy. *Social Text, 25/26,* 56–80.

Foucault, M. (1979). *Discipline and punish: The birth of the prison.* (A. Sheridan, trans.) New York: Vintage Books.

Geertz, C. (1973). *Interpretation of cultures.* New York: Basic Books.

———. (1983). *Local knowledge: Further essays in interpretive anthropology.* New York: Basic Books.

———. (1988). *Works and lives: The anthropologist as author.* Stanford, CA: Stanford University Press.

Goffman, E. (1967). *Interaction ritual: Essays on face-to-face behavior.* New York: Anchor Books.

———. (1989). On fieldwork. *Journal of Contemporary Ethnography, 18,* 123–32.

Jackson, M. (1989). *Paths toward a clearing: Radical empiricism and ethnographic inquiry.* Bloomington: Indiana University Press.

Malinowski, B. (1961). *Argonauts of the western Pacific.* New York: E. P. Dutton. (Original work published 1922).

Marcus, G., & Fischer, M. (1986). *Anthropology as cultural critique: An experimental moment in the human sciences.* Chicago: University of Chicago Press.

Miller, C. (1990). *Theories of Africans: Francophone literature and anthropology in Africa.* Chicago: University of Chicago Press.

Ricoeur, P. (1971). The model of the text: Meaningful action considered as a text. *Social Research, 38,* 529–62.

Rosaldo, R. (1989). *Culture and truth: The remaking of social analysis.* Boston: Beacon.

Theunissen, M. (1984). *The other: Studies in the social ontology of Husserl, Heidegger, Sartre, and Buber.* Cambridge: MIT Press.

Trinh, T. M. (1989). *Woman, native, other: Writing postcoloniality and feminism.* Bloomington: Indiana University Press.

Turner, V. (1975). *Revelation and divination in Ndembu ritual.* Ithaca, NY: Cornell University Press.

———. (1986). *The anthropology of performance.* New York: PAJ Publications.

Tyler, S. (1987). *The unspeakable: Discourse, dialogue, and rhetoric in the postmodern world.* Madison: University of Wisconsin Press.

Van Maanen, J. (1988). *Tales from the field: On writing ethnography.* Chicago: University of Chicago Press.

Wagner, R. (1980). *The invention of culture* (rev. ed.). Chicago: University of Chicago Press.

VII

The Revolution
in Presentation

In the past decade, ethnographers have started to experiment seriously with new (frequently literary) writing forms: poetry, short stories, plays, memoirs, narratives of self, performance texts, responsive readings, comedy, and satire. Richardson calls these evocative representations "creative analytic practices." These writing practices speak to how the self is created in the written text, which is performative. Knowing the self and knowing the other are intertwined— writing about one requires writing about the other. Richardson asks us to understand ourselves reflexively as persons writing from a particular position in time and place. We can never say everything in a single text. This frees us to pursue writing as a method of knowing or coming to know.

PERFORMANCE ETHNOGRAPHY AND ETHNODRAMA

Conquergood sees performing as a moral act, an ethical act. Because the autoethnographic performer is not representing the experiences of another person, many of the ethical pitfalls identified by Conquergood are avoided. The autoethnographic performer is not a custodian, curator, proponent, interpreter, or protector of another culture's performances. The intent, instead, is to create dialogical performance experiences, events (and texts) that interrogate, criticize, empower, and create the conditions for open and honest understanding.

Mienczakowski (1995, 2000; see also Mienczakowski and Morgan 2001) has pioneered the use of ethnodrama, or ethnographic performances based on grounded theory methodology and close-up, traditional fieldwork, interviewing, and participant observation (2000, 468). Ethnodrama is organized by the proposition "that performed ethnography may provide more accessible and clearer public explanations of research than is frequently the case with traditional, written report texts" (471).

Mienczakowski uses postperformance discussions with informants and audience members as a way of making the performance of ethnographic texts more responsive to the demands of praxis and social critique. His method of ethnodrama uses verbatim ethnographic accounts taken from health settings, including a drug and alcohol withdrawal center. These accounts are fashioned into scripts (whole plays), with characters representing different types of staff and clients within the setting. Mienczakowski explores the potential of ethnodrama to provide emancipatory opportunities for health informants and health professionals. Postperformance discussions with audience members, staff, informants, and professionals were used to rework scenarios and reinterpret events. The processes of participant and audience empowerment through forum reconstruction and dialogical interactions were crucial to giving health consumers control over the meaning of their own experiences (Mienczakowski 1995, 361).

The ethnodrama process is "sensitive to the pedagogy of teaching . . . by using the words, stories and advice of people involved in alcohol dependency or other mental health issues, the ethnodrama methodology seeks to tell the truth as they see it, so as to give them voice" (Mienczakowski 1995, 367). Before performances are staged, copies of scripts are distributed, and individuals are invited to comment. The scripts and commentary provide the basis for education workshops and for evaluations of the programs in question. Because they are written in a public voice, in an accessible and unassuming form, they "are instantly open to interpretation by nonacademics" (368). The scripts and performances help correct negative public stereotypes, thereby influencing, informing, and changing public health care policy. This is the "public voice purpose of ethnodrama" (372).

Ethnodramas differ from other forms of performance ethnographic practice "because it is their overt intention . . . to be a form of public voice ethnography that has emancipatory and educational potential" (Mienczakowski 2000,

469). Critical ethnodramas "blur the boundaries and barriers between health care recipients, professionals, policy-makers and the general public" (469). Grounded in local understandings and experiences, these texts provide the basis for the critical evaluation of existing programs. They return the ownership of programs to immediate stakeholders and address audiences previously ignored or unmoved by more traditional approaches (470). This is ethnographic research that turns program evaluation into a participatory-performative process. In so doing, it provides, in its own small way, "limited grounds for Habermas's notion of human communicative consensus/competence" (470).

Ethnodramas focus on crises and moments of epiphany in the culture. Suspended in time, they are liminal moments. They open up institutions and their practices for critical inspection and evaluation.

POETICS—ANTHROPOLOGICAL AND ETHNOGRAPHIC

Anthropologists have been writing experimental, literary, and poetic ethnographic texts for at least forty years. In the literary, poetic form, ethnographers enact a moral aesthetic that allows them to say things they could not otherwise say. In so doing, they push the boundaries of artful ethnographic discourse. Thus, the boundaries between the humanities and the human sciences are blurred. In this blurring, our moral sensibilities are enlivened.

Hymes explores the risks involved in writing poetry, speaking to the courage that is required. He hopes that writing poetry will become part of the reconstruction of anthropological methodology. But the public makes the self vulnerable to criticism from one's peers. Still, he thinks there will be a wider acceptance of such writing, as well as of the writing of novels, the making of films, and perhaps painting and drawing.

The key terms for Hymes are *line* and *shape*. The call to poetry requires an ability to translate complex experience into a brief compass, giving a shape to a series of lines that assume a satisfactory form. The anthropological poet is judged by criteria from two fields at once: poetry and anthropology. The risks are great, for one can fail at one or the other or both crafts. A poem that fails (as poetry) can nevertheless succeed in being true to experience. A wonderful poem, on the other hand, may not be true to experience. This shift from "realist" to experimental, or "messy," texts carries risks for authors and readers alike. Dwell for a few minutes in Hymes's poem "City Night" and see whether you agree that he is a master poet and a master ethnographer.

REFERENCES

Mienczakowski, Jim. 2000. "Ethnodrama: Performed Research—Limitations and Potential." In Paul Atkinson, et al., *Handbook of Ethnography* (pp. 468–76). London: Sage.

———. 1995. "The Theatre of Ethnography: The Reconstruction of Ethnography into Theatre with Emancipatory Potential." *Qualitative Inquiry*, 1: 360–75.

Mienczakowski, Jim, and Stephen Morgan. 1993. *Busting: The Challenge of the Drought Spirit.* Brisbane: Griffith University, Reprographics.

17

Writing: A Method of Inquiry

Laurel Richardson

[...]

WRITING PRACTICES

Writing, the creative effort, should come first—at least for some part of every day of your life. It is a wonderful blessing if you will use it. You will become happier, more enlightened, alive, impassioned, light hearted and generous to everybody else. Even your health will improve. Colds will disappear and all the other ailments of discouragement and boredom.

—*Brenda Ueland, If You Want to Write, 1938/1987*

In what follows, I suggest some ways of using writing as a method of knowing. I have chosen exercises that have been productive for students because they demystify writing, nurture the researcher's voice, and serve the process of discovery. I wish I could guarantee them to bring good health as well. The practices are organized around topics discussed in the text.

Reprinted from *Handbook of Qualitative Research*, 2d. ed., Norman K. Denzin and Yvonna S. Lincoln, eds. (Thousand Oaks, Calif.: Sage, 2000), 923–48. Copyright © 2000 by Sage Publications Inc.

Metaphor

Using old, worn-out metaphors, although easy and comfortable, after a while invites stodginess and stiffness. The stiffer you get, the less flexible you are. Your ideas get ignored. If your writing is clichéd, you'll not "stretch your own imagination" (Ouch! Hear the cliché of pointing out the cliché!) and you'll bore people.

1. In traditional social scientific writing, the metaphor for theory is that it is a "building" (structure, foundation, construction, deconstruction, framework, grand, and so on). Consider a different metaphor, such as "theory as a tapestry" or "theory as an illness." Write a paragraph about "theory" using your metaphor. Do you "see" differently and "feel" differently about theorizing using an unusual metaphor?

2. Consider alternative sensory metaphors for "knowledge" other than the heliocentric one mentioned in the text. What happens when you rethink/resense "knowledge" as situated in voice? In touch?

3. Look at one of your papers and highlight your metaphors and images. What are you saying through metaphors that you did not realize you were saying? What are you reinscribing? Do you want to? Can you find different metaphors that change how you "see" ("feel") the material? Your relationship to it? Are your mixed metaphors pointing to confusion in yourself or to social science's glossing over of ideas?

4. Take a look at George Lakoff and Mark Johnson's *Metaphors We Live By* (1980). It is a wonderful book, a compendium of examples of metaphors in everyday life and how they affect our ways of perceiving, thinking, and acting. What everyday metaphors are shaping your knowing/writing?

Writing Formats

1. Choose a journal article that exemplifies the mainstream writing conventions of your discipline. How is the argument staged? Who is the presumed audience? How does the paper inscribe ideology? How does the author claim authority over the material? Where is the author? Where are you in this paper? Who are the subjects and who are the objects of research?

2. Choose a journal article that exemplifies excellence in qualitative research. How has the article built upon normative social science writing? How is authority claimed? Where is the author? Where are you in the article? Who are the subjects and who are the objects of research?

3. Choose a paper you have written for a class or that you have published that you think is pretty good. How did you follow the norms of your discipline? Were you conscious of doing so? How did you stage your paper? What parts did the professor/reviewer laud? How did you depend upon those norms to carry your argument? Did you elide some difficult areas through vagueness, jargon, calls to authorities, or other rhetorical devices? What voices did you exclude in your writing? Who is the audience? Where are the subjects in the paper? Where are you? How do you feel about the paper now? About your process of constructing it?

Creative Analytic Writing Practices

1. Join or start a writing group. This could be a writing support group, a creative writing group, a poetry group, a dissertation group, or another kind of group. (On dissertation and article writing, see Becker, 1986; Fox, 1985; Richardson, 1990; Wolcott, 1990.)

2. Work through a creative writing guidebook. Natalie Goldberg (1986, 1990), Rust Hills (1987), Brenda Ueland (1937/1987), and Deena Weinstein (1993) all provide excellent guides.

3. Enroll in a creative writing workshop or class. These experiences are valuable for both beginning and experienced researchers.

4. Use "writing up" your field notes as an opportunity to expand your writing vocabulary, habits of thought, and attentiveness to your senses, and as a bulwark against the censorious voice of science. Where better to develop your sense of self, your voice, than in the process of doing your research? Apply creative writing skills to your field notes. You may need to rethink what you've have been taught about objectivity, science, and the ethnographic project. What works for me is to give different labels to different content. Building on the work of Glaser and Strauss (1967), I use four categories, which you may find of value:

- *Observation notes* (ON): These are as concrete and detailed as I am able to make them. I want to think of them as fairly accurate renditions of what I see, hear, feel, taste, and so on. I stay close to the scene as I experience it through my senses.
- *Methodological notes* (MN): These are messages to myself regarding how to collect "data"—who to talk to, what to wear, when to phone, and so on. I write a lot of these because I like methods, and I like to keep a process diary of my work.

- *Theoretical notes* (TN): These are hunches, hypotheses, poststructuralist connections, critiques of what I am doing/thinking/seeing. I like writing these because they open my field note texts to alternative interpretations and a critical epistemological stance. They provide a way of keeping me from being hooked on one view of reality.
- *Personal notes* (PN): These are uncensored feeling statements about the research, the people I am talking to, my doubts, my anxieties, my pleasures. I want all my feelings out on paper because I know they are affecting what/who I lay claim to know. I also know they are a great source for hypotheses; if I am feeling a certain way in a setting, it is likely that others might feel that way too. Finally, writing personal notes is a way for me to know myself better, a way of using writing as method of inquiry into the self.

5. Keep a journal. In it, write about your feelings about your work. This not only frees up your writing, it becomes the "historical record" for the writing of a narrative of the Self or a writing-story about the writing process.

6. Write a writing autobiography. This would be the story of how you learned to write: the dicta of English classes (Topic sentences? Outlines? The five-paragraph essay?), the dicta of social science professors, your experiences with teachers' comments on your papers, how and where you write now, your idiosyncratic "writing needs," your feelings abut writing and about the writing process. (This is an exercise that Arthur Bochner uses.)

7. If you wish to experiment with evocative writing, a good place to begin is by transforming your fieldnotes into drama. See what ethnographic rules you are using (such as fidelity to the speech of the participants, fidelity in the order of the speakers and events) and what literary ones you are invoking (such as limits on how long a speaker speaks, keeping the "plot" moving along, developing character through actions). Writing dramatic presentations accentuates ethical considerations. If you doubt that, contrast writing up an ethnographic event as a "typical" event with writing it as a play, with you and your hosts cast in roles that will be performed before others. Who has ownership of spoken words? How is authorship attributed? What if people do not like how they are characterized? Are courtesy norms being violated? Experiment here with both oral and written versions of your drama.

8. Experiment with transforming an in-depth interview into a poetic representation. Try using only the words, rhythms, figures of speech, breath

points, pauses, syntax, and diction of the speaker. Where are you in the poem? What do you know about the interviewee and about yourself that you did not know before you wrote the poem? What poetic devices have you sacrificed in the name of science?

9. Experiment with writing narratives of the self. Keep in mind Barbara Tuchman's warning: "The writer's object is—or should be—to hold the reader's attention. . . . I want the reader to turn the page and keep on turning to the end. This is accomplished only when the narrative moves steadily ahead, not when it comes to a weary standstill, overlaced with every item uncovered in the research" (in *New York Times*, February 2, 1989).

10. Try writing a text using different typefaces, font sizes, and textual placement. How have the traditional ways of using print affected what you know and how you know it?

11. Write a "layered text" (see Lather & Smithies, 1997; Ronai, 1992). The layered text is a strategy for putting yourself into your text and putting your text onto the literatures and traditions of social science. Here is one possibility. First, write a short narrative of the Self about some event that is especially meaningful to you. Then step back and look at the narrative from your disciplinary perspective and insert into the narrative—beginning, midsections, end, wherever—relevant analytic statements or references, using a different typescript, alternative page placement, split pages, or other ways to mark the text. The layering can be multiple, with different ways of marking different theoretical levels, theories, speakers, and so on. (This is an exercise that Carolyn Ellis uses.)

12. Try some other strategy for writing new ethnography for social scientific publications. Try the "seamless" text, in which previous literature, theory, and methods are placed in textually meaningful ways, rather than in disjunctive sections (for an excellent example, see Bochner, 1997); try the "sandwich" text, in which traditional social science themes are the "white bread" around the "filling" (C. Ellis, personal communication, April 27, 1998); or try an "epilogue" explicating the theoretical analytic work of the creative text (See Eisner, 1996).

13. Consider a fieldwork setting. Consider the various subject positions you have or have had within it. For example, in a store you might be a salesclerk, customer, manager, feminist, capitalist, parent, child, and so on. Write about the setting (or an event in the setting) from several different subject positions. What do

you "know" from the different positions? Next, let the different points of view dialogue with each other. What do you discover through these dialogues?

14. Consider a paper you have written (or your field notes). What have you left out? Who is not present in this text? Who has been repressed or marginalized? Rewrite the text from that point of view.

15. Write your "data" in three different ways—for example, as a narrative account, as a poetic representation, and as readers' theater. What do you know in each rendition that you did not know in the other renditions? How do the different renditions enrich each other?

16. Write a narrative of the Self from your point of view (such as something that happened in your family or in a seminar). Then interview another participant (such as family or seminar member) and have that person tell you his or her story of the event. See yourself as part of the other person's story in the same way he or she is part of your story. How do you rewrite your story from the other person's point of view? (This is an exercise Carolyn Ellis uses.)

17. Collaborative writing is a way to see beyond one's own naturalisms of style and attitude. This is an exercise that I have used in my teaching, but it would be appropriate for a writing group as well. Each member writes a story of his or her life. It could be a feminist story, a success story, quest story, cultural story, professional socialization story, realist tale, confessional tale, or another kind of story. All persons' stories are photocopied for the group. The group is then broken into subgroups (I prefer groups of three), and each subgroup collaborates on writing a new story, the collective story of its members. The collaboration can take any form: drama, poetry, fiction, narrative of the selves, realism, whatever the subgroup chooses. The collaboration is shared with the entire group. All members then write about their feelings about the collaboration and what happened to their stories, their lives, in the process.

18. Memorywork (see Davies, 1994; Davies et al., 1997) is another collaborative research and writing strategy. Stories shared in the group are discussed and then rewritten, with attention paid to the discourses that are shaping the stories in each of their tellings. As more people tell their stories, individuals remember more details of their own stories, or develop new stories. Participants discover what their stories have in common, perhaps even writing what Bronwyn Davies (1994) calls a "collective biography."

19. Consider a part of your life outside of or before academia with which you have deeply resonated. Use that resonance as a "working metaphor" for

understanding and reporting your research. Students have created excellent reports by using unexpected lenses, such as choreography, principles of flower arrangement, art composition, and sportscasting, to view their lives and the lives of others. Writing from that which resonates with your life nurtures a more integrated life.

20. Different forms of writing are appropriate for different audiences and different occasions. Try writing the same piece of research for an academic audience, a trade audience, the popular press, policy makers, research hosts, and so on (see Richardson, 1990). This is an especially powerful exercise for dissertation students who may want to share their results in a "user-friendly" way with those they studied.

21. Write writing-stories (see Richardson, 1997), or reflexive accounts of how you happened to write pieces you have written. Your writing-stories can be about disciplinary politics, departmental events, friendship networks, collegial ties, family, and personal biographical experiences. Writing-stories situate your work in contexts, tying what can be a lonely and seemingly separative task to the ebbs and flows of your life, your self. Writing these stories reminds us of the continual cocreation of the self and social science.

Willing is doing something you know already—there is no new imaginative understanding in it. And presently your soul gets frightfully sterile and dry because you are so quick, snappy, and efficient about doing one thing after another that you have no time for your own ideas to come in and develop and gently shine.

—*Brenda Ueland, If You Want to Write, 1938/1987*

REFERENCES

Agger, B. (1989). *Reading science: A literary, political and sociological analysis.* Dix Hills, NY: General Hall.

————. (1990). *The decline of discourse: Reading, writing and resistance in postmodern capitalism.* Bristol, PA: Falser.

Angrosino, M. V. (1998). *Opportunity House: Ethnographic stories of mental retardation.* Walnut Creek, CA: AltaMira.

Ba, M. (1987). *So long a letter.* (M. Bode-Thomas, trans.) Portsmouth, NH: Heinemann.

Baff, S. J. (1997). Realism and naturalism and dead dudes: Talking about literature in 11th grade English. *Qualitative Inquiry*, 3, 468–90.

Balzac, H. de (1965). Preface to *The human comedy*, from *At the Sign of the cat and racket* (C. Bell, trans., 1897). In R. Ellman & C. Feidelson, Jr. (eds.), *The modern tradition: Backgrounds of modern literature* (pp. 246–54). New York: Oxford University Press. (Original work published 1842).

Banks, A., & Banks, S. P. (eds.) (1988). *Fiction and social research: By ice or fire.* Walnut Creek, CA: AltaMira.

Barley, N. (1986). *Ceremony: An anthropologist's misadventures in the African bush.* New York: Henry Holt.

———. (1988). *Not a pleasant sport.* New York: Henry Holt.

Becker, H. S. (1986). *Writing for social scientists: How to finish your thesis, book, or article.* Chicago: University of Chicago Press.

Behar, R. (1993). *Translated woman: Crossing the border with Esperanza's story.* Boston: Beacon.

———. (1996). *The vulnerable observer: Anthropology that breaks your heart.* Boston: Beacon.

Behar, R., & Gordon, D. A. (eds.) (1995). *Women writing culture.* Berkeley: University of California Press.

Bochner, A. (1997). It's about time: Narrative and the divided self. *Qualitative Inquiry*, 3, 418–38.

Brady, I. (ed.) (1991). *Anthropological poetics.* Savage, MD: Rowman & Littlefield.

Brodkey, L. (1987). *Academic writing as social practice.* Philadelphia: Temple University Press.

Brown, K. M. (1991). *Mama Lola: A Vodou priestess in Brooklyn.* Berkeley: University of California Press.

Brown, R. H. (1977). *A poetic for sociology.* Cambridge: Cambridge University Press.

Bruner, E. M. (1996). My life in an ashram. *Qualitative Inquiry*, 2, 300–319.

Butler, S., & Rosenblum, B. (1991). *Cancer in two voices.* San Francisco: Spinster.

Cherry, K. (1995). The best years of their lives: A portrait of a residential home for people with AIDS. *Symbolic Interaction*, 18, 463–86.

Church, K. (1995). *Forbidden narratives: Critical autobiography as social science.* Newark, NJ: Gordon & Breach.

———. (1999). *Fabrications: Stitching ourselves together* [Online]. Ottawa: Canadian Museum of Civilization. Available Internet: http://www/grannyg.bc.ca/ Fabrications/index.html

Clifford, J. (1986). Introduction: Partial truths. In J. Clifford & G. E. Marcus (eds.), *Writing culture: The poetics and politics of ethnography* (pp. 1–26). Berkeley: University of California Press.

Clifford, J., & Marcus, G. E. (eds.) (1986). *Writing culture: The poetics and politics of ethnography.* Berkeley: University of California Press.

Clough, P. T. (1992). *The end(s) of ethnography: From realism to social criticism.* Newbury Park, CA: Sage.

Crawford, M. A. (1951). *Introduction to* Old Goriot. New York: Penguin.

Daly, K., & Dienhart, A. (1998). Navigation the family domain: Qualitative field dilemmas. In S. Grills (ed.), *Doing ethnographic research: Fieldwork settings* (pp. 97–120). Thousands Oaks, CA: Sage.

Davies, B. (1989). *Frogs and snails and feminist tales: Preschool children.* St. Leonards, Australia: Allen & Unwin.

———. (1994). *Poststructuralist theory and classroom practice.* Geelong, Victoria, Australia: Deakin University Press.

Davies, B., Dormer, S., Honan, E., McAllister, N., O'Reilly, R., Rocco, S., & Walker, A. (1997). Ruptures in the skin of silence: A collective biography. *Hecate: A Woman's Interdisciplinary Journal,* 23(1), 62–79.

Denzin, N. K. (1978). *The research act: A theoretical introduction to sociological methods.* (2nd ed.) New York: McGraw-Hill.

———. (1986). A postmodern social theory. *Sociological Theory,* 4, 194–204.

———. (1991). *Images of postmodern society.* Newbury Park, CA: Sage.

———. (1994). Evaluating qualitative research in the poststructural moment: The lessons James Joyce teaches us. *International Journal of Qualitative Studies in Education,* 7, 295–308.

———. (1995). *The cinematic society: The voyeur's gaze.* Thousand Oaks, CA: Sage.

———. (1997). *Interpretive ethnography: Ethnographic practices for the 21st century*. Thousand Oaks, CA: Sage.

Derrida, J. (1982). *Margins of philosophy* (A. Bass, trans.). Chicago: University of Chicago Press.

DeShazer, M. K. (1986). *Inspiring women: Reimagining the muse*. New York: Pergamon.

Diamond, S. (1982). *Totems*. Barrytown, NY: Open Book/Station Hill.

Diversi, M. (1998a). Glimpses of street life: Representing lived experience through short stories. *Qualitative Inquiry*, 4, 131–47.

———. (1998b). Late for school. *Waikato Journal of Education*, 4, 78–86.

Donmoyer, R., & Yennie-Donmoyer, J. (1995). Data as drama: Reflections on the use of readers theater as a mode of qualitative data display. *Qualitative Inquiry*, 1, 402–28.

Dorst, J. D. (1989). *The written suburb: An American site, an ethnographic dilemma*. Philadelphia: University of Pennsylvania Press.

Edmondson, R. (1984). *Rhetoric in sociology*. London: Macmillan.

Eisner, E. (1996). Should a novel count as a dissertation in education? *Research in the Teaching of English*, 30, 403–27.

Ellis, C. (1991). Sociological introspection and emotional experience. *Symbolic Interaction*, 14, 23–50.

———. (1993). Telling the story of sudden death. *Sociological Quarterly*, 34, 711–30.

———. (1995a) *Final negotiations: A story of love, loss, and chronic illness*. Philadelphia: Temple University Press.

———. (1995b) The other side of the fence: Seeing black and white in a small southern town. *Qualitative Inquiry*, 1, 147–68.

———. (1998). "I hate my voice": Coming to terms with minor bodily stigmas. *Sociological Quarterly*, 39, 517–37.

Ellis, C., & Bochner, A. P. (1992). Telling and performing personal stories: The constraints of choice in abortion. In C. Ellis & M. G. Flaherty (eds.), *Investigating subjectivity: Research on lived experience* (pp. 79–101). Newbury Park, CA: Sage.

———. (eds.) (1996a). *Composing ethnography: Alternative forms of qualitative writing*. Walnut Creek, CA: AltaMira.

————. (1996b). Introduction: Talking over ethnography. In C. Ellis & A. P. Bochner (eds.), *Composing ethnography: Alternative forms of qualitative writing* (pp. 13–48). Walnut Creek, CA: AltaMira.

Ellis, C., & Flaherty, M. G. (eds.) (1992). *Investigating subjectivity: Research on lived experience.* Newbury Park, CA: Sage.

Erikson, K. T. (1976). *Everything in its path: Destruction of the community in the Buffalo Creek flood.* New York: Simon & Schuster.

Fine, M. (1992). *Disruptive voices: The possibility of feminist research.* Ann Arbor: University of Michigan Press.

Fishkin, S. F. (1985). *From fact to fiction: Journalism and imaginative writing in America.* Baltimore: Johns Hopkins University Press.

Flick, U. (1998). *An introduction to qualitative research: Theory, method and applications.* London: Sage.

Fox, M. F. (ed.) (1985). *Scholarly writing and publishing: Issues, problems, and solutions.* Boulder, CO: Westview.

Frank, A. (1995). *The wounded storyteller: Body, illness, and ethics.* Chicago: University of Chicago Press.

Frohock, F. (1992). *Healing powers.* Chicago: University of Chicago Press.

Geertz, C. (1988). *Works and lives: The anthropologist as author.* Stanford, CA: Stanford University Press.

Gerla, J. P. (1995). An uncommon friendship: Ethnographic fiction around finance equity in Texas. *Qualitative Inquiry, 1,* 168–88.

Glaser, B. G., & Strauss, A. L. (1967). *The discovery of grounded theory: Strategies for qualitative research.* Chicago: Aldine.

Glesne, C. E. (1997). That rare feeling: Re-presenting research through poetic transcription. *Qualitative Inquiry, 3,* 202–21.

Goetting, A., & Fenstermaker, S. (1995). *Individual voices, collective visions: Fifty years of women in sociology.* Philadelphia: Temple University Press.

Goldberg, N. (1986). *Writing down the bones: Freeing the writer within.* Boston: Shambala.

————. (1990). *Wild mind: Living the writer's life.* New York: Bantam.

Harper, D. (1987). *Working knowledge: Skill and community in a small shop.* Chicago: University of Chicago Press.

Hills, R. (1987). *Writing in general and the short story in particular.* Boston: Houghton Mifflin.

hooks, b. (1990). *Yearning: Race, gender, and cultural politics.* Boston: South End.

Hurston, Z. N. (1991). *Dust tracks on a road.* New York: HarperCollins. (Original work published 1942).

Hutcheon, L. (1988). *A poetics for post-modernism: History, theory, fiction.* New York: Routledge.

Jacobs, J. (1984). *The mall: An attempted escape from everyday life.* Prospect Heights, IL: Waveland.

Jago, B. J. (1996). Postcards, ghosts, and fathers: Revising family stories. *Qualitative Inquiry, 2,* 495–516.

Jameson, F. (1981). *The political unconscious: Narrative as a socially symbolic act.* Ithaca, NY: Cornell University Press.

Jipson, J., & Paley, N. (eds.) (1997). *Daredevil research: Re-creating analytic practice.* New York: Peter Lang.

Johnston, M. (with Educators for Collaborative Change). (1997). *Contradictions in collaboration: New thinking on school/university partnerships.* New York: Teachers College Press.

Jones, S. H. (1998). *Kaleidoscope notes: Writing women's music and organizational culture.* Walnut Creek, CA: AltaMira.

Karp, D. (1996). *Speaking of sadness.* New York: Oxford University Press.

Kaufman, S. (1986). *The ageless self: Sources of meaning in later life.* Madison: University of Wisconsin Press.

Kondo, D. K. (1990). *Crafting selves: Power, gender, and discourses of identity in a Japanese workplace.* Chicago: University of Chicago Press.

Krieger, S. (1983). *The mirror dance: Identity in a women's community.* Philadelphia: Temple University Press.

———. (1991). *Social science and the self: Personal essays on an art form.* New Brunswick, NJ: Rutgers University Press.

────. (1996). *The family silver: Essays on relationships among women.* Berkeley: University of California Press.

Lakoff, G., & Johnson, M. (1980). *Metaphors we live by.* Chicago: University of Chicago Press.

Lather, P. (1991). *Getting smart: Feminist research and pedagogy with/in the postmodern.* New York: Routledge.

Lather, P., & Smithies, C. (1997). *Troubling the angels: Women living with HIV/AIDS.* Boulder, CO: Westview.

Lawrence-Lightfoot, S. (1994). *I've known rivers: Lives of loss and liberation.* Boston: Addison-Wesley.

Lawton, J. E. (1997). *Reconceptualizing a horizontal career line: A study of seven experienced urban English teachers approaching career end.* Unpublished doctoral dissertation, Ohio State University.

Lee, V. (1996). *Granny midwives and black women writers.* New York: Routledge.

Lehman, D. (1991). *Signs of the times: Deconstruction and the fall of Paul de Man.* New York: Poseidon.

Levine, D. N. (1985). *The flight from ambiguity: Essays in social and cultural theory.* Chicago: University of Chicago Press.

Liebow, E. (1967). *Tally's corner: A study of Negro street corner men.* Boston: Little, Brown.

Linden, R. R. (1992). *Making stories, making selves: Feminist reflections on the Holocaust.* Columbus: Ohio State University Press.

Lockridge, E. (1987). F. Scott Fitzgerald's Trompe l'oeil and The Great Gatsby's buried plot. *Journal of Narrative Technique, 17,* 163–83.

Lyotard, J.-F. (1984). *The postmodern condition: A report on knowledge.* (G. Bennington & B. Massumi, trans.) Minneapolis: University of Minnesota Press.

Margolis, E., & Romero, M. (1998). The department is very male, very white, very old, and very conservative: The functioning of the hidden curriculum in graduate sociology departments. *Harvard Educational Review, 68,* 1–32.

McCall, M. M., & Becker, H. S. (1990). Performance science. *Social Problems, 37,* 116–32.

McCall, M. M., Gammel, L., & Taylor, S. (1994). *The one about the farmer's daughter: Stereotypes and self portraits.* Minneapolis: Country Characters.

McMahon, M. (1996). Significant absences. *Qualitative Inquiry*, 2, 320–36.

Meloy, J. M. (1993). Problems of writing and representation in qualitative inquiry. *International Journal of Qualitative Studies in Education*, 6, 315–30.

Mienczakowski, J. (1996). An ethnographic act: The construction of consensual theater. In C. Ellis & A. P. Bochner (eds.), *Composing ethnography: Alternative forms of qualitative writing* (pp. 244–66). Walnut Creek, CA: AltaMira.

Mishler, E. G. (1989). *Research interviewing: Context and narrative.* Cambridge: Harvard University Press.

Nelson, J. S., Megill, A., & McCloskey, D. N. (eds.) (1987). *The rhetoric of the human sciences: Language and argument in scholarship and human affairs.* Madison: University of Wisconsin Press.

Nicholson, L. J. (ed.) (1990). *Feminism/postmodernism.* New York: Routledge.

Norum, K. E. (in press). School patterns: A sextet. *International Journal of Qualitative Studies in Education.*

Paget, M. (1990). Performing the text. *Journal of Contemporary Ethnography*, 19, 136–55.

Pandolfo, S. (1997). *Impasse of the angels: Scenes from a Moroccan space of memory.* Chicago: University of Chicago Press.

Patai, D. (1988). Constructing a self: A Brazilian life story. *Feminist Studies*, 14, 142–63.

Pfohl, S. J. (1992). *Death at the Parasite Café: Social science (fictions) and the postmodern.* New York: St. Martin's.

Prattis, I. (ed.) (1985). *Reflections: The anthropological muse.* Washington, DC: American Anthropological Association.

Richardson, L. (1985). *The new other woman: Contemporary single women in affairs with married men.* New York: Free Press.

———. (1990). *Writing strategies: Reaching diverse audiences.* Thousand Oaks, CA: Sage.

———. (1992a). The consequences of poetic representation: Writing the other, rewriting the self. In C. Ellis & M. G. Flaherty (eds.), *Investigating subjectivity: Research on lived experience.* Newbury Park, CA: Sage.

———. (1992b). Resisting resistance narratives: A representation for communication. In N. K. Denzin (ed.), *Studies in symbolic interaction: A research annual* (vol. 13, pp. 77–83) Greenwich, CT: JAI.

———. (1993). The case of the skipped line: Poetics, dramatics and transgressive validity. *Sociological Quarterly*, 34, 695–710.

———. (1995). Writing-stories: Co-authoring "The sea monster," a writing-story. *Qualitative Inquiry*, 1, 189–203.

———. (1996a). Educational birds. *Journal of Contemporary Ethnography*, 25, 6–15.

———. (1996b). A sociology of responsibility. *Qualitative Research*, 19, 519–24.

———. (1997). *Fields of play: Constructing an academic life.* New Brunswick, NJ: Rutgers University Press.

———. (1998). The politics of location: Where am I now? *Qualitative Inquiry*, 4, 41–48.

———. (1999a). Dead again in Berkeley. *Qualitative Inquiry*, 5, 141–44.

———. (1999b) Paradigms lost [Distinguished Lecture]. *Symbolic Interaction*, 22, 79–91.

Richardson, L., & Lockridge, E. (1998). Fiction and ethnography: A conversation. *Qualitative Inquiry*, 4, 328–36.

Rinehart, R. (1998). Sk8ing. *Waikato Journal of Education*, 4, 87–100.

Ronai, C. R. (1995). Multiple reflections of child sexual abuse: An argument for a layered account. *Journal of Contemporary Ethnography*, 23, 395–426.

Rose, D. (1989). *Patterns of American culture: Ethnography and estrangement.* Philadelphia: University of Pennsylvania Press.

Rose, E. (1992). *The werald.* Boulder, CO: Waiting Room.

———. (1993). *The worulde.* Boulder, CO: Waiting Room.

Rubin, L. B. (1976). *Worlds of pain: Life in the working-class family.* New York: Basic Books.

Schneider, J. (1991). Troubles with textual authority in sociology. *Symbolic Interaction*, 14, 295–320.

Schwalbe, M. (1995). The responsibilities of sociological poets. *Qualitative Sociology,* 18, 393–412.

Shapiro, M. (1985–1986). Metaphor in the philosophy of the social sciences. *Cultural Critique,* 2, 191–214.

Shelton, A. (1995). The man at the end of the machine. *Symbolic Interaction,* 18, 505–18.

Shostak, A. (ed.) (1996). *Private sociology: Unsparing reflections, uncommon gains.* Dix Hills, NY: General Hall.

Simons, H. W. (1990). *Rhetoric in the human sciences.* London: Sage.

Slobin, K. (1995). Fieldwork and subjectivity: On the ritualization of seeing a burned child. *Symbolic Interaction,* 18, 487–504.

Sparkes, A. C. (1997). Ethnographic fiction and representing the absent other. *Sport, Education, and Society,* 2, 25–40.

Stack, C. B. (1974). *All our kin: Strategies for survival in a black community.* New York: Harper & Row.

Statham, A., Richardson, L., & Cook, J. A. (1991). *Gender and university teaching: A negotiated difference.* Albany: State University of New York Press.

Steedman, K. (1986). *Landscape for a good woman: A story of two lives.* New Brunswick, NJ: Rutgers University Press.

Stewart, K. (1986). *Drinkers, drummers and decent folk: Ethnographic narratives of Village Trinidad.* Albany: State University of New York Press.

Stoller, P. (1989). *The taste of ethnographic things: The senses in anthropology.* Philadelphia: University of Pennsylvania Press.

St. Pierre, E. A. (1997a). Circling the text: Nomadic writing practices. *Qualitative Inquiry,* 3, 403–17.

――――. (1997b). Nomadic inquiry in the smooth spaces of the field: A preface. *International Journal of Qualitative Studies in Education,* 10, 175–89.

Tedlock, D. (1983). *The spoken word and the work of interpretation.* Philadelphia: University of Pennsylvania Press.

Thorne, B. (1993). *Gender play.* New Brunswick, NJ: Rutgers University Press.

Trinh T. M. (1989). *Woman, native, other: Writing postcoloniality and feminism.* Bloomington: Indiana University Press.

Turner, V., & Bruner, E. M. (eds.) (1986). *The anthropology of experience.* Urbana: University of Illinois Press.

Ueland, B. (1987). *If you want to write: A book about art, independence and spirit.* Saint Paul, MN: Graywolf. (Original work published 1938).

Ulmer, G. (1989). *Teletheory: Grammatology in the age of video.* New York: Routledge.

Van Maanen, J. (1988). *Tales of the field: On writing ethnography.* Chicago: University of Chicago Press.

————. (ed.) (1995). *Representation in ethnography.* Thousand Oaks, CA: Sage.

Visweswaran, K. (1994). *Fictions of feminist ethnography.* Minneapolis: University of Minnesota Press.

Walkerdine, V. (1990). *Schoolgirl fictions.* London: Verso.

Weedon, C. (1987). *Feminist practice and poststructuralist theory.* New York: Basil Blackwell.

Weinstein, D. (1993). *Writing for your life: A guide and companion to the inner worlds.* New York: HarperCollins.

Whyte, W. F. (1943). *Street corner society: The social structure of an Italian slum.* Chicago: University of Chicago Press.

————. (1992). In defense of *Street corner society. Journal of Contemporary Ethnography,* 21, 52–68.

Williams, P. J. (1991). *The alchemy of race and rights: Diary of a law professor.* Cambridge: Harvard University Press.

Wilson, C. (1965). *Crazy February: Death and life in the Mayan highlands of Mexico.* Berkeley: University of California Press.

Wolcott, H. F. (1990). *Writing up qualitative research.* Newbury Park, CA: Sage.

Wolf, M. A. (1992). *A thrice-told tale: Feminism, postmodernism, and ethnographic responsibility.* Stanford, CA: Stanford University Press.

Yu, P.-L. (1997). *Hungry lightning: Notes of woman anthropologist in Venezuela.* Albuquerque: University of New Mexico Press.

Zola, E. (1965). The novel as social science. In R. Ellman & C. Feidelson, Jr. (eds.), *The modern tradition: Backgrounds of modern literature* (pp. 270–89). New York: Oxford University Press. (Original work published 1880).

Zola, I. K. (1982). *Missing pieces: A chronicle of living with a disability.* Philadelphia: Temple University Press.

18

Performing as a Moral Act:[1] Ethical Dimensions of the Ethnography of Performance

Dwight Conquergood

For the story of my life is always embedded in the story of those communities from which I derive my identity. . . .The self has to find its moral identity in and through its membership in communities such as those of the family, the neighborhood, the city, and tribe. . . . Without those moral particularities to begin from there would never be anywhere to begin; but it is in moving forward from such particularity that the search for the good, for the universal, consists.

—Alasdair MacIntyre[2]

During the crucial days of 1954, when the Senate was pushing for termination of all Indian rights, not one single scholar, anthropologist, sociologist, historian, or economist came forward to support the tribes against the detrimental policy.

—Vine Deloria, Jr.[3]

Ethnographers study the diversity and unity of cultural performance as a universal human resource for deepening and clarifying the meaningfulness of

---

Reprinted from *Literature in Performance* 5 (1985): 1–13. Used by permission of the National Communication Association.

life. They help us see performance with all its moral entailments, not as a flight from lived responsibilities. Henry Glassie represents the contemporary ethnography's interest in the interanimation between expressive art and daily life, texts, and contexts:

> I begin study with sturdy, fecund totalities created by the people themselves, whole statements, whole songs or houses or events, away from which life expands, toward which life orients in seeking maturity. I begin with texts, then weave contexts around them to make them meaningful, to make life comprehensible.[4]

Joining other humanists who celebrate the necessary and indissoluble link between art and life, ethnographers present performance as vulnerable and open to dialogue with the world.

The repercussions for "thinking," which Clifford Geertz attributes to Dewey, can be transposed to a socially committed and humanistic understanding of "performing":

> Since Dewey, it has been much more difficult to regard thinking as an abstention from action, theorizing as an alternative to commitment, and the intellectual life as a kind of secular monasticism, excused from accountability by its sensitivity to the Good.[5]

This view cuts off the safe retreat into aestheticism, art for art's sake, and brings performance "out into the public world where ethical judgment can get at it."[6]

Moral and ethical questions get stirred to the surface because ethnographers of performance explode the notion of aesthetic distance.[7] In their fieldwork efforts to grasp the native's point of view, to understand the human complexities displayed in even the most humble folk performance, ethnographers try to surrender themselves to the centripetal pulls of culture, to get close to the face of humanity where life is not always pretty. Sir Edward Evans-Pritchard wrote that fieldwork "requires a certain kind of character and temperament. . . . To succeed in it a man must be able to abandon himself to native life without reserve."[8] Instead of worrying about maintaining aesthetic distance, ethnographers try to bring "the enormously distant enormously close without becoming any less far away."[9]

Moreover, ethnographers work with expressivity, which is inextricable from its human creators. They must work with real people, humankind alive, instead of printed texts. Opening and interpreting lives is very different from opening and closing books. Perhaps that is why ethnographers worry more about acquiring experiential insight than maintaining aesthetic distance. Indeed, they are calling for empathic performance as a way of intensifying the participative nature of fieldwork, and as a corrective to foreshorten the textual distance that results from writing monographs about the people with whom one lives and studies.[10] When one keeps intellectual, aesthetic, or any other kind of distance from the other, ethnographers worry that other people will be held at an ethical and moral remove as well.

Whatever else one may say about ethnographic fieldwork, Geertz reminds us, "one can hardly claim that it is focused on trivial issues or abstracted from human concerns."[11] This kind of research "involves direct, intimate and more or less disturbing encounters with the immediate details of contemporary life."[12] When ethnographers of performance complement their participant observation fieldwork by actually performing for different audiences the verbal art they have studied in situ, they expose themselves to double jeopardy. They become keenly aware that performance does not proceed in ideological innocence and axiological purity.

Most researchers who have extended ethnographic fieldwork into public performance will experience resistance and hostility from audiences from time to time.[13] This disquieting antagonism, however, more than the audience approval, signals most clearly that ethnographic performance is a form of conduct deeply enmeshed in moral matters. I believe that all performance has ethical dimensions, but have found that moral issues of performance and are more transparent when the performer attempts to engage ethnic and intercultural texts, particularly those texts outside the canon and derived from fieldwork research.

For three and a half years I have conducted ethnographic fieldwork among Lao and Hmong refugees in Chicago. The performance of their oral narratives is an integral part of my research project and a natural extension of the role of the ethnographer as participant to that of advocate. When working with minority peoples and disenfranchised subcultures, such as refugees, one is frequently propelled into the role of advocate. The ethnographer, an uninvited stranger who depends upon the patient courtesies and openhanded hospitality of the community, is compelled by the laws of reciprocity and human decency to intervene, if he can, in a crisis. Further, the stories my Laotian friends tell make claims on me. For example, what do you do when the coroner orders an autopsy on a Hmong friend and the family comes to you numb with horror because according to Hmong belief if you cut the skin of a dead person the soul is lost forever, there can be no hope of reincarnation? Moreover, that disembodied soul consigned to perpetual limbo will no doubt come back to haunt and terrorize the family.

I have performed the stories of the refugees for dozens of audiences. In addition to academic audiences, where the performance usually complements a theoretical argument I want to make about the epistemological potential of performance as a way of deeply sensing the other, I have performed them before many and varied nonacademic audiences. I have tried to bring the stories of the Lao and Hmong before social service agencies, high schools where there have been outbreaks of violence against refugee students, businessmen, lawyers, welfare case workers, public school teachers and administrators, religious groups, wealthy women's clubs, and so forth. Often I have been gratified to see the way the performance of a story can pull an audience into a sense of the other in a rhetorically compelling way. Many times, however, the nonacademic audiences are deeply disturbed by these performances. I have been attacked, not just in the sessions of discussion and response immediately following these performances. One time the anger and hostility was so heated that I was invited back to face the same group two weeks later for a three-hour session that began with attack and abuse but moved gradually, and painfully, to heightened self-reflexivity (for me, as well as them). The last hour we spent talking about ourselves instead of the refugees.

Here is a partial list of the offenses for which I am most frequently condemned. Members of certain religious groups indict me for collaborating in the "work of the devil." My refugee friends are not Christian, and their stories enunciate a cosmology radically different from Judeo-Christian traditions. Fundamentalist Christians perceptively point out that by the very act of collecting, preserving, and performing these stories, I am legitimizing them, offering them as worthy of contemplation for Christians, and encouraging the Lao and Hmong to hold fast to their "heathenism." Welfare workers despise me for retarding the refugees' assimilation into mainstream America and thereby making the caseworker's job more difficult. From their point of view, these people must be Americanized as quickly as possible. They simply must drop their old ways of thinking, "superstitions," and become American. Developing resettlement programs that involve careful adjustments and blends between the old and new would require too much time or energy or money. Some social workers and administrators clearly emphasize that videotaping ancient rituals, recording and performing oral history are not morally neutral activities. Some public school educators interrogate me for performing in a respectful tone a Lao legend that explains the lunar eclipse as a frog in the sky who swallows the moon. After one performance I was asked, "How do the Lao react when you tell them they are wrong?" When I replied that I do not "correct" my Lao friends about their understanding of the lunar eclipse, the audience was aghast. Some stormed out, but some stayed to chastise me. I've been faulted for not correcting the grammar and pronunciation of the narrative texts I've collected and thus making the people "sound stupid and backward." Weeks after a performance I've received letters from people telling me how angry they were, that they "couldn't sleep" when thinking about the performance, and that it had given them "bad dreams."

In another vein, from audiences who are moved by the performance, I am sometimes challenged in an accusing tone, "How can you go back to being a professor at a rich university? Why don't you spend full time trying to help these people learn English, get jobs, find lost relatives?" In comparison to nonacademic audiences, the criticism from academic audiences pales. Nevertheless, remarks get back to me about how I'm "moving the field off-center." The ostensibly neutral question, "What does this have to do with oral interpretation of literature?" thinly veils deep misgivings. One specialist in eighteenth-century literature was more direct, and I respect him for that. At a Danforth conference, this senior gentleman rose to his feet after my presentation and in authoritative and measured tone declared; "You have confused art and nature, and that is an abomination!"

The one question I almost never get, however, is the "white guilt" accusation, "What right do you, a middle-class white man, have to perform these narratives?" Usually whoever introduces me give some background information about my participant observation research. One time some audience members came in late, after the introduction, and sure enough, one of them was the first to raise his hand after the performance and accuse me of white man's presumptuousness. However, other audience members came to my defense before

I had a chance to respond. They explained to him that I had lived with the people for more than three years, that I was not a weekend commuter from a comfortable suburban house. This information seemed to subdue him.

Even though my ego is probably as vulnerable as the next person's, I take courage in knowing that negative response, more than approving applause, testifies to the moral implications of this kind of work. I can be grateful to my detractors for forcing into my awareness the complex ethical tensions, tacit political commitments, and moral ambiguities inextricably caught up in the act of performing ethnographic materials. Indeed, I began doing this kind of work focused on performance as a way of knowing and deeply sensing the other. Hostile audiences have helped me see performance as the enactment of a moral stance. Now I have become deeply interested in the ethical dimensions of performing the expressive art that springs from other lives, other sensibilities, other cultures.

I agree with Wallace Bacon that the validity of an intercultural performance is "an ethical concern no less than a performance problem."[14] Good will and an open heart are not enough when one "seeks to express cultural experiences which are clearly separate from his or her lived world."[15] I would like to sketch four ethical pitfalls, performative stances towards the other that are morally problematic. I name these performative stances "The Custodian's Rip-Off," "The Enthusiast's Infatuation," "The Curator's Exhibitionism," and "The Skeptic's Cop-Out." These four problem areas can be graphically represented as the extreme corners of a moral map articulated by intersecting axes of ethnographic tensions. The vertical axis is the tensile counterpull between Identify and Difference, the horizontal axis between Detachment and Commitment (see figure 18.1). The extreme points of both sets of continual represent "dangerous shores" to be navigated, binary oppositions to be transcended. The center of the map represents the moral center that transcends and reconciles the spin-off extremes. I call this dynamic center, which holds in tensile equipoise the four contrarieties, "Dialogical Performance."[16] After mapping the five performative stances in order to see their alignments, I will discuss each one in more detail.

THE CUSTODIAN'S RIP-OFF

The sin of this performative stance is Selfishness. A strong attraction toward the other coupled with extreme detachment results in acquisitiveness instead of genuine inquiry, plunder more than performance. Bacon provided a strik-

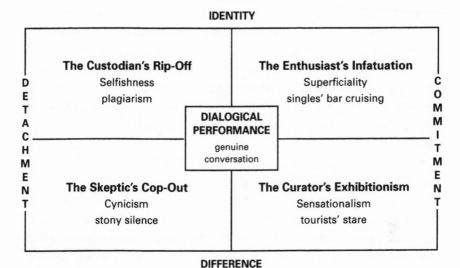

IDENTITY

The Custodian's Rip-Off
Selfishness
plagiarism

The Enthusiast's Infatuation
Superficiality
singles' bar cruising

DIALOGICAL
PERFORMANCE
genuine
conversation

The Skeptic's Cop-Out
Cynicism
stony silence

The Curator's Exhibitionism
Sensationalism
tourists' stare

DETACHMENT

COMMITMENT

DIFFERENCE

FIGURE 18.1
Moral Mapping of Performative Stances Towards the Other*
*This graphic representation is derived from Mary Douglas' method of grid/group analysis. See *Cultural Bias* (1978) and *In the Active Voice* (1982).

ing example of this performative stance when he cited the case of the Prescott Smoki cultural preservation group who continued to perform the Hopi Snake Dance over the vigorous objections of Hopi elders. This group appropriated cherished traditions, reframed them in a way that was sacrilegious to the Hopi, and added insult to injury by selling trinkets for $7.50, all in the name of preserving "dying cultures."[17] The immorality of such performances is un-ambiguous and can be compared to theft and rape.

Potential performers of ethnographic materials should not enter the field with the overriding motive of "finding some good performance material." An analogy from my fieldwork situation would be my performance of some of the stunningly theatrical shaman chants of Hmong healers replete with black veil over face and sacred costume. Not even a Hmong man or woman may perform these sacred traditions at will. You must be called to shamanic per-formance, which typically is signaled by a life-threatening illness, during which you have tremors, "shake" (*oy nang*, the Hmong word for "shaman," is the same word for "shake"). When the shaman shakes and chants, he or she is talking and pleading with the spirits that control the world. These ecstatic per-formances are extraordinarily delicate and dangerous affairs. A Hmong Shaman risks his or her life each time the soul leaves the body and ascends the tree of life on the ecstatic journey onto the spirit kingdom. I have worked with the Hmong for about three years before I was privileged to witness one of these ecstatic trance performances. Now I am not only permitted, but encouraged to videotape them. I have even participated in one of these rituals of affliction as the victim. An elderly shaman "shook"—went into ecstatic performance—for my blind eye. However, I would never try to simulate one of these powerful performances because not only would that be a desecration, it would be perceived by the Hmong as having catastrophic consequences.

THE ENTHUSIAST'S INFATUATION

Too facile identification with the other coupled with enthusiastic commitment produces naïve and glib performances marked by superficiality. This is the quadrant of the quick-fix, pick-up artist, where performance runs aground in the shallows. Eager performers get sucked into the quicksand belief, "Aren't all people really just alike?" Although not as transparently immoral as "The Custodian's Rip-Off," this performative stance is unethical because it trivializes the other. The distinctiveness of the other is glossed over by a glaze of generalities.

Tzvetan Todorov unmasks the moral consequences of too easy and eager an identification with the other:

> Can we really love someone if we know little or nothing of his identity, if we see, in place of that identity, a projection of ourselves or ideals? We know that such a thing is quite possible, even frequent, in personal relations; but what happens in cultural confrontations? Doesn't one culture risk trying to transform the other in its own name, and therefore risk subjugating it as well? How much is such love worth?[18]

"The Enthusiast's Infatuation," which is also the quadrant where "fools rush in where angels fear to tread," is neither innocent nor benign.

Fredric Jameson, to whom we are indebted for naming the Identity-Difference interpretive dilemma,[19] complements Todorov by showing how too easy affirming of identity not only banalizes the other, but seals off the self from any moral engagement:

> if we choose to affirm the identify of the alien object with ourselves—if, in other words, we decide that Chaucer, say . . . or the narratives of nineteenth-century Russian gentry, are more or less directly or intuitively accessible to us . . . then we

have presupposed in advance what was to have been demonstrated, and our apparent comprehension of these alien texts must be haunted by the nagging suspicion that we have all the while remained locked in our own present with its television sets and superhighways . . . and that we have never really left home at all, that our feeling of *Verstehen* is little better than mere psychological projection, that we have somehow failed to touch the strangeness and the resistance of a reality genuinely different from our own.[20]

Secure in our protective solipsism, those of us in this performative stance will never permit the other "to come before us as a radically different life form that rises up to call our own form of life into question and to pass judgment on us, and through us, on the social formation in which we live."[21] Superficiality suffocates self as well as other.

THE CURATOR'S EXHIBITIONISM

Whereas the enthusiasts assumed too easy an Identity with the other, the curator is committed to the Difference of the other. This is the "Wild Kingdom" approach to performance that grows out of fascination with the exotic, primitive, culturally remote. The performer wants to astonish rather than understand. This quadrant is suffused with sentimentality and romantic notions about the "Noble Savage." Performances from this corner of the map resemble curio postcards, souvenirs, trophies brought back from the tour for display cases. Instead of bringing us into genuine contact (and risk) with the lives of strangers, performances in this mode bring back museum exhibits, mute and staring.

Jameson explains that when one affirms "from the outset, the radical Difference of the alien object from ourselves, then at once the doors of comprehension begin to swing closed."[22] The manifest sin of this quadrant is Sensationalism, and it is an immoral stance because it dehumanizes the other. Todorov makes strikingly clear the moral consequences of exoticizing the other in his brilliant case study of the most dramatic encounter with the other in our history, the discovery and conquest of America.[23] He clarifies how the snap-shot perspectives of "Noble Savage" and "dirty dog" can come from the same view-finder:

How can Columbus be associated with these two apparently contradictory myths, one whereby the other is a "noble savage" (when perceived at a distance) and one whereby he is a "dirty dog," a potential slave? It is because both rests on a common basis, which is the failure to recognize the Indians, and the refusal to admit them as a subject having the same rights as oneself, but different. Columbus has discovered America but not the Americans.[24]

Too great a distance—aesthetic, romantic, political—denies to the other membership in the same moral community as ourselves.

The fourth corner of the map is the prison-house of Detachment and Difference in which, according to Jameson, "we find ourselves separated by the whole density of our own culture from objects or cultures thus initially defined as other from ourselves and thus as irremediably inaccessible."[25] Instead of a performative stance, it is an easy bail-out into the no man's land of paralyzing skepticism. This corner of the map is the refuge of cowards and cynics. Instead of facing up to and struggling with the ethical tensions and moral ambiguities of performing culturally sensitive materials, the skeptic, with chilling aloofness, flatly declares, "I am neither black nor female: I will not perform from *The Color Purple*."

When this strange coupling of naïve empiricism and sociobiology—only blacks can understand and perform black literature, only white males John Cheever's short stories—is deconstructed to expose the absurdity of the major premise, then the "No Trespassing" disclaimer is unmasked as cowardice or imperialism of the most arrogant kind. It is only the members of the dominant culture who can hold to this high purity argument regarding cultural intercourse. It is a fact of life of being a member of a minority or disenfranchised subculture that one must and can learn how to perform cultural scripts and play roles that do not arise out of one's own culture. As a matter of sheer survival refugees must learn how to play American ways of thinking and social conduct. "Code-switching" is a commonplace ethnographic term used to describe the complex shifts minority peoples deftly and continuously negotiate between the communication styles of dominant culture and subculture. Todorov, who refers to his own "simultaneous participation in two cultures,"[26] offers a strong rebuttal to the skeptic's position:

> Ultimately, understanding between representatives of different cultures (or between parts of my own being which derive from one culture or the other) is possible, if the will-to-understand is present: there is something beyond "points of

view," and it is characteristic of human beings that they can transcend their partiality and their local determinations.[27]

There is no null hypothesis in the moral universe. Refusal to take a moral
stand is itself a powerful statement of one's moral position. That is why I have
placed squarely on the moral map the skeptic's refusal to risk encounter to
show that nihilism is as much a moral position as its diagonal counterpart,
naïve enthusiasm. In my view, "The Skeptic's Cop-Out" is the most morally
reprehensible corner of the map because it forecloses dialogue. The enthusiast, one can always hope, may move beyond infatuation to love. Relationship
that begin superficially can sometimes deepen and grow. Many of my students
begin in the enthusiast's corner of the map. It is the work of teaching to try to
pull them toward the center. The skeptic, however, shuts down the very idea
of entering into conversation with the other before the attempt, however
problematic, begins. Bacon, who is keenly aware of the "deep and difficult and
enduring problems,"[28] rejects the skeptic's cop-out when facing up to the alternatives for action in the world:

> What, then, do we do? Do we give up performing ethnic materials? Do we say,
> with Anaya, that to the Hispanics belong Hispanic treasures?
>   Surely not, because our world has never before cried out so needfully for un-
> derstanding among us all. Never has a sense of the other seemed more crucial
> for our own humanity. The embodiment of texts of all kinds is ... one real path
> to the understanding of others.[29]

The skeptic, detached and estranged, with no sense of the other, sits alone in
an echo-chamber of his own making, with only the sound of his own scoffing
laughter ringing in his ears.

DIALOGICAL PERFORMANCE
One path to genuine understanding of others, and out of this moral morass
and ethical minefield of performative plunder, superficial silliness, curiosity-
seeking, and nihilism, is dialogical performance.[30] This performative stance
struggles to bring together different voices, world views, value systems, and beliefs so that they can have a conversation with one another. The aim of dialogical performance is to bring self and other together so that they can question,

debate, and challenge one another. It is kind of performance that resists conclusions, it is intensely committed to keeping the dialogue between performer
and text open and ongoing. Dialogical understanding does not end with empathy. There is always enough appreciation for difference so that the text can
interrogate, rather than dissolve into, the performer. That is why I have
charted this performative stance at the center of the moral map. More than a
definite position, the dialogical stance is situated in the space between competing ideologies. It brings self and other together even while it holds them
apart. It is more like a hyphen than a period.

The strength of the center is that it pulls together mutually opposed energies that become destructive only when they are vented without the counter-
balancing pull of their opposite. For example, good performative
ethnographers must continuously play the oppositions between Identity and
Difference. Their stance toward this heuristically rich paradox of fieldwork
(and performance) is both/and, yes/but, instead of either/or. They affirm
cross-cultural accessibility without glossing very real differences. Moreover,
they respect the Difference of the other enough to question and make vulnerable her own a priori assumptions. When we have true respect for the Difference of other cultures, then we grant them the potential for challenging our
own culture. Genuine dialogical engagement is at least a two-way thorough-
fare. Glassie insists that the ethnography's home culture should be as open to
interpretation, questioning, weighting of alternatives, as the host culture.

> Old societies alienated from us by chronology become but academic curios, no
> challenge at all to the status quo. The outward search for alternatives can like-
> wise die into thrills and souvenirs, but when the traveler is serious, the quest
> through space leads through confrontation into culture, into fear, and it can
> prove trying, convincing, profoundly fruitful. The reason to study people, to or-
> der experience into ethnography, is not to produce more entries for the central
> file or more trinkets for milord's cabinet of curiosities. It is to stimulate thought,
> to assure us there are things we do not know, things we must know, things ca-
> pable of unsettling the world we inhabit.[31]

In order to keep fieldwork dialogically alive, Glassie construes it as "intimate
conversation," a description that resonates both literally and metaphorically
with the praxis of ethnography:

Ethnography is interaction, collaboration. What it demands is not hypotheses, which may unnaturally close study down, obscuring the integrity of the other, but the ability to converse intimately.[32]

Todorov makes the same point about the dialogical stance towards textual criticism:

Dialogic criticism speaks not of works but *to* works, rather *with* works. It refuses to eliminate either of the two voices present. . . . The author is a "thou," not a "he," an interlocutor with whom one discusses and even debates human values.[33]

He argues that the honesty of dialogic criticism lies in two voices that can speak simultaneously and interactively. Like good conversation, the event is a cooperative enterprise between two voices, neither of which succumbs to monologue: "as in personal relations, the illusion of fusion is sweet, but it is an illusion, and its end is bitter, to recognize others as others permits loving them better."[34]

Dialogical performance is a way of having intimate conversation with other people and cultures. Instead of speaking about them, one speaks to and with them. The sensuous immediacy and empathic leap demanded by performance is an occasion for orchestrating two voices, for bringing together two sensibilities. At the same time, the conspicuous artifice of performance is a vivid reminder that each voice has its own integrity. The performer of a Laotian cosmological legend stands before an audience in all his Scots-German facticity. Dialogical performance celebrates the paradox of "how the deeply different can be deeply known without becoming any less different."[35] Bacon quoted Auden, who evocatively etched the moral lineaments of dialogical performance: "When truly brothers/men don't sing in unison/but in harmony."[36]

Dialogical performance is a way of finding the moral center as much as it is an indicator that one is ethically grounded. One does not have to delay entering the conversation until self and other have become old friends. Indeed, as the metaphor makes clear, one cannot build a friendship without beginning a conversation. Dialogical performance is the means as much as the end of honest intercultural understanding. But what are the qualities one absolutely needs before joining the conversation? Three indispensables, according to Glassie: energy, imagination, and courage.

Scholars need energy to gather enough information to create full portraits. They need imagination to enter between facts, to feel what it is like to be, to think and act as another person. They need courage to face alternatives, comparing different experiences to help their fellows locate themselves.[37]

If we bring to our work energy, imagination, and courage—qualities that can be exercised and strengthened through dialogical performance—then we can hope not to trample on "the sweet, terrible wholeness of life."[38]

Finally, you don't have to do years of fieldwork with a people before you can perform their verbal art. Fieldwork is enormously time-consuming and labor-intensive; it appeals to a certain kind of person and temperament, but certainly it is not for everyone. Ethnographers would be selfish and arrogant to set themselves up as cultural game wardens, insisting that you have to have "been there" before you understand. Geertz is quite insistent that good ethnography is not dependent on the fieldworker's being possessed of some mystical powers that enable her to "commune with natives"; good ethnography can be done "without recourse to pretensions to more-than-normal capacities for ego-effacement and fellow-feeling."[39] He argues that ethnographic understanding "is more like grasping a proverb, catching an allusion, seeing a joke—or, as I have suggested, reading a poem—than it is like achieving communion."[40]

It is the responsibility of the ethnographer of performance to make performance texts derived from fieldwork that are accessible—and that means performable—for responsible interpreters of texts who have callings other than fieldwork.[41] The ethnographic movement in performance studies will die if it does not reach out to share the human dignity of the other, the other-wise, with audiences larger than a coterie of specialists. If it turns in upon itself, then, quite appropriately, it will become an "inside joke" that only fieldworkers can "get." The ethnographic movement is dependent on the existence of traditional interpreters and teachers of literature, who continue to deepen in new generations of students sensitivity to the other of a Renaissance text, or a contemporary poem, so that when performance texts from nonliterate culture are produced and made available, it will be possible for more voices to join the human dialogue.

NOTES

1. This essay is the result of an ongoing dialogue with three voices other than my own. My transposition of Clifford Geertz' title, "Thinking as a Moral Act: Ethical

Dimensions of Anthropological Fieldwork in the New States," *Antioch Review*, 28 (Summer, 1968), 139–58, explicitly signals the deep impact that essay has had on my own fieldwork project. Wallace Bacon first introduced me to ; "the sense of the other," an idea that changed my life and is a luminous demonstration of "thinking as a moral act." For more than a decade, Mary Strine has given me lists of difficult books that ask hard questions, and insisted that I read them. Particularly the dialogical Marxism of Mikhail Bakhtin, which she introduced to the field, has challenged me, and even though not explicitly cited, I hope its presence is felt by the very nature of the questions that shaped this paper.

2. *After Virtue: A Study in Moral Theory*, 2nd ed. (Notre Dame, Ind.: University of Notre Dame Press, 1984), p. 221.

3. *Custer Died for Your Sins: An Indian Manifesto* (New York: Avon, 1969), p. 98.

4. *Passing the Time in Ballymenone: Culture and History of an Ulster Community* (Philadelphia: University of Pennsylvania Press, 1982), p. xvi.

5. "Thinking as a Moral Act," p. 140.

6. "Thinking as a Moral Act," p. 139.

7. For an incisive historical explanation of this concept, see Beverly Whitaker Long, "A 'Distanced' Art: Interpretation at Mid-Century," *Performance of Literature in Historical Perspectives*, ed. David Thompson (Lanham, Md.: University Press of America, 1983), pp. 567–88. See also the provocative discussion of "moral distance" in Mary Frances Hopkins, "From Page to Stage: The Burden of Proof," *The Southern Speech Communication Journal*, 47 (Fall 1981), 1–9.

8. Quoted in Clifford Geertz, "Slide Show: Evans-Pritchard's African Transparencies," *Raritan*, 3 (fall 1983), 72–73.

9. Clifford Geertz, *Local Knowledge: Further Essays in Interpretive Anthropology* (New York: Basic Books, 1983), p. 48.

10. Ct. Victor Turner, *From Ritual to Theatre: The Human Seriousness of Play* (New York: Performing Arts Journal Publications, 1982).

11. "Thinking as a Moral Act," p. 139.

12. "Thinking as a Moral Act," p. 141.

13. See Jean Speer and Elizabeth Fine, "What Does a Dog Have to do with Humanity?: The Politics of Humanities Public Programming," paper presented at the Eastern Communication Association Convention, Ocean City, Md., 1983.

14. "The Interpretation of Oral and Ethnic Materials: The Ethical Dimension," *Literature in Performance*, 4 (April 1984), 94–97.

15. Bacon, p. 95.

16. I have discussed "dialogical performance" in the philosophical context of the theories of Martin Buber, Mikhail Bakhtin, and Wallace Bacon in "Performance and Dialogical Understanding: In Quest of the Other," *Proceedings of the Ninth International Colloquium on Communication*, ed. Janet McHughes (Tempe: Arizona State University, 1984).

17. Bacon, p. 94–95.

18. *The Conquest of America: The Question of the Other*, trans. Richard Howard (New York: Harper and Row, 1984), p. 168. It is noteworthy that two other books have appeared recently that deal centrally with the concept of "the other": Johannes Fabian, *Time and the Other: How Anthropology Makes its Object* (New York: Columbia University Press, 1983); Michael Theunissen, *The Other: Studies in the Social Ontology of Husserl, Heidegger, Sartre, and Buber*, trans. Christopher Macann (Cambridge, Mass.: MIT Press, 1984).

19. "Marxism and historicism," *New Literary History*, 11 (Autumn 1979), 41–73.

20. Jameson, p. 45.

21. Jameson, p. 70.

22. Jameson, p. 43.

23. Todorov writes, "My main interest is less a historian's than a moralist's, the present is more important to me than the past," p. 4.

24. Jameson, p. 49.

25. Jameson, p. 43–44.

26. "A Dialogic Criticism?" *Raritan*, 4 (Summer 1984), 69.

27. "A Dialogic Criticism?" p. 70.

28. Bacon, p. 96.

29. Bacon, p. 97.

30. The recent explosion of interest in the works of Mikhail Bakhtin now being translated from the original Russian and made accessible to western readers has

given widespread currency to the idea of "dialogue" as a way of being in the world. Two of Bakhtin's works now available in *Imagination*, trans. Caryl Emerson and Michael Holquist, ed. Michael Holquist (Austin: University of Texas Press, 1981), and *Problems of Dostoevsky's Poetics*, ed. and trans. Caryl Emerson for anyone working with Bakhtin: the intellectual biography of Katerina Clark and Michael Holquist, (Minneapolis: University of Minnesota Press, 1984). I also recommend two invaluable scholarly tools, *Mikhail Bakhtin* (Cambridge: Harvard University Press, 1984), and the critical assessment of *Principle*, trans. Wlad Godzich (Minneapolis: University of Minnesota Press, 1984). Clark and Holquist point out in their biography that Bakhtin had a lifelong involvement with performance and theater ranging from the German governess who organized the young Bakhtin brothers in dramatic renderings of the *Iliad* to his dramatic performances in the Nevel Theatre groups long after his university days (p. 21). Todorov concludes his assessment of Bakhtin's lifelong career by arguing that the term that most richly encompasses the scope and depth of his intellectual project is "philosophical anthropology": "I have reserved for this last chapter those ideas of Bakhtin that I value most and that, I believe, hold the key to his whole work: they constitute, in his own terms, his 'philosophical anthropology'" (p. 94).

31. Glassie, pp. 12–13.

32. Glassie, p. 14.

33. "A Dialogic Criticism?" p. 72.

34. "A Dialogic Criticism?" p. 73.

35. *Local Knowledge*, p. 48.

36. Bacon, p. 94.

37. Glassie, p. 12.

38. Glassie, p. xiv.

39. "'From the Native's Point of View': On the Nature of Anthropological Understanding," *Symbolic Anthropology*, eds. Janet L. Dolgin, David S. Kemnitzer, and David M. Schneider (New York: Columbia University Press, 1977), p. 492.

40. "'From the Native's Point of View,'" p. 492.

41. See Elizabeth C. Fin, *The Folklore Text: From Performance to Print* (Bloomington: Indiana University Press, 1984), and Dennis Tedlock, *The Spoken Word and the Work of Interpretation* (Philadelphia: University of Pennsylvania Press, 1983).

19

The Theater of Ethnography: The Reconstruction of Ethnography into Theater with Emancipatory Potential

Jim Mienczakowski

Drink not the third glasse,—which thou can'st not tame
When once it is within thee.

—*George Herbert (1593–1633)*

Drug and alcohol withdrawal centers, more frequently called detox centers by their clients, are not uncommon in the urban terrain of most cities. Situated independently of hospitals or as part of hospital acute provision, they are seldom frequented by those outside the health community. Used to assist in the safe withdrawal from extreme drug and alcohol intoxication, some centers also support health consumers with short postwithdrawal counseling programs. This article reports on an ethnographic study in which health consumers and health professionals within a detox unit contributed data and participated in extensive validation processes in order to see their polyphonic narrative publicly performed by actors. This study was the second stage of an ethnographic research project examining modes of research report construction and transmission that give access and control of the research data and report construction to

Reprinted from *Qualitative Inquiry* 1, no. 3 (1995): 360–75. Copyright © 1995 by Sage Publications Inc.

the study's informants. In so doing, the ethnodrama process described in this article also forms part of a process of reflexive health education and health promotion that possesses emancipatory potential for its informants.

PILOT PROJECT

An ethnographically based pilot project dealing with the health experiences of a community of high-functioning persons with schizophrenia led to the construction of a fictionalized dramatic narrative reflecting health consumer experiences of psychosis and informant attitudes toward treatment regimens. The script/report "Syncing Out Loud,"[1] compiled from a prolonged and intensive research phase, was performed to audiences of health professionals and health consumers as well as to noninformed audiences to voice reflexively health consumer concerns to health service providers and health educators. Each stage of the research's data collection, scripting, and the performances of the research report were subject to processes of informant validation. Scripting sessions were attended by informants, as were rehearsals, and the script was further cooperatively validated via informant group readings and special preview performances to associated health communities. After informant validation of the performances, the play was opened to general audiences.

All performances used elements of Boal's (1979/1985) forum theater techniques, in which auditorium postperformance discussions with informants, health professionals, and general audiences were used to rework scenarios, reinterpret events, and thereby reconstruct and negotiate the individual's understanding of the play's outcomes. These forum elements typically involved the research team, actors, performance director, script constructors, and information representatives. In this way, the performances were also used to further inform the data of the study.

The processes of participant and audience empowerment through forum reconstruction and "dialogical interactions" (Bakhtin, 1984) were crucial to give health consumers control over the social construction of meaning and of their own identities within the report (Alberoni, 1984; MacKinon, 1982). The script, "Syncing Out Loud," interpreted on stage by twenty-two theater and nursing students, was also performed in secure psychiatric settings to audiences who otherwise would not have been able to influence the report data. All performances and discussions were, in keeping with good ethnographic practice, recorded on audio- or videotape (Strauss & Corbin, 1990).

PHASE TWO

The ensuing alcohol-related study, "Busting,"[2] developed the methodologies of the pilot project to adapt the verbatim accounts of informants into an authentic, validated, polyphonic narrative that expressed informant agendas of concern in their own words. Qualitative data were gathered from informants via participant observation and interactionist interview (Denzin, 1970) during an intensive four-month research program in an urban detox unit. Group and individual informant interviewing involved ethnographers and unit staff already working in or familiar with the setting and, where possible, informant gender signification was taken into consideration during the interviewing of women (Warren, 1988). Clinical and participant observations, performed by nursing students in their final year of university training and by qualified nurses pursuing master's degrees, were turned into independent studies by these students. Data from these periods of student observation were also added to the database of the main study.

To deepen their understanding of the nature of the project, actors involved in the project also engaged in observational activities within the detox unit. Their observations formed part of a Stanislavskian (1936, 1983) approach to characterization. To minimize their influence on the setting (Atkinson, 1992; Hammersley, 1992), they entered the detox unit in small numbers and were paired with nursing staff from the unit who would act as their mentors. All students and staff involved in the data collection were also involved in validation processes and in setting up and performing the ethnography.

LOCATION

The detox center, situated in a run-down urban area, was housed between a major police precinct and a railway station and catered to the large street-dwelling population that inhabited the nearby railway arches and riverbanks of the city's red-light area. Its admission policy, however, was that it turned away only the sober—persons who had previously proven violent and persons who had been through detox, within the preceding twenty-four hours. During the research period, significant numbers of housed and waged persons also underwent the voluntary ten-day withdrawal and counseling program offered there.

The detox center, funded by the federal government, covered some five floors of an office building and accommodated a comprehensive drug and alcohol research library. On the upper levels there were dormitory facilities, kitchens, and counseling and interview rooms; on the ground floor was an acute withdrawal ward, where the early hours of withdrawal were monitored to avoid and control client seizures and delirium tremens. The center provided its services free to all clients.

PROJECT

Whereas the pilot project reworked and fictionalized informant experiences and then sought validation of the representations of the world from them, the second project adapted verbatim narrative into a form in which fictionalized account work was used only to link verbatim account work or to give information considered necessary (by the informants) for audience understanding. The preference for nonfictionalized verbatim account work over fictionalized versions of ethnographic interviews and observations was that of the project's informants who, within the "Busting" project, repeatedly demanded that the report be in the actual words of the informants in order to be seen as real by the informed audiences of health consumers and by the informants themselves. Although all fictionalized account work within both the pilot and main projects was extensively validated by informants and perceived as authentic by audiences, in the perceptions of the "Busting" informants fictionalized inclusions were of less worth than direct verbatim transcription.

Logically, in terms of this research the polyphonic narrative was the means by which disempowered health consumers would gain voice within the community. To recontextualize and reconstruct their words unnecessarily and artificially to appease the aesthetic conventions of academic and literary traditions would have been to reduce further the significance of the voices of the informants and thereby act to disempower them. For the narrative to retain its validity in the eyes of the respondents, then, fictionalized inclusions were first agreed on or suggested as necessary by informants (so as to ensure audience understanding of given phenomena) and then determined as plausible and authentic both in their construction and in their actual performance on stage. This entailed validating the need for an inclusion, its literary construction, and its physical and semiotic representation in front of an audience (Mienczakowski, 1994b).

As with the earlier venture, the play "Busting" was performed in a variety of theater spaces, including readings and performances to informants within the research setting. Public performances of the play also involved community drug and alcohol agencies that engaged in intermission health promotion activities with audiences. These activities ranged from alcohol and drug counseling services to demonstrations of the physical effects of alcohol withdrawal. Community police provided free breathalyzer driver alcohol-impairment tests to any willing audience member and a free taxi service home to any driver who was "over the safe limit." Community Services also provided a collage of graphic alcohol-related vehicle accident photographs, which were slide-projected on stage during part of the performance.

Particularly targeted by the health promotion agencies who helped fund the project were teenage and juvenile drinkers. Accordingly, high school students were invited to performances, and their schools were sent packages of support materials and alcohol awareness information for follow-up lessons. The intention behind this was not only to connect with a target audience but to encourage understanding of how the form of drama might have curriculum currency for other teaching areas (Taylor, 1993, 98–102). As with the pilot project, the script was made freely available to audiences at each performance (Morgan & Mienczakowski, 1994).

LEGACY

The construction of ethnographic narratives into a dramatized form is, arguably, a logical extension of the current reinterpretation of ethnographic practice and of the exploration of how ethnographic representations are constructed. As such, ethnography's theatrical heritage has a discernible and recent history. The form described by Paget (1987) as "verbatim theater," for example, can trace its heritage in Europe back to the BBC documentary radio ballads of the 1950s, which culminated in Joan Littlewood's "Oh What a Lovely War," a musical play that used verbatim account work and documentary evidence as a basis for its depiction of class attitudes toward the First World War. The subsequent presentation of oral history techniques on stage by Cheesman (1971), for example, has further extended a methodology through which ethnographically based oral history techniques have been used to develop narratives that accurately and faithfully depict given social phenomena. Mulkay (1985), moreover, has proposed an ethnographic dramatic narrative that uses parody as a form of social analysis, and Richardson and Lockridge (1991), in "The Sea Monster: An Ethnographic Drama," constructed a dramatized narrative to discuss the issues central to the postmodern reconstruction of ethnography. What

JIM MIENCZAKOWSKI

is taking place is not so much a blurring of the boundaries between social science, humanities, and the arts, but a recognition that this blurring has been taking place for some time.

Where the studies "Busting" and "Syncing Out Loud" differ from current reinterpretations of ethnographic practice is in their overt intention not just to blur boundaries, but to be a form of public-voice ethnography that has emancipatory and educational potential. The extensive validation processes inherent in the interactionist data-gathering techniques of the ethnodrama methodology and the reflexive nature of its performance processes overcome some of the structural difficulties inevitable in the ethnographic venture. Of particular significance is the consensual nature of the validation processes, which seek to create a sense of "vraisemblance" (Todorov, 1968) for both the project participants and audiences of the reports. Vraisemblance, explained by Atkinson (1990) as the creation of "plausible accounts" of the everyday world, is one of the major goals of ethnodrama. This is because both textually and in the case of ethnodrama, physically, vraisemblance is sought to evoke belief by representing (perceived) social realities in terms that mask the cultural influences affecting the constructors of the report. The ethnodrama consensual processes, extended through the Bakhtinian (1984) dialogical interactions of the informant group's struggle to create and share meaning, are formally structured through group discussions and extended via forum theater techniques (Mienczakowski, 1994a). This is done to agree consensually that both the written research report and its physical interpretation on stage are in the authentic language of and therefore recognizable and interpretable by informants.

THE ETHNODRAMA PROCESS: PUBLIC VOICE ETHNOGRAPHY

Rorty's (1980, p. 203) iconoclastic invocation to move away from the traditional divisions of academia has undeniable appeal for anyone who is engaged in both ethnographic practice and the performing arts. By suggesting that "if we get rid of traditional notions of 'objectivity' and 'scientific method' we shall be able to see the social sciences as continuous with literature—as interpreting other people to us, and thus enlarging and deepening our sense of community," Rorty is moving toward a pragmatic reconstruction of writing practice, which, in qualitative ethnographic terms, seeks shared cultural understanding through the literary and sociologic representation of individuated and collective experiences. Agger (1991) furthers the reduction of the role of academic boundaries in the construction of meaning by demanding a new form of public voice in which dialogue chances are not monopolized by the imperatives imposed on the individual by "experts," but are potentially seen to exist in a domain where every individual is empowered to participate in scripting, producing, and shaping culture differently. This appeal for a new form of public voice is compounded by Cherryholmes's (1993) recognition that the processes of academic writing are such that reports are consumed and produced in research settings within a methodological and conceptual framework strictly adhering to conventional academic study. This entails the academic reading of texts within the setting in which the research was developed, while conforming to the protocols of other research that they have read (Cherryholmes, 1993, 1–3). Research, consequently, is written in research settings, read in research settings, and interpreted by those familiar with the research genre. In other words, research tends to follow particular patterns of academic tradition as it is by and large produced by universities for the critical consumption of universities (Lyotard, 1984).

As all ethnographic research reports are written by people as opposed to discourses (Scholes, 1985, 1989), their construction is as dependent on the mask of vraisemblance as any other form of research writing. This is simply because all written representations of both social and scientific understandings may be said to succumb to rhetoric, style, and the pragmatics of historic location (Gadamer, 1988; Ricoeur, 1981; West, 1989, 96). Consequently, the ethnographic construction of dramatic scripts, validated by contributors, peers, and informed others, is potentially able to achieve vraisemblance and cultural ingress as effectively, if not more effectively, than some traditional means of research reporting. Moreover, as the research undertaken in the ethnodrama projects described in this article was meant for consumption by both universities and the general public, from its inception it was intended to reconstruct the research report to meet the demands of both. As qualitative research, it has followed both hermeneutic and critical research processes and has been translated into a format amenable to academic reinterpretation, theatrical performance, and consumption by those who contributed to its data. As a result, it is markedly different from some other forms of ethnographic research, particularly those anthropological researches that do not seek their subjects of study as the objects of their deliberations (Mienczakowski, 1994a).

UPDATING TRUTH

The hermeneutic approach to research is guided by a search for truth and meaning, which is governed in both the method and principles of the research. That is not to say that it pursues truth as an absolute, but that it seeks to understand the grounds on which meanings are based. The nihilistic riposte to this notion is that grounded meaning, and therefore truth, can never be attained (Cherryholmes, 1993). Although hermeneutics can be said ironically to recognize the potential "truth" of nihilism, it is also able to embrace such potential in a paradoxic form of "nihilistic hermeneutics" (Gallagher, 1992l; Scholes, 1985, 1989). Such acceptance acknowledges that what hermeneutic research seeks is potentially unachievable but believes that the process of seeking will uncover yet unknown factors that may render the constraints of nihilism conditional or relative in some way. In all events, ethnodrama attempts to render nihilism conditional by continuing to seek validation of its grounded meanings from contributors to the projects throughout and beyond the report-writing stage. Where traditional research, once written, becomes temporarily bound and prone to fundamental readings, ethnodrama, as an extension of forum theater, renegotiates its meanings with every performance. It does this by intentionally updating its authenticity, repeatedly seeking validation from those about whom it is written, and responding to a consensus of informed opinion by changing the research report/script accordingly. The written research report and performances, therefore, represent the current stage of the research findings and are never a definitive, authoritative set of "fixed" social meanings.

PEDAGOGY OR SELF-INTERPRETATION

In terms of pedagogy, the intention is that the ethnodrama process is sensitive to the pedagogy of teaching and theory but mixes the relations to "undermine the conventional transmission model wherein knowledge is produced, conveyed and received" (Lusted, 1986, 2). In fact, the transmissional model for producing, conveying, and receiving knowledge in terms of ethnodrama is one that qualitatively develops its arguments through interpretive dramatic literature and not traditional academic quantitative methodologies. In telling the stories of persons with schizophrenia or alcohol dependency problems, the intention is to be both descriptive and insightful but, above all, useful and explanatory. By using the words, stories, and advice of people involved in alcohol dependency or other mental health issues, the ethnodrama methodology seeks to tell the truth as they see it, so as to give them voice. To do this, it is necessary to interpret other people to ourselves, themselves, and others through a specifically literary and theatrically constructed medium (Rorty, 1980). This is not done without the brethren of scientific methodology and objectivity, but in spite of them.

HIGH-PROFILE ETHNOGRAPHY: "BUSTING" AND REFLEXIVITY
Part of the purpose of this study was to give voice to both health consumers and health workers to reflexively inform health service providers, health educators, and student nurses of the agendas of concern and everyday realities of life within a drug and alcohol detoxification unit.

Reflexivity can be guaranteed within certain parameters because of the predetermined audience mix and selective venues for the performances. Audiences of health professionals, health consumers, health educators, health students, and health service providers were invited to attend, and their interest was encouraged by performing the play in their places of work. To this end, the performances took place in clinical settings and on two different university campuses involved in health education and nurse training (Mienczakowski, 1994a). This was necessary to inform and influence those who "officially" control the content and determination of what is learned (Apple, 1993) or what is practiced.

Before the performance seasons opening at each venue, copies of the script were sent to individuals representative of or significant within the chosen key health groups, and members were invited to comment on the script and contribute to the study's data. In the months preceding performances of the play, versions of the script were used as teaching materials within the schools of nursing and education of the host campuses and as discussion material within alcohol-related clinical settings. Excerpts from the play were also presented to the health community at two major international nursing conventions, where the script formed the basis of nursing education workshops. Further comment was invited from delegates (Morgan & Mienczakowski, 1993).

As ethnodrama is written in a public voice and is translated into performance in an accessible and unassuming form, its agendas were instantly open to interpretation by nonacademics as well as by the academy. To ensure reflexive interest from target groups, the performance aspects of ethnodrama depend on the process being a mode of high-profile ethnography that embraces media coverage and public debate. Both of the performance projects described in this article sought and received wide press and television coverage (Mienczakowski, 1994a). In turn, the media subsequently sought comment on and responses to the project's agendas from health service agencies, who were obliged to address or at least remark on the agendas raised by the plays. In this way, the ethnodrama report-process provokes response rather than passively awaits it.

WHAT DID THE DATA REVEAL?

The processes by which the health consumers involved in drug and alcohol issues become stigmatized have in past years been well documented (Blane, 1968; Kessel & Walton, 1965; Van Meulenbrouck, 1972; Weatherburn & Project Sigma, 1992), but the effects of client stigmatization on health workers are less well investigated.

The social meaning attached to working within drug and alcohol detoxification centers carries a tenacious and irrational cultural imagery of negative stereotypes and stigmatization. This was strongly reflected by the data, which showed clear differentiation between the experiences of women and alcohol and their male counterparts. Furthermore, the data reflected institutional and paradigmatic divisions in the experiences of female and male caregivers, and stigmatization of health carers within alcohol- and drug-related areas and within the institutional funding of treatment issues. The following examples, transcribed from interactionist, open-ended interviews (Denzin, 1970, 1989), later formed part of the narrative of the "Busting" script. Naturally, the names of the respondents have been altered, but the transcriptions are given to demonstrate the strength and range of agendas present in the data. Given in the voices of the respondents, there is little need for an ethnographer to academize and rephrase them to obscure their import, as they are already in the public voice (Mienczakowski, 1994b).

Stigmatization by Association

It's not just us, either. A friend of mine has been working with HIV clients and she says that when she tells people this they sort of back away—as if she's contagious too. And I find that people think that if you're working with these people they think that you have a drinking or drug problem yourself. It got to the stage where I wouldn't tell people where I worked—because if I was at a dinner party or even a drinks party and I told people where I worked they'd say, "Oh, I really only have two glasses of wine with dinner." And it just spoils your spontaneity with anybody. . . . I'd say I worked for the Health Department rather than in drug and alcohol detox. Yeah, if I'm meeting someone for the first time I say I'm just a nurse for the Health Department. This is how you get past it. That's one response because the other response is, "Oh my God! Tell us your horror stories—come on!" (Ginny, senior nurse)

Structural Inequality

I have a fatalism about the work here, that so much is out of our control. One sad and funny thing was that we were totting up how much this client had spent on her alcohol, cocaine, and heroin in the past 18 months and it was about $750,000. I almost cried, but it was also funny. This unit runs on a fraction of that and they're thinking of closing us down because we cost too much! (Ron, guidance counselor)

And because alcohol and psychiatry, I think, are very low down on the bottom of the health structure—because you're not running around doing lots of things all the time—not curing people—not high visibility. We're the Cinderellas of the health budget. They don't put enough money into it; don't make it attractive to good medical staff. And I really think that it's seen as the butt-end of the whole medical service. . . . Believe me, I've worked in hospitals on general medical wards—so I know the difference. (Lisa, senior nurse)

Women, Alcohol, Institutional Provision, and Role Expectation

There are a lot of things wrong with the system. . . . Very few places in town for women in crisis—loads of flop houses for men but they don't accept women. Look, I mean, I've rung around every place I know to find a place for a woman in crisis—be it alcohol or drug abuse or even just domestic violence coupled with the other two, and there is sweet F.A. available for women in this town. We tend to think of alcoholics as dero's on the street—but it can be a woman who can run a house, albeit piecemeal. She may be good at it one minute and hit the piss the next day. With women it is a hidden problem because she's not supposed to get drunk. If she does she's either a "slut," a "whore," a "floosie," a "scarlet woman," and all those nasty words they call you. . . . On the same level, when women do come in [to the detox unit] it seems to be a lot harder for them to come to terms with the fact that they have a serious alcohol problem. People don't make the association, you see? Women are meant to be role models, if they are drunks too they let the side down . . . they are seen as immoral. (Ginny, senior nurse)

You know, women are the silent drinkers, especially in Australia. It's the male thing—drinking. It's accepted, you know? Aussie macho drinkers. Even the adverts. You know the one?

Friend: I've got some bad news for you, your best mate has runoff with the bride.

Bridegroom: Oh, shit!

Friend: I've got some other bad news. He took the beer with him!

Bridegroom: What? The bastard!!!

But then they manage to get some more beer and so they carry on with the party even though the bride isn't there. That's the image of men in Australia. (Sharon, staff nurse)

Female Carers, Male Clients, and Coworkers

The male clients here are just outrageous. They make sexual jokes, a lot of the time. A lot of the men have got inappropriate sexual behavior. It's immature, you know, adolescent. Like one last week, "Oh you are very small, but you probably had a beautiful mother, which would make up for it." A couple of times they'll try to feel your breasts while you are trying to get their blood pressure. Touch you, you know? I tell them, "I find that inappropriate and I feel very uncomfortable." You need to be assertive. Yeah, most of the women here are . . . I think they are really insecure, it's just a facade, yeah? It's part of that macho drinking culture thing. Women as objects. If you're a female carer [caregiver] you're fair game. They don't see the male nurses in the same way. But they mostly come to respect you in time, look up to you. . . . The male nurses don't have to work at it though. (Sharon, staff nurse)

Sometimes I call a male staff down and say I'm just gonna interview somebody and I don't feel quite happy and I'd like you to be hanging round outside. I hate having to do that. The male staff never complain but you know what they're probably think, "Having to do my job and her's too." Anyway, that's how it feels sometimes . . . but we're [women nurses in the unit] not prepared to deal with "head bangers" who might be high on God knows what and HIV positive at the same time. But on the other hand, I had a guy at the weekend I felt very uncomfortable with. It was in the early hours and there were few staff on. You know? And the interview rooms are quiet, a long way from anywhere else, yeah? He never moved towards me or anything. I just felt at risk in the room alone and I just kept the door open deliberately. Just he way he looked at me, I felt, oh, uncomfortable. But I didn't feel I could ask a male staff to nurse-maid me. . . . I think that guy probably hated everybody, personally. (Lisa, senior nurse)

Sections of the above data were included in the play "Busting" without alteration. To reduce further the need to alter verbatim transcription, the play was staged within the same setting and context in which the participant observation and interactionist interviews had taken place (Denzin, 1970). To assist in the creation of vraisemblance, the physical setting for the play echoed that of the research setting, and the actors, after prolonged periods of participant observation, immersed themselves in the correct language, procedures, and behaviors of the detox unit.[3]

VALIDITY AND MIMESIS

Richardson (1993, 1994) refers to the "transgression" of writing ethnography as drama or poetry and asks whether it actually matters whose life is presented in an "ideal-typic" portrait culled from a variety of texts. The important factor is that the text achieves vraisemblance and appears truthful. The philosophical arguments supporting this position are numerous. Davies (1992, 124), for example, compares the real world to a "virtual world," a vast computer simulation in which we are all involved. Like watching a celluloid film played at its correct speed, humankind believes in events as seamless, coherent and continuous and is unable to see the individual photo frames one at a time. In suggesting a computer simulation of consciousness, Davies (1992) raises the notion that "from the viewpoint of the beings within the computer the simulated world would be real" (124–125). Such beings, indeed, would possess no way of knowing that they or their simulated universe were not real.

In effect, the proposition of whether knowledge of their own realness or virtual existence is of any significance or advances any particular cause becomes central to this discussion. Within Richardson's (1994) poetic dramas, the voice of the ethnographer "is distinguished from the voices of the ethnographees" (10). This, in turn, simultaneously invests the narrative with the differential characteristics essential for the audience's acceptance of the truthfulness of the narrative, while also acknowledging the adroitness of the individual ethnographers' influences and craft on the script. This action informs audiences of the scientific practice underlying the ethnographic venture and, in a way, demonstrates the virtual quality of the simulations that they are watching. For what is being witnessed by the audience is the author's deliberate and valid entrance into Geertz's (1988) "theater of language" to create "bewitching verbal structures" so as to inform effectively while pursuing mimesis.[4] This, however, is an essentially different form of ethnographic practice from that proposed via the polyvocal narrative of ethnodrama, which leaves no such distinction of authorial presence to be made. Within ethnodrama, the ethnographer seeks to be the conduit through which the agendas and stories of the informants are channeled and relies on the extended and continual processes of participant validation to redress textual imbalance (Mienczakowski, 1994a; Mienczakowski, Mogan, & Rolfe, 1993).[5]

CONCLUSION

Both "Syncing Out Loud" and "Busting" are full-length plays that contain only informant agendas. Undoubtedly, audiences may recognize artifice in their construction and the use of literary and theatrical constructs in their crafting, but they may also recognize that the ownership and determination of the plays' stories remain with the informants. Moreover, as the meaning of their representations are renegotiated with every performance, their validity is also reconfirmed and recontextualized by each successive audience. So, although the stories may be perceived as crafted, they do not lose authenticity or truthfulness because of it. Furthermore, their fashioning in the authentic words and voice of respondents guarantees a form of accessibility not ensured by styles of report writing that are singularly aimed at academic interpretation.

For the ethnodrama process, or any ethnographic venture, to seek solely to achieve vraisemblance would be meaningless (Atkinson, 1992; Silverman, 1994). Accordingly, the performance scripts are not alone analogous with the accurate reconstruction of given realities (although they do invite audiences to experience the cultural relatives they portray) but they also significantly possess emancipatory and educative agendas as seen from the perspectives of their informants. These agendas, given by the health consumers, health educators, and health service providers within the research site, seek to influence, inform, and change by publicly voicing respondent health concerns. This is the public voice purpose of ethnodrama writing.

NOTES

Authors' Note: Earlier versions of this article were presented to the CES Post Graduate Research Group, King's College, London, October 1994, and at the International IATA/ND Conference, Warwick University, England, August 1994.

1. "Syncing Out Loud: A Journey Into Illness" (Mienczakowski, 1992). The title for this play was derived from a description of schizophrenic thought given by an informant. It is an international play on words reflecting the nature of schizophrenic illness, in which informants think out loud while lacking synchronization in their thought processes.

2. "Busting: The Challenge of the Drought Spirit" (Mienczakowski & Morgan, 1993). The term *busting* is the preferred and accepted health consumer term for ending a period of sobriety.

3. Conversely, the play "Syncing out Loud" was set in an entirely fictitious mental health conference to involve the audience as conference delegates and so, via interactive theater techniques, pull them into the action and experiences presented.

4. Richardson (1994) has, with "Nine Poems," moved far away from what she terms the "subversive repetition of science practices" (p. 10). In relation to ethnodrama, the intention is to present mimesis physically and semiotically in a form through which the "terra exotic," what Richardson calls the "inner experience or inner life of the writer," is controlled and explored by the informants who are telling their stories in their voices. In a sense, this also reduces the distance between boundaries governing the situation of the "self" and of the work of writing (Ellis, 1991), as the authors are no longer the ethnographers but become the informants. Through their validation and participation in constructing both the ethnographic narrative and the authentication of the physical representation of their experiences, they are collaterally situating the ethnography within the self.

5. Although recognizing that all writing is subject to social and cultural intrusion (Gadamer, 1988), the open-ended and revisory nature of the ethnodrama methodology, particularly through extended and continual consensual processes of validation, seeks to reduce the subjective influence of an individual or context-bound writer on the narrative.

REFERENCES

Agger, B. (1991). Theorising the decline of discourse or the decline of theoretical discourse? In P. Wexler (ed.), *Critical theory now* (chap. 5). New York: Falmer.

Alberoni, F. (1984). *Movement and institution* (P. A. Delmoro, trans.). New York: Columbia University Press.

Apple, M. (1993). *Official knowledge: Democratic education in a conservative age.* New York: Routledge.

Atkinson, P. (1990). *The ethnographic imagination: Textual constructions of reality.* London: Routledge.

———. (1992). *Understanding ethnographic texts.* Newbury Park, CA: Sage.

Bakhtin, M. M. (1984). *Problems of Dostoevsky's poetics.* (C. Emerson, ed. & trans.) Minneapolis: University of Minnesota Press.

Blane, H. T. (1968). *The personality of the alcoholic: Guises of dependency.* New York: Harper & Row.

Boal, A. (1985). *Theatre of the oppressed.* (C. A. & M. L. McBride, trans.) New York: Theatre Communications Group. (Originally published in 1979).

Cheesman, P. (1971). Production casebook. *New Theatre Quarterly,* 1, 1–6.

Cherryholmes, C. H. (1993). Reading research. *Journal of Curriculum Studies,* 25, 1–32.

Davies, P. (1992). *The mind of God: Science and the search for ultimate meaning.* London: Penguin.

Denzin, N. (1970). *The research act.* London: Butterworth.

———. (1989). *Interpretive interactionism.* Newbury Park, CA: Sage.

Ellis, C. (1991). Sociological introspection and emotional experience. *Symbolic Interaction,* 14, 23–50.

Gadamer, H. G. (1988). Rhetoric, hermeneutics, and the critique of ideology: Metacritical comments on truth and method. In K. Mueller-Vollmer (ed.), *The hermeneutics reader* (pp. 284–94). New York: Continuum.

Gallagher, S. (1992). *Hermeneutic and education.* Albany: State University of New York Press.

Geertz, C. (1988). *Works & lives: The anthropologist as author.* Cambridge, U.K.: Polity.

Hammersley, M. (1992). *What's wrong with ethnography?* London: Routledge.

Kessel, N., & Walton, T. (1965). *Alcoholism.* Harmondsworth, Birmingham, U.K.: Penguin.

Lusted, D. (1986). Why pedagogy? *Screen Journal,* 27, 2–14.

Lyotard, J. F. (1984). *The post modern condition: A report on knowledge.* Minneapolis: University of Minnesota Press.

MacKinnon, C. (1982). Feminism, Marxism, method and state: An agenda for theory. *Signs,* 7, 133–42.

Mienczakowski, J. (1992). *Syncing out loud: A journey into illness.* Brisbane, Australia: Griffith University Reprographics.

————. (1994a). Theatrical and theoretical experimentation in ethnography & dramatic form. *ND DRAMA: Journal of National Drama,* 2, 16–23.

————. (1994b). Reading and writing research. *NADIE Journal: International Research Issue,* 18, 45–54.

Mienczakowski, J., & Morgan, S. (1993). *Busting: The challenge of the drought spirit.* Brisbane, Australia: Griffith University Reprographics.

Mienczakowski, J., Morgan, S., & Rolfe, A. (1993). Ethnography or drama? *National Association for Drama in Education,* 17, 8–15.

Morgan, S., & Mienczakowski, J. (1993). Re-animation of the research report: Critical ethnography, health education & theatre. In K. MacNamara (ed.), *Shaping nursing theory & practice* (Monograph 2) (pp. 284–90). Melbourne, Australia: La Trobe University Press.

————. (1994). The application of critical ethnodrama to health settings. *MASK,* 16, 15–19.

Morgan, S., Rolfe, A., & Mienczakowski, J. (1993). It's funny, I've never heard voices like that before: Reporting into research performance work in schizophrenia. *Australian Journal Mental Health Nursing,* 3, 266–72.

Mulkay, M. J. (1985). *The word and the world: Explorations in the form of sociological analysis.* London: Allen & Unwin.

Paget, D. (1987). Verbatim theatre: Oral history and documentary techniques. *New Theatre Quarterly,* 12, 317–36.

Ricoeur, P. (1981). *Hermeneutics and the human sciences.* (J. B. Thompson, trans.) New York: Cambridge University Press.

Richardson, L. (1993). Poetics, dramatics, and transgressive validity: The case of the skipped line. *Sociological Quarterly,* 35, 695–710.

————. (1994). Nine poems: Marriage and the family. *Journal of Contemporary Ethnography,* 23, 3–13.

Richardson, L., & Lockridge, E. (1991). The sea monster: An ethnographic drama. *Symbolic Interaction,* 14, 335–40.

Rorty, R. (1980). *Philosophy and the mirror of nature.* Princeton, NJ: Princeton University Press.

Scholes, R. (1985). *Textual power.* New Haven, CT: Yale University Press.

———. (1989). *Protocols of reading.* New Haven, CT: Yale University Press.

Silverman, D. (1994). *Interpreting qualitative data: Methods for analysing talk, text and interaction.* London: Sage.

Stanislavski, C. (1936). *An actor prepares.* (E. R. Hapgood, trans.) New York: Theatre Arts Books.

———. (1983). *Creating a role.* (E. R. Hapgood, trans.) London: Eyre Methuen.

Strauss, A., & Corbin, J. (1990). *Basics of qualitative research.* New York: Russell Sage.

Taylor, P. (1993). Reflecting in the third person and the guided case study. In W. Michaels (ed.), *Drama and education: The state of the art* (pp. 89–102). Sydney, NSW: Educational Drama Association.

Todorov, T. (1968). Introduction, le vraisemblable. *Communications,* 11, 1–4.

Van Meulenbrouck, M. (1972). Serial psychodrama with alcoholics. *Group Psychotherapy and Psychodrama,* 125, 151–54.

Warren, C. (1988). *Gender issues in field research.* (Qualitative research methods Series no. 9). Newbury Park, CA: Sage.

Weatherburn, P., & Project Sigma. (1992). Alcohol use and unsafe sexual behaviour: Any connection? In P. Aggleton, G. Hart, & P. Davies (eds.), *AIDS: Rights, risk and reason* (chap. 9). London: Falmer.

West, C. (1989). *The American evasion of philosophy: A genealogy of pragmatism.* Madison: University of Wisconsin Press.

20

Foreword from *Reflections: The Anthropological Muse*

Dell Hymes

Recent years have seen a great awakening of attention in anthropology to the mote in the eye of the beholder—the ways in which anthropological inquiry is a function of the circumstances and person of the inquirer, and more generally, of the society and culture from which the inquirer comes. Such concerns have always been present, but never before so near the center of the anthropological stage. And never before has there been such an outpouring of concern with uses of language that go beyond normal scientific writing. Until recently, critical reflection on inquiry was intended usually as a corrective, a way to control subjectivity or to compensate for it. Writing that embodied the subjectivity of the inquirer was marginal, represented by a handful of well-known works. Now a second book that describes what the field experience was like for the fieldworker, beside the standard report, is almost a conventional genre. Even more remarkable, the writing and reading of poetry by anthropologists has become a public part of anthropological meetings. The interest in Edward Sapir as a seminal figure of the first half of this century includes an interest in the fact that he wrote and reviewed poetry and had a desire to see

Reprinted from *Reflections: The Anthropological Muse*, ed. J. Iain Prattis (Washington, D.C.: American Anthropological Association, 1985), 11–13.

that poetry definitively published. And a number of anthropologists publish their poems, individually, and in collections such as this.

In this lies the courage, and to use a fashionable term, the risk. The risk is first of all within the field of anthropology itself. Prattis hopes that the writing of poetry will become a part of the reconstruction of anthropological methodology, a hope I share; but to write poems about one's fieldwork is perhaps to give ammunition to one's critics. The apparent objectivity of the standard article and monograph, after all, is a kind of protection of the self. The public poem makes the self vulnerable. One can imagine snide comments from those who think anthropologists should not mix inquiry with poetry or may not have an attitude a poem reveals. Still, I think that there will be wide acceptance and appreciation of such writing, as of the writing of reflective essays and of novels, the making of films, perhaps painting and drawing. The fuller sense of the person behind the work will be welcome. Poetry will enhance the meaningfulness of anthropology to anthropologists.

But what about the meaningfulness of anthropology to others? That is hard to say. It involves a second, greater risk, that of being judged in terms of the craft of poetry as well as the craft of anthropology.

The important kinds of meaning and intention possible in the making of poems must, in the nature of the case, be achieved with varying success. The key terms seem to me to be *line* and *shape*.

It is easy to argue that the writing of effective *lines* is intrinsic to the ethnographic task. Particular experiences of movement, rhythm, taste, smell, color, complexity, and ambience can be addressed in detail and analysis for as many pages as an editor or publisher will permit, but for the translation of a poem—what is to be captured must be captured in brief compass. And with either a rhetorical tautness, or resonance of sound, or both. The call to have poetry affect anthropological methodology could thus be taken to imply that the writing of effective lines should be addressed in all training.

It is harder to argue that the writing of poems themselves is inherent in the ethnographic task. Giving a shape to a series of lines or groups of lines involves a concern for satisfactory form. That concern would seem to be a function of conventions and tastes that do not arise from the ethnographic task itself (much less from the tasks of the archaeologist or physical anthropologist, whose work should also be considered). True, the conventions that organize ethnographic reports may come to an ethnographer from teachers and editors, not direct experience. To a considerable degree, however, they may be said to have a basis in the accumulated experience of a group within a discipline, and to answer to established communicative norms, as well, perhaps, as to shared conceptual assumptions. To shape words into one kind of line rather than another, one kind of verse and stanza rather than another, to one length rather than another, often must involve accumulated experience of kinds of poems, rather than of ethnographic accounts and the field. And we have as yet no systematic warrant for assuming that the poetic shape of our literary world matches the needs of ethnographic experience, let alone arises from the same soil.

Herein lies the greater risk, then—to be judged in terms of criteria that come from poetry, not anthropology. To have one's ability to find pattern, meaningful pattern, in experience be judged *poetically*. And to be judged to fail at the level of craft, or, if one succeeds at the level of craft, to be suspected of failing even more deeply at the level of anthropology. There will be those who judge the poem that is awkwardly shaped as all the more likely to be true to experience.

It may be that the work of anthropologists such as that represented in this volume will lead to the recognition and development of poetic forms found most adequate to the union of the two crafts, ethnographic and poetic. Some of the contributors can be said to be already along that path. Perhaps such forms will be simply a subset of known forms, perhaps adaptations of known forms, perhaps mixed genres somewhat unique. In this volume are haiku, prose poems, rhymed quatrains, as well as, predominantly, verse free lined. The kinds and quantities vary, but there are poems that succeed in mastering the greater risk, being in themselves good poems and also adding to what we know of the anthropologist, and therefore, of anthropology.

To share in the risk about which I have taken the liberty of writing, let me close with a short poem of my own, written five years ago and dedicated to my friend John Szwed. The experience was not in the field but in a museum, the Whitney, on seeing the painting "City Night" by Georgia O'Keefe, as part of an exhibit on the theme of William Carlos Williams and painting. The visual experience crystallized thoughts out of some years of discussion with Szwed, then director of the Center for Urban Ethnography, about the literary dimension of anthropology, a dimension to which he devoted considerable attention. . . .

CITY NIGHT

hovering
below and between
slant stanchions
of a world,

centred,
black, white, black,
seen and seeing
within a world.

sphered light,
what we can imagine as,
precarious,
from beyond a world—

poetry?
as ethnography?
ethnography?
as poetry?

VIII

The Future of Ethnography and Qualitative Research

Where next? Where will the next revolution be? Langellier points us in the direction of personal narrative and performance studies. She regards the proliferation of personal narratives in contemporary cultural and performance studies with both celebration and suspicion. Still, within this complex space, she understands that personal narrative performances are public and political acts, interpretations that intervene between experience and story. Identities are created in the moment of performance. Performance materializes performativity. Every performance is unique, emergent, and reflexive. Performance reworks personal narrative. Performance turns the personal into a cultural performance. These performances are experienced as dramatic, ritual ceremonies. They affirm identities and personal meanings. Personal narrative is liminal, midway between the personal and the public. Performances move the personal out of this liminal state into the public arena. Modernist narratives and performances solidify the self and its meanings, forging linear plots—suffering, pain, and redemption. Postmodernist tales and performances fracture the self, leading to proliferations, breakdowns, and fragmentations.

In these tellings and performances, we extend and transform our own embodiment, for our bodies, like ourselves, always travel with us.

A POLITICS OF POSSIBILITY

Madison (1998, 279–81) offers a case study that shows how performance ethnographies can help enact a politics of resistance and possibility. Like ethnodramas, such performances give a voice to the previously silenced, creating a space for audiences and performers actually to engage in meaningful dialogue and discourse. In 1968, two African-American women employed as cafeteria workers at the University of North Carolina led a strike, protesting for back pay, overtime pay, and better working conditions. The national guard was called in. The Chapel Hill police "circled the cafeteria with guns in hand, and classes were canceled. For the two African-American women who led the strike, it was a difficult time and an unforgettable ordeal. One woman was fired; the other still works in the University cafeteria" (Madison 1998, 279).

In 1993, the university was celebrating its bicentennial, and it was a major statewide event. Madison notes that some people "felt it was time to honor the leaders of the (in)famous 1968 cafeteria workers strike, as well as labor culture on campus. After some time, a performance based on the personal narratives of the two leaders and other service workers was finally scheduled" (279). On opening night, the strike leaders, their partners, children, grandchildren, friends, cafeteria workers, housekeepers, brick masons, yard keepers, and mail carriers "were the honored guests with reserved seats before an overflowing crowd" (298).

Madison observes that although the university never acknowledged the "strike leader's struggle or their contribution to labor equity on campus, almost thirty years later, the leaders, Mrs. Smith and Mrs. Brooks, watched themselves and their story being performed in a crowded theatre" (279).

At the end of the performance, Mrs. Smith and Mrs. Brooks were introduced, and "the audience gave them a thunderous and lengthy standing ovation" (280). Mrs. Smith said that a night like this "made her struggle worthwhile" (280). Her grandchildren reported that they "now understood their grandmother's life better after seeing the performance" (280). The next day, the press reported that "production told a true and previously untold tale" (280). Madison reports that four years later, workers still stop her on campus and "remember and want to talk, with pride and satisfaction, about that night four years ago when their stories were honored in performance" (280).

The performance of these stories helped these workers tell their story, empowering "them before strangers and kin" (280). The performance was an epiphany, a liminal event that marked a crisis in the history of the university. The performance redressed this historical breach and brought dignity and stature to those who had been dishonored by the past actions of the university. The performance allowed these subjects and their families to bear witness to this suppressed history. This performance did not create a revolution, but it was "revolutionary in enlightening citizens to the possibilities that grate against injustice" (280).

At the time of this performance, the campus housekeepers were embroiled in court battle with the university. The "House Keeper's Movement," as "it was called, was reminiscent of the Cafeteria Workers strike in 1968" (281). Once again the workers wanted better pay, better working conditions. At each performance, the House Keeper's Movement set up a table outside the theater "for donations toward court costs, and legal fees" (281). The performances served to bring previously uninformed members of the community into the House Keeper's Movement. For the strike leaders, "the performance did not eradicate inequity, but it did provide a means for their voices . . . and ultimately their fight for fairness to be heard, felt, and joined" (281).

Ethnographic theater such as this moves in three directions at the same time. It shapes subjects, audiences, and performers. In honoring subjects who have been mistreated, evaluation theater contributes to a more "enlightened and involved citizenship" (281). Such performances, like ethnodrama, interrogate and evaluate specific social, educational, economic, and political processes. This form of praxis can shape a cultural politics of change. It can help create a progressive and involved citizenship. The performance becomes the vehicle for moving persons, subjects, performers, and audience members into new, critical, political spaces. The performance gives the audience and the performers "equipment for [this] journey: empathy and intellect, passion and critique" (282).

Such performances enact a performance-centered evaluation pedagogy. Thus, fusion of critical pedagogy and performance praxis uses performance as a method of investigation, as a way of doing evaluation ethnography, as a method of understanding, as a way of collaboratively engaging the meanings of experience, as a way of mobilizing persons for action in the world. Drawing on McLaren and Giroux, this form of critical, collaborative, performance pedagogy privileges the primacy of experience, the concept of voice, and the importance of turning evaluation sites into democratic public spheres. Thus does critical performance pedagogy inform ethnographic practice, which in turn helps create the pedagogical conditions for an emancipatory politics.

Pedagogical performances have artistic, moral, political, and material consequences (Madison 1998, 283–84). In a "performance of possibilities," moral responsibility and artistic excellence combine to produce an "active intervention to . . . break through unfair closures and remake the possibility for new openings" (Madison 1998, 284). A performance of possibilities gives a voice to those on the margin, moving them for the moment to the political center (Madison 1998, 284). Extending Toni Morrison, the best art and the best performance autoethnographies are "unquestionably political and irrevocably beautiful at the same time" (Morrison 1994, 497; also quoted in Madison 1998, 281).

Every performance is political, an act involving potential struggles and negotiations over meaning, identity, and power, a site where the performance of possibilities occurs (Madison 1998, 277). The performance of possibilities "functions as a politically engaged pedagogy . . . [it] centers on the principles of transformation and transgression, dialogue and interrogation" (277–86). Culture so conceived turns performance into a site where memory, fantasy, and desire fuel one another (277).

POETIC ENDINGS

We conclude with three poems written by two gifted anthropologists, Miles Richardson and Anya Royce. Each poet takes us into the sensuous world of anthropologists in the field, shamans, and a tango for one. The poems reflect a dimension to fieldwork and ethnographic writing that is sadly missing from earlier forms of fieldwork. The poems help readers understand the emotional, psychic, spiritual, and transcendental aspects of the lived ethnographic experience—aspects that move us beyond the travel and the living into the experience of the lived.

REFERENCES

Madison, D. Soyini. 1998. "Performances, Personal Narratives, and the Politics of Possibility." In Sheron J. Dailey, ed., *The Future of Performance Studies: Visions and Revisions* (276–86). Annandale, Va.: National Communication Association.

Morrison, Toni. 1994. "Rootedness: The Ancestor as Foundation." In D. Soyini Madison, ed., *The Woman That I Am: The Literature and Culture of Contemporary Women of Color.* New York: St. Martin's Press.

21

Personal Narrative, Performance, Performativity: Two or Three Things I Know for Sure

Kristin M. Langellier

Aunt Dot was the one who said it. She said, "Lord, girl, there's only two or three things I know for sure." She put her head back, grinned, and made small impatient noise. Her eyes glittered as bright as sun reflecting off the scales of a cottonmouth's back. She spat once and shrugged. "Only two or three things. That's right," she said. "Of course, it's never the same things, and I'm never as sure as I'd like to be" (Allison 5).

Aunt Dot's equivocal and embodied knowledge provides a frame for this essay on personal narrative. I use quotations from Dorothy Allison's *Two or Three Things I Know for Sure*—itself a narrative performance piece—compose some of my own stories, and read the scholarly literature to access and assess what we know about personal narrative from the perspectives of performance and perfomativity. I begin by asking "why personal narrative performance now?"

1.

Two or three things I know for sure, and one of them is that personal narrative surrounds us: pervasive, proliferating, multiplying, consolidating, dispersing. "On a daily basis we all act as if we're getting a life" (Smith and

Reprinted from *Text and Performance Quarterly* 19 (1999): 125–44. Used by permission of the National Communication Association.

Watson, *Getting*, 2), and we do this in increasingly ritualistic and public ways by telling our stories and consuming the stories of others. Philosophers identify *homo narrans* and define culture as an ensemble of stories we tell each other (Fisher). Psychologist Arthur W. Frank illuminates the wounded storyteller whose illness calls for stories and asserts that "postmodern times are when the capacity for telling one's own story is reclaimed" (*Wounded Storyteller*, 7). Feminist writer and critic Vivian Gornick names a "memoir boom" among women writers; and Gloria Anzaldúa describes women of color who write to survive: "I write to record what others erase when I speak, to rewrite the stories others have miswritten about me, about you" (169). Sociologist Ken Plummer attributes the creation of the sexual storytelling culture (personal experience stories around the intimate, such as coming out, rape, recovery stories) to the growth of mass media, consumption, and the therapeutic culture—"all locked into conflicts which highlight stories in their warfare" (125). Historian of family culture John R. Gillis argues that the way we display, document, photograph, video-tape, and in all ways narrate "family" sets apart modern Western family life. Indeed, we could say that U.S. culture is on storytelling overload. In performance studies, Carol Benton has pointed out a "preoccupation" and "infatuation" with personal narrative, warning of the dangers of a "talk show" discipline modeled on confessional TV programs.

One way to respond to "why personal narrative now for communication and performance studies?" is to note the "performative turn" in contemporary society and scholarship (Conquergood, "Rethinking Ethnography"). The performative turn responds to the twin conditions of bodiless voices, for example, in ethnographic writing; and voiceless bodies who desire to resist the colonizing powers of discourse (e.g., Frank). Against this disembodiment and silencing, the performance of personal narrative furnishes "identity's body" (Smith) and the "voice of the lifeworld" (Mishler, *Discourse*). Personal narrative situates us not only among marginalized and muted experiences but also among the mundane communication practices of ordinary people. Placed against the backdrop of disintegrating master narratives, personal narrative responds to the wreckage, the reclaiming, and the reflexivity of postmodern times (Bochner; Corey, "The Personal"). Smith and Watson write that "this telling and consuming of autobiographical stories, this announcing, performing, composing of identity becomes the defining condition of postmodernity in America" (*Getting*, 7).

The popular and performance appeal of personal narrative has been matched by voluminous academic interest. Studies often begin with William Labov and Joshua Waletsky's 1967 essay, and Labov's 1972 elaborations. Perhaps most famous is the Labovian duality of fixed referential clauses—recapitulating in temporal order "what happened"?—and free evaluative clauses—"what's the point?", or in more Performative terms, "what's the point of view?" Labov's 1972 elaboration confirmed the structural model of a fully-formed personal narrative with six parts: an abstract ("what, in a nutshell, is this story about?"); an orientation ("who, when, where, why?"); the complicating action ("then what happened?"); evaluation ("so what? How is this interesting?"); a result or resolution ("what finally happened?"); and a coda ("that's it, I've finished and am bridging back to our present situation"). Labov's model (he called it "tentative") embraces the tensions between the structuralism of the 1960s and the post-structuralism which followed, between more traditional, literary approaches to narrative and more performance-based, pragmatic narrative analysis from communication perspectives.

Notably, 1997 marked the thirty-year anniversary of Labov and Waletsky's essay with a special double issue of the *Journal of Narrative and Life History* (Bamberg). It contained a new essay by Labov and forty-six commentaries on his legacy by a remarkable variety of scholars. The multidisciplinary research literature on personal narrative has been described as both healthy heterogeneity and near-anarchy. I will make no attempt here to be exhaustive or definitive, nor will I try to update my review essay (Langellier, "Personal Narratives"; see also Riessman; Mishler, "Models"). Instead, I will map a communication course between macro-philosophical questions about narrative and micro-analyses of conversational storytelling, but with implications for each of these directions. My specific project asks: what do performance and performativity contribute to doing and studying personal narrative? What can we learn about personal narrative in no other way than through performance?

2.

Two or three things I know for sure, and one of them is just this—if we cannot name our own we are cut off at the root, our hold on our lives as fragile as seed in the wind (Allison, 12).

How do we "name our own" as performance? *Performance* is the term used to describe a certain type of particularly involved and dramatized oral narrative. Of special importance is how performance contributes to the evaluative function of personal narrative—the "so what? How is this interesting? Who's interested in this/whose interest is this?" (I usually elicit this insight in the classroom by having one student tell his or her story of a brush with the police, followed by another student's performance of the official police report of the incident.) The focus on performance emphasizes the way telling intervenes between the experience and the story, the pragmatics of putting narrative into practice, and the functions of narrative for participants. From a pragmatic perspective, personal narrative performance is radically contextualized: first, in the voice and body of the narrator; second, and as significantly, in conversation with empirically present listeners; and, third, in dialogue with absent or "ghostly audiences" (Minister). Personal narrative performance is situated not just within locally occasioned talk—a conversation, public speech, ritual—but also within the forces of discourse that shape language, identity, and experience. Atkinson and Silverman, for example, critically examine the locally occasioned research interview within the discursive Interview Society that prizes authenticity and confession.

Let me tell you a story, Dorothy Allison intones. *Let me tell you a story about how I got interested in studying personal narrative as a communication practice. In graduate school I studied phenomenology, one of the interpretive sciences that set the stage for the recent narrative turn. But the first storyteller I loved was my father and the first story I loved was the one he told about me getting run over by the rotary hoe when I was three. The story that scars my body and marks my place as the fifth in a family of ten children, my working class family tenants on the Illinois farm of soy beans, corn, and livestock. I lost my father two years ago. That's how I always say it, "I lost my father," as though he's somewhere around to be found, and the images of searching for him rise in my mind: on the couch or at the kitchen table or among the tangle of blue globe thistle and purple cornflower and climbing morning glories, my perennial bed in Maine he always called weeds, a farmer to the end.*

And in fact he does live on in family stories which I listen to and tell and teach and study. My dad was a good storyteller and funny, performing with dialogue and gesture and eyes that were blind by the time he was my age, herding in his audience like the cows and pigs that often got loose from the pasture. I realized from the beginning that more than self-expression, more than entertainment, more than instruction, and more than everyday aesthetics was at is-

sue in this practice. And I began, with Eric Peterson, to examine the power of family storytelling to maintain a family and to reproduce The Family as a system of social relations within and through generations (Langellier and Peterson, "Family Storytelling," "Critical Pedagogy").

Take one story and follow it all the way through, beginning, middle, end. I don't do that. I never do (Allison, 39).

Two or three things I know for sure, and one of them is that "all narratives have a political function" (Lanellier, "Personal Narratives," 271), so we must "confront performance issues within structures of power" (Diamond, 7). Approaching personal narrative as performance requires theory which take context as seriously as it does text, which takes the social relations of power as seriously as it does individual reflexivity, and which therefore examines the cultural production and reproduction of identities and experience. Although scholars have customarily used the single term *performance* (Hopkins), here I will follow recent developments in performance theory by also considering the contributions of *performativity* to understanding the complex workings of personal narrative (Strine, Pollock).

Personal narrative is performed in the speech act, "let me tell you a story about what happened to me" (Maclean). Like all speech acts, the narrative performative establishes a two-way, double contract: "Let me tell you a story" promises a performance and constitutes an audience; and "a story about what happened to me" re-presents personal experience. In the often-quoted words of Walter Benjamin, "The storyteller takes what he tells from experience—his own or that reported by others. And he in turn makes it the experience of those who are listening to his tale" (87). This re-presentation is enhanced by virtue of performance features that intensify experience, among them narrative detail, reported speech, parallelisms, appeals to the audience, paralinguistics, and gestures (e.g., Fine).

Like all speech acts, the personal narrative performative depends upon context and the shared conventions between partners who accept a new frame of reference. This frame instructs participants to take the discourse in a special way, to distinguish between orders of messages: to recognize the narrator(s) as telling a story about personal experience. On the one hand, the personal narrative contract highlights the interdependence of the telling and the experience, what Annette Martin has called the "reality factor." On the other hand, it differentiates between the telling and the story, between the present act of narrating and the past act being narrated. We distinguish between the self and others "of" the performance (narrator and audience) and the self and others "in" the story (narrator and characters). We concede the strategic ways that performing intervenes between experience and story, the way that narrative mediates experience even when a factual account is promised. In a word, personal experience stories are *made*, not found, by either narrators or researchers. Approaching personal narrative as performance insists on this attention to strategy, situation, and social conventions (Lockford).

Why add performativity to performance? By *performativity*, I highlight the way speech acts have been extended and broadened to understand the constitutiveness of performance. That is, personal narrative performance *constitutes* identities and experience, producing and reproducing that to which it refers. Here, personal narrative is a site where the social is articulated, structured, and struggled over (Butler, Twigg). To study performance as performativity is, according to Elin Diamond, "to become aware of performance itself as a contested space, where meanings and desires are generated, occluded, and of course multiply interpreted" (4). In performativity, narrator and listener(s) are themselves constituted ("I will tell *you* a story"), as is experience (" a story about what happened to me"). Identity and experience are a symbiosis of performed story and the social relations in which they are materially embedded: sex, class, race, ethnicity, sexuality, geography, religion, and so on. This is why personal narrative performance is especially crucial to those communities left out of the privileges of dominant culture, those bodies without voice in the political sense. Theatre theoretician Jill Dolan's shorthand for performativity, "the nonessentialized constructions of marginalized identities" (419), captures these concerns. Performativity reveals that questions about "so what? Who's interested in this? Whose life matters?" to be about competing and conflicting group interests and subject positions.

Thus, when personal narrative performance materializes performativity— when a narrator embodies identity and experience—there is always danger and risk. The performance of personal narrative gives shape to the social relations of identity and experience but because such relations are multiple, complexly interconnected, and contradictory, it can do so in only unstable ways for participants. Performance becomes the means by which we "problematize how we categorize who is 'us' and who is 'them,' and how we see ourselves with 'other' and different eyes" (Madison, "Performance," 282, italics in original). Thus, the *personal* in personal narrative implies a performative struggle for agency rather than the expressive act of a pre-existing, autonomous, fixed, unified, or stable self which serves as the origin or accomplishment of experience (Smith). Performativity articulates and situates personal narrative within the forces of discourse, the institutionalized networks of power relations, such as medicine, the law, the media, and the family, which constitute subject positions and order context; and *performance* implies the transgressive desire of agency and action. From the perspectives of performance and performativity, personal narrative is situated, embodied, and material—stories of the body told through the body which make cultural conflict concrete and accessible (Langellier, "Voiceless").

3.
Two or three things I know for sure, and one of them is the way you can both hate and love something you are not sure you understand (Allison, 7).

Scholars respond to the postmodern proliferation of personal narrative with both approval and alarm. Paraphrasing Michel de Certeau, Smith and Watson write: "we are a postmodern society in which the disappearance of the unproblematic belief in the idea of true selves is everywhere compensated for and camouflaged by the multiplication of recitations of autobiographical stories" (*Getting*, 7). The debate on the consequences of personal narrative pits celebratory against suspicious views. A celebratory vision emphasizes the hopeful project of personal narrative: its human agency and potential for self-transformation through re-storying; its immediacy, emotionality, and embeddedness in experience; and its invitation to empathy and shunning of elitists and experts. Personal narrative can educate, empower, and emancipate. A suspicious view raises concerns over personal narrative's confessions and self-indulgences; its misleading consolations and diversions from material conditions; its inscription of experience within existing structures of domination. Personal narrative can individualize and overpersonalize; it can normalize, naturalize, and moralize. Linda Kaufman describes personal testimony as "fatally alluring" (261). But telling one's story as a personal narrative always carries risk, existential and political: on the double edge and fine line between hegemony and resistance, between recuperation and transgression, disclosure may increase as well as diminish domination (Alcoff and Gray).

But performance and performativity open a pathway through the celebratory and suspicious terrain of personal narrative, a path explored by, among others, feminist theorists and autobiographers (Smith and Watson, *Women*) and performance artists (Carver), a way that is embodied, material, situated, and critical. D. Soyini Madison ("Performance") calls this terrain the "performance of possibilities," the more complicated space that spans both domination and resistance where performance matters because it makes a difference in the world. Efforts such as these do not underestimate the transformative power of personal narrative but neither do they romanticize its claims to resistance. They are critical, but they also specify feminist agency in performance. According to Diamond, "A performance, whether it inspires love or loathing, often consolidates cultural or subcultural affiliations, and these affiliations might be as regressive as they are progressive. The point is, as soon as performativity comes to rest on a performance, questions of embodiment, of social relations, or ideological interpellations, of emotional and political effects, all become *discussable*" (4; my italics).

By "discussable" I include not just experience but also the power relations producing personal narrative—its subjects and practices. If the full meaning of personal narrative as performance is pragmatic, not semantic, we must interrogate not just what experience means, or by what strategies of narrative, but also who and what matters: who speaks to whom for whom under what conditions and with what consequences (Smith)? For example, whose body is speaking in performance: narrator, performer, researcher? Before whom is the speaker revealing or concealing (or both) her or his body? How is personal narrative created, collected, coached, coaxed, or coerced? How is the audience positioned in the text and participating in the performance? What kinds of personal narrative are performed? What kinds of narratives work to empower people, and which do not? How do sites and situations of personal narrative performance enable participation or license consumption? Why perform personal narrative in public, and with what consequences? How do communication norms, such as role-taking, turn-taking, self-disclosure, and body gesture "open up" or "close down" storytelling? How are other voices and bodies arranged in the personal narrative? How does personal narrative performance sit within wider frameworks of power?

Let me tell you a story. More of the story about how I got into studying personal narrative. There's a photograph of me reading to my newborn son in 1983. You can see in the photo that I'm reading Dale Spender's Man Made Language. *Out loud, of course, according to my performance studies training. I'd also read the baby development books on how it doesn't make any difference what you say or read, so long as you do it. No doubt I was trying to get some course preparation done, too. So, sure, we planned to raise a feminist son, but in those early days and months of having crossed a terrifying boundary of experience, feeling untenured/untethered both as a mother and as a professor, my feminist books and friends sustained me, acknowledging the contradictions and disorientations of this most bodily of experiences.*

For me, feminism and women's talk coincided with motherhood, certainly complexly but not as an opposition. Theoretically, I was led to analyses of women storytelling, bringing the critical voice of feminisms into dialogue with phenomenology's interpretive aims. Initially I was interested in the collaborative, conversational practice of personal narrative among women that Eric Peterson and I called "spinstorying" as a way to negotiate identity and effect social change. Some years later, tenured and on sabbatical, I took up more empirical work on narrative performance among women in contemporary quiltmaking culture. Participating in local, regional and state quilt groups, I analyzed Show and Tell as a storytelling practice that insisted upon the relationship of quilts to women's lives and bodies, a counter-narrative to the dominant discourses of traditional quilts, the new art quilts, and the emerging market in quilts. Studies of women storytelling reveal the conflicts of gender performance at the intersection of body, society, and material relations.

Behind the story I tell is the one I don't. Behind the story you hear is the one I wish I could make you hear (Allison, 39).

4.

What can we learn about personal narrative in no other way than through performance? Richard Bauman's (Story) highly influential performance paradigm highlights the evaluative function of narrative, how communication is carried out "above and beyond its referential content" (3) in dialogue with an audience. Significantly, Bauman recasts Labov's text-centered terms of evaluation and reference into the performance constructs of narrative event—the event in which the stories are told—and *narrated event*—the event recounted. Narrative event and narrated event doubly anchor personal narrative in social relations to suggest the vital role performance plays in social life and in relation to other speech events that precede and succeed it. In the speech act, "let me tell you a story about what happened to me," performance enhances, heightens, augments experience, but it does not retreat from the world into a separate realm of fiction or theatre.

Bauman applied the new performance approach to male expressive traditions in Texas in a book-length study based upon fifteen years of fieldwork. He shows, for example, how personal narrative co-occurs with other verbal art; and he charges that a close study of point of view in personal narrative performance, as a way to examine the interdependence of the narrative event and narrated event, is a crucial but neglected area of study. Similarly, Patricia Swain looks to the use of reported speech in performances by an Appalachian woman storyteller. The "good Christian lady" of the title story refers to the storyteller herself but the speech is attributed to another character. Reported speech is a sophisticated form of embedded evaluation which participates in both the narrated event (the narrator's interaction with other characters in the story) and the narrative event (the narrator's interaction with the audience). Swain's work urges further analysis of this strategy, including how reported speech is performed and how gendered norms of a speech community may inform its use.

Sociolinguist Nessa Wolfson has given specific attention to the fact that personal narrative may or not be framed as performance. She asks, under what conditions is it? She focuses on the features that distinguish dramatized reenactments in personal narrative, especially the use of the conversational historical present (CHP) tense. For example, Rhea, a breast cancer survivor who had a mastectomy and then had her mastectomy scar tattooed with a design of Victorian flowers, "breaks through to performance" as she recounts the moment of exposing her tattoo to her gynecologist for the first time:

> and so I'm saying "Wait a minute" [assertively, with hand gesture]
>   You know, I always t-
>   This is how I always start
> I said, "wait a minute" [performs voice and gesture again]
>   Before I open up the little johnny
> I said, "I got a tattoo," all right [she and interviewer laugh].

The alteration of CHP with the past tense ("I'm saying" with "I said"; "I open" with "I said") is a reliable marker of performance that functions as an internal evaluation device to structure the story and heighten its drama (Langellier, " 'You're Marked'"). Wolfson concludes that performance is an interaction variable, only given when the norms for evaluative interpretation are presumed to be shared between narrator and audience.

What we learned about personal narrative through performance is crucial and simple. First, we understand that personal narrative may key a change in the status of discourse to storytelling performance; however, when people engage in personal narrative they do not leave their daily lives behind but transform and extend social relationships. Second, we learn that personal narrative always relies upon the conventions of performance within speech communities and situations: personal narrative is a situated practice rather than an autonomous text. Third, but because every performance is unique and depends upon its particular circumstances and participants, personal narrative is *emergent*, Bauman's term for its potential to rearrange not just text—we know that our personal stories change with each telling—but also social relations within the performance event and perhaps even beyond it. And fourth, we comprehend the *reflexivity* of personal narrative, that is, the way culture exhibits itself and itself and to others in performance. Bauman ("Performance") calls reflexivity a more potent term than reflection, which treats performance as a mirror of some more primary cultural realities (47), and he argues that performance is also reflexive in a socio-psychological sense, constituting the performing self as an object for itself as well as for others (48). Bauman's optimum vision for the performance paradigm thus asks that scholars provide an integrated account of social structure and a wider sense of cultural context as they focus on personal narrative as situated practice.

Let me tell you a story, more of the story about how I got into personal narrative performance studies. A colleague in health communication, Claire Sullivan, came to me with a research problem. She'd been asking research subjects to describe supportive communication during stressful life events by having them respond to questionnaires. And she was frustrated and they were frustrated. She recognized that they wanted to say more, or something different, than the questionnaires allowed. They wanted to tell the story of their crisis. Would I be interested in collaborating on a study of their narratives, in particular breast cancer stories? I said "yes," and we began the study of illness narratives, conducting lengthy interviews with women with breast cancer.

We learned that one in eight women will get breast cancer in her lifetime. We listened to women suture the rupture of breast cancer in their bodies, their lives, their families and friends, their futures. We witnessed how breast cancer calls for stories and how women respond in many different ways. I've wondered how I might answer that call, too. When I'm in the office working with a student who is trying to decide whether or not to research conflict management for a paper, the phone rings, and the caller is trying to decide whether or not to do chemotherapy after her breast surgery.

Claire and I have worked on different analyses of the breast cancer narratives, together and individually (Langellier and Sullivan; Langellier, "'You're Marked'"; Sullivan). At a women's studies conference, we formed a panel with three researcher-researched pairs to talk about our experiences and issues. The next year, again with the participation of survivors, we facilitated a storytelling round among men and women, with and without cancer, about breasts, about getting mammograms, about breast cancer in all our lives. In spring of 1996 we hosted Linda Park-Fuller and her personal narrative performance A Clean Breast of It *for campus and community audiences. I walk in the* Race for the Cure *with two pink signs on my back: one in celebration of Rhea who survives eleven years after breast cancer; one in memory of cousin Mary who died last December. I recall the performance studies conference on personal narrative and HIV/AIDS education (Corey)—and how group story telling may create an opportunity for participants to connect and contribute similar experience to the developing story, to resist the assumption that "this is not my story," to explore new subject positions and to make their own stories.*

I think, "this is the hardest to write because it's less my story; this is the easiest to write because it's less my story."

Two or three things I know for sure, and one of them is that to go on living I have to tell stories, that stories are the one sure way to touch the heart and change the world (Allison, 72).

5.

Having outlined the unique contributions of performance to personal narrative study, next I argue that from the perspective of performativity, much performance analysis has not fulfilled the promise implied by Bauman's vision. In a critique of the performance paradigm, J. E. Limon and M. J. Young assert that there is "minimal or no commentary that takes substantial analytic account of the history and larger sociocultural context of [the] speech setting" (441). Regarding Bauman's study of men's Texas storytelling, they write, "We learn much about the poetics of this verbal art but comparatively little about its relationship to that always fascinating sociocultural process called Texas" (446). Nor, I could add, does it address the power relations around gender at work in the culture of Texas or in academe that have historically privileged white men as cultural representatives of "good" storytellers with "good" stories.

These more macrosociological concerns are echoed from the other end of the spectrum in microsociological critiques of Wolfson's performance studies (Schiffrin). Michael Toolan, for example, supports Wolfson's conclusion that performance is more likely when conversationalists share similarities of race, sex, age, status, attitude, and so on. But if performance shares the task of evaluation, why doesn't performance increase rather than decrease when conversationalist are dissimilar? "Perhaps," Toolan suggests, "evaluation undertakes a larger, more crucial task, than that of performance: the task of articulating the point of the story and persuading the audience of its tellability" (169). The point of a story and its tellability precisely concern the question of what matters and who matters and to whom it matters—concerns of performativity.

Both macro and micro critiques problematize context in personal narrative performance and suggest how narrative event and narrated event participate in wider fields of discourse. Furthermore, we must recognize that the performance frame itself encourages and intensifies a kind of decontextualization. Toolan usefully distinguishes two levels of context: the context of the *situation* and the context of *culture*. Performance can decontextualize the context of situation by making a text stand on its own: an identifiable, self-contained item in a repertoire which is stylized, polishable, and repeatable by a narrator apart from the clarifying marks of the teller and audience's immediate communication. But one cannot decontextualize the context of culture as the markings which shape the story's intelligibility and tellability for a speech community, or what I have called here the issues of performativity that constitute subjects and order context.

To illustrate the distinct contributions of performance and performativity to the workings of personal narrative and subjectivity, let me elaborate an example from anthropologist Barbara Myerhoff's work on ritual, storytelling, and aging among American Jews (Langellier, "Voiceless"). Myerhoff conceptualizes personal narrative as a definitional ceremony, a strategy to show ourselves to ourselves (reflection) and to arouse consciousness of ourselves as we see ourselves (reflexivity) (234). Personal narrative is a performance strategy with particular significance for socially marginal, disparaged, or ignored groups or for individuals with "spoiled identities." Personal narrative as cultural performance has transformative power to assert self-definitions about who matters and what matters: the existence, worth and vitality of a person or group as meanings not otherwise available to an audience. For Myerhoff, personal narrative performance functions as social bonding to create and celebrate a community's identity and values.

Myerhoff continues, however, "That *the ceremonies changed nothing* was signal, and is what distinguished them from social dramas. It seemed, in fact, that their purpose was *to allow things to stay the same,* to permit people *to discover and rediscover sameness* in the midst of furor, antagonism, and threats of splitting part" (263; my emphasis). Definitional ceremonies, while transformative for participants, stop short of transgression, of having effects in the social world. Mark Kaminsky offers an alternative reading of Myerhoff's definitional ceremonies, based in the concerns of performativity. On the one hand, he critiques conceptualizations of personal narrative performance that avoid or veil cultural conflict. On the other hand, he forcefully defends the possibility for definitional ceremonies to effect social change.

Kaminsky argues that Myerhoff's conceptualization depoliticzes and re-enchant Jewish experience by bringing their performances into the hegemonic narrative of Americanization. Definitional ceremonies adhere to a nostalgia for the canonical stories that unify the subject, knowledge, and history to link modernity with traditional society. The consequence, according to Kaminsky, is personal narrative as secular ritual: a machine of cultural production whose input is scraps of beliefs and whose output is a mood of collective elevation and consensus. Performance here evacuates difference, covers over conflict and power interests, and re-stabilizes identity, meanings, and social relations (it "allow[s] things to stay the same"). Linda Kaufman's more pointed critique of a therapeutic model of personal narrative asserts, "writing about yourself does not liberate you, it just shows how engrained the ideology of freedom through self-expression is in your thinking" (269).

When performance engages issues of semantics, the definitions of a self (who am I?) or the bonds of a group (who are we?), it may leave unexamined Madison's questions about "who is 'us' and who is 'them' and how we see ourselves with 'other' and different eyes." The consequences of personal narrative performance that "change[s] nothing" may be to show ourselves to ourselves as we like to think we are—a re-enchantment and depoliticizing of experience and identity. When addressed to the self or self-same others ("to discover and rediscover sameness," as Myerhoff puts it), personal narrative may restore and re-story experience outside the workings of context, power, and identity. But "[performance] is political in its construction of forms of subjectivity that situate social actors in (power) differentiated ways in society" (Mumby 18). If one cannot draw a boundary between performance and social life and if the full meaning of personal narrative is pragmatic, not semantic, then resistance can be determined only within the conditions and consequences of performance in the wider context of culture—not alone from the text, from the narrator's experience, nor the audience's situation.

Myerhoff's conceptualization to the contrary, Kaminsky argues that definitional ceremonies *can* be transgressive, and he re-interprets her definitional ceremonies within the intertwining of religion and politics in the particularities of Jewish cultural history. Clearly, personal narrative performance can critique the underlying assumptions of a story's intelligibility and tellability; can remember how history, society, and culture inform experience; and can destabilize identity by resisting the myth of a unique, unified, and fixed self. Just as clearly, self-definitional stories are crucial for particular situations and audiences, for example, re-storying experience for the self in illness (e.g., Frank, *Wounded Storyteller*; White and Epston; Carilli). Without performativity, however, personal narrative risks being a performance practice without a theory of power to interrogate what subject positions are culturally available, what texts and narrative forms and practices are privileged, and what discursive contexts prevail in interpreting experience. Without it we are vulnerable to the charge that performance makes no difference, that it leaves all material and social conditions unchanged (see Ebert). Performativity asks us to recognize and realize the potential of the performance paradigm.

Two or three things I know for sure, and one of them is that change when it comes cracks everything open (Allison, 48).

Let me tell you another story about how I got into studying personal narrative. I never knew I was French until I moved to Maine. But people kept telling me "you've got to be French." And I am, on both sides, for generations, my people from Canada like the Franco-Americans in Maine. But what does that mean, and what difference does it make? As it turns out, a good deal in Maine where ethnic jokes are still made about dumb Frenchmen, where Frog and Canuck are insults, where the Ku Klux Klan targeted French Catholics (and Jews) in the 1920s, and where North American French dialect was met with hostility in public, and ridicule in schools, including the state university, because it was not Parisian (Doty, Peterson). My second summer in Maine a man from Old Town, the mill town north of Orono with two islands, one called French Island, one called Indian Island, telephoned me. He explained that his wife worked at the University of Maine library and had seen my name on a list, and he told me that Langelier, spelled with one l, was one of his family names.

Gradually, I learned of the migration of one half of Quebec's population to the United States between 1820 and 1920, especially the Northeast, and that they count seven million descendants today. Maine documents up to 40 percent of its population with French cultural heritage. Historically, these Franco-Americans enjoy the distinction of being simultaneously unassimilated and silent. The quiet presence of the French in the Northeast is mirrored at the University of Maine where they remain virtually invisible within the curriculum, as students in the classroom, and on the faculty. Reflecting class differences and education, almost all Franco-American employees are in staff, clerical, and professional positions. Franco-American women especially disappear because they are invisible within "white culture" and muted by the male dominance of their ethnic culture (Langellier, "Responding").

In response, the university has initiated a Franco-American studies program. Collaborations between faculty and community have produced oral history projects on French Island and the first anthology of Franco-American women's writings (Robbins, et al). Off-campus and on-line, a grassroots community of Franco-American women are telling their stories to each other, coming to voice and claiming identity. As I participate in this ongoing effort, my identity is decidedly multiple and unstable, fragmented and fluid, contested and in conflict. I oscillate between the twin risks of overemphasizing the similarities borne of my academic and class privilege. Collaborating with the Franco-American women on curriculum or a conference presentation, for example, I am eligible for grants and travel money for which they are not. Sometimes cultural insider, sometimes outsider, often ally and occasionally enemy, simultaneously oppressor and oppressed, this storytelling teaches me and then teaches me again how the differences of geography, of history, of gender, of religion, of class, make a difference.

This summer I wrote my mother's Franco-American story, a publication without a category on my vita but one which earned me more credibility in the local community than any of my academic publications.

6.

Two or three things I know for sure, and one of them is that I would rather go naked than wear the coat the world has made for me (Allison, 74).

So far I have argued that performance needs performativity to comprehend the constitutive effects of personal narrative, and I have argued, just as strongly, that performativity relies upon performance to show itself. Diamond clarifies that "When performativity materializes as performance in that risky and dangerous negotiation between a doing (a reiteration of norms) and a thing done (discursive conventions that frame our interpretations), between someone's body and the conventions of embodiment, we have access to cultural meanings and critique. Performativity, I would suggest, must be rooted in the materiality and historical density of performance" (4). Below I highlight personal narrative studies that address both concerns of performance and performativity and that clarify how the transformative power of personal narrative is also transgressive.

Madison's ("'That Was My Occupation'") study of the oral narrative of Mrs. Alma Kapper, a sharecropper and domestic worker in Mississippi, uses black feminist thought and the potent constructs of "theories of the flesh" and "specialized knowledge" to ground a critical praxis of personal narrative performance. Theories of the flesh are indigenous performance traditions in which black women theorize themselves. Personal narrative is a way of knowing carved out of experience, experience as it is inflected by particular cultural, geopolitical, and material circumstances. Specialized knowledge re-articulates and re-makes theories of the flesh for critical intervention by the black feminist subject: "the teller's experience is illuminated and made accessible and available as an advocacy discourse for social change and/or affirmation" (215). The authority, knowledge, and power of the critic is directed by the formal and informal theories of the subjects themselves. In this way, theory and experience are interdependent rather than opposed to, or isolated from, one another, thereby altering the dominant relations of power and knowledge. Madison's black feminist narrative analysis echoes similar projects to define situated knowledges (Haraway), such as Anzaldúa's borderlands consciousness and Craig Gingrich-Philbrook's "stand-up theory."

A second example is David Román's study of the performative arena of AIDS discourse, especially artist Tim Miller's performance piece SEX/LOVE/ STORIES. Miller chronicles his experiences as a gay man, beginning his stories with the disclaimer, "I remember so many things, some of the them even happened." Román comments that "what's at stake is not so much a recording of [Miller's] life but, rather, a deliberate displacement of this through performance" (215). Miller's decidedly postmodern performance explores the possibilities of gay male subjectivity and desire in the age of AIDS when the dominant image of being gay is linked to death. Román asserts that Miller's performance intervenes both within the crisis of AIDS and the crisis of representation engendered by AIDS. Moreover, Román argues that Miller's local, free performance workshops in Los Angeles create a community that utilizes performance "to express differences and a self-determined agency in order to engage in the necessary dialogue that may effect social change" (217).

Studies such as these realize the potential of the performance paradigm to examine text/context relations. In an essay that responds to critiques of the performance paradigm, Bauman and Briggs challenge scholars to "displace performance/text as a reified, object-centered event encompassed by a single, bounded social interaction" and to attend to the dialectic between performance and the wider sociocultural and political-economic context (see also Conquergood, "Beyond the Text"). They encourage us to rethink personal narrative performance in terms of *entextualizing* (from experience, from a previous conversation, from an interview) and *contextualizing* (to a new experience, conversation, script). Such a rethinking unavoidably involves issues of performance and social power because it asks us to consider the conditions and the consequences of personal narrative. Who tells what stories to whom under what conditions? Why is this particular story told in this particular way to this particular audience at this particular time and with what consequences?

I tell stories to prove I was meant to survive, knowing it is not true. My stories are not parables, no *Reader's Digest* Unforgettable Characters, no women's movement polemics, no Queer Nation broadsides (Allison, 51).

Let me tell you a story. This is the last part of the story on how I got into studying personal narrative. A few years ago, Eric Peterson and I were invited to join the Narrative Study Group in Cambridge, Massachusetts, organized ten years ago and graciously hosted by Elliot Mishler. The group of narrative scholars from psychology, sociology, anthropology, medicine, education, philosophy—and now communication and performance—meets monthly during the academic year for narrative study at every stage of preparation: audio or videotapes, transcripts, drafts, final copy, published works. And so as often as we can manage, we drive the four-plus hours to Boston. Our work has been received with a good deal of interest, although we struggle to clarify a performance and performativity perspective on personal narrative. Performance is often understood in one of two limiting ways: in the Bauman tradition of situated verbal art (as described above); or as theatre, and thus a "special case" framed outside of communication praxis. Dialogue with the group has influenced our work on narrative analysis, most recently the essay on the politics of methodology in personal narrative research (Peterson and Langellier).

I notice that although other group members are very self-reflexive about their participation in "making stories" as researchers, they rarely tell or write, or indeed perform, their own stories, a practice that has become so prevalent in performance studies that a recent volume calls personal narrative its future (Dailey 199). I wonder: what is this practice in which performance studies scholars engage so "naturally"? Does the "boom" in personal narrative re-enchant performance?

7.

That was what happened. That was it. Do you believe me? (Allison, 3).

Two or three things I know for sure, and one of them is that personal narrative is liminal. A limen is a threshold, a border, a margin, a transitional space, a site of negotiation and struggle. In my attempt to map the terrain of personal narrative in 1989, I began by describing personal narrative as a boundary phenomenon: between literary and social discourse, between written and oral communication, between public and private spheres of interaction, between ritual performance and incidental conversation, between fact and fiction. Today I might restate this boundary in terms of the entextualizing and contextualizing of personal narrative because performance create border crossings, contact zones, and boundary disputes (Conquergood, "Rethinking Ethnography"). In closing I briefly describe **two or three things I don't know for sure**, unresolved challenges facing personal narrative performance theory and practice.

Speaking for myself/speaking for others. No one has stated this boundary dispute more thoughtfully than Darlene Hantzis. "Oddly troubled" by the "turn" to personal narrative, Hantzis worries over "the ease with which the critical practice of personal/political becomes the practice of disclosing personal experiences, not as texts to be interrogated and theorized, but texts to be understood as simple evidence, to be simply affirmed or to be 'honored'" (203).

Hantzis queries the ease of muting critique with two questions: is the turn toward the self as text an attempt to turn away from the problematics of otherness? And does the move to "speak for myself" sanctify experience, render the narrative sacred, and exempt the personal from critique, thereby bracketing the problematics of the self, experience, personal, and telling. Theoretically, Hantzis asks, "if the self, rather than producing personal stories, is (at least partially) produced by them, then that which is taken as 'personal' belongs also to the space of the cultural—marked not by/as individual experience but as socio-political production" (204). In terms of performance practice, she raises concerns about the illusory "safety" for the teller (promised and/or assumed) and the compelled participation of others in the telling. Plummer also alerts us to conditions that may compel performance when he places coaxers, coercers, data collectors, and research collaborators as co-producers of personal narrative. Unresolved problems of speaking for myself are matched—if not intensified—by the problem of speaking for others in ethnographic performance (Alcoff; Pineau et al.).

Individual/community. If personal narrative is not the product of a solitary individual but a group practice, what place does community have in the contact zone of performance? All stories emerge as a practical communication activity as we take up and piece together the bits of our experience into stories. Culture comes already narrated with canonical stories about how lives may (and should be) lived (White and Epston), a narrative briocolage into which we are recruited by virtue of membership in communities—"and we ignore that at our—and others—peril," Hinchman and Hinchman (xxiv) warn. T. Minh-Ha Trinh also reminds us that "The story depends upon every one of us to come into being. It needs us all, needs our remembering, understanding, and creating what we have heard together to keep on coming into being" (119). Narrative performance in Native American culture, for example, may serve communal memory, connection, and interaction between generations rather than the emplotment of self (Murphy). Does personal narrative performance privilege the individual over the community? How are we responsible *to* a community and responsible *for* a community as we engage in personal narrative (Carlin)? What are the (multi)cultural limitations of personal narrative?

Modernism/postmodernism. In this borderland, personal narrative strains in two directions (Plummer). In a modernist, stabilizing drift, personal narrative integrates a life in time and provides unity in an attempt—always frustrated—to fix the self or transform identity. Modernist stories with driving, linear plots—of suffering, coming out, survival—told in unproblematic language assume that one is discovering the truth of the self. These modern tales ultimately fit the archetypal forms of storytelling: journey, homes, consummation. And they continue to be told, perhaps by most people. By contrast, in a postmodern, destabilizing drift, personal narrative contributes to the proliferation of multiple selves: porous, partial, shifting, contingent. Postmodern tales may feature fragmentation, borrowings, and indeterminacies; glitzy, glossy, and high tech strategies that break down grand stories and frustrate unity, essence, and truth. Marvin Carlson describes two kinds of performances—identity and resistant—to suggest how postmodern performances run alongside, rather than replace, modernist stories. Dennis Mumby similarly suggests that we reread the modernism-postmodernism polarity for continuities as well as differences, and that we consider postmodernism as a broadening rather than a rejection of modernism. If the "cash value" of postmodernism lies precisely in its insights into how performance, identity, and power intersect, its vantage point is crucial to theorizing subjectivity and examining personal narrative as self-expression and as self-de(con)struction (Deetz).

Where am I in the stories I tell? (Allison, 4)

What we can learn in no other way than through performance and performativity is just this: the enhancement of experience and the constitution of identity in personal narrative depend upon our bodies as our access to and means of expression. **Two or three things I know for sure**, and one of them is that personal narrative is a privileged form of expressing embodiment. In this essay I have woven three discourses—the personal (my own abbreviated stories), the aesthetic (Dorothy Allison's voice), and the academic—in an attempt to display the embodied act of telling and studying personal narrative. When we move between narrative and literary performance or between narrative and scholarly discourse—what Merleau-Ponty would call a move from one order of expression to another order of expression—we do not leave our bodies behind to enter a separate realm of aesthetics or academia but rather extend and transform embodiment. Frank states that "Just as I write through my body, so *you* read through yours, and none of us begins to know how our bodies, with all that is sedimented in their tissues, affect that writing and reading, thinking and acting" ("Narrative Witness," 106). Performing and studying personal narrative is a way of grasping the world. If, in postmodern times, we are "getting a life" through telling our stories and consuming others' stories in increasingly ritualistic and public ways, the future of personal narrative performance will be shaped by continuing to critically question how it embodies cultural conflict about experience and identity and renders it discussable.

Aunt Dot was the one who said it. She said, "Lord, girl, there's only two or three things I know for sure." She put her head back, grinned, and made a small impatient noise. Her eyes glittered as bright as sun reflecting off the scales of a cottonmouth's back. She spat once and shrugged. "Only two or three things. That's right," she said. "Of course, it's never the same things, and I'm never as sure as I'd like to be" (Allison, 5).

WORKS CITED

Alcoff, Linda. "The Problem of Speaking for Others." *Cultural Critique* 20 (1991–92): 5–32.

Alcoff, Linda, and Gray, Linda. "Survivor Discourse: Transgressive or Recuperative?" *Signs* 18 (1993): 260–90.

Allison, Dorothy. *Two or Three Things I Know for Sure.* New York: Penguin Plume, 1996.

Atkinson, Paul, and Silverman, David. "Kundera's *Immortality:* The Interview Society and the Invention of Self." *Qualitative Inquiry* 3 (1997): 304–25.

Anzaldúa, Gloria. "Speaking in Tongues: A Letter to Third World Women Writers." *This Bridge Called My Back: Writings of Radical Women of Color.* Ed. Cherie Moraga and Gloria Anzaldúa. New York: Kitchen Table, 1983. 165–74.

———. *Borderlands/*La Frontera: *The New Mestiza.* San Francisco: Aunt Lute Books, 1987.

Bamberg, Michael, ed. "Oral Versions of Personal Experience: Three Decades of Narrative Analysis." *Journal of Narrative and Life History* 7 (1997).

Bauman, Richard. *Story, Performance, and Event: Contextual Studies of Oral Narratives.* Cambridge: Cambridge University, 1986.

———. (1992). "Performance." *Folklore, Cultural Performances, and Popular Entertainments: A Communication-Centered Handbook.* Ed. Richard Bauman. New York: Oxford University Press, 1992. 41–9.

Bauman, Richard, and Briggs, Charles L. "Poetics and Performance as Critical Perspectives on Language and Social Life." *Annual Review of Anthropology* 19 (1990): 59–88.

Benjamin, Walter. "The Storyteller." *Illuminations.* Ed. Hannah Arendt. New York: Schocken, 1969. 83–109.

Benton, Carol. "Moving Beyond Performance of Personal Narratives: Implications for an Ethics of Social Interaction." SCA Convention. San Antonio, 20 Nov. 1995.

Bochner, Arthur P. "Perspectives on Inquiry II: Theories and Stories." *Handbook of Interpersonal Communication,* 2nd ed. Ed. Mark L. Knapp and Gerald R. Miller. Thousand Oaks, CA: Sage, 1994. 21–41.

Butler, Judith. "Performative Acts and Gender Constitution: An Essay on Phenomenology and Feminist Theory." *Performing Feminisms: Feminist Critical Theory and Theatre.* Ed. Sue-Ellen Case. Baltimore: Johns Hopkins University Press, 1990. 270–82.

Carilli, Theresa. "Verbal Promiscuity or Healing Art? Writing the Creative/Performative Personal Narrative." *The Future of Performance Studies: Visions and Revisions.* Ed. Sheron J. Dailey. Annandale, VA: NCA, 1998. 232–36.

Carlin, Phyllis Scott. " 'I have to tell you . . .': The Unfolding of Personal Stories in Life Performance." *The Future of Performance Studies: Visions and Revisions.* Ed. Sheron J. Dailey. Annandale, VA: NCA, 1998. 226–31.

Carlson, Marvin. *Performance: A Critical Introduction.* New York: Routledge, 1996.

Carver, M. Heather. "Staging the Self: Feminist Performance Art and Autobiographical Performance." *Text and Performance Quarterly* 18 (1998): 394–400.

Conquergood, Dwight. "Rethinking Ethnography: Towards a Critical Cultural Politics." *Communication Monographs* 58 (1991): 179–94.

———. "Beyond the Text: Toward a Performative Cultural Politics." *The Future of Performance Studies: Visions and Revisions.* Ed. Sheron J. Dailey. Annandale, VA: NCA, 1998. 25–36.

Corey, Frederick C., ed. *HIV Education: Performing Personal Narratives.* Tempe, AZ: Arizona State University and the U.S. Centers for Disease Control and Prevention, 1993.

————. "The Personal: Against the Master Narrative." *The Future of Performance Studies: Visions and Revisions.* Ed. Sheron J. Dailey. Annandale, VA: NCA, 1998. 199–202.

Deetz, Stanley A. "The Future of the Discipline: The Challenges, the Research, and the Social Contribution." *Communication Yearbook 17.* Ed. Stanley A. Deetz. Thousand Oaks, CA: Sage, 1994. 565–600.

Diamond, Elin. "Introduction." *Performance and Cultural Politics.* Ed. Elin Diamond. New York: Routledge, 1996, 1–12.

Dolan, Jill. "Geographies of Learning: Theatre Studies, Performance, and the 'Performative.'" *Theatre Journal* 45 (1993): 417–41.

Doty, C. Stewart. "How Many Frenchmen Does It Take To . . . ?" *Thought and Action* 11 (1995): 85–104.

Ebert, Teresa L. "Ludic Feminism, the Body, Performance, and Labor: Bringing Materialism Back into Feminist Cultural Studies." *Cultural Critique* 23 (1993): 5–50.

Fine, Elizabeth C. *The Folklore Text: From Performance to Print.* Bloomington: Indiana University Press, 1984.

Fisher, Walter R. *Human Communication as Narration.* Columbia: South Carolina University Press, 1987.

Frank, Arthur W. *The Wounded Storyteller: Body, Illness, and Ethics.* Chicago: University of Chicago Press, 1995.

Frank, Arthur W. "Narrative Witness to Bodies: A Response to Alan Radley." *Body and Society,* 3.3 (1997): 103–9.

Gillis, John R. *A World of Their Own Making: Myth, Ritual, and the Quest for Family Values.* New York: Basic Books, 1996.

Gingrich-Philbrook, Craig. "Refreshment." *Text and Performance Quarterly* 17 (1997): 352–60.

Gornick, Vivian. "The Memoir Boom." *Women's Review of Books,* 13.10–11 (July 1996): 5.

Hantzis, Darlene M. "Reflections on 'A Dialogue With Friends: "Performing" the "Other"/Self" OJA 1995,'" *The Future of Performance Studies: Visions and Revisions.* Ed. Sheron J. Dailey. Annandale, VA: NCA, 1998. 203–6.

Haraway, Donna. "Situated Knowledges: The Science Question in Feminism and the Privilege of Partial Perspective." *Feminist Studies* 14 (1988): 575–99.

Hinchman, Lewis P., and Hinchman, Sandra K. *Memory, Identity, Community: The Idea of Narrative in the Human Sciences.* Albany: State University of New York Press, 1997.

Hopkins, Mary Frances. "The Performance Turn-and Toss." *Quarterly Journal of Speech* 81 (1995): 228–36.

Kaminsky, Marc. "Introduction." *Remembered Lives: The Work of Ritual, Storytelling, and Growing Older.* Ed. Barbara Myerhoff. Ann Arbor: University of Michigan Press, 1992. 1–97.

Kaufman, Linda. "The Long Goodbye: Against Personal Testimony, or An Infant Grifter Grows Up." *American Feminist Thought at Century's End: A Reader.* Ed. Linda S. Kaufman. Cambridge, MA: Blackwell, 1993. 258–77.

Labov, William. *Language in the Inner City.* Philadelphia: University of Pennsylvania Press, 1972.

Labov, William, and Waletzky, Joshua. "Narrative Analysis: Oral Versions of Personal Experience." *Essays on Verbal and Visual Arts.* Ed. June Helm. Seattle: University of Washington Press, 1967. 12–44.

Langellier, Kristin M. "Personal Narratives: Perspectives on Theory and Research." *Text and Performance Quarterly* 9 (1989): 243–76.

————. "Responding to Ethnicity: Franco-American Studies in Maine." *Logon Didonai.* Ed. Henner Barthel. Marz: Voraussichtlicher Erscheinungstermin. 93–100.

————. "Show and Tell in Contemporary Quiltmaking Culture." *Uncoverings 1992.* Ed. Laurel Horton. San Francisco: American Quilt Study Group, 1993. 127–47.

————. "Voiceless Bodies, Bodiless Voices: The Future of Personal Narrative Performance." *The Future of Performance Studies: Visions and Revisions.* Ed. Sheron J. Dailey. Annandale, VA: NCA, 1998. 207–13.

————. "'You're Marked': Breast Cancer, Tattoo, and the Narrative Performance of Identity." *Narrative and Identity: Studies in Autobiography, Self, and Culture.* Ed. Donald Carbaugh and Jens Brockmeier (forthcoming).

Langellier, Kristin M., and Peterson, Eric E. "A Critical Pedagogy of Family Storytelling." *Critical Perspectives on Communication and Pedagogy.* Ed. Jaako Lehtonen. St. Ingbert: Rohrig Universistatsverlag, 1995. 71–82.

————. "Family Storytelling as a Strategy of Social Control." *Narrative and Social Control.* Ed. Dennis Mumby. Newbury Park, CA: Sage, 1993. 49–76.

————. "Spinstorying: An Analysis of Women Storytelling." *Performance, Culture, and Identity.* Ed. Elizabeth C. Fine and Jean H. Speer. Westport, CT: Praeger, 1992. 157–80.

Langellier, Kristin M., and Sullivan, Claire F. "Breast Talk in Breast Cancer Narratives." *Qualitative Health Research* 8 (1998): 76–94.

Limon, J. E., and Young, M. J. "Frontiers, Settlements, and Developments in Folklore Studies, 1972–1985." *Annual Review of Anthropology* 15 (1986): 437–60.

Lockford, Lesa. "Emergent Issues in the Performance of a Border-Transgressive Narrative." *The Future of Performance Studies: Visions and Revisions.* Ed. Sheron J. Dailey. Annandale, VA: NCA, 1998. 214–20.

Maclean, Marie. *Narrative as Performance: The Baudelairean Experiment.* New York: Routledge. 1988.

Madison, D. Soyini. "Performance, Personal Narratives, and the Politics of Possibility." *The Future of Performance Studies: Visions and Revisions.* Ed. Sheron J. Dailey. Annandale, VA: NCA, 1998. 276–86.

————. " 'That Was My Occupation': Oral Narrative, Performance and Black Feminist Thought." *Text and Performance Quarterly* 13 (1993): 213–32.

Martin, Annette. "Keynote Address: 'The Power of Performance.'" *HIV Education: Performing Personal Narratives.* Ed. Frederick C. Corey. Tempe, AZ: Arizona State University and the U.S. Centers for Disease Control and Prevention, 1993. xii–xvii.

Merleau-Ponty, Maurice. *Signs.* Trans. Richard C. McCleary. Evanston IL: Northwestern University Press, 1964.

Minister, Kristina. "A Feminist Frame for the Oral History Interview." *Women's Words: The Feminist Practice of Oral History.* Ed. Sherna Berger Gluck and Daphni Patai. New York: Routledge, 1991. 27–41.

Mishler, Elliot G. *The Discourse of Medicine: Dialectics of Medical Interviews.* Norwood, NJ: Ablex, 1984.

————. "Models of Narrative Analysis: A Typology." *Journal of Narrative and Life History* 5 (1995): 87–123.

Mumby, Dennis. "Modernism, Postmodernism, and Communication Studies: A Rereading of the Ongoing Debate." *Communication Theory* 7 (1997): 1–28.

Murphy, Jacqueline Shea. " 'Words Like Bones': Narrative, Performance, and the Reinscribing of Violence in Leslie Marmon Silko's Storyteller." *Journal of Narrative and Life History* 3 (1993): 223–38.

Myerhoff, Barbara. *Remembered Lives: The Work of Ritual, Storytelling, and Growing Older.* Ann Arbor: University of Michigan Press, 1992.

Park-Fuller, Linda. "Narration and Narratization of a Cancer Story: Composing and Performing 'A Clean Breast of It.'" *Text and Performance Quarterly* 15 (1995): 60–67.

Peterson, Eric E. "Diversity and Franco-American Identity Politics." *Maine Historical Society Quarterly,* 34 (1994): 58–67.

Peterson, Eric E., and Langellier, Kristin, M. "The Politics of Personal Narrative Methodology." *Text and Performance Quarterly* 17 (1997): 135–52.

Pineau, Elyse Lamm, Gingrich-Philbrook, Craig, and Mohtar, Laila Fara. "Inside the Aesthetic Frame: Re-Presenting Lies on Stage." *HIV Education: Performing Personal Narratives.* Ed. Frederick C. Corey. Tempe, AZ: Arizona State University and the U.S. Centers for Disease Control and Prevention. 61–69.

Plummer, Ken. *Telling Sexual Stories: Power, Change and Social Worlds.* New York: Routledge, 1995.

Pollock, Della. "A Response to Dwight Conquergood's Essay 'Beyond the Text: Towards a Performative Cultural Politics.'" *The Future of Performance Studies: Visions and Revisions.* Ed. Sheron J. Dailey. Annandale, VA: NCA, 1998. 37–46.

Riessman, Catherine K. *Narrative Analysis.* Newbury Park, CA: Sage, 1993.

Robbins, Rhea Cote, Petrie, Lanette Landry, Langellier, Kristin M., and Slott, Kathryn, eds. *I am Franco-American and Proud of It/Je suis franco-americaine et fiere de l'etre.* Unpublished manuscript, University of Maine, 1995.

Roman, David. "Performing All Our Lives: AIDS, Performance, Community." *Critical Theory and Performance.* Ed. Janelle G. Reinelt and Joseph R. Roach. Ann Arbor: University of Michigan Press, 1992. 208–21.

Sawin, Patricia E. "'Right here is a good Christian lady': Reported Speech in Personal Narratives." *Text and Performance Quarterly* 12 (1992): 193–211.

Schiffrin, Deborah. *Approaches to Discourse: Language as Social Action.* Cambridge: Blackwell, 1994.

Smith, Sidonie. "Identity's Body." *Autobiography and Postmodernism*. Ed. Kathleen Ashley, Leigh Gilmore, and Gerald Peters. Amherst: University of Massachusetts Press, 1994. 266–92.

Smith, Sidonie, and Watson, Julia, eds. *Getting a Life: Everyday Uses of Autobiography*. Minneapolis: University of Minnesota Press, 1996.

Strine, Mary S. "Articulating Performance/Performativity: Disciplining Tasks and the Contingencies of Practice." *Communication: Views from the Helm for the 21st Century*. Ed. Judith S. Trent. Boston: Allyn and Bacon, 1998. 312–17.

Sullivan, Claire F. "Women's Ways of Coping With Breast Cancer." *Women's Studies in Communication* 20 (1997): 31–53.

Toolan, Michael J. *Narrative: A Critical Linguistic Introduction*. New York: Routledge, 1988.

Trinh, T. Minh-Ha. *Woman, Native, Other: Writing Postcoloniality and Feminism*. Bloomington: Indiana University Press, 1989.

Twigg, Reginald. "The Performative Dimension of Surveillance: Jacob Riis' *How the Other Half Lives*." *Text and Performance Quarterly* 12 (1992): 305–28.

White, Michael, and Epston, David. *Narrative Means to Therapeutic Ends*. New York: W. W. Norton, 1990.

Wolfson, Nessa. "A Feature of the Performed Narrative: The Conversational Historical Present." *Language in Society* 7 (1978): 215–37.

22

Performance, Personal Narratives, and the Politics of Possibility[1]

D. Soyini Madison

Opening and interpreting lives is very different from opening and closing books.

—*Dwight Conquergood*, Performing as a Moral Act

You know as well as I, Old Wife, that we have not been scuffling in this waste-howling wilderness for the right to be stupid.

—*Toni Cade Bambara*, The Salt Eaters

I don't want my good name and what I'm telling you to be tossed around up there at that there University like some ol' rag.

—*Bertha Baldwin, 93 year old domestic worker, narrator, and "theorist of the flesh"*[2]

There is a great deal of talk about "the problem of speaking for others"[3] and the ethics and responsibility involved when performing personal narratives, especially of Subjects[4] whose identities and cultural practices are underrepresented

---

Reprinted from *The Future of Performance Studies: Visions and Revisions*, ed. Sheron J. Dailey (Annandale, Va.: National Communication Association, 1998), 276–86. Used by permission of the National Communication Association.

and contested. This "talk," for the most part, is necessary and productive; however, once in a while there are regressions and ramblings that stridently bump up against the more complex and thoughtful deliberations on representations, identity, cultural politics, and fairness. On the surface, these ramblings appear to come from two opposite viewpoints: on the one side are the cynics; and on the other side are the zealots. The cynical believe any attempt toward a self-critical or dialogical performance of an Other is unattainable; and the temporary and tenuous "putting on the 'flesh'" of an Other is ultimately an act of crass appropriation, self-indulgence, and distortion. Therefore, all such performances, reflexive or not, are inauthentic and exploitative. The zealots, however, believe they have cloned the mind, body, and soul of the Other. They speak *for* the Other better than the Other can speak for herself, and they *know* what it means *to be* the Other. In their often new-found awareness, they do not pause to reflect on the consequences of their actions, because they know all the answers. They are loquacious advocates with insider status.

There are important comparisons that need to be made between these two seemingly different perspectives. The cynics, entrenched in uncomplicated suspicion, dismiss the serious work of performers struggling over questions of the politics of representation as dubious and contradictory. The zealots, entrenched in uncomplicated enthusiasm, dismiss this kind of work as well, only their dismissal is due to an arrogance and naïve zeal that overlooks the question in the first place. The cynics uphold the Not Me and disregard the Not Not Me. The zealots uphold the Not Not Me and disregard the Not Me. There is, however, a greater irony of comparisons between the present day cynic and zealot to be made with an earlier tradition of representing Otherness.

Much has been written (from across the Atlantic to our own varied concentrations in Communication Studies) about the long held dispositions toward privileging the written word at the expense of shunning the poetics, oral rhythms, and improvisational expressions of subaltern communities. In privileging canonized print productions above oral practice productions, we observe the tendency (in the Arts and Sciences) to prescribe either our meanings or languages upon Others or to simply ignore them. History and politics notwithstanding, written cultures have also colonized orally—epistemologically and ontologically—by way of the production and representation of knowledge. The contemporary cynic and zealot would be the first to loudly disavow this textual fixation that distorts or casts the Other as invisible. The irony is that in the negation of performance by the cynic and the lack of serious self-critique by the zealot, they ultimately enforce the very tradition they would disclaim. Although the cynic and zealot are often very sincere and well intentioned, one in their suspicion and the other in their enthusiasm, in the end, they too create silence and distortion. When the cynic blatantly nullifies the performance of oral narratives because of a preoccupation with authenticity, important voices and the potential for greater possibilities are obscured; therefore, a form of silence is the result. When the zealot uncritically reveres the performance of oral narratives because of an infatuation with difference, important voices and the potential for greater possibilities are also obscured; but, in this case, a form of misrepresentation is the result.

My hope is that we are able to find that more creative, complex, and slippery terrain between the zealot and the cynic; the space between the fear of authentication and the fear of universalism; the space between absolutely refusing to perform because the stakes are *too* high and absolutely rushing to perform because they *are* so high. In this essay, I am concerned, primarily, with the performance of subversive and subaltern narratives, the challenge of traveling between domains of power, and the "moral responsibility"[5] of artists and scholars in fashioning more humane possibilities for the problems that "beset our world"[6] (Dyson, 153; Hall, 9). I offer some brief thoughts on a *performance of possibilities* that seeks out that more complicated space between the cynic and the zealot.

THE PERFORMANCE OF POSSIBILITIES

In a *performance of possibilities*, I see the "possible" as suggesting a movement culminating in creation and change. It is the active, creative work that weaves the life of the mind with being mindful of life,[7] of "merging text and world,"[8] of critically traversing the margin and the center, and of opening more and different paths for enlivening relations and spaces. The performance of possibilities functions as a politically engaged pedagogy that Lawrence Grossberg describes as, "never [having] to convince a predefined subject—whether empty or full, whether essential or fragmented—to adopt a new position. Rather, the task is to win an already positioned, already invested individual or group to a different set of places, a different organization of the *space of possibilities*" (Giroux & McLaren, 19). Grossberg asks us to consider a model beyond the dichotomous refrain of "domination and resistance"—what Gloria

Anzaldúa describes as a counterstance that locks us in a duel of oppressor and oppressed (561). Grossberg calls for a model "which may enable the mobilization of people's memories, fantasies, and desires, and redirect their investments in politics and the [sic] Other . . . we must collectively articulate a common affective vision of a shared political future, based on a politics of practice—what people do, what they invest in, where they belong"(20). The *performance of possibilities* centers on the principles of transformation and transgression,[9] dialogue and interrogation, as well as acceptance and imagination to build worlds that are *possible*.

The question then becomes, how does a *performance of possibilities* invoke an "investment in politics and the Other" keeping in mind the dynamics of performer, audience, and Subjects while at the same time being wary of both cynics and zealots? We may begin to address the question by critically examining our *purpose* and *assumptions*. Then, we can pointedly elicit responses from our Subjects, people in our field and people in related fields, who are committed to political efficacy, aesthetic virtue, and ethics. Although we understand that assumptions and questions of purpose are ideally enriched, revised, and illuminated as the performance evolves into its many shapes and directions, these initial questions are the impetus for that evolution. It takes time, energy, and courage to undertake each process of probing self-examination, of seeking honest questions, and of collaborating in generative meanings. Because this undertaking does not always follow in this neat order and because it does not stop at the initial questions, these processes will converge and diverge. Without them, however, the issues of purpose and assumptions can not be ethically and productively engaged. Therefore, in a *performance of possibilities* we take the stand that performance *matters* because it *does something in the world* (Langellier, 245–76). And what it "does" for the audience, the Subjects, and ourselves must be driven by a thoughtful critique of our assumptions and purpose.

Only after we answer these questions may we go on to ask three more questions: (1) By what definable and material means will the Subjects themselves benefit from the performance? (2) How can the performance contribute to a more enlightened and involved citizenship that will disturb systems and processes that limit freedoms and possibilities? (3) In what ways will the performers probe questions of identity, representation, and fairness that will enrich their own subjectivity, cultural politics, and art? I will turn now to these three questions as each resonates exclusively with Subjects, audience, and performer.

THE SUBJECTS

The means by which the Subjects themselves will benefit from the performance are explored by examining the arenas of voice, subjectivity, and interrogative field. By voice, I do not simply mean the representation of an utterance, but the presentation of a historical self, a full presence, that is in and of a particular world. The *performance of possibilities* does not accept "being heard and included" as its focus, but only as its starting point; instead, voice is an embodied, historical self that constructs and is constructed by a matrix of social and political processes. The aim is to present and represent Subjects as made and makers of meaning, symbol, and history in their fullest sensory and social dimensions. Therefore, the *performance of possibilities* is also a performance of voice wedded to experience.

Moreover, whether one likes the performance or not, one cannot completely undo or unknow the image and imprint of that voice (inside experience) upon their own consciousness once they have been exposed to it through performance. Performing subversive and subaltern voices proclaims existence, within particular locales and discourses, that are being witnessed— entered into ones own experience—and this witnessing can not be denied. The subjects themselves benefit from this proclamation through the creation of a space that gives evidence that "I am here in the world among you," but more importantly, "I am in the world under particular conditions that are constructed and thereby open to greater possibility." How then does all this benefit the Subjects? Human desire implores that we be listened to, comprehended, engaged, and free to imagine in and with worlds of others. I often quote Barbara Myerhoff who observed "unless we exist in the eyes of others we come to doubt our own existence" (Myerhoff, 103). This idea of existence and self is further illustrated in !Nisa, a !Kung woman, speaking to anthropologist Marjorie Shostak as she expresses the fear of the disappearance of her stories: "I'll break open the story and tell you what is there, this like the others that have fallen out onto the sand, I will finish with it, and the wind will take it away" (Shostak, 233). That we are all social beings where self is necessarily constituted by others reflects Mikhail Bakhtin's words, "nothing is more frightening than the absence of an answer" (111). The nature of Bakhtin's "answer" is a profound giving back that affirms we are real to others (therefore to ourselves) and that we are not alone. This is not to argue that we do not have a Self (or soul) that generates its own will, action, and meaning—"I think therefore I am"—but that the Self is reciprocally joined to other Selves (or souls) for its own being and creations—"I am because We are and We are because I am." This acknowledgment of voice within experience, relative to the social world is just the beginning; a deeper connection is necessary that now takes us a step further into the realm of subjectivity.

Subjectivity requires that we delve more deeply into the desires resonating within the locations of the Other. It is the move beyond the *acknowledgment* of voice within experience to that of actual *engagement*. Audience and performer must now engage the material and discursive world of the Other. Because subjectivity is formed through a range of discursive practices —economic, social, aesthetic, and political—and meanings are sites of creation and struggle, subjectivity linked to performance becomes a poetic and polemic admixture of personal experience, cultural politics, social power, and resistance. We witness Subjects as they work for and against competing discourses and social processes in the quest for security and honor in their locations. The acknowledge Others become Subjects when the audience and performers actually identify with the substance of who they are, where they are, and what they do. We have entered, albeit symbolically and temporarily, in their locations of voice within experience. Through performance, we are tangential, Subject to Subject, in that contested space while, as bell hooks describes, oppressed "people resist by identifying themselves as subjects, by defining their reality, shaping new identity, naming their history, telling their story" (hooks, 43).

How the Subjects themselves benefit from this quality of engagement is illustrated in a student performance of personal narratives by University cafeteria workers at Chapel Hill who went on strike in 1968. The workers protested for back pay, over-time pay, better working conditions, and job descriptions. It was a tumultuous strike: the national guard was called in, the Chapel Hill police circled the cafeteria with guns in hand, and classes were canceled. For the two African-American women who led the strike, it was a difficult time and an unforgettable ordeal. One of the women was fired; the other still works in the University cafeteria.

In 1993, the University was celebrating its bicentennial, and it was a major state wide event. However, some of us felt it was time to honor the leaders of the (in)famous 1968 cafeteria workers strike, as well as labor culture on campus. After some time a performance based on the personal narratives of the two leaders and other service workers was finally scheduled as part of the bi-centennial celebration. For the opening night performance, the strike leaders and the workers were given a special invitation: cafeteria workers, housekeep-ers, brick masons, yard keepers, and mail carriers were honored guests with reserved seats before an overflowing crowd. Although the University never ac-knowledged the strike leaders' struggle or their contribution to labor equity on campus, almost thirty years later the leaders, Mrs. Smith and Mrs. Brooks, watched themselves and their story being performed in a crowded theatre. Their full attention was focused on the stage, and their partners, children, grandchildren, friends, and co-workers were also focused, watching every de-tail of the performance. As I watched them watch themselves in performance, my fears deepened: Did we do justice to their stories? Will they approve of our presentation of them? Will they feel in any way exploited or embarrassed? How is the cast being affected by all this?

At the end of the performance, Mrs. Smith and Mrs. Brooks were intro-duced and the audience gave them a thunderous and lengthy standing ovation as the cast presented them each with a bouquet of roses. After the show, mem-bers of the audience and the press surrounded the two women with admiring questions and accolades. The next day the newspaper stated that "the produc-tion told a true and previously untold tale. . . . 'You can see from the tears in my eyes how I felt about it.' . . . Still clutching the bouquet of cellophane wrapped flowers the cast had given her while singing *This Little Light of Mine*, Mrs. Smith said a night like Tuesday night made her struggle worthwhile." In an-other paper it was reported the grandchildren of Mrs. Smith said they under-stood their grandmother's life better after seeing the performance; "It definitely makes you have more respect for what they've gone through." As I walk across campus four years later, I am stopped from time to time by workers who still remember and want to talk, with pride and satisfaction, about that night four years ago when their stories were honored in performance. It was the narratives of Mrs. Smith, Mrs. Brooks and the other workers "identifying themselves as subjects" and "telling their story" in the mediated space of performance that empowered them before strangers and kin. Performance proclaimed and af-firmed who they were and how they were. Performance also proclaimed that what they did was noticed, appreciated, and that it made a difference.

But what about those performances when the Subjects cannot be present to witness the performances of their stories? Aside from thinking of performance as a movable space that itself can travel to communities and locales where the Subjects work and live (parks, community centers, churches, schools, etc.), we must also remember what is still being communicated even in the absence of their physical presence. The performance strives to communicate a sense of the Subjects' worlds in their own words; it hopes to amplify their meanings and intentions to a larger group of listeners and observers. These listeners and observers are, then, affected by what they see and hear in ways that motivate them to act/think in forms that now beneficially affect (directly or indirectly) either the Subjects themselves or what they advocate. At this point, the audience moves from the performance space to the social world or the interrogative field.

The interrogative field is the point where the *performance of possibilities* aims to create or contribute to a discursive space where unjust systems and processes are identified and interrogated. It is where what has been expressed through the illumination of voice and the encounter with subjectivity motivates individuals to some level of informed and strategic action. The greatest benefit to Subjects is for those who bear witness to their stories to interrogate actively and purposefully those processes that limit their health and freedom. I do not mean to imply that one performance can rain down a revolution, but one performance can be revolutionary in enlightening citizens to the possibilities that grate against injustice. Furthermore, I believe that performance is a most persuasive and poignant "everyday act of resistance" without necessarily succumbing to the simplistic duality of oppressor versus oppressed.

One performance may or may not change someone's world; but, as James Scott reminds us, acts of resistance amass: "rather like snowflakes on a steep mountainside, set off an avalanche. . . . Everyday forms of resistance give way to collective defiance" (192). In the *performance of possibilities*, the expectation is for the performers and spectators to appropriate the rhetorical currency they need from the inner space of the performance to the outer domain of the social world in order to make a material difference. This may mean joining or starting organizations, volunteering, working to influence policy, involvement in protest demonstrations, donating money, resources, services, etc. At the time of our performance for the bicentennial, the campus housekeepers were embroiled in a court battle with the University. "The House Keepers' Movement," as it was called, was reminiscent of the Cafeteria Workers strike in 1968. The housekeepers wanted improved working conditions, better pay, and training for supervisors. Several of the narratives the students performed were from housekeepers' contextualizing the Movement, as well as mediations on their personal lives and futures. At each performance, the House Keepers' Movement set up a table outside the theatre for donations toward court costs and legal fees, announcements about rallies, petitions, sale of Movement paraphernalia, and membership information for faculty, staff and students. Some in the audience knew little or nothing about the housekeepers on campus, least of all their Movement. For the strike leaders and the housekeepers, the performance did not bring forth a utopia or eradicate inequity, but it did provide a means for their voices, subjectivities, and ultimately their fight for fairness to be heard, felt, and joined.

THE AUDIENCE

How the performance will contribute to a more enlightened and involved citizenship is another question arising from the *performance of possibilities*. Creating performance where the intent is largely to invoke interrogation of specific political and social processes means that in our art we are consciously working toward a cultural politics of change that resonates in a progressive and involved citizenship. To regard the audience as citizens with the potential for collective action and change is part of the groundwork upon which a *performance of possibilities* is based. Toni Morrison underscores the symbiosis between art and politics:

> I am not interested in indulging myself in some private, closed exercise of my imagination that fulfills only the obligation of my personal dreams—which is to say yes, the work must be political. It must have that as its thrust. That's a pejorative term in critical circles now; if a work of art has any political influence in it, somehow it's tainted. My feeling is just the opposite; if it has none, it is tainted. The problem comes when you find harangue passing off as art. It seems to me that the best art is political and you ought to be able to make it unquestionably political and irrevocably beautiful at the same time. (497)

Where the intent is both "the political and irrevocably beautiful," art assumes responsibility for political effectiveness in communicating the principle that we are all part of a larger whole; and, therefore, we are radically responsible to each other for all of our individual selves. Linda Alcoff describes a "web" where our social practices are made possible or impossible by agents and events that are spatially far from our own body which in turn, can affect distant strangers: "We are collectively caught in an intricate, delicate web in which each action I take, discursive or otherwise, pulls on, breaks off, or maintains the tension in many strands of a web in which others find themselves moving also" (Alcoff, 20). A *performance of possibilities* strives to reinforce to audience members the "web" of citizenship and the possibilities of their individual selves as agents and change makers.

Striving toward an enlightened and involved citizenship also means that, although formerly the focus was on subjectivity relative to the Subjects, it must now move to intersubjecitivty relative to the audience. Because performance asks the audience to "travel" empathetically to the world of the Subjects and to feel and know some of what they feel and know, two life-worlds[10] meet and the domains of outsider and insider are simultaneously demarcated and fused. I have an identity separate from the Subject, and the performance clearly illuminates our differences. In the space of the performance, I am outsider; in the space of the world, these positions are more than likely *switched*: I am insider and the Subject is outsider. While I see that I am an outsider to the Subject's experience, the performance ironically pulls me inside. I am now in the midst of a profound meeting. Do I remain here at the margins of the meeting, or is the performance beautiful enough and political enough to compel me to travel more deeply inside the mind, heart, and world of the Subject? In this ability to travel across worlds, two identities meet, engage, and become something more. Maria Lugones describes this process of intersubjectivity: "The reason why I think that traveling to someone's 'world' is a way of identifying with them is because by traveling to their 'world' we can understand *what it is to be them and what it is to be ourselves in their eyes.* Only when we have traveled to each other's 'worlds' are we fully subjects to each other" (637). Performance becomes the vehicle by which we travel to the worlds of Subjects and enter domains of intersubjectivity that problematize how we categorize who is "us" and who is "them," and how we see *ourselves* with "other" and different eyes.

As I argue that action beyond the performance space is of essential benefit to the Subjects, so it is to the audience members as well. Ideally, as an audience member consciously re-enters the "web" of human connectedness and then "travels" into the life-world of the Subject where rigid categories of insider and outsider transfigure into an intersubjective experience, a path for action is set. Action, particularly new action, requires new energy and new insight. In the *performance of possibilities*, when the audience member begins to witness degrees of tension and incongruity between the Subject's life-world and those processes and systems that challenge and undermine that world, something more and new is learned about how power works. The question to what extent these life-worlds are threatened and, in turn, resist, is only partially captured in the space and time of performance. The audience, however, as involved citizens who are both disturbed and inspired may seek the answer long after the final curtain. This is a *pursuit of possibility*, a gift of indignation and inspiration, passed on from the Subject to the audience member. The *performance of possibilities* expects the audience member to continue, reaffirmed, or at least to begin honing her skills toward "world traveling." In the *performance of possibilities*, both performers and audiences can be transformed: They can be themselves and more as they travel between worlds.

The performance ambitiously hopes to guide members of the audience and give them equipment for the journey: empathy and intellect, passion and critique.

There are creative tensions at the borders between Self and Other, yet the performance hopes to challenge them to become witness, interlocutor, subversor, and creator. This is the move from transformation to transgression that Dwight Conquergood describes as the unleashing of "centrifugal forces that keep culture in motion, ideas in play, hierarchies unsettled, and academic disciplines alert and on the edge" (138). In 1937, the black artist, activist, and intellectual, Paul Robeson[11] brought light to the particular responsibility of academics to transgress: "There is no standing above the conflict on Olympia Heights. There are no impartial observers. . . . The struggle evades the formerly cloistered halls of our universities and other seats of learning. The battlefront is everywhere. There is no sheltered rear" (52). That we remove and contest this "sheltered rear" is the inheritance of a *performance of possibilities*.

THE PERFORMERS

One of the initial challenges for a performer is the identity of the Subjects. In this meeting with identity the performer is confronted with questions: How is identity formed and what constitutes it? How can performance defer to the ways in which identity changes, transforms itself, and multiplies? Since the performer is transported[12] slowly, deliberately, and incrementally, at each rehearsal and at

each encounter toward the knowledges and life-world of the Subject, the performer is creatively and intellectually *taking it all in* internalizing and receiving partial "maps of meaning"[13] that reflect the subject's consciousness and
context. This receptiveness, however, is never completely without the generative filter of the performer's own knowledges and locales. The process of being transported, of receiving meanings and generating meanings[14] is a more
intimate and, potentially, a more traumatic engagement for the performers
than for the audience members, because the transportation is mentally and
viscerally more intense than traveling to the world of Others; it is making
those worlds your "homeplace."[15] The performer is not only *engaged*, but she
strives to *become*. For the performer, this is not only an endeavor to *live in* an
individual consciousness shaped by a social world, but it is to *live in* that *social world* as well. Of course, by "living in that social world," I do not mean literally changing your address, but I do mean that the performer must first
seriously research all the crucial elements that encompass a cognitive map of
the social, economic, cultural, and political practices that constitute that
world; and, secondly, the performer must be committed—doing what must be
done or going where one must go—to experience the felt-sensing[16] dynamics
of that world: its tone and color—the sights, sounds, smells, tastes, textures,
rhythms—the visceral ethos of that world.

In personal narrative performances, particularly of contested identities,
performers are not only performing the words of Subjects, they are performing their political landscapes. This political landscape is described by Grossberg as "spatial territorialization," that is, "places and spaces, of people,
practices, and commodities. It is in this sense that discourse is always placed,
because people are always anchored or invested in specific sites. Hence, it matters how and where practices and people are placed, since the place determines
from and to where one can speak (or act)"(20). Identity is then constituted by
identification with certain cultural practices and connected to certain locales
that are often ripe with struggle, conflict, and difference just as they are with
creation, empowerment, and belonging. At the same time identity is contingent upon how these practices and locales change over time. Identity is definable yet multiple, contested yet affirmed, contextual yet personal, a matter of
difference and a matter of identification.

As the performer is being transported into domains of spatial territorialization, as well as the domains of the Subject's consciousness, we understand this

process is always partial, contingent, and relative. While some performers more than others have struggled through the complicated tensions between trauma and transformation, any move toward transgression is dangerous without taking on the serious questions of identity conjoined with representation. Performance becomes the vehicle by which a representation is manifest and with it the presentation of an identity; therefore, representation of the Other is a value loaded construction of signification within a specific context. Representation and identity are largely mediated through the performer's body—what it does and says in performance space. Therefore, in the *performance of possibilities*, we understand representation as first and foremost a responsibility. We are responsible for the creation of what and who are being represented; we are representing the represented; and our "representing" most often carries with it political ramifications far beyond the reach of the performance.

Because "how a people are represented is how they are treated," the act of representing is also an act of material consequences (Hall, 27). The body politic responds to individuals and communities by the way they understand them based upon a complex configuration of discourses and experiences none of which is more profound than how these lives enter their consciousness through representations in cultural performances.

Furthermore, because we are leaving the Other vulnerable to our choices of representation and its possible consequences, the responsibility is one that is both moral *and* artistic. That is, we must represent Subjects in a way that interrogates their material. Although political disfranchisement must be our moral impetus, this should not be separate from our concerns with, and investments in, artistic form. Because we are about political efficacy, we must also care about the artistic virtue of our performance and continuously study it, practice it, critique it, respect it, and improve upon it. Alain Locke, the first black Rhodes Scholar and foremost critic and intellectual of the Harlem Renaissance, once said that art must discover and reveal the beauty which prejudice and caricature have overlaid. Art helps us see and realize the unrealized. It is the sensual bridge to another side of imagining. Where there is no art there is no life; it is our special gift for being. Even though we aim to persuade, we can not afford to fall short on our art.

In a *performance of possibilities*, moral responsibility and artistic excellence culminate in the active intervention to *break through* unfair closures and *remake* the possibility for new openings that bring the margins to a shared center. The *performance of possibilities* does not arrogantly assure that we exclusively are giving voice to the silenced, for we understand they speak and have been speaking in spaces and places often foreign to us. Neither are we assuming that we possess the unequivocal knowledge and skills to enable people to intervene upon injustice or that that they have not been intervening through various other forms all the time. We understand that in performing the contested identities of Subjects there must be *caution* and *politics*. We are involved in an ethics guided by caution and a strategy informed by cultural politics. We are not recklessly speaking to and against one location, but to ourselves and our very endeavor. Della Pollack underlines this self-reflexive and self-subversive process: "Debate and revolutionary advocacy also presume a closed mind and a fixed object of persuasion. Dialogue is quite different. It is not a matter of trade-offs, or tolerance but of genuinely opening the self to subversion" (35).

We are involved in the "opening the self" work of *breaking* with the grandest "dialogic" possibility of *remaking*. Audre Lorde's words and work serve as an example: "My work is about difference, my work is about how we learn to lie down with the different parts of ourselves, so that we can in fact learn to respect and honor the different parts of each other, so that we in fact can learn to use them moving toward something that needs being done, that has never been done before."[17]

As we move into the next millennium, I am hoping we find that slippery place in the performance of personal narrative that is not at rest with the polarizing stance of either the dour cynics or the doting zealots. I hope we will always be restless and worried about performing the lives of lived Subjects, about entering body, soul, and mind into spaces—their spaces *and* our spaces—that scare us, condemn us, and confuse us, yet take us beyond.

For audience, Subjects, and performers, the *performance of possibilities* in the next millennium will "specialize in the wholly impossible"[18] reaching toward light, justice, and enlivening possibilities.

NOTES

1. I want to thank professor Genna Rae McNeil for her helpful comments on this essay.

2. Gloria Anzaldúa and Cherrie Moraga discuss "theories of the flesh" as stories that "bridge the contradictions of our experiences"—those root metaphors from the

concrete existence of the "unlettered" that keep us centered and sane. Further elaboration of theories of the flesh is elaborated in " 'That Was My Occupation:' Oral Narrative, Performance, and Black Feminist Thought" (Madison, 1993). Bertha Baldwin is my great aunt who raised my mother. I worked with her on her oral history while completing my dissertation. This was the response she gave me when I first asked her if she would be one of the three women whose life history would comprise my study on performance ethnography.

3. I borrow from Linda Alcoff's important essay entitled "The Problem of Speaking for Others" in *Cultural Critique* (winter 1991–92).

4. I use the term Subjects interchangeably with the term Other, to suggest agency and to borrow from Latina critic Mari Lugones in her article "Playfulness, 'World'- Traveling, and Loving Perception" (1987) when she refers to Others as "subjects, lively beings, resistors, constructors of visions." I am also looking at bell hooks, in *Talking Back* (1989): "Oppressed people resist by identifying themselves as subjects, by defining their reality shaping their new identity, naming history, telling their story." I capitalize both Other and Subjects in keeping with the idea that the literal meanings of these words are displaced to represent individuals whose identities are often contested.

5. In his book, *Reflecting Black*, Michael Dyson writes about "moral responsibility" and that we "must understand moral responsibility against the backdrop of social options, cultural resources, and economic conditions that form the immediate environment within which people must live and make choices. In short, a theory of responsible moral agency must account for the conditions of *possibility* for such agency to be meaningfully exercised." (153)

6. This is a quote from Stuart Hall (9) from the Grossberg essay cited in the reference section.

7. "Mindful of Life" was introduced to me by one of my student/friends, David Dombrowsky, in a one-person performance I was directing with him. It comes from Mark Freeman's *Re-Writing the Self: History, Memory and Oral Narrative* (1993) (3).

8. Edward Said's notion that "the text and the world" must be intimately tied (1983).

9. Dwight Conquergood elaborated on transformation and transgression in his speech at the 1995 Otis J. Aggert Festival, "Beyond the Text: Toward a Performative Cultural Politics."

10. Jürgen Habermas' idea of "life world." Habermas distinguishes the life world from structures of political power and social systems. The life world is social

integration—language and communicative action is celebrated and possible, even when in the midst of struggle.

11. In the late 1930s, Paul Robeson became involved with national and international movements for peace, racial justice, and better labor conditions. He also supported independence for African colonies. This involvement, his friendship with Russia, and his association with Communists brought opposition from conservative groups in the United States. In 1950, the government canceled his passport. In 1958 he finally regained his passport and moved to London. He died in 1963.

12. Richard Schechner's idea of transportation is outlined in greater detail in *Between Theatre and Anthropology* (1985).

13. "Maps of Meaning": I am using this term in the way Grossberg uses it in his essay (see Works Cited) as the layers of signification within specific locales.

14. This idea of receptive and generative meaning is fleshed out in an article by Marion Kleinau "Notes on the Encounter: Toward A Model of Performance Process" (1987): 1–70.

15. bell hooks' idea of "Homeplace" is detailed in her title essay from *Yearning* (1990).

16. I am borrowing this term from Wallace Bacon. It is explained in more detail in *The Art of Interpretation.*

17. This quotation is included in Diedre Mullane's *Words to Make My Dream Children Live*, 296.

18. Nannie Burroughs is an important figure in American history. A black woman educator, historian, journalist, and feminist, she founded the National Training School for Girls and was a founding member of the National Association of Colored Women's Clubs.

WORKS CITED

Alcoff, Linda. "The Problem of Speaking for Others." *Cultural Critique*, (Winter 1991–92): 20.

Anzaldúa, Gloria. "La conciencia de la mestiza: Towards a New Consciousness." *The Woman That I Am: The Literature and Culture of Contemporary Women of Color.* Ed. D. Soyini Madison. New York: St. Martin's Press, 1994.

Bakhtin, Mikhail. *The Dialogic Imagination: Four Essays by M. M. Bakhtin.* Ed. Michael Holquist. Trans. Caryl Emerson and Michael Holquist. Austin: University of Texas Press, 1981.

Bacon, A. Wallace. *The Art of Interpretation.* New York: Holt, Rinehart and Winston, 1979.

Conquergood, Dwight. "Performing as a Moral Act: Ethical Dimensions on the Ethnography of Performance." *Literature in Performance* 5 (1985): 2

———. "Of Caravans and Carnivals: Performance Studies in Motion." *The Drama Review* 39:4 (1995): 138.

Freeman, Mark. *Re-Writing the Self: History, Memory and Narrative.* London: Routledge, 1993.

Grossberg, Lawrence. "Bringin' It All Back Home—Pedagogy and Cultural Studies." *Between Borders: Pedagogy and the Politics of Cultural Studies.* Ed. Henry Giroux and Peter McLaren. New York: Routledge, 1994.

Habermas, Jürgen. *The Theory of Communicative Action, Life-world and System: A Critique of Functionalist Reason.* Vol. II, Trans. Thomas McCarthy. Boston: Beacon, 1987.

Hall, Stuart. "New Ethnicities." *Black Film/British Cinema.* ICA Document T. Ed. Kobena Mercer. London: Institute of Contemporary Arts, 1988. 27–31.

hooks, bell. "Homeplace: A Site of Resistance." *Yearning: Race, Gender, and Cultural Politics.* Boston: South End Press, 1990.

Kleinau, Marion. "Notes on the 'Encounter': Toward A Model of Performance Process." *Essays for Isabel Crouch: Essays on the Theory, Practice, and Criticism of Performance.* Ed. Wallace A. Bacon. Evanston, Ill.: Northwestern University Press, 1987. 1–70.

Locke, Alain. "The Legacy of the Ancestral Arts." *The New Negro.* Ed. Alain Locke. New York: Athenaeum, 1925.

Lorde, Audre. *Sister Outsider: Essays and Speeches.* Freedom, Calif.: Crossing Press, 1984.

Lugones, Maria. "Playfulness, World-Travelling, and Loving Perception." *The Woman That I Am: The Literature and Culture of Contemporary Women of Color.* Ed. D. Soyini Madison. New York: St. Martin's Press, 1994.

Langellier, Kristin. "Personal Narratives: Perspectives on Theory and Research." *Text and Performance Quarterly* 9.4 (1989): 243–76.

Madison, Soyini D. "'That Was My Occupation': Oral Narrative, Performance, and Black Feminist Thought." *TPQ,* 13.3 (1993): 213.

Morrison, Toni. "Rootedness: The Ancestor as Foundation." *The Woman That I Am: The Literature and Culture of Contemporary Women of Color.* Ed. D. Soyini Madison. New York: St. Martin's Press, 1994.

Mullane, Deirdre. *Words To Make My Dream Children Live.* New York: Doubleday/Anchor Books, 1995.

Myerhoff, Barbara. "Life History Among the Elderly: Performance, Visibility and Re-Membering." *A Crack in the Mirror: Reflexive Perspectives in Anthropology.* Ed. J. Ruby. Philadelphia: University of Pennsylvania Press, 1982.

Pollock, Della. "Telling the Told: Performing 'Like a Family.'" *Oral History Review.* 18.2 (1990): 1–36.

Robeson, Paul. *Here I Stand.* Ed. Paul Robeson. Boston: Beacon Press, 1958.

Said, Edward. *The World, The Text, and The Critic.* Cambridge, Mass.: Harvard University Press, 1983.

Schechner, Richard. *Between Theatre and Anthropology.* Philadelphia: University of Pennsylvania Press, 1985.

Scott, James C. *Domination and the Arts of Resistance.* New Haven, Conn.: Yale University Press, 1990.

Scott, Maxwell. "Play Honors Worker's Acts." *The Chapel Hill Herald.* Chapel Hill, N.C. (11/13) 1993: 8.

Shostak, Marjorie. *!Nisa: The Life and Words of a !Kung Woman.* Cambridge, Mass.: Harvard University Press, 1983.

Velliquette, Beth. "Student Play Honors UNC-CH Workers." *The News & Observer.* Raleigh, N.C. (11/13) 1993: 6B.

23

The Anthro in Cali

Miles Richardson

In 1992, thirty years after I had first gone to Colombia to do fieldwork for an anthropological dissertation, I went back. Here are scenes from that return.[1]

I

At *Estancia Paisa*, *"Abierto a las 24 Horas,"* I
offer the lottery vendor, at her station on the corner,
a *tragito* of *aguardiente*. She, broad in the bream.
And tight in the skirt, sips demurely, while
a *compañero* at the crowded table falls asleep;
the guitar player has come and gone, but the school boy,
at his place by the counter, keeps hard to his figuring.

II

Early mass at the Ernita, they come off the street
in assorted disguise: The office-bound in crisp blouse,
stockings, and heels; the homeless adrift in rags and dirt brown;
and the beggars, each from their favorite crouch by the door,
prepared to dispense their blessing,

Reprinted from *Qualitative Inquiry* 5, no. 4 (1999): 563–65. Copyright © 1999 by Sage Publications Inc.

Que Dios le pague, May God repay you,
for any miracle that falls their way.

III

"*¡Hombre!*" the man gestures in open-handed disgust.
At the packed corner where traffic lights are off
because of the *apagón,* the energy-saving blackout,
and distracted by the battle between pedestrian
and car, I have stepped on his heel. Meanwhile,
the dog in mural above the street,
in shoulder-to-shoulder companionship
with his friend, the cat, requests
"*Baja el tono de su agresividad*
and let's learn to live together."

IV

On the foot bridge that crosses the Rio Cali
someone has placed a blind man near the statue
in honor of the writer, Jorge Isaacs. As people
flow around him, he shakes his cup up and down,
up and down, while the soft drink man shouts
from his two wheel cart, "*Limonada, fría, fría*"
and the lottery vendor circling the crowd adds,
"*Del Valle, juega, juega.*" Beneath the bust of *don* Jorge,
frozen in idyllic stone, the heroine, María, listens
chastely to the young man chatting at her shoulder.

V

From a doorway he has occupied during the night,
an old man shakes a plastic curtain over the curb.
In a corner neatly stacked are his straw hat
with a red band around its crown and a stick for walking.
The door has been a perfect fit for his small frame;
now he folds the plastic to make ready for another day,
and in silent admiration I wish him *Buenos días, señor.*

VI

Avenida Belacázar Cinco-Diez. Where we lived in '62.
The Edificio Dominguez, but today it is the daughters
Dominguez. The elegant *señora*, the gracious *doña*,
la madre of these two, the lady we knew, is dead.
I've come back to see what's changed.
If I hadn't returned, would she still be alive?
Things don't stop; they circle. But around what?
Around the past? Around growing old?
Around a place I've yet to discover.

VII

El Señor de la Caña
In *La Ermita*, a cathedral of Neo-Gothic
spire and splendor amid the bustling of downtown Cali,
the Lord Jesus, already judged, judges—the cane stalk
in his hand a baton to bless and a whip to scourge.
Some kneel to flutter crosses over forehead,
mouth, and heart and are on their feet and gone.
Others stay on their knees for the whole story
of *mi culpa, mi culpa, mi grand culpa,*
my guilt, my guilt, my grand guilt; but I,
an Anglo anthro from the Baptist South,
read from a printed petition,
"*Protégé esta aima abatida,*
Shelter this disquieted soul."

NOTE

1. Scene VI comes from a longer report of the return (Richardson, 1998).

REFERENCE

Richardson, M. (1998). The poetics of a resurrection: Re-seeing 30 years of change in a Colombian community and in the anthropological enterprise. *American Anthropologist, 100,* 11–21.

24

Shaman

Anya Peterson Royce

Raven saw his shadow
far below
a black shape skimming
the rabbitbrush and sage.

Winging high, he felt
cool, dry air caress
his sleek feathers,
ate the desert
in his flight.

Ancient head bowed,
Raven headress brushing
deerskin covered knees,
the shaman sat,
a husk emptied of spirit.

He sat,
knees drawn up, unmoving

Reprinted from *Qualitative Inquiry* 8, no. 2 (2002): 264. Copyright © 2002 by Sage Publications Inc.

in the clearing
marked by sacred pollen.

Raven flew, tugging
against that invisible
tether—
    Let me go, old man,
    your strength flows away like sand;
    you are smoke in the wind of my wings.

Worn now by his
fractured twin-self,
the shaman threw the pollen again,
summoned Raven by the burning sage,
felt his powerful wings
become frail bones, earthbound.

Struggle over, he whispered—
    One day soon, you and I
    will fly like arrows into the sun;
    our ashes will fall like snow on the hot sand.

25

Tango for One

Anya Peterson Royce

Muscles bunch, dense,
thick with tension,
rippling to a pulse.
Shoulders drive down,
feet, calves, thighs arc,
stretching upward
to meet them
somewhere in the torso—
tango for one.

Buried in that solid throb of ribcage,
the heart, exiled,
at home and homeless.
Bound by tango rules,
kissed by tango promise,
it paces out *un paso solitario.*
It would shimmer in a blur
of changed directions,

Reprinted from *Qualitative Inquiry* 8, no. 2 (2002): 265. Copyright © 2002 by Sage Publications Inc.

all shifting right angles to itself;
dip and sway in
that formal tango way;
fly across the floor
in a hundred tiny steps,
feet stitching a tapestry
unraveled as quickly as it is formed.

Legs weave around each other—
sinuous and molten,
a reverie for one.
Then still as a stone,
only flare of nostril,
beat of pulse in marble neck,
a single bead of sweat
slipping between rigid shoulder blades
betray the *tanguera*.

About the Editors

Yvonna S. Lincoln is University Distinguished Professor of Higher Education and the Ruth Harrington Chair of Educational Leadership in the College of Education at Texas A&M University. She is the coauthor, editor, or coeditor of numerous books, including *Effective Evaluation, Naturalistic Inquiry, Organizational Theory and Inquiry, Fourth Generation Evaluation, Representation and the Text,* and *The Handbook of Qualitative Research, First and Second Editions.* She is the recipient of the 1987 Paul Lazarsfeld Award for Outstanding Contributions to Research and Scholarship in Evaluation Theory; the 1990 Distinguished Researcher Award, Division J of the American Educational Research Association; the 1991 Sidney Suslow Distinguished Research Award of the Association for Institutional Research; and the 1993 Research Achievement Award from the Association for the Study of Higher Education. She is the coeditor of the journal *Qualitative Inquiry.*

Norman K. Denzin is distinguished professor of communications, college of communications scholar, and research professor of communications, sociology, cinema studies, and humanities at the University of Illinois, Urbana–Champaign. He is the author of numerous books, including *Interpretative Ethnography, The Cinematic Society, Images of Postmodern Society, The Recovering Alcoholic,* and

The Alcoholic Self, which won the Charles Cooley Award from the Society for the Study of Symbolic Interaction in 1988. In 1997, he was awarded the George Herbert Award from the Society for the Study of Symbolic Interaction. He is past editor of *The Sociological Quarterly,* editor of *Cultural Studies: Critical Methodologies,* coeditor of *The Handbook of Qualitative Research, Second Edition,* and series editor of *Cultural Studies: A Research Annual* and *Studies in Symbolic Interaction.*